RENAISSANCE TRANSACTIONS

RENAISSANCE TRANSACTIONS

Ariosto and Tasso

Edited by Valeria Finucci

Duke University Press

Durham & London

1999

© 1999 Duke University Press

All rights reserved

Printed in the United States of America

on acid-free paper ⊗ Typeset in Quadraat

Library of Congress Cataloging-in-

Publication Data appear on the last

printed page of this book.

Contents

III   ACTING OUT FANTASIES

Acknowledgments

This book is the result of long conversations I had a few years ago with Dino Cervigni on the appeal of Renaissance culture, specifically of chivalric romances and epics, to our imaginary. I gratefully acknowledge here his spur to "say more." As the volume took shape, I was lucky to share in the generosity and creative criticism of all the contributors and of the two anonymous press readers. This project has been collaborative in every sense.

I would like to thank for their encouragement and enthusiasm Edward Mahoney, Ronald Witt, Elizabeth Clark, Anna Ferrarotti, Marina and Kevin Brownlee, and David Aers. The executive editor of Duke University Press, Reynolds Smith, was a very supportive colleague. My editorial task has been facilitated by the wonderful assistance of Maura High, who proved adept at solving all possible linguistic difficulties and cross-references.

On the personal level, the shaping of this book went along at times with frightening intimations of my mortality. I must record a profound debt to Emma Ciafaloni, Rusty Hood, Antonio Laurenza, and Rosamaria Preparata. In my year at Villa I Tatti, the Harvard University Renaissance Studies Center in Florence, their transcontinental presence over the phone gave a new meaning to medical care and personal empathy. Along the same lines, my greatest debt goes to Dr. Allan Friedman. Space is too short to express my gratitude for his sense of humor, solicitude, and professionalism. This book is dedicated to him with admiration and respect.

Introduction
Ariosto, Tasso, and Storytelling

VALERIA FINUCCI

Historically speaking, the first critical controversy in narratology took place in Italy in the sixteenth century and focused on two successful authors and two strikingly different fictional styles: that of Ludovico Ariosto (1474–1533)—whose narrative in *Orlando furioso* (1532) is characterized by digressions, romance plots, and an interlaced structure—and that of Torquato Tasso (1544–1595)—whose narrative in *Gerusalemme liberata* (1581) has a more linear epic line leading toward a conclusion. This "quarrel" has been considered the first sustained, historically important debate on what constitutes literature, or at least, modern literature. Critics have asked whether Ariosto can be credited with inventing a new genre specific to Italian culture, the chivalric romance, or whether Tasso can claim the greater achievement, for reaching the epic heights of Homer and Virgil, thereby making it possible for a literature written in Italian to reach the level of its classical Greek and Latin antecedents. The crux of this debate is the definition of what is a more truly important and readable literary piece: one with authorial interventions, enticing micronarratives, and a mixture of entertaining heroic and erotic actions—such as the *Orlando furioso*—or one with a unified, more objective, and possibly moral, macronarrative—such as the *Gerusalemme liberata*.[1]

This sixteenth-century battle between the "ancients" and the "moderns," masterfully replayed by Daniel Javitch in *Proclaiming a Classic*, has been linked recently to the current debate between modernism and postmodernism.[2] In "The Origins of Postmodernism," Ronald McKinney

---

1. For a thorough account of this debate, see Weinberg.
2. Javitch, *Proclaiming a Classic*.

suggestively connects today's question on whether postmodernism is revolutionary or reactionary to the core question posited by the Ariosto/ Tasso supporters and detractors. Although he does not draw "the simplistic conclusion that Ariosto is a proto-Postmodernist and Tasso a proto-Modernist" (232), it is significant that the question is even posed, because it shows that Ariosto and Tasso, whose readerly and critical fortunes have shifted more than once throughout the centuries, are still central to the debate on what constitutes modern narrative. Why do these two writers' own preoccupations with the culture, the sexual and bodily discipline, the political understandings, and the religious practices of the early modern period resonate with us today, so much so that they are at the center of sweeping critical rereadings of the Cinquecento canon?

Ariosto has been the subject of an intense and mostly celebratory critical interest lately, more so on this side of the Atlantic than could perhaps have been anticipated. One has only to follow the punctual bibliographical updates by Robert Rodini (or Rodini and Di Maria) to realize how staggering the output on Ariosto is, although such was not the case earlier in the century, nor during the century before, for that matter. What does this writer, whom Francesco De Sanctis famously denigrated as the creator of a "world empty of everything that is noble and lofty— without religion, without fatherland, without morality" (487), offer to our postmodern imagination?

First, there is Ariosto's famous irony, which, cast in contemporary terms, makes him an author who shares our own skepticism regarding the power of reason. Then there are the rhetorical devices that entice us: his exposure of the artificialness and fictionality of the literary piece; his fragmentation of material—the *varietà*, as he wrote, of plotlines ("varie file e varie tele / uopo mi son che tutte ordire intendo," 2.30); his authorial intrusions, meant to move the narrative forward and sideways; his fabulist bent for hyperrealistic and hyperbolic events; and his virtuosity in accelerating, suspending or, frequently, interrrupting the tempo.[3]

---

3. Javitch was not joking when he saw in the *Furioso* a series of superbly truncated and restarted narratives. See *"Cantus Interruptus."*

As for Tasso, embraced by his contemporaries, worshiped by Romantics, analyzed by Freud, he has most recently been studied for reasons that he himself, perhaps, would have dismissed: because of his tortured outlook on reality. To be sure, Tasso was the first to discourage his own, and others' doubts, and his lengthy rewriting of the Liberata into the Gerusalemme Conquistata attests to his desire to feel in tune with the ideology he had planned to represent but that at times seemed to escape him.[4] That he failed—that the reader always knows where the good and the bad lie in the Liberata, and yet is attracted by the way the marginal subverts a seemingly seamless master discourse—is a measure perhaps of how easily Tasso can be taken for a modern representative of what Sciascia, Eco, and Gianni Vattimo have publicized as the "pensiero debole," a thought that is not nihilistic but is not sufficiently "strong" to give us definitive truths.[5] Such linking has recently been proposed by Francesco Erspamer in "Il 'pensiero debole' di Torquato Tasso." Erspamer argues that Tasso's patent ideological desire to show one moral, one truth, and one religion was at odds with his taking up the poetics of mannerism, where doubts serve to uncover the truth, signs do not necessarily "mean," reason—although eventually victor—is challenged by dissimulations, and lies, by provoking discontinuity, allow for a different reading of the Liberata.[6] Given the recent celebrations for the four-hundredth anniversary of Tasso's death and the host of articles sure to follow the event, my belief is that we will see more examinations of Tasso's ruptures.

In today's climate of doubts and fragmentation, both Ariosto's bemused attitude toward history and Tasso's search for unequivocable truths and a structure that stands through anguished personal and moral choices make for fruitful investigations. We are, after all, still living through, and trying to make sense of, many of the situations that faced

4. Interpretations of Tasso's thwarted personality have been many. For a recent study, see Ferguson.

5. See Vattimo and Eco. For a similar argument on this side of the Atlantic, see Rorty.

6. For a study of mannerism in this context, see Hauser.

the early modern readers of these texts: the skirmishes in the name of religion that were played out in battlefields outside Jerusalem in Tasso are still being played out today, in the same spots; the genocide of innocent people in Paris at the hands of Rodomonte in Ariosto doubles other, more present, senseless killings, like those in Rwanda; ethnic separation and phobias, endlessly staged and never resolved by the two authors, are still issues not judiciously tackled today; and class distinctions still overdetermine relations of power. Today, history is being called upon to make sense of our present. The *Furioso* and the *Liberata* crowd our fantasies and speak to our fears because the stories in them haunt, tease, satisfy, and bewilder us.

This collection of essays situates itself at the crossroads of the current reexamination of our two Renaissance authors. My aim in putting together this volume was to foster a dialogue among colleagues of various critical schools so that new perspectives could come out and long-held assumptions on history, culture, ethics, gender, and genre could be problematized. Needless to say, this is not a collection on the postmodernity of the epic and the romance, although two contributors, Javitch and Finucci, use the term in their essays; rather, it showcases, through a broad range of concerns, how and in what ways two canonical authors who defined more than one genre in their times (in fact, they defined three—chivalric romance, romance, and epic—and were instrumental in the establishment of a fourth, theater) speak to us today.

Some of the essays revisit the Ariosto-Tasso controversy delineated above, as in the volume's first part, "Crossing Genres." An interest in Ariosto's epicity, although one revised and adapted, is central to both Ronald Martinez's and Daniel Javitch's contributions. In "Two Odysseys: Rinaldo's Po Journey and the Poet's Homecoming in the *Orlando furioso*," Martinez reconstructs the paladin Rinaldo's journey along the River Po in the final cantos of the *Furioso* as a Ulyssean, epic journey of return, although one in the style of Ariosto. Martinez argues that Ariosto's aim is just as much to delineate a journey of self-discovery as to foreground a cultural itinerary. Moving sweepingly from Homer to Virgil and Dante at the epic level, and from Pulci to Morgante and Boiardo at the romance level, Martinez marks the changes in the topos of the hero's return throughout the centuries, culminating in Ariosto's insertion of bourgeois-mercantile aims in a previously well-defined heroic quest: domestic ruses and comic moments, such as the emphasis on jealousy, take the place of epic trials. Thus, rather than moving the hero from romance to epic, as was usually done in the tradition of the hero's homecoming, in Rinaldo's journey Ariosto accommodates both genres and celebrates Arthurian romances and Carolingian epics; both in short, the *Iliad* and the *Odyssey*.

Working with the same interlaced romance and epic strands in his essay, "The Grafting of Virgilian Epic in *Orlando furioso*," Javitch revises his earlier assessment that Ariosto—finding himself more in tune with the intertwined narratives of Ovid—only ironically and somehow skeptically borrowed from Virgil and then just to endow his work with classical features.[7] Why, Javitch asks himself now, would Ariosto clearly want his readers to know that he is integrating the romance material of his times and explicit Virgilian sources? By breaking the epic's continuous flow with romance interruptions, that is, by adapting the material from the *Aeneid* to the demands of a multiplot romance structure, Ariosto shows how well two such diverse genres can be fused together structurally, how captivatingly amatory and heroic acts ("arme e amore") can succeed each other and be part of each hero's characterization, and most of all how good he was at working in both genres. Tasso does not hybridize the romance and the epic as Ariosto did but seamlessly fuses the two narrative strands. In the succeeding centuries, readers were accustomed to thinking that Tasso's method was more enticing because it was homogenous. But we in our postmodern times are more primed than others, according to Javitch, to enjoy Ariosto's ways because they are so clearly idiosyncratic. I would like to add that perhaps hybridization itself, this citing, mingling, adapting, and playful reenacting of other stories locates Ariosto strangely in place in our days of "literary exhaus-

7. See Javitch, "The *Orlando Furioso*," and "The Imitation."

tion," to borrow from John Barth, where the compulsion to repeat comes from the self-conscious realization that there are only a given number of forms and genres available for literary use. The pleasure of the text, then and now, and with a few necessary adjustments, comes as usual from the remaking of the already read, the recycling of the *déjà vu*.

Whereas Martinez and Javitch work on the modified epic ambitions of well-publicized Ariostan romance episodes, Jo Ann Cavallo proposes in her essay, "Tasso's Armida and the Victory of Romance," that there is more of a romance interest, and less of an epic one in Tasso's concluding canto. Cavallo argues that romance wins out in the *Liberata* and that it constitutes, in fact, the poem's last choice. Indeed, Tasso leaves us not with the Christian conquest of Jerusalem but with the future probable marriage between Rinaldo and a reconstructed Armida. If women are always left behind in the classical stories of wandering heroes destined to high positions of power (not only in the works of Homer and Virgil but also in Ariosto's), why does Tasso reintroduce Armida at the end? Cavallo asks. She then retraces the motif of the temptress through the entire Italian chivalric romance tradition, starting from *Orlando innamorato* and *Mambriano* and shows that Tasso, by opting not to separate sexuality and dynastic marriage, chooses not to make woman dual: either an evil, promiscuous seductress *à la* Alcina or a chaste, marriageable virgin *à la* Bradamante. Cavallo thus revises powerful current arguments that Tasso, bent on delineating a resonant political teleology, wanted to expurgate romance from his epic.[8] For her, Tasso rejects interlacing but considers romance and epic as belonging in the same genre.

The next part of the book, "The Politics of Dissimulation," concentrates on subversive strategies enacted in the *Furioso* and the *Liberata* when issues of honesty, honor, historical truthfulness, and authorial self-representation are in the forefront. Making Tasso more a representative of the "pensiero debole" than an epic writer at work, Sergio Zatti looks at the uses of deception in the *Liberata* as ways of enlarging the text in the mannerist mood. In "Epic in the Age of Dissimulation: Tasso's

8. See, for example, Zatti, *L'uniforme*.

Gerusalemme liberata," Zatti examines an array of motifs related to deception, such as false speeches (those of Alete and Armida), unacknowledged feelings (the buried love pangs of Erminia), hidden purposes (the task of Eustazio), body transvestism (the taking up of armors by Erminia and Clorinda), and the in/out, inside/outside veil and cloth of language. Zatti argues that for Tasso the multiplicity itself of romance plots versus a more linear epic line inscribes error, fiction, and dissimulation; the language of romance is a language of deceit; and the "locus amoenus" of romance plots functions as another opportunity for digression and errantry. Even the text is perceived by Tasso as the legitimization of a deception, Zatti notes, so that the author's choice can paradoxically only be between dissimulating dishonestly, like Armida, or dissimulating innocently, like Erminia. Feminine discourse then embodies a language of dissimulation, although perhaps a necessary one, for it alone opens the way to the Christian and historical truth that was the purpose of Tasso's writing.

Like Zatti, Walter Stephens works on Tasso's lies and dissimulations to arrive at the representation of authorship. Concentrating first on the figure of the trickster Vafrino, Stephens, in his essay, "Trickster, *Textor*, Architect, Thief: Craft and Comedy in *Gerusalemme liberata*," shows that, unlike Homer's Dolon, Vafrino is not a failed trickster. His purpose, in fact, is to discover the missing part in the "tessitura" that makes Tasso's text. He is thus a surrogate author, a master of illusions, a contriver of textual tricks. Like Vafrino, Tasso steals/constructs his plot from material written elsewhere. But even Vafrino, Stephens argues, gets upstaged by Erminia, a revised Homeric Helen, who although seemingly incompetent at the beginning ("errante ancella," in Tasso's telling words) soon demonstrates how she can manipulate those around her. Erminia is also a figure for the author, in that she alone, like Tasso, knows each hero's prowess and name. Stephens constructs the figure of the "vafro" and "vafra" by working through the similarities between texts and textiles, "tela" and conspiracy. For Tasso and Homer women are weavers, Stephens argues, just like Penelope, verbally devious and artistically good. The fact that the Erminia story does not end (she is neither killed, like Clorinda, nor domesticated, like Armida) means that she comedically resists her own author and the epic world he portrays.

If lies are problematic in Tasso, could one doubt that the concept of honor and truth is at least as shifty and unstable in Ariosto? Katherine Hoffmann contrasts honor to pride and avarice in "'Un così valoroso cavalliero': Knightly Honor and Artistic Representation in Orlando furioso." Starting from a reading of canto 26 in which honor, which gives the knights a sympathetic identity, is no longer conquered in the battlefield but in brawls, Hoffmann suggests that Ariosto longed for a past where honor was still the sine qua non of knighthood. She reads this first at the political level, by showing how much Ariosto felt that in his times honor had collapsed into avarice, "impero" had turned into the bed of greed, and both state and church had become mired in corruption. Hoffman then links honor to art and aesthetic achievements, and to the project itself of the Furioso, considered not opportunistic like the "stile avaro" of self-serving prince-flatterers. She argues that Ariosto walks a thin line between the golden age of the past and the expedient present, between praise of his patrons and a critique of them, showing how morality and honor (personal, aesthetic, and political) can become easy prey to greed and avarice.

In the volume's third part, "Acting Out Fantasies," the focus is on performance, real or imagined. Working on subjectivity and with an eye on gender, Valeria Finucci considers how masculinity fares with Ariosto. In "The Masquerade of Masculinity: Astolfo and Jocondo in Orlando furioso, canto 28," she examines the novella in which Astolfo and Jocondo exact a Don Juanesque revenge for having been cuckolded. This revenge takes the shape of an endless search throughout Europe for a woman who does not betray—a task that involves more than a thousand sexual encounters—until the two men settle on a young servant whom they share in equal installments. Canto 28 has been read as a fantasized (and negative) account of women's pernicious sexual appetites and as a fantasized (but positive) telling of men's extravagant sexual performances. Finucci, however, sees it as a story of perplexing characterizations of masculinity, one that puts masculinity on trial, so to speak, and deessentializes it.

She demonstrates how difficult it is to read Renaissance constructions of gender through our modern eyes: what today we understand as effeminacy may have not appeared as such then; what then was an overriding fear—cuckoldry, which clearly undermined property and genealogical lines—does not have the same echo in our times. By looking at the two men's actions through psychoanalytical lenses (working, that is, on narcissism, doubling, fantasy, and repetition), Finucci demonstrates that just as femininity, in culture, is something made up, put on by women to conform to social requirements, so masculinity is not only unstable but also unhinged, both a performance and a masquerade.[9]

Bridging two genres, the chivalric romance and the theater, Eric Nicholson reconstructs the significance of various and unorthodox stagings of the *Furioso* to the development of the theater and the relevance of the *Liberata* to the founding of yet another genre, the melodrama/opera. In "Romance as Role Model: Early Female Performances of *Orlando furioso* and *Gerusalemme liberata*," Nicholson argues that a new figure, that of the upstart actress, both revered and reviled, became important when the Italian stage adopted scenes from the chivalric romances. As we know, unlike in the English theater, where transvestite boys played women's parts, in the Italian theater women were on the stage as early as 1542.[10] In fact, by 1570 there were already calls from above to limit the use of actresses; women dressed as boys (and boys dressed as women) were thought to foster lascivious behavior. This eventually led to Pope Sixtus V's 1588 ban against women appearing in public theaters. But, as Nicholson shows, the actresses' presence was instrumental to the transformation of romance into theatrical plots. Actresses, in fact, used representations of the *Furioso* to further a more female agenda: they revised the Marganorre episode, for example, so that no woman could be the victim of that man's misogyny. Tasso, on the other hand, whose plots

---

9. For a corresponding take on the masquerade of femininity in Ariosto, see Finucci, "The Female Masquerade." The classic text on the subject is that of Rivière.

10. Although plenty of work still needs to be done on the subject, some is already coming out. See Clubb and Nicholson.

were easier to act and sing, became more melodramatic, and actresses appearing in stage versions performed scenes that made them appear pathetic rather than powerful. Monteverdi's music was instrumental in making the Gerusalemme liberata key to the development of opera. By having women play dying, vanquished characters, Monteverdi was also able to recuperate the attacks on gender morals brought by actresses performing in assertive roles, such as those playing the Furioso scenes. What Nicholson suggestively shows in reading gender through a historicization of the Italian theater is that actresses played strong roles when the stage first allowed women to represent female parts, because the women themselves were responsible for devising the words, gestures, and tricks of the parts they performed, and thus they came up with confident, even somewhat "camp" performances. When the acts, however, started to be written down, a task taken up by men, as in Monteverdi's preoperatic pieces, gender roles became normalized, and actresses ended up playing more vanquished, abandoned, and doomed characters. Thus Nicholson sets the stage for a feminist study of the early modern Italian theater, one that would be useful to compare with the more substantial output on the still transvestite English stage.

Moving to Tasso, in " 'Dal rogo alle nozze': Tasso's Sofronia as Martyr Manqué" Naomi Yavneh argues that epic is a field reserved exclusively to men in Tasso; women can only have a romance ending, even when a more heroic/hagiographic one, as in the episode of Sofronia in canto 2 of the Liberata, would seem perfectly in tune with the events. Retracing the controversy over the worship of images and the church's explanation that idolatry does not come from the things we worship but from what we do with them, Yavneh reads the episode of Sofronia's condemnation to death as a story typical of martyred virgins. But Tasso refuses in the end to grant a privileged status in his epic to the heroics of virginity and chooses instead to portray Sofronia as a damsel in distress waiting for the saving grace of marriage.[11] To better accomplish her movement from bride of Christ to bride of Olindo, Tasso, who had earlier character-

---

11. For the heroism displayed by some of the condemned martyrs, see Schulenberg.

ized Sofronia as having manly courage (martyred virgins had "masculine strength" according to church fathers), now feminizes her, according to Yavneh, by reaffirming Saint Paul's teaching that a true Christian woman can only be subordinate to man. The demise of Sofronia's power is exemplified, as for all female martyrs, by taking care that she—soon to be married—no longer embodies the erotics of chastity.

Following up with an inquiry on gender relations in the *Furioso*, Constance Jordan links the woman question not to culture, as is often done, but to history. In "Writing beyond the *Querelle*: Gender and History in *Orlando furioso*," Jordan studies the figure of the woman warrior Bradamante and concludes that in Ariosto gender is just as undecidable as readings of history are. She argues that Ariosto moves beyond the treatment of the woman question present in the contemporary *querelle des femmes* and questions tenets of Renaissance thoughts through new readings of history that problematize society, its morality, and its politics. The new Ariostan woman is embodied in Bradamante, who alone is given the task of seeing history, as in the episodes of Merlin's tomb, where she understands the importance of woman to kinship; of Tristan's castle, where she sees how culture affects gender; and of Cassandra's tent, where she comprehends the ties between woman and property. Bradamante's sense of justice makes her a good reader of history, Jordan shows, because she recognizes that there are many ways of reading it, that signs are not necessarily truthful, that understandings that are not judgmental often do not come first, and that there is nothing definite in a world in flux. Endowed with virtues such as mercy, chastity, and a clear ability to manage things, Bradamante stands, for Jordan, as the idealized androgynous woman in the prowoman discourses of the time, for in emphasizing her agency Ariosto shows that all positive qualities have to be managed for good results, just as history cannot be read either positively or negatively and with no provisions for nuances and adaptations.

From Javitch's call for the saving grace of hybridization to Finucci's psychoanalytical examination of masculinity; from Zatti's experimentation with the "pensiero debole" to Nicholson's hyperreal theatrical performances; from Jordan's ironic readings of history to Yavneh's historicization of a fictional martyrdom; from Cavallo's accentuation of the power of romance to Hoffman's rewriting of the politics of honor; and from authorial weaving in Stephens to authorial homecoming in Martinez, these essays have brought ashore, I trust, original ways of reading Tasso and Ariosto in the context of our present preoccupations. They also pave the road, hopefully, for future investigations of other, not yet canonized or only cursorily studied, chivalric romances—both those written by men and those, recently recovered, written by women.[12]

Works Cited

Ariosto, Ludovico. *Orlando furioso*. Ed. Marcello Turchi. Milan: Garzanti, 1974.

Barth, John. "The Literature of Exhaustion." *Atlantic Monthly*, August 1967, 29–34.

Clubb, Louise. "Italian Renaissance Theater." *The Oxford Illustrated History of Theatre*. Ed. John Russell Brown. Oxford: Oxford UP, 1995. 107–41.

De Sanctis, Francesco. *History of Italian Literature*. Trans. Joan Redfern. New York: Harcourt, Brace, 1931.

Eco, Umberto. *Semiotics and the Philosophy of Language*. Bloomington: Indiana UP, 1984.

Erspamer, Francesco. "Il pensiero debole di Torquato Tasso." *La Menzogna*. Ed. Francesco Cardini. Florence: Ponte alle Grazie, 1989. 120–36.

Ferguson, Margaret. *Trials of Desire: Renaissance Defenses of Poetry*. New Haven: Yale UP, 1983.

Finucci, Valeria. "The Female Masquerade: Ariosto and the Game of Desire." *Desire in the Renaissance: Psychoanalysis and Literature*. Ed. Valeria Finucci and Regina Schwartz. Princeton: Princeton UP, 1994. 61–88.

———. "Moderata Fonte e il romanzo cavalleresco al femminile." *Moderata Fonte, Tredici canti del Floridoro*. Ed. Valeria Finucci. Modena: Mucchi, 1995. ix–xxxix.

Hauser, Arnold. *Mannerism: The Crisis of the Renaissance and the Origin of Modern Art*. New York: Knopf, 1965.

Javitch, Daniel. "*Cantus Interruptus* in the *Orlando Furioso*." *Modern Language Notes* 95 (1980): 66–80.

———. "The Imitation of Imitations in *Orlando Furioso*." *Renaissance Quarterly* 38 (1985): 215–39.

———. "The *Orlando Furioso* and Ovid's Revision of the *Aeneid*." *Modern Language Notes* 99 (1984): 1023–36.

———. *Proclaiming a Classic: The Canonization of Orlando Furioso*. Princeton: Princeton UP, 1991.

12. For a reconstruction of the genre of the chivalric romance written by women, see Finucci, "Moderata Fonte."

McKinney, Ronald. "The Origins of Postmodernism: The Ariosto-Tasso Debate." *Philosophy Today* 13 (1989): 232–44.

Nicholson, Eric. " 'That's How It Is': Comic Travesties of Sex and Gender in Early Sixteenth-Century Venice." *Look Who's Laughing: Gender and Comedy*. Ed. Gail Finney. Langhorne, Pa.: Gordon & Breach, 1994. 17–34.

Rivière, Joan. "Womanliness as a Masquerade." *Formations of Identity*. Ed. Victor Burgin, James Donald, and Cora Kaplan. London: Methuen, 1986. 35–44.

Rodini, Robert. "Selected Bibliography of Ariosto Criticism, 1980–87." *Modern Language Notes* 103 (1988): 187–203.

———. "Selected Bibliography of Ariosto Criticism: 1986–1993." *Annali d'Italianistica* 12 (1994): 299–317.

Rodini, Robert, and Salvatore Di Maria. *Ludovico Ariosto: An Annotated Bibliography of Criticism, 1956–1980*. Columbia: U of Missouri P, 1984.

Rorty, Richard. *Consequences of Pragmatism: Essays: 1972–1980*. Minneapolis: U of Minnesota P, 1982.

Schulenberg, Jane. "The Heroics of Virginity: Brides of Christ and Sacrificial Mutilation." *Women in the Middle Ages and the Renaissance*. Ed. Mary Beth Rose. Syracuse: Syracuse UP, 1986. 30–72.

Vattimo, Gianni, and Pier Aldo Rovatti, eds. *Il pensiero debole*. Milan: Feltrinelli, 1983.

Weinberg, Bernard. *A History of Literary Criticism in the Italian Renaissance*. Chicago: U of Chicago P, 1961.

Zatti, Sergio. *L'uniforme cristiano e il multiforme pagano: saggio sulla Gerusalemme liberata*. Milan: Saggiatore, 1983.

I
CROSSING GENRES

Two Odysseys: Rinaldo's Po Journey
and the Poet's Homecoming in *Orlando furioso*

RONALD L. MARTINEZ

Rinaldo's journey from Paris to Lipadusa frames the concluding episodes of the 1516 *Orlando furioso*, leading directly into the final exordium and its presentation of the narrator arriving by ship in port after the long, forty-canto excursion of his poem.[1] As the longest and most complex episode in the poem, Rinaldo's episode offers narrative, ethical, and cultural implications I propose to discuss in this essay. Beyond the intrinsic interest of Rinaldo's character and of the two *novelle* he hears on the subject of jealousy, the final position of the episode makes it important for critics interested in epic and romance closure;[2] more recently, Dave Henderson has suggested that in its original form the episode was composed as early as 1507, making it one of the germs of the *Furioso*. The poem began, then, with its end.

In the midst of a journey that had begun with Charlemagne in Paris, and continued via the Ardennes, the city of Basel, and the headwaters of the Rhone, Rhine, Danube, and Po, an anonymous Mantuan host delays Rinaldo and proposes he drink of the testing cup that would determine if his wife, Clarice, is faithful. To compensate for the delay, Rinaldo's host offers him overnight passage down the Po to Ravenna in a swift riverboat furnished with an informative helmsman, who narrates for the paladin the tale of Anselmo's comeuppance as a sequel to the host's own tale of misfortune caused by jealousy.[3] After a refreshing night's sleep

---

1. Studies of these cantos include Ceserani, Santoro, Moretti, Wiggins, Sherberg, Casadei, Zatti, Hoffman, Martinez, and Henderson. For the 1516 version, see Casadei *Il percorso*.

2. The tension between epic closure and romance deferral in the conclusion of the *Orlando furioso* (OF) has interested numerous readers: see Nohrnberg; Parker; Zatti; Marsh; Quint, "Boat"; Sitterson; Quint, "Death"; and Casadei, "Breve analisi."

3. For Rajna (580) a parallel is the poem by Antonio Fregoso, *La cerva bianca*, which reports a

on the boat, Rinaldo continues overland to Urbino, Rome, and Ostia, and from there by sea to Trapani, site of Anchises' tomb, arriving finally in Lipadusa, though too late to save the life of Brandimarte, killed, at the tragic climax of Ariosto's narrative, by Gradasso wielding Orlando's sword, Durindana.

But the place where Rinaldo wakes up during his passage is also important: the neighborhood of Ferrara, including the island of Belvedere. Passing it, Rinaldo prophesies a future Estense golden age of good government, liberal studies, and courtly manners. Although the Gascon Rinaldo is hardly Ferrarese, his arrival near Ferrara has the quality of a homecoming—indeed he refers to a previous visit. Readers have therefore intuited that the journey suggests Ariosto's own cultural itinerary as well—not merely the derivation of chivalric literature from France, but recall of accomplishments by the Renaissance courts of Mantua, Ferrara, Urbino, and Rome. In this sense, the transition to the narrator's homecoming from the sea, opening the subsequent and concluding canto in the 1516 *Furioso*, is the logical pendant to Rinaldo's journey down the Po. The poet's homecoming is also a return to his cultural springs.

Wings of Oars: Ulysses in Homer, Pulci, Boiardo, and Dante.

Preparing a previous study of this episode with an eye on the theme of destroying chastity with money, I was struck by parallels between Rinaldo's journey and another famous voyage of homecoming, that of Homer's Odysseus, sent home to Ithaca from Scheria, the island of the utopian Phaeacians ruled by King Antinous and Queen Arete. Like Odysseus, conveyed in the sure, swift ships of the Phaeacians—ships as fast as chariots or birds—Rinaldo's host offers him a perfectly safe journey in a ship as fast as a hunting falcon.[4] Like Odysseus, who sleeps a deep

---

banquet offered Fregoso by Apuano and a subsequent riverboat journey with a chatty helmsman. Fregoso, however, does not sleep.

4. See *Odyssey* 13.85–98: "She ran on / very steady and never wavering; even the falcon, / that hawk that flies lightest of winged creatures, could not have paced her, / so lightly did she

sleep, very like death, as he returns to his home (*Odyssey* 13.70–125), Rinaldo sleeps between his journey's beginning in Mantua and his arrival near Ferrara—the future home of Este rule and of the poet Ariosto, perhaps not by accident itself compared, in terms of the island *delizia* of Belvedere, to the island of the Phaeacians in stanzas Ariosto added for the 1532 edition (OF 43.56–59).[5] Like Odysseus, whose last nights before sailing are spent hearing two principal tales—the tale of Troy sung by Demodokos, and Odysseus's wanderings related by himself—Rinaldo hears a pair of stories, one before, one as he sets out on his journey.[6] The narrative functions exercised by Demodokos and Odysseus are represented in Ariosto's episode by the helmsman and by the Mantuan host who tells his own story, while Rinaldo retains Odysseus's function as auditor, an attribute Rinaldo displays in the related episode of Ginevra earlier in the *Furioso*. Finally, like Odysseus, for whom the journey home to Ithaca is the turning point in his journey when his wanderings finally become his homecoming, Rinaldo's journey, though not taking him home, does return the poem to its origin in the culture of the Po valley.

In proposing these parallels, I am not overlooking the difficulties in documenting Ariosto's direct knowledge of Homer's text, in any language.[7] I take it as probable that like his predecessor, Boiardo, he had a

---

run on her way and cut through the sea's waves. / She carried a man with a mind like the Gods for counsel . . . / but now he slept still, oblivious of all he had suffered." The Phaeacians point out that their ships suffer no danger because of Poseidon's protection: "nor is there ever / any fear that they may suffer damage or come to destruction" (*Odyssey* 8.562–63). Compare OF 43.51–52, 43.56, and 43.63 ("con maggiore [fretta] al logoro non scende / falcon ch'al grido del padrone risponde").

5. Ariosto refers to "la patria di Nausicaa" (Scheria) and evokes the topics of the golden age. Giamatti, *Earthly Paradise*, discusses the topic, but omits Ariosto's mention of the Phaeacians (*Odyssey* 7.117, 8.248–49) and his description of Alcina's island (the love of bathing and changing clothes, OF 7.31) and Logistilla's orchards (OF 10.63).

6. That storytelling is itself a conveyance is of course a topos: cf. Apuleius, *Metamorphoses* 1.2; Boccaccio, *Decameron* 6.1.7, but especially Boiardo's Fiordelisa (*Innamorato* 1.12.3) (OI) and Doristella (2.26.20.8: "Perchè parlando se ascurta il camino").

7. Ariosto might have read the *Odyssey* in the Latin translation of Rafaello da Volterra, pub-

working understanding of the principal episodes in Homer's narrative,[8] and certainly of an episode in the poem as crucial as Odysseus's return to Ithaca—one that was, in addition to its structural importance, significant in the tradition of Neoplatonic glosses on the Homeric poems and in Aristotle's discussion of epic form in the *Poetics*.[9] Still, my case rests not on the Homeric text alone, but on the complex tradition accreted around the figure of Ulysses in Latin literature,[10] in the text of Dante's *Commedia*, and in the tradition of *cantastorie* and chivalric romance, notably Pulci and Boiardo.

For even granting that Ariosto has drawn from Homer in fashioning Rinaldo's voyage down the Po (I will discuss his very significant modifications later),[11] the adoption of the Homeric model is scarcely unmediated.[12] In the chivalric tradition it is precisely the figure of Rinaldo

---

lished in Rome in 1510, or learned about the poem from Boiardo, who worked with Greek (see Reichenbach 192–97). In his *Satira* 6 Ariosto refers several times to Ulysses (134, 173–74, 201).

8. See Lansing, Fachard, and King; Boiardo mentions the Cyclops at 1.6.28; 3.3.28 (*orco*), the Sirens at 2.4.36–39, and his Circella evokes Circe; the Lestrigoni, are at 2.18.33. Boiardo's episode of the Cyclops and Norandino is continued by Ariosto, whose principal Homeric borrowing is of Alcina as Circe, mediated through Virgil, Ovid, Boethius, and Boiardo; Astolfo's control of the winds (38.29–30) plays on the failure of Odysseus's crew to do so (all these episodes were of course the object of Neoplatonic commentary on the story of the *Odyssey*; cf. Buffiere 365–418). Ariosto several times refers to both Ulysses and Penelope (OF 13.60; 33.28; 36.70; Penelope, 13.60, 35.27). For Orlando's return to "sanity" in the OI and Odysseus's return, see Cannon 127; she considers Ulysses a model for Orlando (Cannon 42–43, 51–53, 93–95).

9. See Aristotle, *Poetics*, ch. 24. Rajna (567) notes that Ruggiero swimming for conversion on the island with the hermit recalls Odysseus swimming from his raft-wreck to Scheria.

10. Relevant passages from Cicero and Horace, stressing the stoic Ulysses who suffers, endures, and is prudent, are cited and summarized in Defaux 23–68, 153–63; and see Castiglione 4.47.

11. Other possible parallels are Rinaldo's uncharacteristic tipping of the boatman (43.147), recalling Odysseus's gift to Demodokos, *Odyssey* 8.474–81 (both heroes are typically impoverished). Ariosto also refers to the Cyclopes (OF 43.185) next to whom the Phaeacians formerly resided (*Odyssey* 6.5).

12. See Javitch, "Imitation."

who draws to himself the reputation and practices of a wandering and curious Odysseus, whose reputation, seriously damaged under Roman culture because of his role in the destruction of Troy, began to be rehabilitated in the Quattrocento. But the ambivalence Dante expresses for Ulysses did not disappear. The Renaissance, which knew and praised the prudent and durable stoic Ulysses, as well as the Neoplatonic Ulysses, who exemplified the return of the soul to its home, still hesitated before the wily and crafty Ulysses, master of dangerous stratagems and virtuoso of lies, *fandi fictor*.[13]

Ariosto found the link between Rinaldo and Dante's Ulysses fully formed in Pulci's *Morgante*. Late in the poem, after the rout of Roncevaux and death of Orlando, Rinaldo announces to Charlemagne that he is going exploring past the pillars of Hercules to the antipodes, "to search the whole world like Ulysses" (28.29.3–4).[14] Pulci's comparison sets the seal on Rinaldo's extensive wanderings thus far in the poem, an odyssey in themselves: to Egypt to see the pyramids (25.122), thence through the Hellespont to Mount Olympus and Mount Zion in the Holy Land and all the way to "India" to see Prester John. Finally he returns to Egypt through the pillars of Hercules "and above all he commended Ulysses / who went to the other world to see" (25.130). These journeys are completed with the narrator's decision to bring Rinaldo to the scene of the massacre at Roncevaux, though he arrives too late to affect the outcome (25.115). Leaping through the air on a demonically driven Baiardo, Rinaldo's voyage to Roncevaux occurs within a context whose exemplary figure is, as Dieter Kremers showed, Dante's curious Ulysses.[15] With his lengthy Rinaldo episode (248 stanzas), Ariosto in fact imitates Pulci's

---

13. On Ulysses' reputation in Latin culture, see Stanford, Kremers, Defaux, and recently Boitani, who takes Ariosto to be an enthusiast for the adventuresome Ulysses: but Ariosto mentions Ulysses' treachery in the death of Astyanax (OF 36.70). Defaux's study presents a more complete picture of the Renaissance Ulysses, giving equal weight to both prudent and deceitful aspects.

14. See *Morgante* 28.33.7–8: "come disotto in quell'altro emisspero / erano e guerre e monarchie e regni, / e che e' passassi alfin d'Ercule i segni."

15. See Kremers, esp. 90–120.

lengthy closure to the *Morgante* (217 stanzas), and as David Quint has pointed out, the journey by river, land, and sea to Lipadusa in Ariosto's poem imitates Rinaldo's journey in Pulci's poem.[16]

Boiardo's treatment of Rinaldo does nothing to undermine the identification of Rinaldo with Ulysses found in the *Morgante*, although in the *Orlando innamorato* it remains inexplicit. In 2.5.40–56 Rinaldo is drawn away from his duel with Gradasso by a phantom figure of Gradasso himself, who leads him on board a ship that soon departs from shore, en route to a pleasance designed by Angelica. Boiardo's language ("He has turned his stern [Volto ha la poppa] to the wind of Seville") echoes the setting out of the ship of Ulysses and his crew in the *Inferno* ("turning our stern [Volta la nostra poppa] to the morning") and his ship likely adopts the same route, passing Seville on the right, then what is now Gibraltar, and heading out to sea on a leftward, southwesterly course.[17]

Although generally speaking Ulysses is identified by Boiardo with his Orlando, who defeats a Polyphemus figure (1.6.28–34), it is Boiardo's Rinaldo who is chosen by Angelica to rescue Brandimarte and Orlando, given drugs by Dragontina that, like Circe's, transmute them from whom they are (1.6.45). More important for the structural links of the *Innamorato* and the *Furioso*, Rinaldo's distraction from his duel with Gradasso anticipates Rinaldo's pretext for departing Paris in canto 42 of the *Furioso* —the need to seek Baiardo, still in the possession of Gradasso, now on Lipadusa with the other combatants. Thus, although Ariosto certainly associates Ulysses' voyages "following the sun" with other characters in the poem, notably the globe-girdling Ruggiero and Astolfo, Rinaldo as voyager in cantos 42–43 of the *Furioso* demonstrably evokes the tradition of a Rinaldo-Ulysses established by Pulci and Boiardo.[18]

16. See Quint, "Death," 80–81.

17. Charles Ross points out in his translation of *OI* that Rinaldo sails west beyond the pillars of Hercules, then doubles back east (886). Rinaldo also sails back from the Danube via Cyprus; for the relation of this itinerary to the story of Ulysses, see Corti 119–22. Translations in the texts and notes are by the author, with the exception of Dante's *Inferno*, where I follow Durling and Martinez.

18. Ariosto establishes links between Rinaldo, Ruggiero, and Astolfo: Astolfo is of course both Ruggiero's predecessor on Alcina's island and the successor to the hippogriff, while

Despite the immediate parallels from the chivalric poems, Dante's Ulysses remains fundamental to establishing the Odyssean parameters for the journeys, in the *Furioso*, of Rinaldo and of the narrator. Dante's Ulysses describes his own journey through the Mediterranean, seeing "the one shore and the other" (l'un lito e l'altro) until reaching the present straits of Gibraltar

> which Hercules marked with his warnings so that one should not go further; on the right hand I had left Seville [da la man destra mi lasciai Sibilia], on the other I had already left Ceuta [da l'altra m'avea lasciata Setta].[19]

Ariosto in turn casts Rinaldo's journey in the language and rhythms of Dante's Ulysses, which in effect mark off the principal stages in Rinaldo's journey, from when he leaves Paris ("Lascia Parigi," 42.43.7), to his speedy crossing of the Alps once he hears of the duel, leaving Verona and Mantua behind ("Verona a dietro, a dietro Mantua lassa," 42.69.7), to his descent of the river past Estensi landmarks, leaving behind Melara on the left shore and Sermide on the right ("Restò Melara nel lito mancino; / Nel lito destro Sermide restosse," 43.53.5–6).

There can thus be little doubt about the close relation of Rinaldo's voyage with the narrator's, which includes the same cities (Ferrara, Mantua, Urbino; cf. 46.10) and which features the ladies and poets who were Ariosto's patrons and fellows. Ariosto's episode, in anticipating the narrator's return home in the exordium to canto 46, also echoes in this sense the intervention of the narrator in the *Morgante* (he names himself at *Morgante* 25.115), the more so for Pulci's remark, at canto

---

Ruggiero's first flight on the flying beast—a descendant of the high-leaping Baiardo of the *Morgante* (see Pulci, and Ariosto's comparisons of the fliers to Phaethon, both probably deriving from Dante's Geryon; cf. Ascoli 135–68) takes place in *Orlando furioso* 4.50, upon which the narrator returns to tell of Rinaldo's voyage to Scotland (4.51). In the *Cantari di Rinaldo di Montealbano*, Rinaldo is the best-traveled paladin; the reputation of *viator* that Sherberg ("Ariosto's Rinaldo") assigns to him is closely related to the identification with Ulysses.

19. Dante (Alighieri, *Inferno*, 403, 405) is recalling classical instances, of course, from Ovid's Icarus (*Metamorphoses* 8.220–25) and Statius's Ulysses in the *Achilleid* (1.675–81); see also *Metamorphoses* 12.101–3.

24.1–2, of a link to Rinaldo "called out" of Egypt ("it is meet that you should call me out of Egypt"), but also to Homer the fabulist, who, like the poets mentioned by Ariosto's Saint John, was thought to have "too much exalted the wanderings of Ulysses" (24.2). In *Morgante* 28.130–31, the parallels are explicit, the narrator asserting that he "do[es] not wish again to tempt Abila and Calpe" (the Strait of Gibraltar), though "if [he] wished to go farther than Ulysses, there is a lady in heaven who will ever shield [him]." Ariosto's reference to "she who has escorted me over this long sea" (46.1.3–4) echoes Pulci's use of the invocation of the Virgin as his home port in the *Morgante* (28.2.6–8), and in his anxiety about being lost at sea reenacts the insistent fear of Homer's Odysseus that he would "lose the day of his homecoming" (*Odyssey* 1.9, 168, 413).[20] In consulting his *carte*, a word that conflates a navigator's charts with the poet's pages—Ariosto betrays the fact that his journeys were literary, performed by scanning Ptolemaic geographies in Ferrarese libraries and the pages of the poets that were his exemplars. In this sense Ariosto's ship, too, like those of the Phaeacians, "moved swift as thought, or as a winged creature" (*Odyssey* 7.36).

Indeed, the simile in Homer of the vessel as a bird is closely related to the prophecy made by Tiresias, in Hades, of Odysseus's last journey to a place where his oar will be taken for a winnowing fan. Tiresias's account of "oars, which act for ships as wings do" (*Odyssey* 11.125, 23.272) is the origin of the famous trope used in Virgil, Ovid, and the medieval Latin rhetorical tradition to describe the oars of the ship as wings (*remigium alarum*).[21] This metaphor becomes the emblem of the last journey of Ulysses in Dante's poem, and may be taken as the emblem of the continuity between the voyage of Ulysses and those of the several Rinaldos and their narrators.[22] As the figure was for the rhetoricians an instance

20. See Casadei "L'esordio."

21. See Raimondi, Freccero, and Gorni.

22. For the "wings of oars" in connection with the flights of Ruggiero and Astolfo, see Ascoli 145–46 and 135–62; also 378. For the implications of Tiresias's prophecy for the evolving Renaissance figure of Ulysses, see Boitani 17–23.

of an elegant "reciprocal" metaphor (there may be both "oars of wings" and "wings of oars") it may stand as an exemplary instance of the metamorphic power of poetry itself,[23] though in its final misprision as a winnowing fan it marks the limit of all sailing and is thus a sign of death. In its combined figuration of tropical discourse and of the extraordinary literary/nautical journey, the *remigium alarum* trope links Rinaldo's journeys on the one hand to storytelling, and thus to Odysseus as a notorious inventor of fables, including the account of his own journey told to the Phaeacians; and on the other hand to the narrator's own verbal journey brought to completion in Ariosto's canto 46.[24] The prophecy of Odysseus's last journey and the journey as narrated in the Latins and Dante are thus themselves troped together, or transumed, into Ariosto's text.[25]

Beyond the Mark: This Story's About You

Ariosto's lengthy episode follows Rinaldo from his first decision to pursue Angelica as far as Cathay, corresponding to Rinaldo's decision, in Pulci, to follow the track of Ulysses to the antipodes, to his arrival at Lipadusa—in the case of Pulci, Roncevaux. This linking of the episode to the universal madness inflicted by love and jealousy—the madness that drives Orlando to explode at the poem's center—points to the morally therapeutic dimensions of Rinaldo's journey. Rinaldo's reeducation begins with a drink from the stream of *disamore* to cure him of jealousy and concludes with the tale of Anselmo, which confirms Rinaldo's decision to reject the cup that would have tested the chastity of Clarice. In the context of his voyage through Italy to Lipadusa, Rinaldo's rejection

---

23. Raimondi 32–33.

24. Numerous readers (see Raimondi, Freccero, Musa, and Gorni) argue that for Dante Ulysses' "wings of oars" both parallel and contrast with the pilgrim-poet's own audacious voyage, requiring both metaphorical sails (as in *Paradiso* 1) and metaphorical wings (as in *Purgatorio* 27.123). For the self-projection of Dante's pilgrim—and of Dante himself—into the figure of Ulysses, see Lotman, Shankland, Scott, Ferrucci, Boitani, and Corti.

25. See Barkan 41–48 for the use of transumption in narrative and history.

of the cup marks his refusal to transgress a dangerous limit: a refusal springing in part from consciousness of his own shortcomings and the awareness that he too is being tested. How does this series of events echo the homecoming of Ulysses?

With the host's regret that he inquired "beyond the limit" (oltre la meta) of what it was lawful to know about his wife's fidelity, Ariosto links the drinking of the cup to the temptation of Adam (43.8), and, indirectly, to Dante's account of the transgression of Ulysses beyond the limits set so that explorers "should not go further" (più oltre non si metta).[26] The cup of jealousy is also allusively the bitter cup of Christ's passion (cf. 42.7, "let this wine be taken from before me" and Luke 22:42, "remove this chalice from me") and, given the context of fidelity, the cup of faith that forms part of Saint John's iconography.[27] In Ariosto's case the mad desire of Dante's Ulysses to know the antipodes is posed rather of the more domestic ambition of desiring to know the wife's chastity. Nevertheless, there is a sense in which the geographical *hybris* of Dante's Ulysses is indeed at stake here in terms of the narrator's need to reach the limit, the closure of his poem. Or, in the terms of the exordium to canto 46, for the navigating epic poet to furl sails and reach port lest he be lost at sea.[28]

In Ariosto's account, the testing horn of chastity is explicitly linked to the romances of Tristan. In the context of allusion to Homeric materials, however, the cup also suggests the cup of Circe, versions of which Ariosto had already employed in the episodes of Astolfo and Ruggiero involving Alcina; both knights fall under her sway, with Astolfo transformed into a myrtle bush. Within the two *novelle* told to Rinaldo, both

---

26. Dante established the parallel between the "trapassar del segno" of Adam's sin and Ulysses' transgressive journey beyond the pillars of Hercules: the canto of *Inferno* and *Paradiso* share the same number, and Dante again recalls his Ulisse and his "folle varco" just after his interview with Adamo (*Paradiso* 27.82–83). Boccaccio noticed the link; see his gloss, quoted in Boitani 47; see also Kremers 90–120 and Damon 37–42.

27. For the link of the Mantuan host's cup to the cup of faith, see Ascoli 327, 337.

28. Pulci refers to Homer's Ulysses as too much exalted (24.2), and to the danger of foundering in the sea (23.1), passages which bracket his beginning of the *aggiunta* to the *Morgante*.

Melissa and Manto tempt with the cup of dangerous knowledge that would destroy domestic complacency: in this sense the stories replicate the tension in the Ulysses story between pursuing experience and returning home. Neoplatonic allegories of the Ulysses story saw in the Circe episode the resistance of Ulysses' human reason to the bestializing effects of the passions.[29] But in the context of Rinaldo's episode, the cup rather tests Rinaldo's ability to restrain jealous curiosity after his therapeutic drink concluding canto 42.[30]

Such a link between fountain and cup had already been authorized by Boiardo's use of Dragontina's cup of forgetfulness, drawn from a river, to enchant Orlando in the *Innamorato*, with explicit reference to Circe and her "goblet of enchantment" (1.6.45, 1.6.52), an episode thematically and structurally parallel to the attempted seduction of Rinaldo (who has just drunk of *disamore*, "unloving") by Angelica (who has drunk from *amore*) at the outset of the lengthy and fruitless pursuit that ends only with Rinaldo's drink at *Orlando furioso* 42.63. The continuity of fountain and cup may also be deduced from the establishment of the "fountain of unloving" by Merlin in order to cure Tristan of the love philter he drank with Isolde, which brings us back to Ariosto's etiology of the cup offered Rinaldo as the testing cup from the Tristan story (42.103, 43.28). For in the *Tavola ritonda* the episodes of the love philter and of Isolde's chastity test are closely linked by the narrative: where the love philter irrevocably binds, the testing cup scandalizes and divides.

Philters, magic cups, and enchanting fountains are thus part of one system. Indeed, we might say that cups, rivers, and fountains are part of one system, just as the waters that emerge from the fountain of the

29. Horace pairs the episodes of Circe and the Sirens with Ulysses' return in his *Epistolae* 1.2.16–26; the juxtaposition was commonplace. For the Boethian and Neoplatonic traditions of interpreting the transformations imposed by Circe (enslavement to vices, and loss of humanity; metemsomatosis into the bodies of animals), see Buffiere, 507–16; Lamberton 278–79).

30. In the *Odyssey*, Odysseus drains the cup with impunity, since he is protected by the moly furnished him by Hermes; in Ovid and Boethius the drinking is omitted, though implied, while for Horace Ulysses refuses the cup; cf. *Epistolae* 1.2.25–26.

chaste ladies in Ariosto's palace of the mournful *oste* are probably to be thought of as linked to the "fountain of unloving," the Po river system, and the cup that tests chastity—Ariosto's chaste ladies are all evidently winners in this test. That these fountains cause the remembering and forgetting of *folle amore* suggests their link to the fundamental topic of the Ulysses narrative: the quest of the protagonist to return home, or, in negative terms, not to forget it: as in Boiardo's Dragontina-Circella episode, the various Circe, Calypso, Lotofagi, and Sirens are all designed to erase the memory of the homeland through gratification and pleasure.[31]

The emphasis on chastity itself in the offer to Rinaldo also suggests a Homeric counterpart: the long test of the chastity of Penelope by the absence of Odysseus. Ariosto, praising Isabella d'Este in canto 13,[32] compares her to Penelope in being as faithful as Ulysses, a gesture that anticipates Rinaldo's evenhandedness to men and women in his answer to his host (43.47–49). Told in two different versions, the tale of Ovid's Cephalus, mediated by Niccolò da Correggio's *Fabula di Cefalo*, is the basis for the two narratives about the imprudence of testing wifely chastity. The *Odyssey* shares with Niccolò da Correggio's *Fabula* and with Ariosto's

---

31. Homer's Circe gives Odysseus's men drugs that "make them forgetful of their own country" (*Odyssey* 10.236), and Circe herself warns that if Odysseus hears the Sirens he "has no prospect of coming home" (11.41–42); such is also the effect of the "Fount of laughter" ("Fontana del riso") in the *Orlando innamorato*; cf. Cannon 121–29. Boiardo and Ariosto's two fountains have been variously traced (see Ponte) to Claudian, Poliziano, Sannazaro, and Petrarch (*Canzoniere* 135, vv. 60–90). In light of Rinaldo's "purification" from jealousy, Dante's Letè and Eunoè are relevant: Boiardo's rivers restore and delete memory of Love, as Dante's rivers do for bad deeds and good.

32. Compare OF 13.60: "Sol perche casta visse, / Penelope non fu minor d'Ulisse"; in this she equals her husband, Francesco Gonzaga, who defeated the French on the Taro. For Isabella d'Este Gonzaga, often grouped with Alfonso and Ippolito, her brothers (cf. 13.68), see also 13.59, where she is the benefactress of Mantua ("aprica / fara la terra che sul Menzo siede, / a cui la madre d'Ocno il nome diede"); implied as the paragon of chastity because she is carrying the name of Zerbino's Isabell, 29.29; 41.67, and 42.84, where she is the second pillared lady (just before the Mantuans Elizabetta and Leonora Gonzaga), and where she is presented as bringing good to Ferrara. For Henderson, Isabella was the focus of the earliest version of the fountain episode.

tales for Rinaldo the ruse of presenting the testing husband (or a surrogate) disguised in order to tempt the spouse. As Odysseus is accused by a Scherian of being a most unheroic merchant (*Odyssey* 7.158–64), both da Correggio's Cefalo and Ariosto's *oste* disguise themselves as merchants setting out to "buy" a chaste wife: even Boiardo's Rinaldo could be taunted by Orlando for having once disguised himself as a merchant (OI 1.28.5) in order to kidnap a princess for Charlemagne.[33]

In addition to narrating the degradation of the wife into merchandise, Ariosto mentions, as part of Saint John's revelation of authorial distortions of truth, that just as Virgil lied in having made Dido unchaste, so Homer lied in making Penelope chaste.[34] Given that Ulysses' account of his adventures to the Phaeacians was a proverbial instance of fiction, what Erasmus, using Plato's phrase, called *apologus Alcinoi*,[35] it is reasonable to suppose that a lying Homer and a lying Odysseus are closely related: indeed, it is the existence of a character like Odysseus *fandi fictor* that accounts for that unreliability of narrators of which Saint John speaks. In this light, the staging of several tales of chastity threatened and destroyed at the end of the 1516 *Furioso* might appear a confirmation of Saint John's recommendation that the statements of poets be read in reverse—undermining the claims of Penelope's chastity and implicitly reversing the outcome of the *Odyssey* itself.

But Ariosto's *novelle* are more complex still than this, focusing closely

33. Boiardo refers to an episode (OI 1.28.5) from the anonymous romance *Innamoramento del Re Carlo Magno* (princeps, 1481); see Bruscagli's note (1, 495) pointing out that Orlando joined in the venture as well.

34. For a precedent, see Horace, *Satires* 2.5.81–83, claiming that Penelope, like Ulysses himself, would have gladly sold herself for money: the premise is closely related to the presuppositions of the *novelle* Rinaldo hears, which depict avarice ravaging chastity; this is an instance of the "impoverished" Ulysses. For Rinaldo's poverty, see OI 2.9.32–40.

35. Defaux (44–49, 155–57) points out that Erasmus included the phrase *apologia Alcinoi* in the *Adagia* in reference to Ulysses' reputation as a liar; the notion goes back to Plato's Socrates, who compares his myth of Er to Ulysses's tales for the Phaeacians; to Lucian's *Vera historia*, and to Juvenal (*Satires* 15.13–26), where Ulysses is the "mendax aretalogus" who takes in the Phaeacians with outrageous lies about his travels.

on the folly of wishing to *know* the chastity of the wife: that is, on the folly of suspicion, of going *plus ultra* in surveillance of the wife, as Ariosto warns in his fifth *Satira* (5.283–88). As I have argued elsewhere, the second *novella* in particular emphasizes how the husband's need to know is tyrannical[36] and his umbrage hypocritical, since he cannot himself pass the test arranged for him by his wife, Argia. The impasse presented by the wife's unchastity and the husband's tyranny is broken only by the exposure of Anselmo's hypocrisy and Argia's pardon. In the fact that both spouses "test" each other we can detect traces of the mutual testing of Odysseus and Penelope in the last ten books of the *Odyssey*, but Ariosto's conclusion, with its emphasis on a reconciliation that springs acknowledged mutual fragility and forebearance, adapts to Christian humanism Homer's portraits of Odysseus and Penelope as equal to each other in wary resourcefulness.

That Ariosto's jealous men are hypocrites, unable to "see the beam in their own eye" (OF 43.128.3)[37] points to the emphasis throughout the whole episode on consciousness of faults in the self. Ariosto has designed the episode so that the *fabulae* that Rinaldo hears are not only about Rinaldo and his host, but, given the close intertextual links with the question of spying on wives in Ariosto's fifth *Satira*, and the presence of both Ariosto and Alessandra Benucci, whose figures are concealed in the episode of the fountain of chaste ladies, about the narrator and the author as well. As I have suggested elsewhere, this presentation of character, narrator, authorial figure, and reader as common addressees of the message of the *novelle* stages the Horatian commonplace *de te fabula*: "what are you laughing at? . . . [T]he story's about you" (*Satires* 1.1.69). The ensemble of tale and frame strongly underlines the moment of embarrassed self-recognition: Rinaldo, upon hearing of Anselmo's comeuppance, blushes and laughs (43.144), just as the host and his wife

---

36. Martinez passim. Sherberg, "Ariosto's Rinaldo," 150, points here to a possible parallel, in Anselmo's attempt to know the future, to Dante's Amphiaraus (a Theban) who "volle veder troppo davanti" (*Inferno* 20.38).

37. "[O]r quella che era una festuca, è una trave"; cf. Matthew 7:5.

had both turned pale at the moment her infidelity was revealed (43.40). Rinaldo's comment on the tale emphasizes the ethical symmetry of the outcome ("she made him fall into the same net") and refers to Argia's fault as "a lesser fault," which echoes an earlier exchange about laying blame between narrator and imagined reader just after Orlando's onset of madness: "Brother, you point out those of others, but see not your own fault" (24.1.3), which itself evokes Horatian and Petrarchan precedents.[38] Ariosto's text, which had earlier mentioned Morgana's cup as designed to inform Arthur "of Guinevere's fault" (43.28) itself suggests the poetic precedent underlying this iteration of *fallo*: Dante's reference to "il primo fallo scritto di Ginevra" (*Paradiso* 16.15) and its dramatic realization in the *Inferno*, the Guinevere-inspired fatal reading of Paolo and Francesca, at the end of which the reader sees evidence of the poet-pilgrim's own overinvestment in the pathos of Francesca's narrative.

The tendency of these last tales to turn the tables on male complacency and implicate Rinaldo as auditor and "reader," as well as Ariosto as narrator and author, also raises the question of the relationship between the *Furioso* and the *Odyssey* in terms of narrative devices. In Homer's poem, it is during Ulysses' sojourn in Scheria with the Phaeacians that he hears the tale of Troy and relates his own wanderings: he is both the teller and the tale told, both active and passive in relation to his own story; and this singular doubling of his identity seems to prepare and announce his return home. As writers on Homer's account have pointed out,[39] what is at stake in the episode of Scheria is precisely the constitution of the fame, the *kleos* of Odysseus, which is to say the text of the

---

38. See Martinez 94–95, for the use of a closely related passage from Horace, *Sermones* 1.3.19–20 ("quid tu? nullane habes vitia"); for the reproach of the moralizing narrator in OF 24.3 in the context of universal madness, see Durling 168–69.

39. See Segal 23–35, Ferrucci, and Pucci 214–45. The testing cup presented to Rinaldo evokes the opening scene of the *Cantari di Rinaldo* (1.6–12) where Aymon, Rinaldo's father, is interrupted when drinking from Charlemagne's cup by "il traditor Ginamo di Baiona" (Ganelon). Ginamo claims Aymon's sons for his own, so accusing Rinaldo of illegitimacy and Rinaldo's mother of unchastity; this event, the origin of Rinaldo's difficulties with his father, helps define his rebellious role and character.

Odyssey itself, in contradistinction to the different account in the *Iliad*. In this sense, the constitution of the *Odyssey* as a new "version" of the events at Troy (analogous to those listed by Ariosto's Saint John) is gestated during the sojourn on Scheria.

In the case of Ariosto's poem, Rinaldo (like Rodomonte, earlier, listening to the tale of Giocondo) is twice a listener of a tale for which his recent cure from jealousy gives him a role as a potentially suspicious husband.[40] But unlike Ulysses, Rinaldo does not himself narrate. This function, we saw, is taken over by the chatty helmsman or, at another level, by the narrator and poet inscribed among the sculptured poets in the underground Mantuan palace of canto 42. Rinaldo as reader and listener, and Ariosto as narrator and writer divide up the cycle of communication.[41] I will return later to the implications for the "figure of the poet" of the Homeric model here proposed, and to a rationale for the diffraction of the figure of the poet into author, narrator, and auditor.

Sources of Eloquence: Coming Home

The convergence of a Homeric Odysseus with the Latin and Dantesque Ulysses is itself a chief part of Ariosto's extensive muster and review of materials and sources in cantos 42–43 and 46. In this section, I propose that the exordium to canto 46, where the poet returns and is met by the ladies, poets, and friends who have been his faithful readers, concludes a broader thematics of homecoming in cantos 42–43. As noted earlier, full homecoming is primarily at the level of the poet, who, like Ulysses, feared he might be one whose "day of homecoming has perished" (*Odyssey* 1.165–68; OF 46.1). Perhaps the strongest element in the homecoming is the poet's covert self-insertion as one who sustains the fame of his lady: in this sense there is no home like the poet's self, and no situation

---

40. Rinaldo is repeatedly a listener and a reader in the first book of the *Orlando innamorato*; see 1.8.27–52; 1.12.5–89; 1.xiii.30–45; 1.16.2–16. For Odysseus's assumption of these roles, see Ferrucci 48–50.

41. Sherberg, "Ariosto's Rinaldo," 86, 181.

closer to the making of the poem than this immediate derivation of inspiration from his and (it is implied) from the ladies, variously related to the Este court, found extolled in the fountain of chastity. The connection of the poets and ladies in the fountain of chastity and those in the exordium remains unmistakable even in the 1532 edition, and not only because of the common thread of poetry and patronage: members of the house of Correggio are featured in both locations, as is the poet, first mute and concealed, and then—as the narrator—publicly celebrated.[42]

As readers have suggested, Rinaldo's voyage presents a recapitulation both of the late Gothic and humanist culture of the Valpadane courts, and of Ariosto's own migrations from Ferrara to Urbino and Rome. Indeed, as we descend from France we descend into Latin culture (we might think of this descent or *calata* as benign, reversing the violent descents of French armies described in the Rocca di Tristano), and we touch on locations rich in cultural and literary memory: Virgil's Mantua, Dante's Ravenna, Castiglione's Urbino: later points, such as Trapani, site of Anchises' tomb (43.149), also associated with the Cyclopes (43.185), suggest turning points in the epic journeys of Aeneas and Odysseus.[43] Inflecting the voyage as an Odyssean *nostos* enriches the episode, for the thematics of homecoming are emphasized at several levels. First, we find frequent reference to the myths of civic origins (Mantua and Ferrara); second, we find allusions, which also attribute textual filiation, to the cardinal texts of chivalric and romance traditions, the *matières* of France and Britain, as well as to the *matières* of Troy and Rome, and to the canonical texts of Virgil and Ovid in Latin, and of Dante, Pulci, and Boiardo in the vernacular. Finally, but most significant, are the traces of the more

---

42. For a study of the list and Ariosto's revisions of it, see Casadei, "L'esordio." The Correggi are also featured because of the role of Niccolò da Correggio's text in the two last *novelle* of the Orlando furioso; see Martinez passim.

43. See Ceserani, "Due modelli culturali," 501. Sherberg, "Ariosto's Rinaldo," 179, sees Rinaldo transformed from a French knight, "Franco cavalier," to an Italian one as he effects his journey; the whole episode, he claims, is "an allegory of the evolution of Italian narrative." For French romance in the Mantuan court, see Woods-Marsden.

bourgeois tradition of prose *novella* and vernacular drama suggested by the use of Boccaccio and Niccolò da Correggio. In their weave, the cantos exhibit much of what constitutes Ariosto's literary culture.[44] A third form of "return" is formal. Narrative closure is achieved by cycling back to the origins of the *Orlando furioso* in Boiardo's poem, and to earlier portions of the *Furioso* itself: for example, the episode of Rinaldo's adventure in Scotland. The homecoming is thus complex, and conducted both intratextually and metatextually, involving a return to the sources of patronage, literary inspiration, local history, and Ferrarese civic pride. As Ulysses' task was to remember his homeland and return to guarantee his own fame, the narrative of his sufferings and triumphs, Ariosto's return marks the completion of the poem and memorializes those named in it, guaranteeing the fame of author and patrons alike: indeed the fame of the whole Po valley as the cradle of Mantuan and Ferrarese Renaissance culture.[45]

Ariosto's homecoming to the shore and Rinaldo's previous anticipation of the Ferrarese golden age compose a sort of textual monument (echoing the pavilion of chaste ladies), and suggest that we include Ariosto's homecoming in the tradition of poet's *nostoi*, of which the most illustrious examples for Ariosto are Virgil's intention to return the laurels to the Mincio and raise a temple to Caesar, Dante's hope of returning to Florence to receive the laurel crown in San Giovanni, and Sannazaro's return to the Sebeto and Naples from Arcadia.[46] That Rinaldo's river journey seems to be among the earliest parts of the poem composed is consonant with this function. That Rinaldo should, in the stanzas added in 1532 (43.56–59) refer to a previous journey to Ferrara, making the

---

44. Sherberg, "Ariosto's Rinaldo," 182, noting especially echoes of Dante, suggests these cantos are self-consciously "literary."

45. The poet and Alessandra had to be inserted after 1513, when he had met her, and probably close to the publication date of the 1516 edition; see Henderson.

46. These "returns to the source" derive, as Quint, "Origin," 32–42, showed, from Virgil's epyllion describing the descent of Aristaeus to his mother, and the source of rivers, where he discovers from Proteus how to resurrect his bees, at *Georgics* 4.315–558. Virgil's episode derives from Telemachus's query of Proteus regarding Odysseus's return, *Odyssey* 4.365–570.

present voyage literally a return, seems also to underscore the poet's own compositional "return" to this episode in concluding the final version of the poem.[47]

Ariosto's emphasis on local myths of origin just as he closes his poem suggests yet another form of homecoming. The two tales narrated to Rinaldo take place in and near Mantua, and exploit the fluvial setting; the traditional mythical origins of Mantua and Ferrara are mentioned (OF 43.11, "dragon of Agenor," 43.32; "serpent's jaw," 43.74; "sown serpent's teeth," 43.79). Not only is the Theban origin of Mantua given, but the origin of the parent city of Thebes is invoked as well through mention of Cadmus, who slew the dragon (43.97), and "men born of serpent's teeth."[48] By the same token the Ferrarese, descendants of Paduans fleeing Attila, are ultimately the relics or survivors of Troy ("reliquie troiani"); so we also hear of the judgment of Paris (43.23), which became the remote origin of the Trojan war when Venus bribed Paris with the promise of Helen.[49] More substantively, the tale of Argia, Anselmo, and Manto, with its account of snakes beaten, and the prostrations of the faery brood into serpent form, echoes both the story of Theban Tiresias, punished with a sex change for separating copulating snakes, and the Theban foundation myth, by which the citizens originated from the teeth of serpents sown by Cadmus.[50] Why such myths should be emphasized will be discussed in my conclusion.

Myths of civic origin are accompanied by allusions to literary origins.

47. Henderson dates the episode (in part) to 1507.

48. Ariosto drew these accounts from Ovid, Dante (see below) or from numerous accounts in Statius's *Thebaid*: Theban topics link the two Rinaldo adventures (cf. OF 5.5.3), while the wife of Anselmo is named after the Argive wife of Theban Polynices, Argia. For the importance of Tiresias, also a Theban, see below.

49. "[R]eliquie di Troia che dal flagello d'Attila camparo," echoes the suicide's account of Dante's Florence, *Inferno* 13.148-49 ("quei cittadin che poi la rifondarno / sovra'l cener che d'Attila rimase"), and proud Troy, in *Purgatorio* 12.60-61 ("reliquie" and "cenere e . . . caverne" used in consecutive lines).

50. For Tiresias's sex change, see Ovid, *Metamorphoses* 3.322-38. The prostration of Cadmus, part of Ovid's account (4.576-603), is recapitulated in Dante, *Inferno* 25.97-135.

Ariosto's invocation of the testing horn sent by Morgan le Fay to Guinevere as the model of the oste's *nappo*, following hard upon the scene of Brandimarte's Roland-like death at Lipadusa [51] bring to mind the *chanson de geste* and Arthurian romance. In the Tristan tradition, the testing horn, destined by Morgana for the court of Guinevere, is diverted by Sir Lamorat, who hates Tristan, to the court of King Mark and Queen Isolde. In this way, just as the adventures of Tristan and Lancelot are interwoven in the prose Tristan versions, the testing horn links the two chief courts of adulterous romance, where chivalry was based on maintaining the illusion of the queens' chastity—the exposure of which supposed chastity is also a theme of the two *novelle* told to Rinaldo. Such a courtly link also ties in with Rinaldo's earlier defense of a different Ginevra in Scotland, since Ariosto's Caledonian forest of adventures is modeled on the desert forest of Dirnadant, where Tristan tries to kill Lamorat, again because of the testing cup sent to disgrace Isolde.[52]

In his emphasis on the theme of the embarrassing testing horn as a background to his *novelle*, Ariosto in one sense continues the tradition that denies the chastity of Penelope, challenging what Homer wrote; he also appears to be rereversing Boiardo's polemical preference for the amorous (and adulterous) courts of the Arthurian poems over the rough-

51. Quint, "Death of Brandimarte," 81, argues that Ariosto's immediate precedent for the death of Brandimarte is the *Morgante*, not the *Chanson de Roland*. But Orlando's formal lament for Brandimarte (44.170–74), reminiscent of Charlemagne's for Roland, and for which there is no real equivalent in Pulci's poem (though see 27.151.4, spoken by Rinaldo), suggests Ariosto has the older Roncevaux account in mind as well.

52. See the *Tavola ritonda* 57 ("diserto di Anderlantes") in *Tristan and the Round Table*; *Tristano Riccardiano* 151–57 ("diserto di Nerlantes"). E. G. Gardner pointed out long ago that the Ginevra story also recalls the episode of Mador de la Porte in the *Mort le roi artu*, where Guinevere innocently offers the brother of Mador de la Porte a poisoned apple: symbolically, the episode suggests Guinevere's guilt for her relapse into adultery with Lancelot after his return from the quest for the Grail. Anselmo's decision to murder Argia echoes Boccaccio's Bernabò, who decides to murder his wife Zinevra, falsely accused by Ambrogiuolo after a "test" of her chastity sanctioned by her husband; see *Decameron* 2.9.33–37; this tale is echoed by Lurcanio's calumny of Ginevra in the Dalinda episode, the pendant to the two tales in 42–43.

and-tumble *chansons de geste*,[53] in this sense again reversing the fame, the *kleos*, of the two traditions, as if he, too, had drunk of the fountain of *dis-amore*. The Tristan-Artù materials also underscore the biblical archetypes Ariosto keeps in play, a "return" to the moral sources, the fundamental written code, of the society: as the Mantuan host's error was like the overweening desire of Adam, the "first fault written down of Guinevere" echoes the fault of Eve—and Anselmo, "caught in the same fault," is Adam all over again.

Ariosto's inclusion of his literary origins includes, of course, Boiardo, whose poem the *Orlando furioso* is designed to conclude. This is vividly true of the material involving Rinaldo, whose final adventure is elaborately prepared in the latter half of the *Furioso*.[54] Rinaldo is the last of the knights in love, and his disillusion puts an end to the passions Angelica first awakened when she appeared at Charles's court with her brother Argalia: the beginning not only of Boiardo's poem, but of Ariosto's as well, given that Ariosto picks up his narrative at a point where Boiardo had brought his questing knights back to Paris after an initial cycle of fruitless pursuits of Angelica (cf. OI 3.4.40; OF 1.10–12). Thus the last sight we have of Rinaldo in the *Innamorato* has him searching on foot for Boiardo, in which guise he appears for the first time in the *Furioso*, at 1.10–12. At the same time, Rinaldo's decision to pursue Boiardo, even after Angelica is lost to him, and his tardy arrival on Lipadusa to find Gradasso dead, echo Rinaldo's missed duels with Gradasso over Boiardo in the *Orlando innamorato*. Drinking of the "fountain of unloving" at Sdegno's request, Rinaldo completes a final reversal of a cycle begun by Boiardo (his first drink of the sane fountain is at OI 1.3.35) and also reiterates, even as it concludes, Boiardo's use of the two fountains for

53. See Boiardo, OI 2.18.1–2 and 2.26.2–3, where Arthur's court is compared favorably with Charlemagne's, and where Tristano and Lancilotto are exalted and regretted; and note Bruscagli's observations in Boiardo, OI (ed. Riccardo Bruscagli), 1.18–20.

54. *Orlando furioso* 27.7–9 views Orlando mad and Rinaldo departing once more from Paris after Angelica in an effective summary of the poem thus far; 31.90–92 summarizes Gradasso's desire for Boiardo and the incomplete duel with Rinaldo from Boiardo's poem, here resumed, though soon interrupted at 33.84–89.

prolonging the game of approach and avoidance between Rinaldo and Angelica. This completes another cycle; as we saw, the fountains are versions of the two potions, Isolde's unifying potion of love, and the divisive goblet of jealousy offered by Rinaldo's Mantuan host.

Richest of all, these completed "cycles" for the theme of voyaging and homecoming are internal to the tissue of the *Furioso* itself. Sergio Zatti has recently recalled Donald Carne-Ross's conception of the poem as organized in terms of the "circular motion of the quest." [55] Thus it is that Rinaldo's voyage to Scotland, near the poem's opening, is juxtaposed closely to Ruggiero's abduction by the hippogriff to Alcina's island and her Circean charms (cf. 4.50–52); while Astolfo's aerial travels had themselves begun in Rinaldo's presence (in the *Orlando innamorato*) when Alcina's whale sailed off with Astolfo. These latter two journeys are, as Ascoli argued, all themselves modeled on the travels of Dante's Ulysses "following the sun," which thus emerges as the archetypal exoteric quest of the poem. Such extra-European expeditions give rise, in canto 15.21–23, to Logistilla's prophecies of future Argonauts and their transatlantic crossings, which Boitani claims are Ariosto's contributions to a post-Columbian updating of the exploits of Ulysses in the political and imperial terms imposed on them by the Spanish empire.[56] Ariosto himself, however, pointedly withdraws from the exoteric, expansionist quest with his narrator's return in the exordium to canto 46.

The placement of limits on the narrative concerns the homeward tendency of Ariosto's encomiastic vocation. For if the poet orchestrates, in canto 46, the termination of his figurative voyage, one aspect of that determination concerns the drawing of the earth's limits toward Ferrara.

---

55. Zatti 39–60, esp. 49–50; also Ascoli 378.

56. In 1516 Charles V adopted as one of his official *imprese* the pillars of Hercules and the motto *plus ultra* (calqued from the French *plus oultre*) with reference to Ulysses (perhaps through Dante and Pulci, surely known to the *inventor* Luigi Marliano) as a bold explorer; for discussion, see Rosenthal. Charles's intentions were imperial and geopolitical, announcing the new golden age of Hapsburg hegemony. See Ariosto, OF 15.21–25 (added 1532); Quint, *Romance*; Boitani 44–68.

In Rinaldo's vision of the future Ferrara, the island of Belvedere exceeds in amenity the Hesperides as well the island of the Phaeacians, Nausicaa's, where Odysseus finds a place to rest. The Estensi have in a sense set the westernmost limits of exploration in Ferrara itself, and brought the gardens of the Hesperides, and the columns of Ulysses, to the island of Belvedere, which though a landlocked river island is in one sense the island destination of the poet's praise, as Ithaca is the island destination of Ulysses and Lipadusa the island destination of Rinaldo. On the other hand, in the narrative in canto 46 it is the pavilion of Cassandra (in juxtaposition to the *padiglione* of the chaste ladies) with its encomiastic paeans to Ippolito d'Este, that is brought from Constantinople, at the eastern reach of the Mediterranean, to Italy to serve as the marriage pavilion of Ruggiero and Bradamante, betrothed by Rinaldo. The force of these geographically balanced encomia is that far-flung marvels have been brought within the limits of the Ferrarese duchy by Este *virtù*, indeed by the "Herculean" power of the household (see 43.59.7–8), obviating any need to go to the antipodes: the world's extremes are gathered symbolically in Ferrara, probably in implied contrast here with the real westward push of the Spanish empire under Charles V.[57] But in a more immediate sense such a contraction of the world is the act of the poet's imagination, which returns to its literary and geographic origins in the same gesture.

Rinaldo descends into Italy from the Rhaetian Alps, an important part of the Po watershed; indeed he traverses a part of Europe where the Rhine, Rhone, and the Danube originate. Since he arrives in Mantua, he plausibly follows the course of the Mincio itself from Benaco (Lake

---

57. The pillars of Hercules, the limit broached by Dante's Ulysses, figure prominently, along with the garden of the Hesperides (another of Hercules' labors) in delimiting spheres of action in Ariosto's poem. Ariosto (like Ptolemy, like Dante) thinks of the distance from the Ganges or Nile to the Hesperides or pillars of Hercules as the extent of the known or civilized world: this domain Andrea Doria will purge of pirates (15.31); the new Argonauts (and Ulysses) will exceed it (15.22); within this domain women are famous (37.6); and Agramante is offered cities by Charlemagne if he will be baptized (38.12–13); over this domain Orlando defends and pursues Angelica (1.7). Here resonate the deeds of knights like Rinaldo (4.60, in Scotland). For the pillars on Renaissance maps, see Conley 155–63.

Garda; 43.11); this flows of course into the Po; and the voyage is itself marked by the articulations in the river, the three rightward shifts first toward Ferrara rather than Venice (43.53: "Melara left behind on the leftward shore"), then on the Po di Primaro (43.63), and then, past Argenta and the future site of the Bastia, the "morta gora" or stagnant canal that leads south to Ravenna (43.146). In this system, with its tributaries, canals, and ramifications, the generous stream ("fecondo canale") deriving from the fountain of chaste ladies is itself the exemplary ekphrastic origin of chaste fecundity whose waters also must end up in the Po. Not only in their iconography as cornucopiae, or "horns of plenty," the ladies are the source of poetic achievement since they materially underwrite it with patronage, while the poets reciprocate with praise; that the poets are linked to the mythic origins of poetry, to Virgil's Mantua and to the Po, confirms this supposition.[58] Ariosto here establishes for his text a mythology of the Po valley as a cradle of poetry, a view arising from the transformation of Cygnus into a swan as he lamented the fall of Phaethon into the Eridanus—Cygnus, who became a swan, a bird symbolic of melancholy love lyric.[59] The origin of such a poetics is Petrarch's canzone "Nel dolce tempo della prima etade" (Petrarch 23) where he represents himself as Cygnus, and originates the kind of praise for which Ariosto literally stands in the fountain of chaste ladies.

58. References to archaic poets such as Linus and Orpheus, Parnassus and Helicon, and the birth of Pegasus, "cavallo alato" (a pun for Marco Cavallo), alternate with mention of Virgil as the poet of Mantua, the Reno—a tributary of the Po—as well as the Isauro and, most notably for Ariosto's choice of tales, Niccolò da Correggio and Timoteo Bendedei, whose poetry might halt, Ariosto exaggerates, the flow of the Po itself: "ambi faran tra l'una e l'altra riva / fermare al suon d' lor soavi plettri / il fiume ove sudar gli antiqui elettri."

59. Ascoli (341, 373) points to a mythology of the Po as closely connected with Este patronage, given that the two brothers are at one point offspring of the "Tindareo cigno" (3.50.4) (offspring of Tyndarus, husband of Leda, mother of the Gemini, consort of Jove in the form of a swan, Latin *cygnus*). OF 3.34.7–8 are linked to 42.92.7–8 by the rhymes "plettro/i" and "elett(r)o/i." Manto's son, according to the Virgilian etiology for Mantua, was Ocnus. The Po is the model for the river of fame and oblivion in OF 35.12–23, where swans, vultures, and crows (true poets against mere flatterers) determine one and the other; note the mention of the Po at 35.6.

In this sense the river comes to stand both for the stream of patronage and for what it makes possible, the stream of eloquence,[60] a stream that can only become copious through patronage bestowed by the chaste court ladies represented in the underground palace of the Mantuan host. Because of the important literary precedents that are evoked, Rinaldo's voyage on this river of eloquence, which flows both from the great divide of the Alps and from patronage, becomes Ariosto's instance of the journey to the literary source like that described by Quint, who cites the influential instance of Aristaeus's descent from Virgil's *Georgics* as the archetype for Renaissance versions.[61]

Here, too, the figure that best organizes this complex itinerary to literary founts is the voyage of Dante's Ulysses, for many readers, as we saw, the chief figure, in the *Commedia*, of the journey of Dante's pilgrim—which might well be considered in itself a journey to the source—through the various stages of the underworld ("dark and obscure places," OF 42.58.8; "dark places," *Inferno* 16.82, 24.141).[62] Rinaldo's journey down the Po echoes Ulysses' nautical voyage filtered through Dante, but given the swampy conditions [paludi] around Mantua and the Po estuary generally (43.60, "these swamps" and 70: "the swamp and lake enclosed by the bridled Mincius"),[63] it also echoes the descent of Dante's pilgrim to "the swamp called Styx" (7.106)[64] and the watercourse ("gorgo," *Inferno* 17.118) guarded by Geryon (compare "swamps

---

60. For the river as a figure of poetry, used of Virgil, see Macrobius, *Saturnalia*, 5.1.10; it was also commonly said of Homer, from whom Macrobius is polemically transferring it. Dante recalls it in his remark to Virgil (*Inferno* 1.80) "che spandi di parlar sì largo fiume."

61. See Quint, *Origin and Originality*, 32–42. Sannazaro's *Arcadia*, where the Tiber, and the poet's little Sebeto, are the rivers of interest, and Tasso's cave of the magus of Ascalon are other examples furnished by Quint. In his underground return from Arcadia to Naples, Sannazaro echoes not only the descent of Aristeus to his mother's cavern, but also the pilgrim Dante's passage through the earth (*Arcadia* 12.20–35).

62. See note 24.

63. See also 37.9, of Issabella d'Este: "che'l Menzo fende e d'alto stagni serra"; 43.11: "un chiaro fiume laco / che poi si stende e in questo Po declina."

64. See also "livida palude," *Inferno* 3.98; "Questa palude ch'el gran puzzo spira," 9.31; "quei de la palude pingue" 11.70.

and watercourses" [stagno e gorgo], OF 43.61). Even the articulation of Rinaldo's journey into stages determined by the branching of the Po, first to pass Ferrara, then branching south at Bastia to head toward Ravenna—might echo the articulations of the pilgrim's infernal journey, requiring oarsmen or *galeotti* like Charon or Flegiás, at each stage ("a single oarsman," *Inferno* 8.17; "well did I know the oarsman," *Purgatorio* 2.27). The *Inferno* itself, in its triple or quadruple division (incontinence, violence, and two kinds of fraud), is echoed in the terms Guido del Duca uses to describe the descent of the Arno, past the bestialized inhabitants (pigs, curs, wolves, foxes) of Arezzo, Florence, Lucca, and Pisa in *Purgatorio*, canto 14. The same passage echoes the account of the origin of the Mincio in Lake Benaco in canto 20 of the *Inferno*, also articulated in stages, with the river changing its name as it falls into the Po:[65] a precedent with a direct impact on Ariosto's conception of the river's descent from Benaco to Mantua, and on the inclusion of Manto, Dante's character, in the *novella*. With the strong emphasis throughout the tale of Manto on magical transformation, Ariosto rejects Dante's correction of Virgil's account (*Aeneid* 10.92) and returns to the story of Mantua founded by the river god Ocnus, the son of Manto, the Theban sorceress.

Ariosto's Ferrara, which Rinaldo declares will be a place of "love and courtesy" (43.61.6), a "city of good venture" (bene avventurata), stands in contrast to Dante's degenerate towns along the Arno, the "wretched ditch" (sventurata fossa), where Guido del Duca, in a passage promi-

---

65. The Styx is itself a "lago," cf. *Inf.* 8.54; Virgilio's account of the founding of Mantua begins with a river source, cf. 20.61: "suso in Italia bella giace un laco" and compare 43.11: "un chiaro fiume laco / che poi si stende e in questo Po declina"; see *Inferno* 20.61–93; and OF 42.86.4–6, in praise of Sadoleto and Bembo ("sì gloriosa la terra di Manto, / che di Virgilio, che tanto l'onora, / più che di queste, non si darà vanto"). For the "horns" of the Po, see Virgil, *Georgics* 4.37–373: "et gemina auratus taurino cornua vultu / Eridanus, quo non alius per pinguia culta / in mare purpureum violentior effluit amnis." Ariosto at OF 43.54 makes the horns into a *bivium*—"de le due corne prese il destro." The "horns" of the Po ironically echo the content of the tales Rinaldo hears: see Ceserani 500–502 and Martinez 98; the river itinerary thus refers again to Hercules, establisher of the pillars, chooser at the *bivium*, and winner of the Hesperidean apples.

nently featured by Ariosto in beginning his poem, says that "love and courtesy" (*Purgatorio* 14.110) had once held sway. Rinaldo's voyage, the associations of which with Dante's poem in other respects [66] have been observed, is thus also a superimposition of Ulysses' nautical journey (which ends, of course, in a descent "sotto le acque") to the antipodes and Dante's descent through Hell: the echoes of Geryon in the figure of Gelosia (pushed back into Hell by Sdegno, like Dante's *lupa*) would seem to announce this dimension of Rinaldo's journey.[67]

The extent to which the Rinaldo episode layers references to Ariosto's literary tradition is discernible in the personification of Gelosia as a summary of monstrous personifications. She is the first important personification since Discordia (OF 14.84–84) and the Beast of Avarice (OF 26.31–33)—ass, lion, wolf, and fox—both of which she recalls. Her many eyes recall Ovid's Argus and his surveillance of Io; her snaky locks are those of Virgil's Allecto, a Fury, and like a Fury she brings strife and dismay; her long, barbed tail echoes Dante's Minos and Geryon. Her despair and self-gnawing recall Dante's Ugolino, Ovid's *Invidia* and Virgil's chained Furor. But as the final and supreme *prosopon* of the poem, Gelosia—given her expression of a cumulative literary experience—seems excessively subjective and personal, as if the focus of the poem were overbalancing toward personal sexual jealousy: the poem winds down,

---

66. Sherberg, "Ariosto's Rinaldo," focuses on recollections of Paolo and Francesca, underscoring reading and writing (see also 43.40); for Dante's pilgrim seized by pity ("pietà mi giunse," *Inferno* 5.72), see Rinaldo "di pietà vinto," 43.47. For parallels with Ugolino, see 43.140, "O terra . . . perchè allor non t'apristi?" (cf. *Inferno* 33.66), and "Rode . . . e si manuca" (42.58) of Gelosia, compared to *Inferno* 32.127 ("come'l pan per fame si manduca"). For the pilgrim's journey in general, see "tomare/tomi/pomi" of the pilgrim's need to descend, *Inferno* 15.63, compared to OF 43.8 (rhymes "tomo," "pomo").

67. Tasso's extra-Mediterranean journey, that of Ubaldo and Guelfo on the ship of Fortune to the Isole Fortunate to recover Rinaldo seduced by Armida, is also a superposition of the nautical odyssey (see Quint, *Romance*, 191–94) and the journey of Dante's pilgrim (Armida's island is a mountain, with a garden at its summit, etc.). Tasso also follows the model of Pulci's return of Rinaldo to Roncevaux, discoursing along the way with an ambiguous figure, Astarrotte; in Tasso's poem the demon's role is taken by the magus of Ascalon, and by Fortuna herself.

in its 1516 conclusion, into a private and domestic sphere. Ariosto's own insertion of himself as Alessandra Benucci's poet and "sustainer" in the temple of chastity marks jealousy as particularly germane to the narrator-poet himself, as he reiterates with Petrarchan citation: "understand what I say, for I understand myself" (43.5).

The Humblest Lot: Going with the Flow

In addition to making the literary canon serve the poet's subjective investment in the problem of jealousy, the high-serious canon of Virgilian and Dantesque etiologies and sources is one that Ariosto decisively tempers through these cantos. Between the lofty exemplars of Dante and Virgil, Ariosto has turned, in his *novelle*, to originals less exalted, and arguably more bourgeois, realistic, and domestic: to Ovid's domestic tragedy of Cephalus and Procris and its native Ferrarese adaptation by Niccolò da Correggio, to the Ovidian (as well as Statian) stories of Tiresias and Manto, with "Aesopic" and folkloristic overtones, and, especially, to Boccaccio's *Decameron*. As Rajna pointed out, Ariosto models Anselmo's decision to murder the unfaithful Argia on the tale of Bernabò, who decides to murder his wife, Zinevra, when she is defamed by Ambrogiuolo's lies (Anselmo himself is very like the dried-up Riccardo da Chinzica in the tale that follows); it is with good reason, then, that Rinaldo proclaims the tale of Anselmo to be a native product ("qui tra voi rimane," OF 43.71.4). The lover figures in the two tales are reckless spendthrifts, like Boccaccio's Federigo degli Alberighi and Nastagio degli Onesti,[68] and Argia's father attempts to raise her free of corrupting influences, like Filippo Balducci, raised away from noxious moral influences (*Decameron* 4, proem); the Aesop-like Moor who offers to seduce Anselmo recalls aspects of Frate Cipolla's Guccio Im-

---

68. See *Decameron* 5.8 (Nastagio degli Onesti), 5.9 (Federigo degli Alberighi), in which both of the lovers spend themselves into penury attempting to win over their lady loves. Ariosto also draws, for the long and extenuating wanderings of Argia's lover, on Boccaccio's Arcita in the *Teseida*, set partially at Thebes.

bratta.[69] Speaking more broadly, Boccaccio has furnished his own "fertile canal" as a source for the ladies' fountain of patronage, the "Valley of the Ladies," which introduces a book of vengeance against the outrages of men.[70] The very emphasis on the *novella* and the theatrical *fabula*, closely allied by Ariosto's time, with the tales of the Mantuan host and Anselmo/Argia constituting the poet's final word so to speak of the 1516 edition, significantly alters the epic-romance dialectic of the poem and tips the poem's engagement in the direction of the generically comic, with the corresponding subjects of aged avarice, youthful erotic intrigue, and final reconciliation, all within the typical confines of the bourgeois household.[71]

Rinaldo's passage from the fountain of unloving (according to Boiardo, one of the four Merlin had had built in Europe), to the battlefield of Lipadusa, with its anticipations of Roncevaux, might well be read as a movement from the evasions of romance to the crisis of epic, culminating with death in battle and the defeat of the traditional enemy. At the same time, much militates against such a reading: the monster of jealousy, with her evocations of the Fury and Dante's wolf, seems drawn if not narrowly from Latin epic, then from poems of high seriousness and

69. See Guccio Imbratta's "barba grande e nera e unta," *Decameron* 6.10.18, and the Moor at OF 43.135: "bisunto e sporco." The Moor is "d'attristar, se vi fosse, il paradiso," just as Guccio Imbratta can destroy all the virtues of Solomon, Aristotle, and Seneca, *Decameron* 6.10.16.

70. The implicit irony that the *novelle* themselves risk undercutting chastity is balanced by one of Ariosto's sources here, Boccaccio's "Valle delle donne" (*Decameron* 6, conc. 25–28), where we find a similar "fecondo canale" (OF 42.96) alluding to the female body and introducing a book of tales in which the ladies avenge slights from men. This is a precedent for the "lessons" against surveillance imparted to Rinaldo. For the "Valley of Ladies," see Stillinger.

71. The Mantuan host uses an explicitly theatrical metaphor (43.10, "vo' levarti da la scena i panni"). In transforming da Correggio's play (written in *ottava rima*) into his narrative, Ariosto had the precedent of Boiardo's rendition of Plautus's *Captivi* in his tale of Ziliante and Manodante, *Orlando innamorato* 2.9–13. For the *Cefalo* as a "comic" and domestic form of the "heroic" Orpheus tale (Pyle, Tissoni-Benvenuti), see Martinez, 89. Zatti (57) suggests that Anselmo's quest for knowledge about his wife (43.119) constitutes a bourgeois reduction, or, better, an "Erasmian" version of the chivalric quest.

cosmic struggle, while the allegorical duel between Rinaldo's jealousy and his personified Wrath is ultimately an ingenious variant on one of the founding scenes of epic and allegorical literature, Achilles' struggle between Wrath and Athena in the *Iliad* (1.187–222).[72] On the other hand, Orlando's military readiness for the ordeal on Lipadusa is the result of the romance device of the pilotless ship, which arrives carrying the full armor abandoned by Ruggero, along with Balisarda. The arrival of Balisarda supplants the loss of Durindana after Orlando's madness (OF 24.58) in a round-robin of swords that Vinaver has identified as typical of interlaced romances.[73] Ariosto has contrived to fashion a romance scene with epic detail, and an epic scene arranged with romance instruments. In this sense the journey, rather than shifting from romance to its epic roots, acts to level or reduce to analogous impurity those roots, attributing equal weight to the Arthurian and Carolingian, to the Iliadic and Odyssean.

Just as important is the fact that Rinaldo's journey, although it might seem to begin with the romance quest (first pursuing Angelica, then Boiardo), and to conclude with the epic scene of Brandimarte's death, in fact evades or blunts a clear teleology, just as Rinaldo's original impetus, broken by the narrative of the Mantuan knight, fails to get him to Lipadusa on time. Rinaldo's tardiness, rather than merely undercutting the character, is the narrator's ploy for multiplying the goals of the paladin's journey, which remain suspended between the vision of future Ferrarese glories and the tragic death of Brandimarte. To put it another way, by way of summarizing a poem itself so brilliantly about shifting objects of desire and mutable human identities—about, in short, *le passage* in Montaigne's sense—Ariosto has located the helmsman's narrative within the moving flow of the river that represents eloquence, poetry, and both the diachrony and dissemination of the literary tradition.

In emphasizing the domestic and the local, in the very emphasis on the Boccaccian *novella* as the dominant genre (a double dose, two tales

72. See Whitman 15–20.
73. Vinaver 68–98, esp. 85–86.

to Rinaldo), Ariosto seems to have come to a different idea of the quest and its hero. The poet returns as a private citizen and minor courtier: he meets friends, fellow poets, ladies who are his peers and relations. Alfonso and Ippolito, who loomed large in the poem's opening formal encomia, no longer figure here. In Rinaldo's sobered mindfulness of Clarice, in the poet's return to his friends, in the bourgeois reconciliation of Anselmo and Argia, Ariosto's poem finds a center of gravity which despite the heroic duel of Rodomonte and Ruggiero that finally concludes it is decidedly not epic. Thus one consummation of the imitation of Ulysses in the episode is the repudiation of the heroic, exploratory desire characteristic of the Ithacan. But this refusal, too, is part of the legend of Ulysses. In the last book of the *Republic*, Plato includes as part of the narrative of Er, the resurrected soldier who has traveled to Hades, the sight of Odysseus choosing the lots for reincarnation. Reversing his usual opportunism, he chooses last, and in welcoming the lot of the obscure private citizen renounces ambition and the quest.[74]

All this points, of course, to the profound alterations that Ariosto has made in his model of Ulysses' sleeping return to Ithaca at the turning point of the *Odyssey*, as well as in the model of Aristaeus's descent to the source or rivers or Dante's journey through the underworld. In dramatic ways, Rinaldo's journey is nothing like these, indeed turns them inside out. Rinaldo does not descend into the earth, nor does he aim for faraway destinations across trackless seas. Rinaldo's journey is distinct from those of Ulysses and Dante in that it is fluvial, not oceanic, hewing to the actual course of the Po and its system of canals, given with sharp detail by a native of the Valpadane region; it is superficial, not a descent or *katabasis*; and it is within the confines of the Mediterranean and, indeed, for its most significant portion landlocked, within the confines of Italy. It is even psychologically inward: the task the jealous husbands set for themselves, knowing the thoughts of the wife, is one of entering

74. Ascoli (144–45) points out that Ariosto makes a similar withdrawal from the quest in *Satira 6*, when he inquires for a master to teach Virginio Greek so he might read Homer's *Odyssey*, but himself chooses to provide for his son rather than imitate Ulysses.

into the mind of another, of knowing secrets, and we have secret confessions of the author himself. Like the poet's drawing of the Hesperides and Constantinople to Italy and to Ferrara, this inland and inward journey (from Mantua to Ravenna, the part of Rinaldo's journey that involves storytelling) might appear the focus of the episode. But there is a dispersive, ramifying tendency as well: as we saw, Ariosto arranges for the inland destination to be an island, like Odysseus's Ithaca, like Lipadusa: the river island of Belvedere where the Estensi will, Rinaldo prophesies, recreate the golden age. The poem's destinations fan out in multiple dimensions: both in the sea and inland, both in the narrative present and in the envisioned future.

Such multiple outcomes are possible only with a narrative style that can fuse, and metamorphose, epic, romance, and bourgeois *novella*. As an example, consider how Ariosto weaves delicately through the whole episode a series of uses of the idea of the horn. We might say that the assimilation of the *matière de Bretagne* to the local environment of the Po valley is rendered textually in the punning shift from the "cimier di Cornovaglia" (the Cornish—that is horned—helmet), which, beyond the inevitable nod to cuckoldry, alludes to the derision of Cornish knights in the Tristan romances, to the *corno* or branching of the Po that articulates Rinaldo's journey, and to the cornucopia, the "horn of Amalthea" that the patronesses hold in their hands in the fountain of chastity: a feminization of the phallic *corno* through association with the nurse of Jove, Amalthea, and the ladies' own "fertile canal."[75] A similar metamorphic poetics is evident in the characters: Ariosto's Melissa, in the Mantuan host's tale, is a mutation of Ovid's Aurora, but, given her offer of a drinking cup, we cannot avoid the traditional association of Melissa the sorceress with Circe the transformer of men.[76] The question of whether the capricious Mantuan Melissa is also the Melissa who fosters Bradamante offers an undecidable choice between two Melissas or one Melissa

75. See Ceserani 500–2; Martinez 98.
76. For this tradition (Plato, *Republic* 10.620c) see Defaux 37, 154, who cites Ficino's translation of Plato; Boitani 24–25.

who changes her nature; the poem proposes either a puzzling multiplication or a puzzling metamorphosis. Arguably, Ariosto doubles (but also transforms) the Melissa of the first tale with the sorceress Manto in the second precisely because Manto, too, was, in Dante's poem, enigmatically doubled.[77] Manto herself is in constant metamorphosis: her weekly subjection to the serpent's form echoes her kinship with the brood of Cadmus, founder of Thebes, himself changed to a serpent, and to the Mantuans as Cadmeids generally, born from dragon's teeth. Her changes also mark her as the daughter of Tiresias, who was changed from a man to a woman because he struck copulating snakes with his wand (a gesture imperfectly recalled by Argia's lover, who saves the Manto-snake from a beating).[78] Thus it is with perfect logic that Manto takes on shapes such as the revenue-producing dog that compasses the seduction of Argia, but also perhaps, with a shift of gender, the sodomitic Ethiop who is compared to wise old Aesop.[79]

If the figure of Manto (who, like Atlante and Alcina, effects magical transformations) is as some readers have suggested to be taken as a reflection of the poet,[80] then Ariosto would seem to be proposing for himself a figure of the poet as a protean shape-shifter[81] whose deepest kinship is not with the melancholy Mantuan host or the hypocritical

---

77. She is mentioned in *Inferno* 20.55 among the soothsayers; and in *Purgatorio* 22.113 as the daughter of Tiresias in Limbo.

78. *Metamorphoses* 3.322–40; Dante, *Inferno* 20.40–45. Tiresias's shifts of gender were interpreted in medieval allegories as expressions of active and passive principles in generation, and as changes in the seasons: thus, of the mutations of time itself. For Proteus also in this sense, as seen through Neoplatonic interpretation, see below.

79. Boiardo's episode of Febosilla (OI 2.26), transformed from a serpent back into a fairy, is generally held a model for Ariosto's transformations of Manto; see also the mutations of the protean Balisardo, 2.10.22–32) and, for the revenue-producing dog (also linked to Petitcreu, the dog that accompanied Isolde and Tristan), the stag that moults golden horns (1.22.56–59).

80. See Schiesari; also Martinez 110–11.

81. Such a poet figure is Proteus himself, in the wake of Sannazaro, who in the *Arcadia* (6.46–54) identifies Lacinio, a thievish magus with "magichi versi" as a Proteus; or Ennius, who

Anselmo, but with the amorous couples and their helpers, especially the grateful Manto, the *genius loci* of Virgil's countryside.[82] This figure of the poet is Ovidian rather than Virgilian, or, to adopt Quint's typology, Protean rather than Orphic: Protean in representing, through tales of metamorphosis and passion, the world of endless generation and flux, where the Orphic poet is bound rather to loss, mourning and monumentalizing his love.[83]

We might also consider another typology here, that opposing the poetry of ceaseless becoming and multiplicity to a transcendent world of aniconic Being and Truth: in other terms, the opposition between Homer and Plato, between *mythos* and *logos*. In Roberto Calasso's formulation, Homer is the "bearer of the knowledge of metamorphosis" and thus of the "realm that is the enemy of philosophy."[84] Again, in Calasso's formulation it is precisely Odysseus, with his ruses, disguises,

---

presented himself as the reincarnation of Homer, and Ovid's Pythagoras, who recapitulates the *Metamorphoses* in book 15, and who remembers fighting at Troy in a previous life as Euphorbus. Ariosto's debts to an Ovidian poetic have been noted by Javitch "Rescuing Ovid."

82. For Manto in this sense, see Poliziano's *Sylva* "Manto" (*Poeti* 1062–97), recalling that Manto conceived her offspring Ocnus out of the river Tiber, and who has Manto appear to the infant Virgil to predict his glorious destiny; there is a related telling of the myth in the Latin sapphics on behalf of Cardinal Mantuano interpolated by Poliziano into his *Fabula de Orfeo* (Poliziano 162–63). See also Pontano's "Ad Antimachum Mantuanum . . ." where in Pontano's personal mythology Melissa is one of the nurses of Virgil (*Poeti*, 707).

83. Quint, 40. In the Renaissance, Proteus normally represents the multiplicity of the generable, and the disposition to form of prime matter; for Servius on Virgil, Eclogues 4.390 he represents the passions. See Giammatti, "Proteus Unbound"; Wind 191–217; Nohrnberg 569–89, 643; Quint, 35–39. Odysseus's cave of nymphs on Ithaca, where he hides the gifts given him by the Phaeacians, is sacred to Phorkys, called the "Old man of the sea" (*Odyssey* 13.96), as Proteus had been earlier (4.385); see note 82 above.

84. For this paragraph, see Calasso, *Quarantanove gradini*, 490; *Le nozze*, 395; *Quarantanove gradini*, 491; *Le nozze*, 407, respectively (translations mine). Ariosto mentions King Proteus of Egypt at 46.82, in connection with the passage of Cassandra's needlepointed *padiglione* to Menelaus in exchange for Helen, who according to the account in Herodotus was never in Troy at all. This account of course made Homer a liar, like other authors of Ariosto's Saint John.

and fictions, who embodies in his character the realm of fable, metamorphosis, and a "falsehood more coherent than truth." For the realm of metamorphoses is revealed "through the knowledge of he who treats of the simulacra by transforming himself into them." Odysseus marks the end of the heroic age because he "carried to victory for the first time the mediated over the immediate, deferral over presence, the curve of the mind over rectilinear thrust."[85]

In Ariosto's poem the poet's diffraction of himself into the figure of the narrator, returning home, like a weary Odysseus, to his friends and fellows; into the covert author, confessing his place as the singer of Alessandra Benucci; into his character Rinaldo, confronting his own jealousies and bridling them; and into the shape-shifting Manto, transmuting herself and those around her in a ceaseless play of simulacra, represent an alternative to the closure represented by the tragic death of Brandimarte. If Ariosto's poem moves toward closure as death—in the foretold death of Ruggiero, in the anticipated death of the narrator (and aged poet)—it also disperses itself into the flux of metamorphosis that is literary tradition, while emphasizing the Protean "varie ac multiformis . . . animal" (varied and many-shaped animal) that has for so many readers appeared the chief subject of Ariosto's art.

Works Cited

Alighieri, Dante. La divina commedia. Ed. Natalino Sapegno. Milano-Napoli: Riccardo Ricciardi, 1957.

——. Inferno. Ed. and trans. Robert M. Durling with intro. and notes by Ronald L. Martinez and Robert M. Durling. New York: Oxford UP, 1996.

Apuleius of Madaura. Metamorphoses. Ed. and trans. J. Arthur Hanson. 2 vols. Cambridge, Mass.: Harvard UP, 1989.

Ariosto, Ludovico. Cinque canti. Ed. Lanfranco Caretti. Turin: Einaudi, 1977.

——. Orlando furioso. Ed. Santorre Debenedetti and Cesare Segre. Bologna: Commissione per i testi di lingua, 1960.

85. For emphasis on the poem's movement toward closure as death, see Quint "Death of Brandimarte," 80–84; for the relative emphasis on deferral and suspension, see Ascoli 361–79.

———. *Opere*. Ed. Giuliano Innamorati. Bologna: Zanichelli, 1967.

Arnaldi, F. et al., eds. *Poeti latini del Quattrocento*. Milan-Naples: Riccardo Ricciardi, 1964.

Ascoli, Albert R. *Ariosto's Bitter Harmony*. Princeton: Princeton UP, 1986.

Barkan, Leonard. *Transuming Passion: Ganymede and the Erotics of Humanism*. Stanford: Stanford UP, 1991.

Boccaccio, Giovanni. *Decameron*. Ed. Vittore Branca. Milan: Mondadori, 1976.

Boiardo, Matteo Maria. *Orlando innamorato*. Trans. Charles Ross. Berkeley: U of California P, 1989.

———. *Orlando innamorato*. Ed. Riccardo Bruscagli. 2 vols. Turin: Einaudi, 1995.

Boitani, Piero. *The Shadow of Ulysses: Figures of a Myth*. Trans. Anita Weston. Oxford: Clarendon, 1994.

Buffiere, Félix. *Les Mythes d'Homère et la pensée grecque*. Paris: Belles Lettres, 1956.

Calasso, Roberto. *Le nozze di Cadmo e Armonia*. Milan: Adelphi, 1988.

———. *I quarantanove gradini*. Milan: Adelphi, 1984.

I cantari di Rinaldo di Monte Albano. Ed. Elio Melli. Bologna: Commissione per i testi di lingua, 1973.

Casadei, Alberto. "Breve analisi sul finale del primo *Furioso*." *Studi e problemi di critica testuale* 44 (1992): 87–100.

———. "L'esordio del canto XLVI del *Furioso*: strategia compositiva e varianti storico-culturali." *Italianistica* 15 (1986): 53–93.

———. *Il percorso del 'Furioso': Ricerche intorno alle redazioni del 1516 e del 1521*. Bologna: Il mulino, 1993.

Castiglione, Baldessar. *Il libro del cortegiano*. Ed. Giulio Carnazzi. Milan: Rizzoli, 1987.

Cavallo, Joanne. *Boiardo's 'Orlando Innamorato: An Ethics of Desire*. London: Associated U Presses, 1993.

Ceserani, Remo. "Due modelli culturali e narrativi nell '*Orlando furioso*." *Giornale storico della letteratura italiana* 161 (1984): 481–506.

The Classical Heritage, vol. 5: *Homer*. Ed. Katherine Callen King. Garland Reference Library in the Humanities. Vol. 1531. New York: Garland, 1994.

Conley, Tom. *The Self-Made Map: Cartographic Writing in Early Modern France*. Minneapolis: U of Minnesota P, 1996.

Corti, Maria. "La 'favola' di Ulisse: invenzione dantesca?" *Percorsi dell'invenzione: il linguaggio poetico e Dante*. Turin: Einaudi, 1993. 113–46.

Curtis, Renée L., ed. *Le roman de Tristan en prose*. Critical ed. Vol. 1. (Munich, 1963); vol. 2 (Leyden, 1976), vol. 3 (Cambridge, 1985).

Damon, Phillip. "Dante's Ulysses and the Mythic Tradition." *Medieval Secular Literature: Four Essays*. Ed. W. Matthews. Berkeley: U of California P, 1965. 25–45.

Gérard Defaux, *Le Curieux, le glorieux et la sagesse du monde dans la première moitié du XVIe siècle* (*L'exemple de Panurge, Ulysse, Démosthène, Empédocle*). Lexington, Ky.: French Forum Publishers, 1983.

Erasmus, Desiderius. *Praise of Folly*. Trans. Betty Radice. Penguin, 1971.

Faccioli, Emilio. "Il palazzo ducale di Revere e un episodio dell 'Orlando furioso." *Civiltà mantovana* 1 (1966): 7–12.

Fachard, Denis. "L'immagine dell'eroe: reminiscenze omeriche nell 'Innamorato e nel Furioso." *Etudes de lettres* 1 (1989): 5–40.

Ferrucci, Franco. *The Poetics of Disguise: The Autobiography of the Work in Homer, Dante, and Shakespeare*. Trans. Ann Dunnigan. Ithaca: Cornell UP, 1980.

Freccero, John. "Dante's Prologue Scene, II: The Wings of Ulysses." *Dante Studies* 84 (1966): 12–25.

Gardner, Edmund G. *The Arthurian Legend in Italian Literature*. New York: Dutton, 1930.

Giammatti, A. Bartlett. *The Earthly Paradise and the Renaissance Epic*. Princeton: Princeton UP, 1966.

———. "Proteus Unbound: Some Versions of the Sea God in the Renaissance." *The Disciplines of Criticism*. Ed. P. Demetz and G. Rimanelli. New Haven: Yale UP, 1968.

Giovenale. *Satire*. Ed. Luca Canali and Ettore Barelli. Milan: Rizzoli, 1960.

Gorni, Guglielmo. "Le 'ali' di Ulisse, emblema dantesco." *Lettera nome numero*. Bologna: Il mulino, 1990. 175–98.

Henderson, Dave. "The Northern Italian Court as Poetic Artifact: Arrogation of Court(ier)ly Power in the *Orlando furioso*." Paper presented at the Sixteenth-Century Studies Conference, St. Louis, La., Oct. 27, 1995.

Hoffman, Kathryn. "The Court in the Work of Art: Patronage and Poetic Authority in the *Orlando furioso*." *Quaderni d'italianistica* 13 (1992): 113–24.

Homer. *The Iliad of Homer*. Trans. Richmond Lattimore. Chicago: U of Chicago P, 1951.

———. *The Odyssey of Homer*. Trans. Richmond Lattimore. New York: Harper, 1965.

Horace. *Satires and Epistles*. Trans. Niall Rudd. Penguin, 1973.

Javitch, Daniel. "The Imitation of Imitations in *Orlando furioso*." *Romance Quarterly* 38 (1980): 215–39.

———. "Rescuing Ovid from the Allegorizers." *Comparative Literature* 30 (1978): 97–107.

Kremers, Dieter. *Rinaldo und Odysseus: Zur Frage der Diesseitserkenntnis bei Luigi Pulci und Dante Alighieri*. Heidelberg: Carl Winter, 1966.

Lamberton, Robert. *Homer the Theologian: Neoplatonist Allegorical Reading and the Growth of the Epic Tradition*. Berkeley: U of California P, 1986.

Lansing, Richard H. "Ariosto's *Orlando furioso* and the Homeric Model." *Comparative Literature Studies* 24 (1987): 311–25.

La leggenda di Tristano. Ed. Luigi di Benedetto. Bari: Laterza, 1942.

Looney, Dennis. "Ariosto the Ferrarese Rhapsode: A Compromise in the Critical Terminology for Narrative in the Mid-Cinquecento." *Interpreting the Italian Renaissance: Literary Perspectives*. Ed. A. Toscano. Stonybrook, N.Y.: Forum Italicum, 1991. 138–50.

Lotman, Jurij. "Il viaggio di Ulisse nella Divina Commedia di Dante." *Testo e contesto: Semiotica dell'arte e della cultura*. Ed. S. Salvestroni. Cambridge, Mass.: Harvard UP, 1980. 81–102.

Marinelli, Peter. *Ariosto and Boiardo: The Origins of Orlando Furioso.* Columbia: U of Missouri P, 1986.

Marsh, David. "Ruggiero and Leone: Revision and Resolution in Ariosto's *Orlando furioso.*" *Modern Language Notes* 96 (1981): 144–51.

Moretti, Walter. "Gli ultimi canti del *Furioso:* il viaggio dell'Ariosto nel mondo dell' 'avarizia.' " *Studi in onore di Lanfranco Caretti.* Ed. W. Moretti. Modena: Mucchi, 1987. 25–43.

Nasone, Publio Ovidio. *Metamorfosi.* Ed. P. B. Marzolla. Turin: Einaudi, 1979.

Nohrnberg, James. *The Analogy of the Faerie Queene.* Princeton: Princeton UP, 1976.

Padoan, Giorgio. "Ulisse 'fandi fictor' e le vie della sapienza." *Il pio Enea, l'empio Ulisse: tradizione classica e intendimento medievale in Dante.* Ravenna: Longo, 1977. 170–99.

Papagno, Giuseppe, and Amedeo Quondam, eds. *La corte e lo spazio: Ferrara estense,* 3 vols. Rome: Bulzoni, 1982.

Parker, Patricia. *Inescapable Romance: Studies in the Poetics of a Mode.* Princeton: Princeton UP, 1979.

Petrarch, Francesco. *Petrarch's Lyric Poems: The "Rime sparse" and Other Lyrics.* Trans. and ed. Robert M. Durling. Cambridge, Mass.: Harvard UP, 1976.

Plato. *The Collected Dialogues.* Ed. E. Hamilton and H. Cairns. Princeton: Princeton UP, 1961.

Poliziano, Angelo. *Stanze; Fabula di Orfeo.* Ed. Stefano Carrai. Milan: Mursia, 1988.

Ponte, Giovanni. "Le fontane d'Ardenna nell '*Orlando innamorato.*" *Giornale storico della letteratura italiana* 129 (1952): 382–92.

Pulci, Luigi. *Morgante e lettere.* Ed. D. de Robertis. Florence: Sansoni, 1962.

Quint, David. "The Boat of Romance and Renaissance Epic." In *Romance: Generic Transformation from Chrétien de Troyes to Cervantes,* ed. Kevin Brownlee and Marina Scordilis Brownlee. Hanover, N.H.: UP of New England, 1985. 178–202.

———. "The Death of Brandimarte and the Ending of the *Orlando furioso.*" *Annali d'italianistica* 12 (1994): 75–85.

———. *Epic and Empire: Politics and Generic Form from Virgil to Milton.* New Haven: Yale UP, 1993.

———. *Origin and Originality in Renaissance Literature: Versions of the Source.* New Haven: Yale UP, 1983.

Raimondi, Ezio. "Per una immagine della *Commedia.*" *Metafora e storia.* Bologna: Il mulino, 1972. 31–37.

Rajna, Pio. *Le fonti dell'Orlando furioso.* Florence: Sansoni 1900.

Rebhorn, Wayne. *Foxes and Lions: Machiavelli's Confidence Men.* Ithaca: Cornell UP, 1988.

Rosenthal, Earl. "Plus Ultra, Ne Plus Ultra, and the Columnar Device of Emperor Charles V." *Journal of the Warburg and Courtauld Institutes* 34 (1971): 204–28.

Sannazaro, Iacopo. *Arcadia.* Ed. Francesco Erspamer. Milan: Mursia, 1990.

Santoro, Mario. *L'anello di Angelica: nuovi saggi ariosteschi.* Naples: Federico ed Ardia, 1983.

———. *Letture ariostesche.* Naples: Liguori, 1973.

Segal, Charles Paul. "The Phaeacians and the Symbolism of Odysseus' Return." *Arion* 1 (1962): 17–64.

Schiesari, Juliana. "The Domestication of Woman in *Orlando furioso* 42 and 43, or A Snake Is Being Beaten." *Stanford Italian Review* 10 (1991): 123–43.

Scott, J. A. "*Inferno XXVI*: Dante's Ulysses." *Lettere italiane* 23 (1971): 145–86.

Shankland, Hugh. "Dante's 'Aliger' and Ulysses." *Italian Studies* 32 (1977): 21–40.

Tristan and the Round Table: A Translation of 'La Tavola Ritonda.' Intro. and notes by Anne Shaver. Binghamton, N.Y.: Medieval and Renaissance Texts and Studies, 1983.

Sherberg, Michael. "Ariosto's Rinaldo: The Fall of Man and the Rise of Literature." Diss. University of California–Los Angeles, 1985.

———. *Rinaldo: Character and Intertext in Ariosto and Tasso.* Saratoga, Calif.: Anima Libri, 1993.

Sitterson, Joseph. "Allusive and Elusive Meanings: Reading Ariosto's Vergilian Ending." *Renaissance Quarterly* 45 (1992): 1–17.

Stanford, W. B. *The Ulysses Theme: A Study in the Adaptability of a Traditional Hero.* Oxford: Blackwell, 1954.

Stillinger, Thomas. "The Language of Gardens: Boccaccio's 'Valle delle Donne.' " *Traditio* 39 (1983): 301–21.

Tasso, Torquato. *Gerusalemme liberata.* Ed. C. Varese and Guido Arbizzoni. Milan: Mursia, 1972.

———. *Rinaldo.* Ed. Luigi Bonfigli. Bari: Laterza, 1936.

Il Tristano Riccardiano. Ed. E. G. Parodi. Bologna, 1896.

Vergili Maronis, P. *Opera.* Ed. R. A. B. Mynors. Oxford: Clarendon, 1969.

Vinaver, Eugène. *The Rise of Romance.* Oxford: Oxford UP, 1971.

Wiggins, Peter de Sa. *Figures in Ariosto's Tapestry: Character and Design in the 'Orlando Furioso.'* Baltimore: Johns Hopkins UP, 1986.

Wind, Edgar. *Pagan Mysteries in the Renaissance.* New York: Norton, 1968.

Woods-Marsden, Joanna. *The Gonzaga of Mantua and Pisanello's Arthurian Frescoes.* Princeton: Princeton UP, 1988.

Zatti, Sergio. *Il Furioso fra epos e romanzo.* Lucca: Maria Pacini Facci, 1990.

The Grafting of Virgilian Epic
in *Orlando furioso*

DANIEL JAVITCH

Commentary on imitations of the *Aeneid* in *Orlando furioso*, ever since Lodovico Dolce itemized them in 1542, has usually identified the passages or episodes in the Latin poem that Ariosto modeled himself on, and then considered the sameness and difference between the Italian and Latin texts, without much accounting for the difference. The tendency, moreover, has been to isolate the Italian passages ostensibly imitative of the *Aeneid*, and to disregard what surrounds them.[1] Such a dyadic focus (*x* in the *Furioso* is modeled on *y* in the *Aeneid*) not only fails to account for the complexity of Ariosto's imitations (cf. Javitch, "Imitation"), it leads readers to neglect his much more impressive achievement, namely his ability to integrate the language and matter of Virgilian epic (not to mention the poetry of Ovid and of other Latin authors) with the different material and narrative structure of his chivalric romance. Indeed, there is reason to believe that Ariosto wanted his readers to appreciate this integration or grafting more than his imitations as such. Almost every time he imitates the *Aeneid*, the poet highlights that the context of these imitations belongs to the matter and form of romance.

---

1. As I have argued elsewhere (Javitch, *Proclaiming*, 34–36, 51–53), Dolce wanted to establish clear links between the *Furioso* (OF) and the *Aeneid* as often as he could in order to affirm the prestigious epic ancestry of the Italian poem. But much later commentators have continued to treat Ariosto's use of Virgil in the isolated and unilateral manner initiated by Dolce, even though they ceased to do it for the honorific motives that had prompted the sixteenth-century editor. The constraints of annotations to each octave in modern editions of the poem encourage what I call the dyadic approach to Ariosto's imitations. Emilio Bigi's edition is one of the very few to recognize and identify the plurality of models that Ariosto was imitating, even when the *Aeneid* was the dominant one.

Often, the narrative matter into which Ariosto blends his imitations of Virgil consists of the rewriting of scenes and episodes from prior chivalric romances.

Consider, as an initial example, the description of Orlando when we first meet him inside Paris under siege, sleeplessly tossing and turning in his bed and obsessed with thoughts of his absent Angelica. The simile used to describe his conflicting thoughts (8.71) is borrowed from the one used in the *Aeneid* (8.20–25) to describe Aeneas, awake at night, anxiously casting his mind back and forth while contemplating the impending war with Latium. In his commentary on Ariosto's imitations Lodovico Dolce identified this borrowing, and then also observed that the description a few octaves later (8.79) of the peaceful sleep enjoyed by all except the tormented Orlando was drawn from *Aeneid* 4.522–27 ("Nox erat et placidum carpebant fessa soporem Corpora per terras. . . .") when Virgil describes how the world is peacefully at rest, in contrast to Dido's tormented night before her lover's departure from Carthage. Dolce's claim was valid, even though Ariosto was primarily imitating the sequel to the simile describing Aeneas's conflicting night thoughts in which Virgil describes how, in contrast, night had brought peaceful slumber to all beings ("nox erat et terras animalia fessa per omnis," *Aeneid* 8.26).[2] When Aeneas does eventually fall asleep, he has a dream vision of the river god Tiber, whereas in the *Furioso* we are told of Orlando's tormenting dream of Angelica (8.80–83), a dream which prompts him to leave Paris in search for her. Ariosto's recognizable imitations of Virgil's poem in this episode deserve to be noted but what needs more attention —precisely because it so often remains undiscussed—is that Orlando's insomnia, his lament about the absent Angelica, his sudden departure

2. It is very likely that Ariosto wanted to allude to *both* moments in the *Aeneid*, the eve of Dido's suicide, and the eve of war with Latium. As Lawrence Rhu has pointed out to me, the double allusion would go hand in hand with the poet's desire to bring together the military and the amatory in the episode as a whole. Ariosto may have also had in mind Virgil's own source for his simile, book III of the *Argonautica*, where Medea is described passing a sleepless night on the eve of Jason's frightful ordeal with the bulls, and her throbbing and fluttering heart is compared with light reflected from water (3.756ff.).

from Paris wearing an armor that makes him *incognito*, all this is a rewriting of the very similar episode at the beginning of Boiardo's *Orlando innamorato*, describing Orlando's noctural departure from Paris after his infatuation with Angelica (1.2.22–28). In fact, what distinguishes Ariosto's quite patent imitation of Orlando's nocturnal departure in the *Innamorato* are the various elements that he borrowed from the *Aeneid*—including the idea of a dream sequence—and grafted with the Boiardan matter. In other words, an early reader of *Furioso* 8 would recognize the imitation of Boiardo's account of Orlando's lament over the absence of Angelica and his nocturnal departure, but would be further impressed by Ariosto's ability to work into this romantic episode (in the sense, too, of being typical of romance) very fitting imitations of Virgil's epic.

Ariosto's felicitous inclusion of Virgilian similes at moments in his narrative involving typical situations of chivalric romance is but a part of his effort to combine the strains of romance and Virgilian epic. One can best discern his desire to mix the two strains in his more sustained imitations of the *Aeneid*, also regularly inserted into episodes which rewrite or borrow matter from prior romances. Melissa's mission to extricate Ruggiero from the toils of the enchantress Alcina (7.51ff.) can serve as a representative example. The *maga* Melissa flies over to Alcina's island where, after disguising herself as his mentor, Atlante, she urges Ruggiero to abandon Alcina and to resume his heroic duties, as well as meet his responsibilities to his future descendants, a progeny that will result from his union with Bradamante. Commentators have been quick to point out that Melissa's appeal to Ruggiero was modeled on Virgil's account of Mercury's mission, on Jupiter's orders, to fly down to Carthage and persuade Aeneas to abandon Dido and resume his duty to found Rome (*Aeneid* 4.259ff.). Ariosto could not introduce into his fictional world a pagan divinity to rescue his protagonist, but had to resort to a magician, the agent of supernatural power that in chivalric romance replaces the divinities of ancient epic.[3] But the idea of having Melissa

3. In the first extensive definition of romance, the *Discorso intorno al comporre dei romanzi* (1554), G. B. Giraldi Cinzio had pointed out that writers of this genre could not represent a Christian God interfering in the struggles or predicaments of their protagonists in the

fly to Alcina's island and use magical subterfuge to retrieve the truant hero was itself imitative of a prior romance. In fact, what has been, until modern times, much more rarely observed is that the other text Ariosto imitates in this episode is canto 7 of Cieco's *Mambriano*, specifically the sorcerer Malagigi's mission and successful appeal to Rinaldo to disenthrall himself from queen Carandina and depart from her island (7.77ff.). That Ariosto partly modeled his rescue operation on the one in Cieco's romance is made evident by peculiar similarities in both episodes. For instance, both magicians fly to their respective islands on the backs of demons turned into horses. Like Malagigi, Melissa has to hide upon arriving on Alcina's island and has to resort to subterfuge. Both magicians disguise themselves before confronting the truant heroes (in marked contrast with Mercury's very direct encounter with Aeneas).[4] When Malagigi finds the occasion to address his truant cousin, he brings up the setbacks suffered by the Christians during Rinaldo's absence, including the news that his own home town, Montalbano, is under siege, and then chides Rinaldo for having forsaken his spouse, Clarice, for the "meretrice" Carandina (7.83–84). Malagigi's first sermon, aside from being monitory, does not initially correspond to Mercury's in *Aeneid* 4,

---

way that ancient epic writers had depicted pagan divinities, but, to observe decorum, had to replace them with magicians or daemonic agents. "Gli scrittori che ne' romanzi hanno spiegate cose cristiane, finte da loro," writes Giraldi, "hanno introdotte le fate, ed invece di que' Dei antichi falsi e bugiardi (come disse Dante), hanno fatto venire spiriti infernali e si hanno finte le incantagioni, col mezzo delle quali hanno fatto venire nelle loro composizioni quelli medesimi effetti che avevano fatto prima colla forza de' lor Dei i Poeti greci e latini" (84). Or, as James Nohrnberg has more recently put it: "In the epic the heroic is shadowed by the divine; in the romance, it is shadowed by the daemonic, that is, by the kind of animistic forces that pass through nature and are controlled by magicians" (9).

4. Rajna commented briefly on Ariosto's borrowing from Cieco's *Mambriano* (186–87), and Emilio Bigi notes it in his edition of the *Furioso*, but I found more useful, and I am indebted to, Jo Ann Cavallo's discussion of the similarities between Malagigi's rescue of Rinaldo in *Mambriano* 7 and Melissa's extrication of Ruggiero, in her paper "When Duty Calls: Variations on a Theme in Virgil, Cieco da Ferrara, and Ariosto," part of the proceedings of the Philology and Criticism Seminar held at the Italian Academy for Advanced Studies, Columbia University, in February 1994.

but a little later, when the repentant Rinaldo seems to falter, Malagigi exhorts him once more by invoking his responsibility to his children:

> Ma se Clarice tua non ti commuove,
>   La qual sta cinta da tanti perigli,
>   Commover ti dovriano i cari figli.   (7.89)

(But if your Clarice does not stir you, / beset as she is by so many dangers, / your beloved children must stir you.)

This final admonition does recall the last part of Mercury's speech to Aeneas, when the messenger god states that if Aeneas's personal glory doesn't motivate him (there is nothing, obviously, about his obligations as a husband), then he should consider the destiny of his son:

> si te nulla movet tantarum gloria rerum
> nec super ipse tua moliris laude laborem,
> Ascanium surgentem et spes heredis Iuli
> respice, cui regnum Italiae Romanaque tellus
> debentur.   (*Aeneid* 4.272–76)

(If the glory of such a fortune does not stir you, and for your own fame you do not shoulder the burden, have regard for growing Ascanius and the promise of Iulus your heir, to whom the kingdom of Italy and the Roman land are due.)

It is, of course, these same lines that we find much more explicitly imitated in the *Furioso* when Melissa delivers her sermon to the truant Ruggiero (note the emphasis, as in Virgil, on the dynastic obligation):

> Se non ti muovon le tue proprie laudi,
> e l'opre escelse a chi t'ha il ciel eletto,
> la tua succession perche defraudi
> del ben che mille volte io t'ho predetto?   (7.60)

(Though you do not care for your own fame, and for the shining deeds for which Heaven has elected you, why must you defraud your own descendants of the good that I have predicted to you a thousand times?)

It is possible that Cieco's partial and rather vestigial imitation of Mercury's encounter with Aeneas may have inspired Ariosto to imitate the same scene in *Aeneid* 4 but he did so much more explicitly (aside from the octave cited above, see 7.53). This difference between Cieco's and Ariosto's imitations of Virgil needs to be emphasized. If prior Renaissance romances had begun to use the *Aeneid* as a model for some of their heroic episodes, they did so less discernibly than Ariosto, because, while duplicating actions or situations in the *Aeneid*, they did not imitate the specific language and verse in which Virgil narrated them. For example, on the comparatively few occasions in *Orlando innamorato* when Boiardo borrows scenarios from the *Aeneid* there are few, if any, echoes or reprises of Virgil's language in the Italian verse. A reader might notice an extended simile borrowed from Virgil, but there is nothing in Boiardo's narrative like the more sustained and conspicuous rewriting of Virgil's lines that one can discern in Ariosto's imitations.[5] What is new in Ariosto's poem is the explicitness and extent, at the textual level, of the imitations of the *Aeneid*, as well as the artistic skill with which he manages to embed them in his romance plot.

5. Consider, as an example, the virtual absence of linguistic traces of the imitation in *Orlando innamorato* (OI 1.5.32–55, when Rinaldo boards a boat that is carrying off a figure he mistakes for Gradasso, an action modeled on the scene in *Aeneid* 10.633–88, where Turnus also boards a boat in pursuit of a phantasm of Aeneas. See the recent discussion of Boiardo's rewriting of Virgil's episode in Looney 80–89.

Ettore Paratore's analysis of Boiardo's use of the *Aeneid* corroborates my claim. Despite some of the similarities he finds between a few of the heroic encounters in the *Innamorato* and those in the *Aeneid* (e.g., Orlando's reproach to Agricane before their duel at 1.18.32–33 and Aeneas's taunts to Turnus before their final encounter), Paratore cites no explicit imitations of Virgil's lines on Boiardo's part in these cases. In her more meticulous analysis of Boiardo's appropriation of various Latin poets, Cristina Zampese compares, at one point (p. 240f.) Boiardo's account of Agricane's single-handed fighting inside the walls of Albraca (*Innamorato* 1.xi) with Turnus's similar rampage inside the Trojan camp (*Aeneid* 9.691–818). While she shows that there are some echoes of the Latin epic in Boiardo's narrative, the imitation is not very sustained, and, except for a borrowed simile, these occasional echoes seem barely discernible in comparison to the manifest verbal reprises in Ariosto's similar imitation of Turnus's exploits when he describes Rodomonte's rampage inside the walls of Paris (cantos 16–18), an imitation which I discuss below.

After Ariosto imitates Mercury's rebuke to Aeneas, the action takes a non-Virgilian turn and one not even inspired by the scene in the *Mambriano*. Melissa cannot count on her exhortation alone to make Ruggiero give up his sensual involvment with Alcina. To help him regain rational self-control (which, incidentally, both Aeneas, and Cieco's Rinaldo achieve by their own volition), she resorts to the magic "ring of reason." After placing the ring on Ruggiero's finger (7.65) Melissa returns to her proper identity and tells him that she has been sent by his loving Bradamante who has provided the magic ring to counter Alcina's "incanto." The ring also exposes that Alcina is a hag beneath her beautiful appearance, a revelation that quickly makes the hero lose all his desire for her (7.74). There is, it hardly needs saying, nothing like this in *Aeneid* 4. The scenario of exposing the evil, corrupted nature of a bewitching female in order to convince an infatuated knight or knights of the enchantress's undesirabilty is a characteristic one in chivalric romance. In fact, the scene I am describing in canto 7 would make readers recall the one in Boiardo's *Innamorato* when Angelica relies on the very same magic ring to disenchant Orlando and other knights entrapped by the enchantress Dragontina (1.14 38ff.).[6] My point is that after a Virgilian phase, namely the speech exhorting Ruggiero to resume his heroic obligations, the episode consists, once more, of characteristic romance action. Not that the reader forgets the Virgilian "turn" in the episode. On the contrary, what distinguishes Ariosto's treatment of a rather typical scenario in chivalric romance—the retrieval of a knight enamored of and entrapped by an enchantress—is that it is enriched ("dignified," those might say who rate epic higher than romance) by the Virgilian supplement worked into it.

By grafting his imitations of the *Aeneid* in episodes that are typical of Arthurian romance, that is, episodes involving (as the one discussed above) amatory themes, magic, and enchantment, Ariosto makes his blend of Virgilian and romance strains more conspicuous than when

6. In his comment on OF 7.65, when Melissa puts the ring on Ruggiero's finger, Emilio Bigi notes the echo of *Innamorato* 1.14.43. Cf. also Rajna 185–87.

these imitations turn up in sequences that derive more from the Carolingian *chansons de geste*—for example, during the account of the siege of Paris and of the battling between Charlemagne's forces and Agramante's. This military action in and outside Paris described in cantos 15 to 19 is, in fact, the part of the *Furioso* most replete with imitations of the *Aeneid*: Rodomonte's assault on Paris, his rampage inside the walls, and his eventual retreat are modeled on Turnus's exploits inside the Trojan camp and his forced exit in book 9 of the *Aeneid*; Dardinello's display of valor and his eventual death at the hands of Rinaldo imitate the *aristeia* of the young Pallas and his fatal duel with Turnus in *Aeneid* 10; the arrival of Rinaldo with British troops to relieve the besieged Parisians (16.28ff.) recalls Aeneas's return with aid from Evander; the night sortie of Cloridano and Medoro is modeled, in large part, on the nocturnal exploits of Nisus and Euryalus in *Aeneid* 9. A number of these heroic exploits are repeatedly interrupted by the narrator's shifts to the fantastic Middle Eastern adventures of Astolfo, and then to the amatory misfortunes of Grifone in Damascus. This shifting back and forth in cantos 15 to 19 from Carolingian *gesta* to fantastic and amatory adventures of a more Arthurian type constitutes a large-scale example of Ariosto's successful conflation of epic and romance. What I'd like to dwell on in particular is how the Virgilian imitations that recur in the military sequences are modified precisely because Ariosto has to accommodate them to the demands of the romance's multiple plot structure.

Consider, as a representative example, the segmented account of Rodomonte's rampage within the walls of Paris, his destruction of its inhabitants and buildings, his confrontation with a phalanx of Christian knights, and his eventual forced exit from the city. This series of events is modeled on the exploits of Turnus inside the Trojan camp (*Aeneid* 9.691–818) before he, too, attacked by the entire garrison, is forced to leap into the Tiber. Although Ariosto's imitation of Virgil's narrative is particularly discernible in the segment when Rodomonte, surrounded by the enemy and showered by missiles, is forced to leap into the Seine (see OF 18.21–25 and *Aeneid* 9.789–815), verbal imitations of Virgil's description of Turnus's exploits are evident when Rodomonte's rampage is initially described (e.g., at 16.23 Rodomonte, compared to a tigress attacking a herd, specifically recalls the description of Turnus at *Aeneid* 9.730: "immanem veluti pecora inter inertia tigrim"). Later, when Carlomagno reproaches his knights for not counterattacking Rodomonte (17.7–8), he echoes the same reproach that Mnestheus levels at the Trojans fleeing before Turnus (*Aeneid* 9.781–85). While these textual echoes make Ariosto's imitation clearly recognizable, the most striking difference is that Rodomonte's "aristeia" (if it can be so called) inside Paris is discontinuous and spread over three cantos, whereas Turnus's assault inside the Trojan camp is narrated with much more intensity, and takes up a little less than the last hundred lines of *Aeneid* 9. The single-handed destruction caused by Rodomonte is regularly interrupted by narrative switches to the military action *outside* Paris (e.g., at OF 16.28) or to the altogether separate adventures of Grifone in the Middle East (e.g., at 17.16) which take up a whole canto and the beginning of another before the final phase of Rodomonte's attack on the Parisians is resumed (18.8). Obviously, Ariosto chose to dispense with Virgil's narrative continuity while incorporating Rodomonte's Turnus-like heroics into the multiple plotlines of his romance. Nor is the breaking up of the heroic exploits inside and outside Paris solely dictated by the need of *entrelacement*. Ariosto's interruptions are very abrupt, so abrupt and annoying that they cannot but seem to be highly deliberate ploys to frustrate the reader. Having proposed elsewhere why Ariosto made his interruptions so frustrating, here I simply want to say that the suddenness of the breaks, occurring as they do in the middle of suspenseful combats, highlight even further how Virgil's continuity has been forsaken.[7] In this regard, one of the most notable interruptions in the account of the war in and around Paris occurs when the outstanding feats of the young Saracen prince Dardinello are described (18.47ff.), a display of valor which is itself an imitation of the *Aeneid*, modeled on the *aristeia* of the young

7. See Javitch, "*Cantus interruptus*," where I argue that Ariosto sought to deprive his readers of continuity and fulfillment in order to duplicate the frustration of desire and expectation constantly experienced by the characters in his poem.

Pallas just before he fights the much stronger Turnus and is killed by him (*Aeneid* 10.439–509). To the extent that Ariosto's imitation is recognized, it contributes to the sense of Dardinello's impending doom, even as he overcomes one Christian knight after another. But, at the point when, after his many successes, Dardinello encounters the more formidable Rinaldo, just before the moment of tragic pathos when, like the young Pallas, he will meet his death, Ariosto suddenly interrupts the action (18.58–59) and resumes his account of Grifone's revenge in Damascus, which was broken off fifty octaves earlier. The narrator then leaves the reader deprived of the sequel to Dardinello's fatal encounter with Rinaldo, the equivalent of Pallas's death at the hands of Turnus, for nearly one hundred octaves, making this imitation of the *Aeneid* the one that most conspicuously flouts the continuity and concentration of Virgil's narrative.

As is well known, the multiplicity of plotlines in romance and the discontinuity this produced had already became objects of criticism twenty years after Ariosto's death, and were increasingly disparaged as neo-Horatian and neo-Aristotelian principles of poetic unity and continuity became normative in the later Cinquecento. Even Ariosto's widely acclaimed poem was criticized for its too frequent and too sudden interruptions, and specifically targeted in these attacks was the breaking up of accounts of heroic combat, like the ones narrated during the siege of Paris. When, in one of the better known of these critiques, Antonio Minturno condemns the untimely interruptions perpetrated by *romanzatori*, one can infer that Ariosto's interrupted account of Rodomonte's rampage inside Paris is the kind of narrative he has in mind. In opposition to those who claim that the shifts of plotlines in romance offer pleasurable variety, Minturno asserts that the romancer's habit of suspending the narrative in the middle of a battle or of a storm produces pain rather than pleasure. He suggests that epic poets would not shun this sort of suspension if they thought it had artistic virtue, and he then brings up Virgil's account of Turnus inside the Trojan camp in *Aeneid* 9, maintaining that the Latin poet could have interrupted his account of those exploits had he thought it would have produced more pleasure: "Virgil, for example could have left Turnus shut up in the Trojan fort and passed to the council and the assembly of the gods, and then returned to liberate Turnus, not without injury to his enemies, if he had thought that leaving off of his narrative could reasonably delight." [8]

Minturno suggests that Virgil did not deem such interruption as satisfying as the continuous account we have in *Aeneid* 9. He does so, I would propose, to criticize indirectly Ariosto's fragmentation of his account of Rodomonte inside Paris when he imitated Virgil. Given that Minturno's censure of the discontinuity of romance is preceded by a disapproving account of Ariosto's decision to write a *romanzo* rather than an epic, this implicit critique of the interrupted narration of Rodomonte's exploits in cantos 17 and 18 would be apparent to any reader familiar with Ariosto's episode.

Obviously Minturno's neo-Aristotelian biases made him unsympathetic to Ariosto's disregard of Virgilian continuity, but his critique strongly suggests that those who liked the procedures of romance appreciated Ariosto's modification of Virgilian norms. The neoclassical principles that Minturno and others were ushering in became dominant for so long in Western poetics that even now it is difficult for us to perceive Ariosto's discontinuous narrative, especially when he is recognizably imitating Virgil, as anything other than an impoverishment. We should, instead, try to appreciate Ariosto's narrative procedure as an alternative way of presenting heroic action. To be sure, by being quite suddenly interrupted, these segments of heroic action have different readerly effects, but not necessarily worse ones. It could be argued (as it was, by Cinquecento defenders of the *romanzo*) that while the interruptions disengage readers, they only do so momentarily, that the deferral can be a source of pleasure, and that the technique does allow for greater *varietà*, less monotony. This is not the occasion to argue for the virtues of

---

8. "[S]iccome potuto avrebbe Virgilio lasciar Turno racchiuso dentro al forte de' Trojani, e passarsene al consiglio, ed alla ra[d]unanza degl'Iddii, e poi tornare a liberar Turno non senza danno de' nimici; se questo tralasciamento stimato avesse, che ragionevolmente dovesse dilettare" (Minturno 35). The translation is from Gilbert 288–89.

Ariosto's discontinuous mode of narration. But Ariosto confirmed such a mode was viable, and, by making it work, his break up of continuous Virgilian narrative demonstrated that romance and epic could be fused structurally as well as thematically.

Not only does the Italian poet fragment Virgilian continuity when he describes Rodomonte's Turnus-like heroics, but when they're stopped, Ariosto carries Rodomonte's story back to a romance context. It will be recalled that Virgil's account of Turnus inside the Trojan camp closes, as does book 9, with Turnus being forced to jump into the Tiber. But Ariosto does not bring Rodomonte's actions to an end with the knight's dive into the Seine, nor does this scene close a canto, but occurs after the start of a new one (18.25). That's because, unlike the *aristeia* in epic, the actions of protagonists in chivalric romance may be interrupted but they are never brought to a close. They are always relaunched by new encounters and challenges. So it is with Rodomonte, and what follows his forced exit from Paris is totally un-Virgilian. After a brief digression about the figure of Discord making her way with Pride and Jealousy, and a dwarf to the Saracen camp, we are told that, as Rodomonte pulls himself out of the river, he is met by this same dwarf, sent to him by Doralice, and learns from him that his mistress has been carried off by Mandricardo. Jealousy, Discord, and Pride then take possession of Rodomonte and goad him into a fit of jealous madness. As he storms off searching for a mount (18.37) his story is then suspended for five cantos. Not only, then, does Ariosto depart from the model of *Aeneid* 9 by refusing to close Rodomonte's exploits with his dive into the river; the Saracen's Virgilian heroics turn into the ravings of a betrayed lover. In good romance fashion, martial matters cannot be long sustained before they give way to amatory preoccupations. The Virgilian element in the account of Rodomonte at Paris is not only modified by the formal exigencies of romance, but it is also altered by the *romanzo's* thematic imperative to combine *arme* and *amori*. Actually, the formal and thematic demands are inseparable. The accommodation of Virgilian epic matter in the ongoing interlaced plots of romance not only entails breaking up the continuity of Virgil's episodes but also depriving them of closure, opening them up by carrying forward the actions of the protagonists. These actions do not usually continue to be military, not simply because knights cannot keep fighting perpetually, but because their martial heroics regularly give way to amatory or simply more private desires. In other words, by intertwining *arme* and *amori*, which he does by attending to the erotic preoccupations or susceptibilities of his warriors, Ariosto is able to meet the *romanzo*'s formal demand of propelling ever forward its plotlines.

The way in which such collocation of the military and the amatory significantly modifies borrowings from the *Aeneid* in the *Furioso* is perhaps best illustrated by the outcome of Cloridano's and Medoro's night expedition. This episode, which begins in the last part of the same canto where we see Rodomonte disappear in a fit of jealous rage, is prompted by the desire of the two Saracen soldiers to retrieve the body of their liege, Dardinello. The comradeship of the two soldiers, their courageous decision to make the sortie, their killing of the sleeping enemy sodden with wine, the eventual ambush by an enemy night patrol make very recognizable Ariosto's imitation of the similar night expedition of Nisus and Euryalus in the *Aeneid* (9.176ff.). Although this final episode of canto 18 is perhaps Ariosto's most sustained imitation of the *Aeneid*, it is also modeled on the night expedition of Dymas and Hopleus in Statius's *Thebaid* (10.347ff.), itself an imitation of the Virgilian episode. In fact, in both Ariosto's and Statius's stories, but not in Virgil's, the young warriors act out of love and duty to their dead sovereigns. I do not want to dwell on how Ariosto's imitation of the *Aeneid* is modified by the copresence of the *Thebaid* as a subtext, but on how Ariosto chooses to resolve his version of the night expedition. In both the Latin epics, it will be recalled, the pairs of warriors are killed. Virgil's account of Euryalus's death at the hands of the furious Volcens is especially pathetic (*Aeneid* 10.431–37). But when his counterpart Medoro, in the same dire situation, is about to be killed by Zerbino, the latter's characteristic "gentilezza" moves him to spare the young Saracen ("ma come gli occhi a quel volto mise / gli ne venne pietade, e non l'uccise," 19.10). This act of "pietade" marks the beginning of a happier fortune for Medoro. Whereas Virgil's story of the death of the two warriors is concluded with an account of the desperate, inconsolable grief of Euryalus's mother,

Medoro's survival is followed by his rescue and healing at the hands of the princess Angelica, who falls totally in love (for the first time!) with the young soldier (19.26). Medoro survives the expedition that took the life of Cloridano, not to achieve great military deeds but to become the object of Angelica's love, and eventually her husband.

Some readers have seen in this comedic modification of the tragic Virgilian matter a parodic intent on the part of Ariosto.[9] I would disagree. That is to say, I do not believe that Ariosto placed his imitation of Virgil and Statius in a context that clearly turns into more comical romance to mock his epic models. Ariosto's modulation of Medoro's fatal sortie into a love story with a *lieto fine* seems to me to be yet another brilliant instance of Ariosto's ability to accommodate Virgilian epic matter to the thematic and formal demands of romance. Irreverent parody was not Ariosto's aim here, any more than it was at the end of canto 7, when Melissa exhorts Ruggiero to abandon Alcina for the sake of his glorious Estensi descendants, another Virgilian imitation that has also been mistaken as ironic because of its fantastic romance context.[10] Not that Ariosto never resorts to parody. I have argued, as have numerous critics before me, that the whole sequence of Astolfo's adventures in cantos 34 and 35, from his visit to Hell, his journey to Earthly Paradise, to his ascent to the moon with Saint John as his guide, constitutes a parodic rewriting of Dante's *Commedia* (Javitch, "Orlando Furioso," 1032–34). But

9. For instance, Maria Cristina Cabani maintains in a recent discussion of the Cloridano and Medoro episode that the "lieto fine" of Medoro's near fatal outing, as well as Angelica's unexpected choice of the obscure young Moor as her lover, "getta una luce comico-ironica sulla stessa vicenda classica della coppia eroica." And she concludes that "la scelta di funzionalizzare narrativamente all'interno di una struttura romanzesca e con un lieto fine comico-borghese . . . un episodio epico-tragico che, isolato e chiuso in se stesso, si svolgeva originariamente, nelle due fonti latine, con l'andamento di un dramma, costituisce un'aperta irreverenza verso i modelli" (Cabani 81).

10. A recent example of such an interpretation is to be found in Watkins, esp. 94–98. In a way quite characteristic of modern comparisons of Spenser and Ariosto, Watkins is keen to show that Spenser recast in a much more serious vein a number of Ariosto's Virgilian imitations in the account of Ruggiero's carnal involvement with and eventual abandonment of Alcina in cantos 6 and 7, a line of approach which virtually compels him to argue that these imitations in the *Furioso* are irreverent parodies of the *Aeneid*.

Ariosto's particular combination of the Virgilian and the *romanzesco*, even when it leads the poet to stress amorous rather than heroic drives, does not result in such a parodic reduction of Virgil's epic perspective. Rather it serves to complement it.

The inclination to ascribe a parodic as well as a satiric intent to some of Ariosto's adaptations of Virgil reflects the *unease* that late-twentieth-century readers have had with Ariosto's imitations of the *Aeneid* generally.[11] These readers often find inauthentic or incongruous the encomiastic celebration of the Este dynasty, the military heroics, and other Virgilian features of the *Furioso*. Robert Durling epitomizes this attitude when he maintains that Ariosto's use of Virgil is "an effort to demonstrate the impossibility of a modern *Aeneid* in sixteenth century Italy" (106, but see also 112–14). One wonders, however, whether it is not these readers' own profound skepticism about Virgilian heroism in their time that is being projected on Ariosto. I think that such a projection takes place when readers claim that the Virgilian imitations and passages are there in the *Furioso* to diminish their context. For example, Patricia Parker sees the Virgilian simile describing Orlando when we first meet him at VIII.71 (in the passage I initially discussed) as serving to bring out the reduced heroism of Orlando in comparison to Aeneas. "This use of Virgilian echoes," she then writes, "to point up the reduced or diminished

11. Over ten years ago I myself maintained that Ariosto's treatment of Virgilian epic was critical and revisionary, in an argument about the inspiration Ariosto derived from Ovid's skeptical revision of the *Aeneid* in books 13 and 14 of the *Metamorphoses* (Javitch, "Orlando Furioso," 1025–260). Convinced that Ariosto and Ovid had kindred sensibilities and intentions, I believed that their kinship extended to Ariosto's skeptical treatment of Virgil's epic and its ideology. I could not appreciate, as I do now, that Ariosto's imitation of Virgilian epic, no less than his imitation of Ovidian myth, was part of his general effort to endow his chivalric romance with recognizably classical features, to show that the matter and the language from both ancient poems could be successfully recycled and blended with the *romanzesco*. To be sure, the formal and stylistic affinities between the *Furioso* and the *Metamorphoses* made the grafting of Ovidian myth somewhat less challenging and, one might argue, less conspicuous than that of Virgilian epic. But if the imitations of the *Aeneid* stand out more in their romance contexts, it is not because they are incongruous but, in part, because Ariosto wanted the conflation to be visible and admired.

context of romance occurs throughout the *Furioso*" (40). Such views may also be influenced by the practice of modernist poets like Pound or Eliot whose quotations of, or allusions to, classical poetry do often have an ironic, contrasting relation to the verse that surrounds them. But Ariosto did not share these twentieth-century poets' despairing view of the modern condition, and even if his representation of errant knights and their susceptibilities is quite often humorous, there is no evidence that he deemed the world of his protagonists inherently inferior to that of ancient heroic poetry. It seems anachronistic therefore to confuse his use of Virgil with the modernist technique of quoting classical poetry to decry, by contrast, the impoverishment of contemporary life.

If one takes a longer historical perspective, the tendency to view the imitations of Virgil in Ariosto's poem as having a contrasting rather than a complementary relation to the surrounding narrative can also be seen to stem from ingrained (originally neoclassicist) notions about the difference and superiority of ancient epic in comparison to chivalric romance. As a result of this hierarchization of the two genres, their mixture in the *Furioso* has been mistakenly evaluated in high/low terms. The two most frequent assumptions are either that the inferiority of romance is accentuated by being juxtaposed to Virgilian passages or episodes, or that those epic moments are debased by the conjunction. Hence, the tendency to see Ariosto's accommodation of epic conventions to the formal and thematic demands of romance as an anticipation of later (i.e., seventeenth- and eighteenth-century) mock-heroic or burlesque versions of epic. The neoclassical legacy of privileging epic over romance has impeded readers from appreciating their mixture in positive terms; it has certainly prevented some readers from seeing that, far from accepting the superiority of one genre to the other, Ariosto sought to display his mastery of both and, by grafting them together, to surpass both classical and medieval traditions of narrative poetry, and thereby assert his modernity.

I doubt that for Ariosto's courtly and other sophisticated readers chivalric poetry was deemed so inferior to classical epic that they perceived the fusion of the two strains as serving to ennoble the "poema cavalleresco" or to belittle or mock epic. The grafting of Virgilian and chivalric matter, much like the infusion of Ovidian myth in Ariosto's narrative, would have appealed to these readers as another manifestation of the new blend of overtly classical and late medieval, "gothic" elements they were enjoying in contemporary painting and architecture. Learned readers, on the other hand, did consider Virgilian epic superior to chivalric romance, and Ariosto may well have imitated the Aeneid as often as he did to redeem his chivalric poem in their eyes. Certainly, his successful conflation of classical epic and chivalric matter contributed to the appeal the poem had for a broad and diversified audience, including courtly and learned, as well as unlearned and lesser-born readers. Far from being an "effort to demonstrate the impossibility of a modern Aeneid," Ariosto's fusion of Virgilian and medieval romance elements was an effort to demonstrate how these two narrative strains could be effectively united to produce a new sort of heroic poetry whose originality lay in this very syncretism.

Ariosto's particular combination of the Virgilian and the romanzesco was unprecedented and also unrepeatable. While he demonstrated that the chivalric romanzo could indeed incorporate Virgilian epic, his particular syncretism became impossible to reproduce as heroic poetry in the Cinquecento was increasingly made to conform to neoclassical principles of unity and uniformity, and purged of what were seen as the deficiencies of chivalric romance. In particular, Torquato Tasso's epic practice and theory established new standards that rendered Ariosto's hybridization of romance and epic unacceptable. Not that Tasso ceased to imitate the Aeneid in his epic on the First Crusade, but because the larger narrative context in which these imitations are to be found in the Gerusalemme liberata is so similar to the imitations that one no longer senses that Virgilian episodes have been grafted but rather completely and therefore imperceptibly assimilated.

The difference between Tasso's and Ariosto's imitations of the Aeneid can best be illustrated by comparing both poets' integration of the same

Virgilian episode. I am referring to the account of the funeral procession held for Brandimarte in canto 43 of the *Furioso* (43.166–85), and Tasso's description of Dudone's funeral at the end of canto 3 of the *Liberata*, both imitations of Pallas's funeral procession in the *Aeneid* (9.22ff.). The numerous verbal and other parallels between the obsequies held for Brandimarte and Pallas's funeral in the *Aeneid* have been noted frequently since the sixteenth century.[12] Once again, however, what is more remarkable than Ariosto's imitation of Virgil as such is his ability to insert this solemn epic account into a typical romance narrative largely devoted to Fiordiligi's premonition and grief-stricken reaction to the news of her husband's death, to her journey from north Africa to Sicily, and the simultaneous transportion of Brandimarte's body from Lipadusa to Agrigento (43.154–66).

After the description of the military funeral, Ariosto resumes his account of Fiordiligi's mourning for her spouse, tells of her building a tomb for him, and concludes their love story with her refusal to leave this sepulchre, and her eventual death there (43.182–85). This ending was probably inspired, as Rajna originally pointed out, by the end of the story of Febus and the daughter of the king of Norbellanda who also decided to be buried alive with her dead lover, after repenting for her cruelty to him (Rajna 562–63). Again we can observe here Ariosto's typical procedure of ending an extensive imitation of the *Aeneid* not on an epic note but with a modulation into romance. And, again, for those who may not appreciate the romance ending, he highlights it by rewriting a prior version of it in the well-known *Roman de Palamede*.[13] The actual transition

12. For example, Bardin, Brandimarte's old servant, shown weeping at the bier (OF 43.168) recalls Pallas's aged squire Acoetes grieving for his master (*Aeneid* 11.30–31; 85–86). Alberto Lavezuola was the first commentator to bring out the numerous parallels between this funeral and Pallas's in his "Osservationi" on Ariosto's imitations appended to the 1584 de Franceschi edition of the *Furioso*. For useful recent observations, see Emilio Bigi's comments, especially on the specific verbal reprises Virgil's account in octaves 169, 172, 175, and 178. (Bigi 1802–6).

13. See, too, *Cantari di Febus-el-Forte* for another account of this reunion-in-death in *Dal roman de Palamedes ai Cantari di Febus el Forte*, ed. Alberto Limentani (Bologna, 1962), 282–85.

from the epic pomp of the funeral to Fiordiligi's "romantic" death in the tomb is so smoothly achieved (43.182–83) as to appear seamless, yet the narrative shifts in typical fashion from military matters to those of the heart.

On the other hand, the funeral obsequies held for Dudone in canto 3 of the *Liberata* occur right after the initial skirmish between the crusaders and the pagans that results in Dudone's death at the hands of Argante. Before Dudone is buried, Tasso devotes some stanzas to Goffredo, who chooses to halt the fighting and gives orders for setting up the Christian camp outside Jerusalem. But unlike Ariosto's prolonged account of Fiordiligi in Africa and other matters that interrupt the sequence to Brandimarte's death, Tasso's narrative never leaves the scene of military action and only as much time elapses as is needed for the Christian warriors to pitch their tents before the rites for the dead Dudone are carried out. Tasso's description of Goffredo and the funeral speech he delivers at Dudone's bier (3.67–70) actually echoes Orlando's oration at the burial of Brandimarte (e.g., OF 43.170) at the same time that it imitates Aeneas's final obsequies for Pallas (e.g., *Aeneid* 9.36–38). Tasso invokes both Ariosto's imitation of Virgil and the original Latin poem to make readers aware of his departures from and critique of Ariosto. The main differences—apart from the fact that Dudone's death and funeral occur early in the poem, not like Brandimarte's near the end of the *Furioso*—are the stylistic register and the context. One is hardly aware that Tasso is imitating anyone, because the funeral obsequies for Dudone are identical in tone and content to the martial actions represented before and after. Tasso's imitation is camouflaged, so to speak, because it blends right in with the rest of Tasso's epic narrative. No amatory or romance elements complement or open up Tasso's military scenario (the funeral procession is immediately followed by the expedition to gather lumber for building the siege machines) as they did in Ariosto's, nor is it conceivable that Tasso might so compromise the unity of tone and action he has so deliberately sought to achieve. Whereas Ariosto's imitations of Virgil, standing out as they did because of the romance context surrounding them, aimed to make us admire his ability to master and conjoin two different generic codes, Tasso's imitations reveal quite the opposite: their complete assimilation with a surrounding narrative whose generic code is the same as Virgil's. Tasso's practice, in short, aimed to show how one could truly fuse modern and Virgilian heroic poetry, in contrast to Ariosto's hybridization.

I suggested earlier that Ariosto's grafting of Virgilian epic and romance has been deemed incongruous by modern readers because of ongoing (though unavowed) neoclassicist prejudices. One could argue that Tasso's overgoing of Ariosto played a significant role in shaping those prejudices. In the light of the uniformity and consistency that obtained between Tasso's imitations of Virgil and his ongoing poetic narrative, Ariosto's accommodation of Virgilian matter within his romance could (and was made to) seem inept, incongruous, at best problematic. The sort of generic hybridization still freely practiced by Ariosto was not only rendered outmoded by Tasso's practice but was eventually deemed artistically inferior and illicit by Tasso's champions. Yet a more dispassionate and historically open view must recognize that what Ariosto and Tasso display are two different uses of the classical in the sixteenth century. Even though Tasso's model has been more lasting, in these postmodern times, receptive as they are to difference and to generic hybridization, we should revalue Ariosto's masterful coinjoining of the Virgilian and the romanzesco and acclaim his achievement in the way his first readers did, before literary tastes were corrected.

Works Cited

Ariosto, Lodovico. *Orlando furioso.* Ed. Emilio Bigi. 2 vols. Milan: Rusconi, 1982.

Boiardo, Matteo M. *Orlando innamorato.* Ed. Aldo Scaglione. Turin: UTET,1962.

Cabani, Maria Cristina. "Gli amici amanti: coppie epiche e sortite notturne nei poemi fra Cinque e Seicento." *Riscrittura Intertestualita Transcodificazione.* Ed. E. Scarano and D. Diamanti. Pisa: Tipografia Reditrice Pisana, 1994.

Cavallo, Jo Ann. "When Duty Calls: Variations on a Theme in Virgil, Cieco da Ferrara, and Aristo." Paper presented at Philosophy and Criticism Seminar, Italian Academy for Advanced Studies, Columbia University, February 1994.

Cieco, Francesco. *Mambriano.* Ed. Giuseppe Rua. 2 vols. Turin: UTET, 1926.

Dolce, Lodovico. "Brieve dimostratione di molte comparationi et sentenze dall'Ariosto in diversi autori imitate." *Orlando furioso di M. Ludovico Ariosto. . . .* Venice: G. Giolito, 1542.

Durling, Robert M. "The Epic Ideal." *Literature and Western Civilization. The Old World: Discovery and Rebirth*. Ed. David Daiches and Anthony Thorlby. London: Aldus Books,1974.

Gilbert, Allan. *Literary Criticism: Plato to Dryden*. Detroit: Wayne State UP, 1962.

Javitch, Daniel. "Cantus interruptus in the Orlando Furioso." *Modern Language Notes* 95 (1980): 66–80.

——. "The *Orlando Furioso* and Ovid's Revision of the Aeneid." *Modern Language Notes* 99 (1984):1023–36.

——. "The Imitation of Imitations in Orlando Furioso." *Renaissance Quarterly* 38 (1985): 215–39.

——. *Proclaiming a Classic: The Canonization of Orlando Furioso*. Princeton: Princeton UP, 1991.

Lavezuola, Alberto. "Osservationi sopra il Furioso . . . nelle quali si mostrano tutti i luoghi imitati dall'autore nel suo Poema." *Orlando Furioso di M. Ludovico Ariosto*. . . . Venice: F. de Franceschi, 1584.

Limentani, Alberto, ed. *Dal Roman de Palamedes ai Cantari di Febus-El-Forte*. Bologna: Commissione per i testi di lingua, 1962.

Looney, Dennis. *Compromising the Classics: Romance Epic Narrative in the Italian Renaissance*. Detroit: Wayne State UP, 1996.

Minturno, Antonio. *L'arte poetica del Sig. Antonio Minturno*. . . . Venice: G. A. Valvassori, 1563.

Nohrnberg, James. *The Analogy of the Faerie Queene*. Princeton: Princeton UP, 1976.

Paratore, Ettore. "L'Orlando Innamorato e l'Eneide." *Il Boiardo e la critica contemporanea*. Ed. Giuseppe Anceschi. Florence: Olschki, 1970.

Parker, Patricia. *Inescapable Romance: Studies in the Poetics of a Mode*. Princeton: Princeton UP, 1979.

Rajna, Pio. *Le Fonti dell'Orlando Furioso*. Florence: Sansoni, 1900.

Romizi, Augusto. *Le fonti latine del Furioso*. Turin: Paravia, 1896.

Tasso, Torquato. *Gerusalemme liberata*. Ed. Lanfranco Caretti. Turin: Einaudi, 1971.

Virgil. *The Aeneid of Virgil*. Ed. R. D. Williams. 2 vols. London: Macmillan/St Martin's, 1973.

Watkins, John. *The Specter of Dido: Spenser and Virgilian Epic*. New Haven: Yale UP, 1995.

Zampese, Cristina. *Or si fa rosso or pallida la luna: la cultura classica nell'Orlando innamorato*. Lucca: Pacini Fazzi, 1994.

Tasso's Armida and the Victory of Romance

JO ANN CAVALLO

The first person to offer an interpretation of Armida is Torquato Tasso himself, who in the "Allegoria" published with the Ferrarese edition of 1581 places her squarely within a traditional moralistic framework. Tasso draws a parallel between Armida and Ismeno as "ministers of the Devil" ("ministri del Diavolo") who "strive to keep the Christians from fighting" ("procurano di rimuovere i Christiani dal guerreggiare") and as "diabolic temptations that lie in wait for the two faculties of our soul from which all sins proceed" ("due diaboliche tentazioni, che insidiano à due potenze dell'anima nostra, dalle quali tutti i peccati procedono"). Armida is, more specifically, "the temptation that lays traps for the appetitive faculty" ("la tentatione, che rende insidie alla potenza, che appetisce"). In the same essay, the Christian hero Rinaldo is designated as the figure who provides the arm of the crusading army whose head is Goffredo. Armida and Rinaldo are thus assigned allegorical roles that put them at odds with each other on both moral and political grounds. If as readers of the *Gerusalemme liberata* we follow Tasso's allegorical indications, then we would expect Rinaldo's departure from Armida's garden in canto 16 to represent a permanent victory of reason over the appetites and of Christian piety over the forces of the devil.

Armida's literary precedents also lead the reader to assume that Rinaldo will renounce the alluring female obstacle on a permanent basis as he gives himself over to duty. The situation can be traced back to the *Odyssey*, where Odysseus leaves Circe and then Calypso in order to return to Ithaca.[1] In Virgil's elaboration of Homer, Aeneas leaves Dido in order

---

1. Homer may not have moralized, but his commentators and imitators usually did. See

to found the Roman empire. Tasso was keenly aware of the many Renaissance chivalric episodes that were patterned on *Aeneid* 4, such as those of Rinaldo and Carandina (*Mambriano*), Ruggiero and Alcina (*Orlando furioso* [OF]), Corsamonte and Ligridonia (*Italia liberata*), and Alidoro and Lucilla (*Amadigi*), and he wrote his own version of the episode in the story of Rinaldo and Floriana (*Rinaldo*).[2] In the *Gerusalemme liberata*, however, although Tasso uses elements from previous romance epics, he presents an ending that is so radically different that it challenges the basic assumptions of all its precedents. In order to explore the implications of this ending in terms of Tasso's poetic enterprise, I would first like to place Armida within the context of the Italian Renaissance epic.

The first Italian epic to fascinate readers with dangerous, seductive females that provide a model for subsequent poets was Boiardo's *Orlando innamorato*, which introduced the alluring Angelica as well as actual *maga* figures like Dragontina and Alcina.[3] Yet Boiardo blurred the conventional distinction between woman and enchantress in the chivalric romance by having Angelica make use of both feminine and magical arts in trying to achieve her goals. At her appearance in Charlemagne's court in the opening canto of the poem, her beauty alone is so overwhelming that every knight without exception, even King Charlemagne, falls in love with her. Yet when Rinaldo, due to the magic of Merlin's fountain, becomes immune to her feminine charms, she turns to witchcraft to seduce him. She creates a splendid pleasure palace and garden paradise on a deserted island in the middle of the sea, she has the magician Malagigi transport Rinaldo there in an unmanned boat, and, while attractive maidens provide him with every luxury at table, she waits offstage for her cue to

Yarnall. Unfortunately, Yarnall refers to Armida only in passing, listing her along with Ariosto's Alcina and Spenser's Acrasia.

2. One could perhaps add to this list the story of Massimissa and Sofonisba in Petrarch's *Africa*, even though it was written in Latin. For Petrarch's use of *Aeneid* 4 in this episode, see Kallendorf.

3. Boiardo could have found the name Alcina in Barberino's *Guerino detto il Meschino*. This earlier Alcina was a prophetess-enchantress who lived in the Apennine mountains, but she was unable to seduce the hero Guerino.

act out the role of Circe to this Carolingian Odysseus. Angelica's magical site, however, fails to override the effects of the Fountain of Merlin. Although Angelica's maidens tell him that he is powerless to leave ("sei pregione," 1.8.12), he simply boards the ship and sails off.

Angelica's failure as a would-be Circe keeps her one step this side of an enchantress such as Dragontina, who offers all knights who arrive at her magical palace a potion that immediately causes them to fall into a state of oblivious erotic enchantment and makes them forget their public duty, their past, their very identity. Dragontina is, however, linked to Angelica not only by the particular version of the Circe story that is depicted on the walls of her loggia, but also by the fact that it is ultimately Angelica who frees Orlando from Dragontina with her magic ring and leads him to Albraca under the "spell" of her beauty.[4]

The first chivalric romance to adopt the innovative techniques and themes of the *Innamorato* is the *Mambriano* by Francesco Bello (also known as Cieco da Ferrara).[5] Early in the poem, Bello replays the narrative situation in which a Carolingian knight is enticed by an enchantress on a pleasure palace complete with a fountain and a garden that seemed an earthly paradise ("sembrava un terrestre paradiso," 1.46).[6] The *maga* Carandina is attended by maidens who resemble sirens ("ognuna risembrava una sirena," 1.30). The knight in question is Rinaldo, who in the *Innamorato* had resisted Angelica's attempts to play Circe at her island pleasure palace. While Boiardo had combined *maga* and *donna* by suggesting Angelica's affinity to both Circe and Dido, Bello underscores Carandina magical powers, calling her a more powerful *maga* than Circe and Medea (1.32). Yet as the episode proceeds, Carandina will reveal herself to be much closer to Virgil's Dido than to either of the enchantresses

---

4. Other seductive sites of the *Innamorato* (OI) are the Fountain of Love, Morgana's underwater realm, Falerina's garden, Alcina's island, the Narcissus fountain, and the Fonte del Riso. For more detail, see Cavallo.

5. Praloran 77. Written between 1490 and Bello's death in 1496, the *Mambriano* was published posthumously in 1509.

6. Praloran has noted that the early part of the poem (and consequently the episode in question) is typically Boiardan (77).

to which Bello compares her in this passage. Indeed, Bello turns the *Innamorato*'s Virgilian allusions into an outright imitation of the *Aeneid*'s story of Dido and Aeneas, thus providing the first of a series of imitations of *Aeneid* 4 in the Italian Renaissance epic, which will lead to Tasso's account of Armida and Rinaldo.

Carandina first appears to Rinaldo in a dream posing as a damsel in distress and offering him fame ("fama," 1.74), adventure/fortune ("ventura," 1.75), and wealth ("tesoro," 1.77). Although her original intention was to entice Rinaldo from France to her island so that her lover Mambriano could fight him, Carandina soon transfers her affection to the more valorous Rinaldo. She is more fortunate than Angelica, since she succeeds in gaining Rinaldo's love in return and in keeping him on her island for some time. It is important to note that, despite her powers as a *maga*, Carandina seduces Rinaldo with feminine rather than magical arts. Nevertheless, a demon who later tells Malagigi of her seduction describes it as though Carandina had used the same method as Boiardo's Dragontina, accusing her of having given him water from the river of Lethe in order to place him under her spell and erase from his mind the priorities of a Christian knight: religion, country, and family.[7]

In order to free Rinaldo from private passion and reinstill in him a sense of duty, Malagigi arrives at Carandina's island in the guise of Virgil's Mercury. We recall that in the *Aeneid*, Mercury first reminded Aeneas of his glorious deeds and fame, and then elaborated on Jupiter's rhetorical question ("But if the brightness of such deeds is not enough to kindle him, if he cannot attempt the task for his own fame, does he—a father—grudge Ascanius the walls of Rome?"), turning it into an imperative:

> si te nulla movet tantarum gloria rerum
> [nec super ipse tua moliris laude laborem,]
> Ascanium surgentem et spes heredis Iuli

---

7. :The passage reads: "Costei già tolse dal fiume di Lete / Tanta acqua, che ne fece un beveraggio / Al tuo cugin, non per trargli la sete, / Ma per tenerlo a l'isola del Faggio, / E per saziar le sue voglie discrete, Poi per ridur quel baron franco e saggio, / Non solamente a scordarsi il battesmo, / Ma Montalban, Clarice e sè medesmo" (6.7)

respice, cui regnum Italiae Romanaque tellus
debetur. (4.264–69)

(If the brightness of such deeds is not
enough to kindle you—if you cannot
attempt the task for your own fame—remember
Ascanius growing up, the hopes you hold
for Iülus, your own heir, to whom are owed
the realm of Italy and land of Rome.)

By referring to Aeneas's son by his two given names, Mercury evoked both the feeling of private, paternal love of a father for his young son ("Ascanius growing up") and the more dynastic mission of a ruler who must pass on a kingdom to his descendents ("Iülus, your own heir").[8] While Mercury's speech had an immediate effect, Malagigi's rhetoric of persuasion is needed at various moments.[9] After evoking the suffering of his fellow Christians and countrymen at the hands of the Saracens (7.83), Malagigi moves to a more intimate tie, reminding Rinaldo of his failings toward his wife, Clarice (7.84). Rinaldo seems persuaded to put duty before desire, but then, when Malagigi asks Rinaldo to help him put Carandina to sleep by magic in order to escape, the knight resists. Even after Malagigi resorts to the promise of glory (7.88), Rinaldo remains hesistant. It is at this point that Malagigi employs both the formal structure and the content of Mercury's climactic verses:

> Ma se Clarice tua non ti commove,
> La qual sta cinta da tanti perigli,
> Commover ti dovriano i cari figli. (7.89)

(Though you are not moved by Clarice, who is surrounded by so many dangers, your dear sons should move you.)

According to Malagigi, it is the welfare of Clarice rather than the promise of glory that constitutes the second highest priority. And while

8. See Greene's analysis of this episode.

9. Mercury will return once again in a dream to urge on the sleeping Aeneas, signaling reluctance on the hero's part, but Malagigi's intervention is much more extensive.

the fate of one's children represents the highest priority in both texts, Bello privileges immediate familial ties over dreams of dynasty by focusing exclusively on a father's concern for his beloved children who are in danger.

Although the separation of the lovers is permanent, Carandina is treated with sympathy by the author. She will later reappear in the narrative to seek Rinaldo and will eventually marry her first lover, Mambriano. By transforming her from the dangerous enchantress who detains Rinaldo on the Isola del Faggio to the wife of Mambiano who will rule with him in his eastern kingdom, Bello provides a happy ending for his heroine, which contrasts with the suicide of Dido but does not compromise the integrity of his Christian hero. This suggests a double perspective that many readers have detected in Virgil's original: a moralistic stance with regard to the hero who must put duty over pleasure, along with a sympathetic treatment of the woman who has temporarily detained him.

When Ariosto attempts his own imitation of *Aeneid* 4, his Dido figure is the Boiardan enchantress Alcina. When Astolfo and his fellow Christian knights encountered Alcina singing to a vast public of fish, her first impulse was to kill the knights; yet Astolfo's beauty enchanted her, and she decided instead to whisk him away on her whale (OI 2.13.54–64). When Ariosto picks up the story of Alcina, he narrates the seduction of a new victim, Ruggiero, who was transported by the unbridled hippogriff to Alcina's island and was then seduced by the enchantress's magically sustained beauty (OF 7.18).

Whereas in the *Mambriano* Malagigi had disguised himself as a merchant to free his younger cousin Rinaldo, here Melissa takes on the form of Ruggiero's guardian, Atlante. In her speech, Melissa appeals primarily to Ruggiero's ego by stressing the prospects of glory and fame. She, too, incorporates the structure and content of Mercury's exhortation into her speech when she asks:

> Se non ti muovon le tue proprie laudi,
> e l'opre escelse a chi t'ha il cielo eletto,

la tua succession perché defraudi
del ben che mille volte io t'ho predetto?   (7.60)

(Though you care nothing for your own renown and for the shining
deeds for which Heaven has appointed you, why must you defraud
your own posterity of all the good which I have a thousand times
predicted to you?)

Whereas Bello had intensified the sense of paternal love inherent in
Virgil's verses, Ariosto moves in the opposite direction, to underscore
exclusively the dynastic aspect. Ruggiero's descendents are referred to
merely as "la tua succession." And rather than end the exhortation with
this rhetorical question, Ariosto immediately follows it with an encomi-
astic passage on the Estense family (especially brothers Ippolito and
Alfonso) that continues for three and a half stanzas. Ariosto can take
the time to flatter his patrons at this moment because Melissa's speech
has a merely preparatory function. Ruggiero's attraction to Alcina will
be dispelled completely the instant Melissa puts the spell-breaking ring
on his finger: "si parte / de l'animo a Ruggiero ogni pensiero / ch'avea
d'amare Alcina" ("Ruggiero could no longer find in himself the slightest
inclination to love Alcina," 7.74). Although Melissa speaks both before
and after using the ring, Ariosto makes clear that just as Ruggiero's
earlier enamorment was exclusively the result of magic ("per incanto,"
7.18), so is his recovery: "quando il suo amor per forza era d'incanto, /
ch'essendovi l'annel, rimase vano" ("His love had been wrought out of
enchantment, and, with the ring, the spell was broken," 7.70).

Ruggiero, in fact, like the *Orlando innamorato* knights, is unable on his
own account to break free of erotic enchantment. There is no testing of
the will here, as there was in Virgil and Bello, and the reader is made to
doubt the hero's control of his appetites, a doubt confirmed in the next
episode in which Ruggiero attempts to rape Angelica after having freed
her from the Orca. Alcina, in the meantime, revealed to be old and de-
crepit, cannot even choose to follow Dido's fate because she is a *fata*, and
is left to suffer and eventually (in the *Cinque canti*) to seek revenge.

By the time Torquato Tasso wrote his *Rinaldo* in 1559, it was practically de rigueur for the *poema eroico* to include an episode in which the hero is tempted to succumb to the allure of a seductive female. In contrast to the typical Renaissance seductress, Rinaldo's "temptress" Floriana is a noble woman rather than a *maga*.[10] As Rinaldo himself will later acknowledge, her means of seduction was not magic but her beauty, her courtesy, and her other virtues: "l'alta sua beltà, la cortesia, / e l'altre sue virtù" (9.92). Moreover, Tasso does not contrast Floriana with his future wife, Clarice; on the contrary, he creates a parallel between the two women. Although they are of different religions, both women are young, beautiful, courteous, articulate, and forthright, with strong character and leadership traits (Clarice presides over a group of noble knights; Floriana is the queen of Media). And in contrast to Alcina, who had a thousand other lovers before Astolfo and Ruggiero, Floriana is, like Clarice, a virgin when she meets Rinaldo. Moreover, Floriana's aunt had foretold that she will bear Rinaldo two noble sons. This reference to future progeny not only further distances Floriana from the figure of the seductress, but it creates dynastic expectations previously associated with the hero's destined wife.

The garden in which Rinaldo and Floriana consummate their desire is not a place of magic or deceitful artifice. On the contrary, the setting is naturalistic and the scene suggests the golden age later described by the chorus of the *Aminta*, in which passionate love reigned supreme. Floriana's name recalls Flora, the goddess of flowers and spring (Ovid, *Fasti* 5.195). Their love delights Venus, who laughingly rains down on them pleasure in abundance ("rise Venere in cielo, e i suoi diletti / versò piovendo in lor larga e cortese," 9.80).

Rinaldo's liberation comes about when Clarice appears to him in a dream and describes the negative effects that his love affair will have on his reputation as a knight.[11] To press home her point, she uses the struc-

10. I should note that this humanization of the seductress also occurs in Bernardo Tasso's *Amadigi*, in the episode of Lucilla and Alidoro.

11. She states: "[A]hi! si dirà Rinaldo in Media or bada, e lascivi pensier ne l'ocio cova, / e per una pagana e lancia e spada / posto in non cale, ei preso ha legge nova" (9.86).

ture of Mercury's climactic exhortation, but alters the content so that honor is now seen as the highest priority:

> Ma se 'l mio duol non curi, e non t'aggrada
> l'amor, crudele, il proprio onor ti muova.   (9.86)

(Though you care nothing for my pain, and my love does not please you, you cruel man, let your own honor move you.)

In this way, Clarice distinguishes between Rinaldo's love for the "pagan" Floriana, which has led him to idleness and disregard for his own religion, and his love for her which spurs him on to seek fame and which preserves his honor. Her reasoning convinces Rinaldo, who wakes from the dream and hurriedly dons his armor (9.87).

Yet what in the chivalric tradition was stated as an absolute hierarchy of duty over love becomes in the *Rinaldo* a question of correct timing. We recall that the oracle in the temple of love had given Rinaldo this advice:

> — Segui, Rinaldo, il tuo desir primiero
> di venir chiaro in arme; e fia tua moglie
> Clarice allora, e pago il tuo pensiero.   (5.67)

(Follow, Rinaldo, your first desire to become famous in arms, and then may Clarice become your wife, and your desire satisfied.)

While fame comes before the fulfillment of desire in time, love comes before fame in importance. The oracle does nothing but reiterate the priorities that Rinaldo had set for himself at the end of canto 1. Clarice had invited Rinaldo into her castle, but after much deliberation he declined and set off to create a name for himself. This was not, however, a contest between private passion and public duty, but rather an affirmation of the knight's need to seek adventure in order to be more worthy of his lady: "prima ha disposto illustri imprese / condur al fin per farsi grato a quella" ("He decided to first undertake illustrious undertakings to make himself pleasing to her," 1.93). The beloved is not rejected as inimical to chivalry; on the contrary, to become worthy of her love becomes the knight's ultimate goal. (The poem, in fact, ends with the marriage of Rinaldo and Clarice.) This attitude is informed by a courtly love ethos that draws its inspiration from the romances of the Breton cycle.

Despite the value given to love and personal achievement in the poem, the Rinaldo and Floriana episode adheres to the pattern established in the Virgilian precedent of Aeneas and Dido. At the same time, Tasso has shown too much sympathy for Floriana to condemn her to the same fate as Virgil's Carthaginian queen. Floriana's aunt—none other than "Medea l'incantatrice" (10.28)—arrives and prevents her from committing suicide by giving her a drink from the healing waters of Lethe. Tasso goes against literary tradition by transforming Medea, traditionally a symbol of the evil of which a spurned woman is capable, into an elderly matron ("un'antica matrona," 10.27) who understands pain and administers essential relief to her desperate niece. This domestication of Medea is consonant with Tasso's positive rendering of the "seductress" who had been depicted as an evil *maga* by Ariosto. In fact, the resolution of the episode is more in line with Bello's treatment of Carandina. While Bello gave Carandina happiness through marriage to the pagan hero Mambriano, Tasso has Medea transport Floriana to a happy island ("isola del Piacer") beyond the pillars of Hercules where anyone who approaches becomes joyful and free of care ("null'è che l'uom mai punto annoi, / lieto divien ciascun che vi s'appresse," 10.33). This "isola del Piacer" represents both a golden age outside Christian morality and a blissful resting place that makes mortal life seem a real burden—even for heroes. We can also assume that Floriana will bear Rinaldo the noble twins that, according to her aunt, were destined to perform great deeds ("due gemelli, che ad alte e nuove imprese / già destinava il lor benigno fato," 9.59). Tasso, then, has not only reversed the tragic suicide of Dido (as well as the revenge of Medea), but he has also granted to Floriana the establishment of an alternative dynasty.

While the opening verses of Il Rinaldo announced a poem about "i felici affanni e i primi ardori / che giovanetto ancor soffrì Rinaldo" ("the happy anguish and the first fervour [of love] that Rinaldo suffered while young," 1.1), the Gerusalemme liberata is introduced as a poem about "l'arme pietose e 'l capitano / che 'l gran sepolcro liberò di Cristo" ("the reverent armies and the captain who liberated Christ's great sepulcher," 1.1). Tasso has replaced Rinaldo's youthful ardors with the First Crusaders' liberation of Jerusalem. One thing that the two poems have in common, however, is an episode in which the hero, named Rinaldo, is side-tracked from duty by an alluring female in a garden setting. In the latter poem, the one hero whose participation in the First Crusade is necessary for a Christian victory is detained on an island by the seductress Armida. Given not only the poem's subject matter but also Tasso's own historical circumstances (the Council of Trent was reopened in 1562–63), we can almost expect a retreat from the sympathetic treatment of the seductress that we found in Il Rinaldo.[12] In actuality, as the remainder of this essay will argue, Tasso departs in an even more radical way from the pattern of Aeneid 4 and its Renaissance imitations in the Gerusalemme than he did in the Rinaldo.

Armida is a woman ("donna," 4.23) who is well versed in both feminine and magic arts ("gli accorgimenti e le più occulte frodi, / ch'usi o femina o maga, a lei son note," 4.23). Like Boiardo's Angelica, Tasso's donna-maga appears before a group of Christian knights with the sole mission of removing them from their power base and leading them to a prison. Even though her uncle Idraote has admitted that she already surpasses him in demonic art ("già ne l'arti mie me stesso avanze," 4.24), she too relies exclusively on her feminine charms or arte feminil (4.25). In fact, she expects to accomplish more with her sweet actions and beautiful visage than Circe or Medea did with their magic arts ("far con gli atti dolci e co 'l bel viso / più che con l'arti lor Circe e Medea," 4.86). She also intends to carry out the familiar role of the siren by putting even the most alert minds to sleep ("e in voce di sirena a i suoi concenti / addormentar le più svegliate menti," 4.86).[13]

12. Tasso is often, and, as I shall argue below, erroneously, considered a spokesman for the Counter-Reformation. Giamatti, for instance, states: "Either a man is saved, through rigid adherence to absolute values and his sense of duty, or he is damned. He serves the spirit or he wallows in sensuality. There is no middle ground" (The Earthly Paradise 192).

13. Tasso continues in the next stanza to emphasize the fact that Armida's arts here are ex-

Like Angelica, Armida aims to elicit feelings of pity as well as attraction by resorting to a false story which puts her in the role of a damsel in distress.[14] She is a better actress than Angelica, however. While Boiardo's seductress told Charlemagne of her exile "con vista allegra e con un riso" ("radiant and with a smile," 1.1.23), Armida bows before Goffredo, silent and bashful ("vergognosetta") until the leader has been reassured, and she proceeds with much more elaborate and doleful account of her exile.[15]

Armida is not assisted by a brother, and rather than propose a joust, she openly asks for their aid. In this she recalls Trissino's Elpidia. In book 6 of L'Italia liberata da' Goti, a beautiful damsel appeared before the Christian knights who were trying to free Italy from the barbarians, and she requested their aid to help her avenge her father's death and win back her kingdom.[16] She told the assembled knights how the captain of the Goths had killed her father by treachery because he refused to marry her off to the Goth's repulsive son. Her mother then died of grief, leaving Elpidia to seek vengeance through the Captain of the Italians. In return for his help, she offered herself in marriage to a knight of the captain's choosing. Tasso's Armida not only uses elements of Elpidia's story, but she also intensifies them in her pleas for help. The description of the unwanted spouse goes from "il più brutto" ("the ugliest")

---

clusively those of a *donna* not of a *maga*: "Usa ogn'arte la donna" (4.87). The effect, however, is to gather men in her net like fish: "onde sia colto / ne la sua rete alcun novello amante" (487).

14. Both begin with a one-stanza *captatio benevolentiae* (cf. OI 1.1.24 and GL 4.39). Both also mix truth with falsehood. For example, the knight who accompanies Angelica is her brother as she says, just as Armida really is from Damascus and does have an uncle. Migiel notes that Tasso never tells us Armida's real history, and we cannot therefore determine how much of her story is a lie. Interestingly, Fasani notes that Armida's tale of exile contains textual echoes of Tasso's own autobiographical poetry.

15. Cossutta notes the incongruity of Angelica's demeanor and her story (223).

16. Whereas Angelica was surrounded by four giants, Elpidia is surrounded by four noble knights: "Apparve una bellissima donzella, / Ch'avea le veste di colore oscuro; / E venia sopra un palafren morello, / Con quattro nobil cavalieri intorno" (57).

to "sotto diforme aspetto animo vile" ("beneath a misshapen exterior a base mind"), and from "il più sciocco" ("the stupidest") to "né mai troppo alto intese" ("nor did he comprehend anything too high," 4.46). The interesting thing about Trissino's precedent is that Elpidia's story was indeed legitimate, her request was granted, and the epic's hero Corsamonte is destined to become her future husband.

When Armida later falls in love with Rinaldo, she whisks him away to a garden paradise she has created in the Fortunate Islands, but she does not use magic to make Rinaldo desire her. In fact, he had already begun to fall in love with her in canto 4, although Tasso specifies that the passion was just under his skin and had not yet penetrated his heart.[17] During the time that Rinaldo spends on her island, Armida practices magic only when she is away from him and attending to her other matters (16.26).

Rinaldo's liberation will come about thanks to the visit of two fellow crusaders. If in the *Orlando furioso* Melissa's speech is preparatory and the real transformation in Ruggiero takes place afterward through the magic ring, here the transformation of Rinaldo takes place immediately, and the subsequent speech, limited to two brief stanzas, functions simply as a reinforcement. Ubaldo's rhetorical questions to Rinaldo— "Qual sonno o qual letargo ha sí sopita / la tua virtute? o qual viltà l'alletta?" ("What slumber or what lethargy has so lulled your manhood? or what commonness allures it?" 16.33) — echo the earlier part of Mercury's speech to Aeneas ("What have you in mind? What hope, wasting your days / in Libya?"). The climactic moment of Mercury's exhortation, however, is missing—and with good reason. Since Rinaldo was designated to be the progenitor of the Estense family, any allusion to these verses might have brought up the question of Rinaldo's dynastic suc-

---

17. Tasso says of Rinaldo: "a lui colpi d'amor più lenti / non hanno il petto oltra la scorza inceso" ("in him the blows of love, being lighter, have not cut into his breast beyond the outer shell." 5.12). Tasso also singles out Goffredo and Tancredi as the only two knights who are not enamored of her: "Questi soli non vinse: o molto o poco / avampò ciascun altro al suo bel foco" (5.65).

cession. This, in turn, would have led to curiosity regarding the identity of Rinaldo's future consort, something that Tasso is not quite ready to disclose in canto 16. By way of contrast, in the *Furioso*, when Ruggiero arrives at Alcina's island, readers already know that he is destined to marry Bradamante. Likewise, in the *Rinaldo*, Tasso's hero met Floriana only after he had promised his love to Clarice. But the crusader whom Tasso has invented as the new progenitor of the Estense family is still without a designated consort. Earlier, Peter the Hermit had foretold of Rinaldo "ben di lui nasceran degni i figli" ("sons worthy of him will be born," 10.75), as if no female participation were necessary for procreation.

Ubaldo's speech nevertheless completes the scene by turning Rinaldo's initial feeling of shame to disdain (*sdegno*). Ripping off his exotic clothes, he exits the labyrinthine palace. While in the *Rinaldo*, Floriana became aware of Rinaldo's departure when it was already too late, here Armida sees her Rinaldo escaping and tries to retain him. After attempting in vain to hold him by magic, she decides to resort to her "vaga e supplice beltà" ("lovely and suppliant beauty," 16.37), and runs down to the shore after him. At first, Tasso tells us that Rinaldo is impenetrable: "resiste e vince; in lui trova impedita / Amor l'entrata, il lagrimar l'uscita" ("he struggles and overcomes; Love finds the entrance closed, and tears the exit," 16.51). Yet the definitive sound of these two verses is overturned in the following stanza. Although Love is barred entrance by reason, compassion ("pietate") gets through, and now it becomes hard for Rinaldo to hold back his tears: "a freno / può ritener le lagrime a fatica" ("he can scarcely hold his tears in check," 16.52).[18] Although Armida criticizes him for having dry eyes (16.57), after she faints, Tasso intervenes to tell Armida to open her eyes so that she can see the tears in Rinaldo's: "il pianto amaro / ne gli occhi al tuo nemico or ché non miri?" ("Why do you not see now the bitter tear in the eyes of your enemy?" 16.61).

By shifting from love to compassion, Tasso can represent an inner

---

18. In the Aminta, Tasso links compassion and love when Dafne says, "La pietà messaggiera è de l'amore, / come 'l lampo del tuono" (4.1).

conflict in his hero that is not one of the appetites against reason, but rather of Courtesy ("cortesia") and Pity ("pietà") against harsh Necessity ("dura necessità"). Both choices, in this case, are laudable, but one must take precedence. Rinaldo departs, yet as Fortuna's boat flies across the sea, he follows the precedent of Aeneas and Bello's Rinaldo by looking back at what he has left behind: "Vola per l'alto mar l'aurata vela: / ei guarda il lido, e 'l lido ecco si cela" ("the golden sail flies over the open sea: he looks to the shore, and lo, the shore is hidden," 16.62). For the liberators who had to pass through a series of allegorical monsters, Armida's garden was just another enchanted trap like Falerina's garden or the Fonte del Riso.[19] For Rinaldo, on the other hand, Armida herself was a woman rather than a witch. These two alternate perspectives, moral allegory and literal realism, create a rift at the core of this episode. But on which side is Tasso?

Returning to the passage on Armida and Ismeno in the "Allegoria," it may be that what Tasso leaves unsaid is more revealing than what he actually tells us. He explains the allegorical significance of Ismeno's enchanted forest in all its details. Yet, at the point in which, to complete the parallel discourse, Tasso should turn to the allegory of Armida's garden, he instead passes the task of interpretation on to the reader. If we follow Tasso's own indications in the "Allegoria," then Rinaldo's departure from Armida's garden should represent, literally, a victory of Christian piety over the forces of the devil and, allegorically, of reason over the appetites. Indeed, the pressure from both the episode's allegorical features and its classical and Renaissance precedents is so strong that some critics treat Rinaldo's separation from Armida as permanent.[20] But this is not the way the story goes.

19. In fact, the liberators encounter a series of elements that were earlier used in the *Innamorato*'s enchanted sites, even the name of the "fonte del riso."

20. Moretti writes that Rinaldo's "odyssey" ends with his return to Jerusalem in canto 17 (28). Brand speaks of a "final scene of shame and return to duty" in both the *Rinaldo* and the *Gerusalemme* (68). Residori writes that "l'uscita dal mondo romanzesco grazie alla guida del Mago" signals "il punto finale della 'peripezia' di un personaggio, Rinaldo" (470).

As canto 17 opens, Armida flies by chariot to the pagan camp while Rinaldo arrives at a nebulous site where he finds a suit of armor and a sword awaiting him. The Mago d'Ascalona is there in the guise of a custodian ("quasi custode"). Following a preparatory speech, the *mago* shows Rinaldo a shield which contains the images of his forefathers. His lineage is described as the "fertil d'eroi madre e felice" ("fecund and fortunate mother of heroes," 17.86) that will never tire of giving birth ("non è né fia di partorir mai stanca," 17.86). After this metaphor in which the lineage itself acts as a mother figure, the *mago* says he regrets not being able to tell Rinaldo about his descendants ("così potessi ancor scoprire a pieno / ne' secoli avenire i tuoi nepoti," 17.87). He claims that the reason he cannot do so is the limit of his vision ("Ma l'arte mia per sé dentro al futuro / non scorge il ver che troppo occulto giace," 17.88). This implies that his vision gets murkier as it gets farther from the present. Yet, although the *mago* does not even identify either Rinaldo's consort or children, he seems to have no qualms about jumping ahead several centuries to tell of Rinaldo's descendant Alfonso II d'Este, the poem's dedicatee.[21]

The Estense genealogy stirs Rinaldo's military instincts, and the shield succeeds in awakening his desire to emulate the valor ("virtù") of his ancestors. His reaction is pure martial instinct:

> Questa è la serie de gli eroi che viva
> nel metallo spirante par si mova.
> Rinaldo sveglia, in rimirando, mille
> spirti d'onor da le natie faville,
>
> e d'emula virtù l'animo altèro
> commosso avampa, ed è rapito in guisa
> che ciò che imaginando ha nel pensiero,
> città abbattuta e presa e gente uccisa,
> pur, come sia presente e come vero,
> dinanti agli occhi suoi vedere avisa.   (17.81–82)

21. Migiel points out that in this genealogy, "Tasso does not appear hesitant to proclaim a story of fathers and sons" (151). This is not, in my view, because women do not matter, but rather because the identity of one particular woman matters far too much.

(This is the procession of heroes that seems as if it moves alive in the breathing metal. Rinaldo in gazing awakens a thousand impulses of honor from his inborn sparks: and his proud spirit being moved with emulative virtue takes fire and is rapt away in such manner that that which he has in his mind through imagining [the city laid low, and taken, and its people killed] he thinks he sees before his eyes even as if it were present and as if it were true.)

He arms quickly, thinking that he is heading for victory ("s'arma frettoloso, e con la spene / già la vittoria usurpa e la previene," 17.82), yet the enemy remains unspecified. Indeed, the hurriedness with which he arms himself ("s'arma frettoloso") recalls the way in which Ariosto's Ruggiero disarmed when intending to rape Angelica: "Frettoloso . . . l'arme si levava" (10.115), highlighting the instinctual (as opposed to rational) motivation of his actions. At this point Carlo takes advantage of Rinaldo's martial instinct by handing him Sveno's sword and calling for revenge on Solimano (17.83).

Critics have generally taken the *mago*'s speech at face value. In comparing the *Rinaldo* to the *Gerusalemme liberata*, Sherberg writes: "In the first poem Rinaldo must undertake a romance challenge, to rescue Clarice from Mambrino, while in the *Liberata* he must rise to the challenge of epic destiny, freeing Jerusalem in order to win his rightful place in the Este line" (189–90). That is certainly the impression that the *mago* gives by posing as a guard ("quasi custode") of Rinaldo's arms and relating his genealogy. But it is all a hoax. Although the Christian forces do need Rinaldo in order to succeed in their mission, Rinaldo's dynastic succession has nothing at all to do with the liberation of Jerusalem. On the contrary, not only will his participation in the crusade delay his dynastic destiny, but his "liberators" are attempting to lead him away from his destined consort.

Tasso tells us that Rinaldo listened joyfully ("lietamente") to the *mago*'s genealogy, and "del pensier de la futura prole / un tacito piacer sentia nel petto" ("he felt a secret pleasure in his breast at the thought of his future progeny," 17.95). But can Rinaldo know at this point that his future wife is Armida?

Tasso has already given us an indication of the future in canto 16 when Rinaldo makes the following promise to Armida just prior to his departure:

> Fra le care memorie ed onorate
> mi sarai ne le gioie e ne gli affanni,
> Sarò tuo cavalier, quanto concede
> La guerra d'Asia e con l'onor la fede.   (16.54)

(In joy and in sorrow you will be among my dear and cherished memories; I shall be your knight, as far as the war with Asia permits, and fealty with honor.)

Thus, at the very moment in which he leaves Armida to return to the crusade, Rinaldo reasserts his adherence to the tenets of knight errancy by designating himself as her "cavaliere." Indeed, all his re-Christianization under the guidance of Peter the Hermit will not interfere with his promise to Armida.[22] After the liberation of Jerusalem, Rinaldo, newly elected leader of the knights errant, recalls "che si promise in fede / suo cavalier quando da lei partia" ("that he faithfully pledged himself her knight when he parted from her," 20.122). As he follows her fleeing figure, Armida arrives in a "chiusa opaca chiostra" ("dark and sheltered spot," 20.122) that, as Chiappelli has pointed out, recalls the representation of a garden (186).[23] In this site, however, there are no allegorical monsters and no magical artifice. Armida sees Rinaldo just as she is about to commit suicide and, turning away from his "amato viso"

---

22. When in Ismeno's forest Rinaldo disregards the voice of Armida and cuts the tree, critics are quick to attribute his success to his renunciation of Armida and her garden of love. Tasso, however, specifies that Rinaldo is "accorto sí, non crudo" ("not cruel, but fully aware," 18.33). In other words, it is because Rinaldo recognizes that he stands before an illusion and not the actual woman that he can move against it.

23. Chiappelli notes several verbal echoes of earlier love scenes in the reunion of canto 20 (16.50 and 20.123; 16.18 and 20.130; 14.67.5–8 and 20.136.3–6; 14.59.8, 14.76.6, 16.10.5–6 and 20.136; 14.66.1–8, 16.25.1 and 20.121.5–8), 186–87. For eroticism in the *Gerusalemme*, see also Jonard.

("beloved face"), she faints. Whereas earlier, Armida "cadde tramortita" ("fell in a faint," 16.60), here Tasso describes her like a languishing flower: "Ella cadea, quasi fior mezzo inciso, / piegando il lento collo" ("She fell, like a flower half cut, letting her neck bend limply," 20.128). And whereas earlier Rinaldo stood and debated what to do before finally leaving her lying on the sand, now, even before the verse is completed, Rinaldo has already caught her in his arms. Tasso highlights the sheer physicality of this moment:

> Ella cadea, quasi fior mezzo inciso,
> piegando il lento collo; ei la sostenne,
> le fe' d'un braccio al bel fianco colonna
> e' intanto al sen le rallentò la gonna,
>
> e 'l bel volto e 'l bel seno a la meschina
> bagnò d'alcuna lagrima pietosa.   (20.128–29)

(She fell, like a flower half cut, letting her neck bend limply; he held her up; he made of one arm a prop for her lovely side, and meanwhile loosened her gown about her bosom. And he bathed with a pitying tear the poor girl's lovely bosom and her lovely face.)

While in the earlier scene Rinaldo's tears were not observed by the unconscious Armida, here it is precisely his tears on her beautiful face *and* beautiful breast that bring Armida back to consciousness.

Moreover, this scene reverses the opening encounter of the two, in which Armida was face to face with the sleeping figure of Rinaldo: now Rinaldo lovingly beholds the unconscious figure of Armida as he holds her in his arms. It is now Rinaldo's strong arm rather than Armida's magic sash that acts as a belt:

> E con man languidetta il *forte braccio*,
> ch'era sostegno suo, schiva respinse;
> tentò più volte e non uscì d'impaccio,
> ché *via più stretta ei rilegolla e cinse*.
> Al fin raccolta entro quel *caro laccio*,
> che le fu caro forse e se n'infinse.   (20.130)

(And with languid hand she pushed away in scorn the brawny arm that was her prop. She tried many times and could not escape from his embrace, for far more straitly he encircled and bound her again. At last, [she] settled within that welcome embrace [for it was welcome perhaps, and she was pretending about it].)

Echoing Tasso's earlier authorial intervention telling Armida to look into Rinaldo's eyes, Rinaldo now tells Armida himself: "Mira ne gli occhi miei, s'al dir non vuoi / fede prestar, de la mia fede il zelo" ("Behold in my eyes the sincerity of my faith, if you do not wish to trust my words," 20.135). The zeal (*zelo*) of Rinaldo's faith (*fede*) refers obviously to the ardor of his love for Armida. He is borrowing religious language to express the depth of his passionate love.

While Rinaldo's desire for Armida is alluded to in somewhat oblique fashion, Armida's desire is stated simply and directly: "Così l'ira che 'n lei parea sì salda, / Solvesi, e restan sol gli altri desiri" ("So is dissolved the wrath that seemed in her so firm, and only her other passions are left behind," 20.136). Although Tasso has stripped Armida of her diabolical and allegorical connotations (i.e., as minister of the devil and as a temptation to the sensitive appetite), he does not strip her of her sexuality.

It is the phrase that immediately follows this reference to Armida's desires that has attracted the most critical attention: "Ecco l'ancilla tua" ("Behold your handmaid"). Because the phrase echoes the words of the Virgin Mary in Luke 1:38, critics have spoken of a sudden transformation of Armida into a Marian figure.[24] The verse is indeed crucial, since Rinaldo's proposal of marriage to Armida is conditional upon her conversion to Christianity, yet, coming as it does on the heels of Tasso's

24. Johnson-Haddad sees a linear progression in Armida "from whore to Virgin Mary" (214). Del Giudice states: "The reader, although accustomed to Armida's changeability, is nonetheless shocked by this discordant statement and by Armida's final transformation to a Marian *ancilla* and suspects that this phase too is a *fictio*" (48). Likewise, Walter Stephens: "As a character, Armida is inconsistent: her sudden conversion cannot be explained in psychological or mimetic terms" (175). Tillyard calls this a "surprising and scantily motivated reversal" (408). Getto seems to think that this final scene is a failed seduction attempt, referring to it as a final attempt at seduction on the part of Armida (203).

affirmation of her desires, it hardly turns her into a religious figure.[25] Armida does not repeat the words of the Virgin Mary ("Ecce ancilla Domine"); she pledges herself to the man she loves ("Ecco l'ancilla tua"). Armida's submission, moreover, does not come *ex nihilo*. She had already declared to Rinaldo in canto 16 that she was prepared to be his "sprezzata" ("despised") *ancilla* (16.48 and 49), his servant ("serva," 16.49), and his "scudiero o scudo" ("shield bearer or shield," 16.50) if he would only allow her to follow him.

Critics have treated this phrase as a direct quotation from the Bible, whereas Tasso had already found the same expression used in the *Italia liberata* without any overt religious connotations. In the earlier epic, Elpidia offered herself in marriage to the knight of the Captain's choosing: "E prenderò colui per mio consorte, / Che mi sia dato da la vostra altezza" ("I will take as my consort whoever is given to me by your excellency," 58). The exact words that she uses to signal her obedience to Captain Belisardo are: "Signor mio caro, *ecco la vostra ancella*, / Parata a far di sè quel, ch'a voi piace" ("My dear lord, behold your handmaid, prepared to do that which pleases you," 59).

While Elpidia gave Captain Belisardo the power to choose a husband for her, Armida, using the intimate *tu* form, signals to Rinaldo the power she confers upon him as the husband she has chosen herself: " 'Ecco l'ancilla tua; d'essa a tuo senno / dispon," gli disse "e le fia legge il cenno" ("Behold your handmaid; dispose of her at your discretion," she said, "and your command shall be her law," 20.136). As Stephens notes, "Armida's words allusively declare her the 'body' of Rinaldo, in covert response to his overt proposal of matrimony" (194).

To concentrate exclusively on the submissiveness of Armida, however, is to miss the power of the scene in which each lover submits to the other. Rinaldo had at that moment just declared himself the champion and servant of Armida: "non a gli scherni, al regno io ti riservo; / nemico no, ma tuo *campione e servo*" ("I am not preserving you for mockeries, for

---

25. When Rinaldo had left Armida in canto 16, he specified two impediments: the war and religion. Now that the war is over, the only thing keeping them apart is the difference of religion.

my rule—no enemy I, but *your champion and your servant*," 20.134; italics mine). If for the female the phrasing stems ultimately from a sacred source, for the male the lexicon comes from the courtly chivalric sphere. Both lovers, using different code words, are making the same pledge of themselves to their beloved.

Armida's acceptance of Rinaldo's religion is not meant to fit the mold of a Pauline- or even Clorinda-style conversion.[26] It is, rather, an example of the conversion for love common in the chivalric epic. In the *Aspramonte*, the Saracen knight Galaciella converts to Christianity for love of Rugiero II and marries him. This couple takes on added significance when Boiardo designates them the parents of Rugiero III, whom he hails as the progenitor of the Estense family. Their history is intended to be replayed when Rugiero, raised as a Saracen, will convert to Christianity for love of Bradamante. Although the poem was interrupted shortly after the narration of their enamorment in OI 3.5, Niccolò degli Agostini's fourth book of the *Orlando innamorato* (1506) quickly brings the destined events to completion. The lovers find themselves alone in the woods, where Bradamante will agree to consummate their desire only after Rugiero has converted, received baptism, and exchanged marriage vows with her:

> prima vo che rineghi Macometto
> e poi me sposarai con la tua mano
> così di me potrai prender diletto
> anzi che si partiam di questo prato.   (4.7.19)

(First I want you to renounce Mohammad, and then you will give me your hand in marriage; in this way you can take your pleasure with me before we leave this meadow.)

The baptism of Rugiero by the hand of Bradamante gives Agostini leave to describe an extended amorous encounter beginning in the very next stanza:

---

26. Regarding the other two female protagonists, Clorinda converts for religious reasons, and Erminia, we are led to believe, will convert out of love for Tancredi.

Poi posersi a seder sul verde prato
sol per venir a l'ultimo diletto
che suol far ogni amante al fin beato
senza haver un de l'altro alcun rispetto
fronte con fronte il fiato con fiato
volto con volto & poi petto con petto
l'ardentissime fiamme in modo estingue
ch'in bocca ognun de lor havea due lingue.   (4.7.35)[27]

(Then they sat down on the green meadow to arrive at that high-
est pleasure that makes every lover blessed, without any inhibitions
toward each other, forehead to forehead, breath to breath, face to
face, and then chest to chest, they quenched the burning flames of
desire with two tongues in each mouth.)

In the *Furioso*, Ruggiero plans to follow this same pattern of conversion
for love when he and Bradamante head to Vallombrosa where he intends
to be baptized (canto 22). But Ariosto diverts the action, and goes on to
adopt the other model of conversion.[28] Tasso simply returns to the tra-
ditional pattern of conversion for love in his story of the Estense origins.

By the time that Armida speaks her famous "ancilla tua" line in canto
20, the more important conversion has already taken place—it is not a
religious conversion from paganism to Christianity, but a secular conver-
sion from seductress to *innamorata*. There are, in fact, two conversions,
first from enemy to lover ("di nemica ella divenne amante," 14.67) when
she sees him, and then from master to servant when she is about to
lose him.

While the magical garden of Armida and the enchanted forest of Is-
meno were considered negative opposites of the city of Jerusalem, this

27. Ariosto's sterner moral stance can also be glimpsed by the context in which he uses the
same topos of two tongues in each mouth. While Boiardo had used the phrase to describe
the lovemaking of Fiordelisa and Brandimarte, Ariosto reserves it for the illicit love between
Alcina and Ruggiero.

28. Ariosto turns the conversion into a personal experience by delaying it until Ruggiero is
alone at sea and facing death.

new natural setting of canto 20 is not unlike the pastoral setting that Erminia discovered as she fled earlier in the poem from the scene of battle. Although the forest once again provides an image of Arcadia, it is not, however, characterized by its frugality and simplicity of needs, as in the case of Erminia's shepherds. Rather, the natural setting in which Rinaldo and Armida declare their love for each other is closer to Floriana's garden and to the golden age of sexuality described in the *Aminta*.[29] Tasso, in effect, not only refuses to distinguish between a good and bad love, but he ultimately collapses the differences between the golden age's earthly paradise and the false gardens of sensuous delight characteristic of the Renaissance epic.[30]

When in canto 16 one of the sirens had invited Rinaldo's liberators to a life of leisure, she explicitly linked Armida's garden paradise to the golden age:

> Questo è il porto del mondo, e qui è il ristoro
> de le sue noie, e quel piacer si sente
> che già sentì ne' *secoli de l'oro*
> l'antica e senza fren libera gente.   (15.63)

(This is the haven of the world; and here is surcease from your troubles, and that pleasure known that once was known in the golden age by the ancient race of men, free and unbridled.)

Although one of the knights had referred to the girls as "false Sirene," her statement is actually true. The knights had already been told that Armida has taken Rinaldo to the Fortunate Islands. This correspondence between a golden age in the distant past and the geographical location of westward-lying islands comes down from the classical tradition.

---

29. By way of contrast one could think of Poliziano's *Stanze*, in which Iulio thinks that the golden age ended when "Lussuriosa entrò n'e petti e quel furore / Che la meschina gente chiama amore" (1.21).

30. In the *Romance of the Rose*, Genius also describes an age where men did whatever they pleased, there was eternal springtime, and love was free and unembarrassed. This is discussed in Levin 37.

Levin has pointed out that these faraway islands also served the function of the Elysian fields, providing an apt place for the heroes of antiquity to enjoy their afterlife.[31] Tasso had already used this latter idea in *Il Rinaldo* when he has Medea carry Floriana in her chariot to these Blessed Islands. Tasso, moreover, spells out in advance what the siren tells the knights when he describes the *isole Felici* toward which Lady Fortune is guiding Carlo and Ubaldo as both the site of the golden age and the resting place of heroes:

> ed eran queste l'isole Felici,
> così le nominò la prisca etate,
> a cui tanto stimava i cieli amici
> che credea volontarie e non arate
> quivi produr le terre, e 'n più graditi
> frutti non culte germogliar le viti.
>
> . . . .
> e qui gli elisi campi e le famose
> stanze de le beate anime pose. (15.35–36)

(And these were the Fortunate Isles: so the early ages named them, that thought the heavens so favoring to them that they believed the earth brought forth her goods there voluntarily and untilled, and the vines untended burst forth with the finest fruits . . . and here they placed the Elysian fields and the famous Mansions of the Blest.)

Whereas earlier poets had commonly said how enchanted gardens *resembled* a terrestrial paradise (e.g., Carandina's garden), Tasso actually put his lovers there.

It may not be a coincidence that at about the time Tasso was writing this portion of the *Gerusalemme*, he was also at work on the *Aminta*. When

31. Levin writes: "Horace had suggested an escape from history to geography, when he proposed that the faithful should leave strife-torn Rome and seek the Islands of the Blest. There, according to Hesiodic tradition, the golden age continued to exist" (58).

the *Aminta* was first performed, the Estense's own version of the garden-paradise at Belvedere provided the backdrop for both the actors and the public. At the end of the first act, the chorus explains the characteristics of the golden age in a way that, according to Levin, codified "the example of hedonistic behavior presumably set by the first generation of men into a single precept, a golden law (46).

Yet whereas Levin goes on to doubt the seriousness of the *Aminta*'s hedonism based on the morality of the *Gerusalemme*, I would instead question the seriousness of the moralizing in the later poem based on the hedonism of the *Aminta*.

By redeeming sexuality in the reunion scene of Rinaldo and Armida, Tasso goes against the tendency of Cinquecento writers to equate sexuality with the illicit. In fact, Tasso elsewhere attacks the *Furioso* on this very point. In the "Apologia in difesa della *Gerusalemme liberata*," he complains that Ariosto's Ruggiero does not try to earn Bradamante's love, "ma quasi pare che la disprezzi e ne faccia poca stima: il che non sarebbe peraventura tanto sconvenevole, se il poeta non fingesse che da questo amore e da questo matrimonio dovessero derivare i principi d'Este" ("but seems almost to disdain her and hold her in little regard, which in itself would not be that unseemly were it not for the fact that the poet imagines that the Este dynasty arises from this love and this marriage," 421). On the other hand, sexual desire characterizes Ruggiero's reaction to Alcina and Angelica: "Né solo facilmente si piega a' piaceri d'Alcina, e arde, e s'accende, come s'avesse nelle vene acceso il solfo; nella qual cosa poteva forse aver parte l'incanto, benché egli nol dica espressamente; ma delibera di godersi d'Angelica ignuda." ("Not only does he give in to the pleasures of Alcina, and burn, and become enflamed, as though he had sulpher in his veins, which could perhaps in part be attributed to the spell, although he does not say it directly, but he intends to take his pleasure with the naked Angelica" 421).

Tasso counters Ariosto by creating a female character who is not only as seductive and enchanting as Angelica, Dragontina, Morgana, and Alcina, but who is also destined for the dynastic role of Bradamante. And by turning the episode of the hero's passionate interlude into the beginning of a dynastic union, Tasso also rejects a polarized view of the woman as either evil seductress or chaste virgin.[32] A. Bartlett Giamatti wrote about the centrality of the woman to the epic: "The epic is often concerned with exile and the way back, and woman is always at the center. She is often both the goal and the obstacle. She is the Penelope who waits and the Circe who delays. Sometimes she is both the reason we wander and the object we seek, because only where she is are we at home" (Exile 4).

Tasso, however, as far as I know, is the only epic poet to merge woman as obstacle and woman as goal into the very same person.[33] In so doing, he creates a character who not only departs from literary precedent, but who also defies Tasso's own allegorical interpretation of her in the "Allegoria."

Indeed, whereas allegory was traditionally the means to arrive at the core of the text's meanings, Tasso has turned allegory into a wrapper which conveniently covers his story. In fact, Tasso said in a 1576 letter to Scipione Gonzaga that the allegorical aspects of his poem only came to mind in the course of writing.

Io, per confessare a Vostra Signoria illustrissima ingenuamente il vero, quando cominciai il mio poema non ebbi pensiero alcuno d'allegoria, parendomi soverchia e vana fatica. . . . Ma poi ch'io fui

---

32. Tasso refuses to judge Armida. Not so the poem's critics. Even Del Giudice, who notes the polymorphism of Armida, concludes that she thereby "embodies the Tassian concept of the chaos and void of Hell" (29).

33. Yarnall's comment regarding Spenser's Faerie Queene could be applied to the epic at large: "[T]he bad women are sexual and the good women are pure" (132). Tasso was obviously well aware of the controversial nature of such a radical rewriting. In a letter to Luca Scalabrino, he attempts to divert Sperone Speroni away from a reading of cantos 16 to 20: . . . Io non vo' padrone se non colui che mi dà il pane, nè maestro; e voglio esser libero non solo ne' giudicii, ma anco ne lo scrivere e ne l'operare . . . Perchè non gli mostraste i miei sonetti, avendovene io pregato? . . . e sovra tutto pregatelo che pensi a i dubbi che ho mossi intorno a la partita d'Erminia," ("I do not want masters, unless they feed me, nor teachers; and I want to be free not only in my judgments but also in my writing and my doing. . . . Why didn't you show him my sonnets, as I asked you to do? . . . And above, all, remind him to think about the doubts that I have expressed about Ermiria's departure.") Rome, May 4, 1576 (Epistolario 32–33).

oltre al mezzo del mio poema, e che cominciai a sospettar de la strettezza de' tempi, cominciai anco a pensare a l'allegoria, come a cosa ch'io giudicava dovermi assai agevolar ogni difficultà. (*Epistolario* 38)[34]

(To ingenuously confess the truth to your Lordship, when I began my poem, I had not given allegory any thought, considering it to be an unneccessary and useless chore. . . . But then when I got beyond the middle of my poem, and I began to suspect the narrow-mindedness of the times, I began to think about allegory as something that could go a long way in smoothing out every difficulty.)

In a June 1576 letter to Luca Scalabrino, Tasso admits to having constructed a shield to protect his story of love and enchantment: "Mostrerò ch'io non ho avuto altro fine che di servire al politico; e con questo scudo cercherò d'assicurare ben bene gli amori e gl'incanti" (I will show that my only purpose was political; and with this shield I will try to assure a good supply of love and magic). In this view, the literal sense does not serve to illustrate the allegory; rather, it is the allegory which, like a shield, serves to protect the literal sense. Tasso leads his readers along, giving the impression that his elaborately rich narrative is the surface under which one will find a moralistic kernel. Yet as the story reaches its conclusion, Tasso lays down the shield of allegory and the literal sense comes to the fore in all its humanity.[35]

When Chiappelli says that the reunion of Rinaldo and Armida in canto 20 is just a simple love story ("solo una storia d'amore"), he is absolutely right. But while Chiappelli finds that this love story has no connection to the rest of the poem, I would like to argue on the contrary that it radically affects the poem as a whole, not only on a thematic and allegorical

---

34. He continues that he found it, but not as distinctly and so precisely throughout and that his Lordship will have a chance to see it for himself.

35. Clearly, then, I disagree with critics who treat Tasso's poem as a straightforward allegory, such as Brand, who says that Tasso "is careful to stress the allegorical significance of the incident, and to try to improve morally on his models" (105).

level but on a structural level as well. Rather than offer a world of moral hierarchies, Tasso returns to the idea of temporal succession that he first presented in the *Rinaldo*. At the moment in which the finite goal of liberating Jersualem is accomplished, the role of Armida changes. Armida may have been an obstacle and a digression with respect to Goffredo's liberation of Jerusalem, but when the war is over she becomes the goal and end point for Rinaldo.

No wonder Tasso was so nervous about the reaction to his poem.[36] But he need not have been so worried. Critics, equating Armida's garden and Ismeno's wood with romance, have generally agreed that with the destruction of Armida's garden and Ismeno's wood, romance digression gives way to epic closure. Fichter writes: "Just as Rinaldo must first be truant to his cause before he can be redeemed, so the poem must first represent itself as romance before its epic structure can be discerned" (115).[37] Those who have noted Rinaldo's return to Armida have seen the final episode as ambiguous or confusing, but have not recognized it as subversive of the poem's ostensible morality.[38] In fact, not until Zatti's study of the tensions between unity and diversity in the poem has anyone noted the extent to which Tasso identified with the enemies of Goffredo and the "truant" elements that he supposedly intended to stamp

---

36. One way to see what Tasso regarded as potentially transgressive would be to check the *Liberata* against the *Conquistata* for deletions and modifications. See Olini.

37. Residori sees Tasso's use of the *mago* as part of this program of giving a place to romance only to reaffirm epic morality: "di concedere il massimo credito alle ragioni del romanzo per dare più rilievo all'affermazione della moralità epica" (471).

38. Of the critics who have acknowledged this "happy ending," some have considered it "ambiguous," "inconsistent," "unconvincing," or "unpoetic," while others have statedly refused to speculate as to its meaning. The few critics who have given serious consideration to the reunion of Rinaldo and Armida have focused on a single perspective. While Chiappelli points out the continued sensual, erotic nature of Armida and Rinaldo's final scene, dismissing it as a mere love story with no relation to the main plot (185), Stephens, on the other hand, demonstrates Tasso's emphasis on the marriage of the couple, considering Armida's conversion as part of "a discourse that betrays both a nostalgic idealization of marriage and deep anxieties about the human body" (193). Each seems to treat sensuality and marriage as irreconcilable in Tasso.

out (*L'uniforme cristiano*).[39] Zatti makes an analogy between Tasso's efforts to exorcise romance from his poem and Goffredo's efforts to exorcise the demons of diversity ("Tasso contro Ariosto").[40] I would take this a step further and say that Tasso does not have any intention of renouncing the elements of romance from his poem, and he purposefully retains them at the end. In his theoretical writings, Tasso did not see himself as an enemy of romance per se. On the contrary, he maintained that the elements of romance—more precisely, *gli incanti e gli amori* (magic and love)—were essential to a successful epic.[41] In another letter from 1576, this one written to Luca Scalabrino, Tasso states emphatically that love constitutes "heroic" material:

> Io voglio difender contra tutto il mondo, chè l'amore è materia altrettanto eroica quanto la guerra; e 'l difenderò con ragione, con autorità d'Aristotele, con luoghi di Platone che parlano chiaro chiaro chiaro, chiarissimamente chiaro." (*Epistolario 29*)

(I want to maintain, against the entire world, that love is just as heroic a subject as war, and I will defend it with reason, with the authority of Aristotle, and with passages in Plato that speak clearly, clearly, clearly, extremely clearly.)

Likewise, he writes to Scipione Gonzaga: "Quanto a gli amori e a gli incanti, quanto più vi penso, tanto più mi confermo che siano materia per

39. Zatti's revisionist view of Tasso comes in the wake of critical reassessments of Virgil's *Aeneid*. Whereas centuries of interpretation and commentary (especially strong in medieval and Renaissance Italy) had considered the *Aeneid* as an account of the moral education of the hero, since the 1960s critics have pointed out Virgil's ambiguous relation to his hero and his deep sympathies toward the "enemy" figures of Dido and Turnus. See Commager.

40. Zatti writes: "La volontà di canto epico del Tasso si consolida come una faticosa conquista sulle struggenti nostalgie del libero mondo romanzesco. . . . Il codice romanzesco perde progressivamente di autonomia e di legittimità, fino a coincidere con quello spazio dell'errore dove Satana sconta la sua emarginazione necessaria, ma anche vive, orgogliosamente, la sua irriducibile alterità" (211). Quint also speaks of "the assimilation of romance into . . . epic structures of meaning," *Epic and Empire* 253.

41. Tasso puts romance and epic elements on equal footing not only by refusing to put them into separate genres, but by foretelling that at some point Rinaldo's (and consequently Armida's) progeny will combine with Goffredo's line.

sè convenevolissima al poema eroico; parlo de gli amori nobili, non di quelli de la Fiammetta, nè di quelli che hanno alquanto del tragico" ("As for love and magic, the more I think about it, the more I am sure that they are extremely appropriate material for a heroic poem; I speak of noble loves, not those of Fiammetta, or those that have something tragic about them," *Epistolario* 35).

The fact that Tasso refused to consider romance and epic as two separate genres was not, as some critics have maintained, a way of effacing romance, but rather a way of conserving romance as part and parcel of the heroic poem he was writing. What he objected to in romance was not its central elements of love and magic, but rather the technique of interlacing that overtaxed the reader's memory and the poet's intervention in poems and elsewhere which upset the sense of verisimilitude created by a consistent third-person narrator ("Discorsi sul poema eroico," 373).

Thus, while romance was traditionally treated as a parenthesis within the epic structure, the ending of Tasso's poem gives us an opportunity to view the relation in reverse: the epic struggle to free Jerusalem was a long but nevertheless temporary effort at whose completion the knights are free to transform back into their "natural" state. Just as Goffredo is freed from his promise to God, Rinaldo is freed from his duty to Goffredo. While Goffredo "il gran Sepolcro adora e scioglie il voto" ("adores the great Sepulcher, and discharges his vow," 20.144), Rinaldo is in the woods making a new vow to Armida.[42] With the epic closure, romance is allowed to extend into an indefinite and happy future.

With regard to the *Rinaldo*, Sherberg points out that "by not writing an ending to the knight's exile [Tasso] never reintegrates him into the Christian fold" (192). Sherberg goes on to see the reconcilation of Rinaldo and Goffredo in the *Gerusalemme liberata* as a way of making "amends for the errors" of his earlier poem: "In this way Tasso paints a new portrait of himself as poet, apologizing for representing Rinaldo the rebel, for adding to an autonomous cycle that historically had sanctioned contempt for authority and invited its audience to participate in

---

42. That Goffredo enters the temple still covered with blood is problematic in its own right. See Benedetti 472–76.

that scorn" (192).[43] I would argue instead that the *Gerusalemme liberata* does not aim to reverse the *Rinaldo's* antiauthoritarianism, but that it does a better job in concealing it.[44] Moreover, the *Gerusalemme liberata* goes even farther than the *Rinaldo*: while Tasso ended the earlier poem with the hero's sanctioned marriage to a French Christian maiden, Tasso has his new Rinaldo marry the enchantress from Damascus who had been the single greatest threat to the Christian cause.

If from the perspective of canto 16, Armida may have seemed to be a temporary obstacle to the epic fulfillment of the *Gerusalemme liberata*, from the endpoint, that is, just eight octaves away from the conclusion of canto 20, it is rather the crusade that, for the hero Rinaldo, has provided a parenthesis in his career.[45] He divests himself of the role of holy crusader to return to the role of a knight errant now, however, with the mission of founding a dynasty. And unlike Aeneas, who will marry the rather bland Lavinia and die after three years of rule (or Ruggiero, whose early death was foretold prior to his first appearance in the *Orlando innamorato*),[46] Rinaldo's future with Armida is projected indefinitely into a

43. He continues: "In the new light of his age Tasso appears to believe two things: first, that romance, while formally indistinguishable from epic, is ethically inferior, and second, that by participating in romance he had endangered his reputation as a poet and his society in general." Regarding the account of Rinaldo's return to the *avventurieri* and Armida, Sherberg then cautiously concedes that "Tasso appears to signal that repressed romance will resurface yet again, and he appears to sanction its reappearance as well" (193).

44. For personal and political events that could have led Tasso to harbor antipapal and antiimperial sentiments—and, at the same time, to conceal those feelings—see Ferguson. Quint provides further information about Tasso's troubles with papal and imperial authority, although his argument takes a very different line ("Political Allegory").

45. One could make a similar case for the story of Erminia and Tancredi, who thanks to the epic closure are apparently united. See Murtaugh, who argues that Tasso treats love as a unifying and positive force in the case of Erminia and Tancredi, noting also that their encounter contains textual allusions to the *Aminta*. However, she completely disregards the reunion of Armida and Rinaldo, referring to the encounter between Erminia and Tancredi as the *last* encounter between love and arms in the poem, and concluding that Tasso thereby subsumes this "romance" episode into the epic structure of the poem.

46. Regarding Ruggiero's foretold death, Quint has noted that the four years of life that Ariosto allotted to him from the moment of his baptism in the *Furioso* of 1516 were expanded

"happily ever after" in which creating a dynasty will not be a burden to bear but rather a pleasure to enjoy.

Works Cited

Ariosto, Ludovico. *Orlando furioso*. Ed. Marcello Turchi. Milano: Garzanti, 1974.

Barberino, Andrea da. *Guerino detto il Meschino*. Venice: Baroni, 1689.

Bello, Francesco. *Il Mambriano*. Ed. Giuseppe Rua. Turin: UTET, 1926.

Benedetti, Laura. "La vis abdita della Liberata e i suoi esiti nella Conquistata." *Lingua e stile* 30 (1995): 465–77.

Boiardo, Matteo Maria. *Orlando innamorato*. Trans. Charles S. Ross. Berkeley: U of California P, 1989.

Brand, Peter. *Torquato Tasso: A Study of the Poet and His Contribution to English Literature*. Cambridge: Cambridge UP, 1965.

Cavallo, Jo Ann. *Boiardo's "Orlando Innamorato": An Ethics of Desire*, Rutherford, N.J.: Fairleigh Dickinson P, 1993.

Chiappelli, Fredi. *Il conoscitore del caos: una "vis abdita" nel linguaggio tassesco*. Rome: Bulzoni, 1981.

Commager, Steele, ed. *Virgil: A Collection of Critical Essays*. New York: Prentice-Hall, 1966.

Cossutta, Fabio. *Gli ideali epici dell'umanesimo e l'Orlando innamorato*. Rome: Bulzoni, 1995.

Del Giudice, Luisa. "Armida: Virgo Fingens (The Broken Mirror)." *Western Gerusalem: University of California Studies on Tasso*. New York: Out of London P, 1984.

Fasani, Remo. "Il racconto di Armida: dalla finzione alla realtà." *Il Tasso e il mondo Estense*. Florence: Olschki, forthcoming.

Ferguson, Margaret W. *Trials of Desire: Renaissance Defenses of Poetry*. New Haven: Yale UP, 1983.

Fichter, Andrew. *Poets Historical: Dynastic Epic in the Renaissance*. New Haven: Yale UP, 1982.

Getto, Giovanni. "Il fascino di Armida." *Nel mondo della "Gerusalemme."* Florence: Vallecchi, 1968.

Giamatti, A. Bartlett. *The Earthly Paradise and the Renaissance Epic*. Princeton: Princeton UP, 1966.

———. *Exile and Change in Renaissance Literature*. New Haven: Yale UP, 1984.

Greene, Thomas M. *The Descent from Heaven: A Study in Epic Continuity*. New Haven: Yale UP, 1963.

Johnson-Haddad, Miranda. " 'Like the Moon It Renews Itself '": The Female Body as Text in Dante, Ariosto, and Tasso." *Stanford Italian Review* 11 (1992) 203–15.

---

to a total of seven years in the 1532 edition (Cinque canti, 23, note 19). Seven years are admittedly better than four, but they are nothing compared to the sense that Tasso gives us that Rinaldo has an open future with Armida.

Jonard, Norbert. "L'erotisme dans la *Jérusalem délivrée*." *Bergomum: Bollettino della Civica Biblioteca* 78.3–4 (1984): 43–62.

Kallendorf, Craig. *In Praise of Aeneas: Virgil and Epideictic Rhetoric in the Early Italian Renaissance.* Hanover, N.H.: UP of New England, 1989.

Levin, Harry. *The Myth of the Golden Age in the Renaissance.* Bloomington: Indiana UP, 1969.

Migiel, Marilyn. *Gender and Genealogy in Tasso's Gerusalemme Liberata.* Lewiston, Pa.: Edwin Mellen, 1993.

Moretti, Walter. "La diversità del Tasso nella Ferrara dell'Ariosto." *Esperienze letterarie* 17.2 (1992): 19–30.

Murtaugh, Kristen Olsen. "Erminia Delivered: Notes on Tasso and Romance." *Quaderni d'italianistica* 3.1 (1982): 12–25.

Olini, Lucia. "Dalla 'Gerusalemme terrena' alla 'Gerusalemme celeste': Rinaldo e Armida vs. Armida e Riccardo." *Bergomum: Bollettino della Civica Biblioteca* 80.3–4 (1985): 69–87.

Ovid, *Fasti.* Trans. Sir James George Frazer. Loeb Classical Library. London: Heinemann; New York: Putnam, 1931.

Poliziano, Angelo. *Stanze.* Ed. and trans. David Quint. Amherst: U of Massachusetts P, 1979.

Praloran, Marco. "*Maraviglioso artificio": tecniche narrative e rappresentative nell'Orlando innamorato.* Lucca: Pacini Fazzi, 1990.

Quint, David. *Epic and Empire: Politics and Generic Form from Virgil to Milton.* Princeton: Princeton UP, 1993.

——. "Political Allegory in the *Gerusalemme Liberata*." *Renaissance Quarterly* 43 (1990): 1–29.

——. Introduction. *Cinque Canti: Five Cantos.* Trans. A. Sheers and D. Quint. Berkeley: U of California P, 1996.

Residori, Matteo. "Il Mago d'Ascalona e gli spazi del romanzo nella *Liberata*." *Torquato Tasso e la sua fortuna.* Special issue of *Italianistica* 24.2–3 (1995): 453–71.

Sherberg, Michael. *Rinaldo: Character and Intertext in Ariosto and Tasso.* Stanford French and Italian Studies 75. Saratoga, Calif.: Anma Libri, 1993.

Stephens, Walter. "Saint Paul among the Amazons: Gender and Authority in *Gerusalemme liberata*." *Discourses of Authority in Medieval and Renaissance Literature.* Ed. K. Brownlee and W. Stephens. Hanover, N.H.: UP of New England, 1989. 169–200.

Tasso, Bernardo. *L'Amadigi.* Ed. Lodovico Dolce. Venice: Zoppini, 1581.

Tasso, Torquato. "L'Allegoria." *Il Goffredo, overo Gierusalemme Liberata, poema heroico del Sig. Torquato Tasso con l'allegoria universale dell'istesso.* Venice: Fusconi, 1651. Trans. Lawrence F. Rhu. In *The Genesis of Tasso's Narrative Theory: English Translations of the Early Poetics and a Comparative Study of their Significance.* Detroit: Wayne State UP, 1993.

——. "Apologia in difesa della *Gerusalemme liberata*." *Prose.* Ed. Ettore Mazzali. Milano: Ricciardi, 1959.

——. "Discorsi sul poema eroico." *Prose.* Ed. Ettore Mazzali. Milano: Ricciardi, 1959.

——. *Epistolario.* 2 vols. Lanciano: Carabba, 1912.

——. *Gerusalemme liberata*. Ed. Anna Maria Carini. 2 vols. Milan: Feltrinelli, 1961.

——. *Rinaldo*. Ed. Michael Sherberg. Ravenna: Longo, 1990.

Tillyard, E. M. W. *The English Epic and Its Background*. New York: Oxford UP, 1954.

Trissino, Giovan Giorgio. *L'Italia liberata da' Goti. Tutte le opere*. Verona: Vallarsi, 1729.

Virgil. *The Aeneid of Virgil*. Trans. Allen Mandelbaum. 1971. Reprint, Berkeley: U of California P, 1981.

Yarnall, Judith. *Transformations of Circe: The History of an Enchantress*. Urbana: U of Illinois P, 1994.

Zatti, Sergio. "Tasso contro Ariosto." *Studi in onore di Bortolo Tommaso Sozzi*, ed. Aldo Agazzi. Bergamo: Centro Studi Tassiani, 1991. 203–16.

——. *L'uniforme cristiano e il multiforme pagano: saggio sulla Gerusalemme liberata*. Milan: Il Saggiatore, 1983.

II
THE POLITICS OF DISSIMULATION

Epic in the Age of Dissimulation:
Tasso's *Gerusalemme liberata*

SERGIO ZATTI

The themes I wish to consider here may be counted among those that best justify the *Gerusalemme liberata*'s placement among so-called mannerist texts. These themes absorb from mannerist literature the principle of a self-reflexive moment, wherein the semantic referent appears inscribed in the act of textual enunciation.[1] In other words, I wish to argue that the theme of dissimulation—the disguising of bodies, sentiments, or intentions—plays such a large role in the *Gerusalemme liberata* because Tasso's text is itself born from a discourse of dissimulation:

> O Musa, tu che di caduchi allori
> non circondi la fronte in Elicona,
> ma su nel cielo infra i beati cori
> hai di stelle immortali aurea corona,
> tu spira al petto mio celesti ardori,
> tu rischiara il mio canto, e tu perdona
> s'intesso fregi al ver, s'adorno in parte
> d'altri diletti, che de' tuoi, le carte.
>
> Sai che là corre il mondo over più versi
> di sue dolcezze il lusinghier Parnaso,
> e che'l vero, condito in molli versi,
> i più schivi allettando ha persuaso.
> Così a l'egro fanciul porgiamo aspersi
> di soavi licor gli orli del vaso:

---

1. On the subject, see Ulivi, Sozzi, and Scianatico. For a different interpretation, see Erspamer.

succhi amari ingannato intanto ei beve,
e da l'inganno suo vita riceve.²

The Lucretian ascendancy of these verses was almost too familiar to theoreticians of Counter-Reformation poetics who were torn between instruction and delight.³ Masked beneath the pleasure of writing, Tasso's work displays a didactic purpose: it dissimulates a deceit intended to bring health (and this is, let us note, not a simple question of dosing out poetic alchemies, as in the Horatian *miscere utile dulci*, but a vertical relationship of "above" and "below," of "outside" and "inside"). The simile of the drinking glass does nothing more than develop, on a different semantic register, intentions already declared in two complementary metaphors, that of the embroidery, which embellishes the discourse of historic and religious truth, and that of "other" delights that adorn the pages of this epic and Christian poem.

But in this forced compromise the awareness of a textual "error" inevitably accepted and undertaken is most acutely revealed, so much so that the muse, abandoning the canonical function of inspirer, must become the indulgent accomplice of a poet who requests pardon in advance for his deviance.⁴ To say what this error, and its dissimulation, consists of

2. "O Muse, that do not wreathe your brow on Helicon with fading bays, but among the blessed choirs in Heaven above possess a golden crown of deathless stars: breathe into my breast celestial ardors, illuminate my song, and grant me pardon if with the truth I interweave embroiderings, if partly with pleasures other than yours I ornament my pages. // You know that the world flocks there where feigning Parnassus most pours out her sweetnesses, and that the truth in fluent verses hidden has by its charms persuaded the most froward. So we present to the feverish child the rim of the glass sprinkled over with sweet liquids: he drinks deceived the bitter medicine and from his deception receives life" (*Liberata*, 1. 2–3). Hereafter references to cantos and octaves appear directly in the text. Translation by Nash.

3. The verses of *De Rerum Natura* 1.936–42 recur, among others, in Ammirato and Denores (reprinted in Weinberg). See also Speroni 736. Tasso may have been able to read a version in his father Bernardo's *Amadigi*: "Come talor un medico, che vuole / gabbar l'infermo per fargli salute, / celar l'amaro sotto il dolce suole, / acciocch'egli di ber non lo rifiute; / così sotto figmenti di parole, / di chimere da noi non conosciute, / danno i poeti molti documenti / al volgo ignaro, ed all'inferme menti" (51.1).

4. On criticism born of this protasis, see Guastavini, *Risposta*, 5.288–89. Guastavini de-

would require too long a discussion—which in any event I have already attempted elsewhere.[5] Such a discussion would turn precisely on the structure of compromise of which the whole poem is an expression, for it is balanced between Christian ideology—the straight path leading to the liberation of Jerusalem—and "pagan" temptations that render this path full of obstacles and labyrinthine; between the will to epic unity, which constitutes the narrative scheme declared by the poet, and the dispersive romance variety, which represents its deviant fascination. What kind of operation is Tasso performing at the opening of his tale? Does he celebrate pedagogic authoritarianism or, rather, use his verses as a convenient safe-conduct for the irrational? In a period anguished by dissimulation at court and in the political and religious realms, he tortures himself by casting his poetry as the legitimation of a deception. If every *fictio* presupposes a truth at the same time that it dissimulates it, the aim of the deception is what counts: will his poetry be Armida's dishonest simulation ("fa manto del ver alla menzogna") or Erminia's innocent fraud ("nasconde [amore] sotto il manto dell'odio")?

A possible answer may emerge if we contextualize the author's discourse within other components of Tasso's text that contribute to a broad and conspicuous thematics of concealment in the *Liberata*: these include false and tempting speeches (Alete's mellifuous embassy in canto 2 or Armida's deceitful tale in canto 4); repressed sentiments (Erminia's in canto 3) or masked intentions (Eustazio's in cantos 4 and 5); and the disguising of bodies (by Erminia, when she first puts on Clorinda's armor and then the shepherdess's clothes; by Clorinda herself, whose changed armor generates Tancredi's tragic misunderstanding). But I also propose to show how different phenomenologies of "dissimulation"[6] take on relevant formal and structural functions in the *Liberata*:

---

fended Tasso from the accusation of following the old, authoritative thesis of poetry as fiction and cover of truth.

5. See my book *L'uniforme cristiano*.

6. While establishing a conceptual distinction between simulation and dissimulation, I should also point out that their complementarity often becomes a substantial synonymic

1. The theme's linguistic cloak obeys the same dialectic of above/below, outside/inside belonging to the poem's rhetoric of compromise. In fact, the "textual" metaphor[7] materializes itself in the various disguisings of characters and orients the conceptual movement of the protasis, because friezes and ornaments correspond to the *cloak* and the *veil* beneath which each person's identity is dissimulated, since they contaminate the truth of writing;

2. The epic discourse that programmatically "dissimulates" (when it does not explicitly banish) the romance code, still makes use of the modern chivalric tradition of "marvelous" amplification of the *fabula*. Conceived under the sign of error or misunderstanding, betrayal or fiction, the idea of variety and of the multiple that the epic unity would still like to discipline comes up again at the text's surface and expands its structural plot: such is the case, for example, of the instances of "courtesy" opportunistically advanced by the Christian Eustazio, entrapped by Armida, against the superior mission of the crusade. These, as we shall see, tend to inscribe the chivalric code within a discourse of dissimulation.

II

Let us begin the investigation with an episode that is minor, but is located emphatically on the threshold of the narrative action. The embassy of Alete and Argante (2.57–end), sent by the king of Egypt to gauge

---

coincidence in the *usus scribendi* of many sixteenth-century authors. In this essay it will be inevitable sometimes to use this semantic contiguity. The most essential definition of difference that I know of is Accetto's canonical text, *Della dissimulazione onesta* (1641): "La dissimulazione è una industria di non far veder le cose come sono. Si simula quello che non è, si dissimula quello che è." In his critical edition of this text, Nigro demonstrates that such a conceptual distinction is also present in Tasso's "Malpiglio," although not rendered terminologically explicit (51, n. 1).

7. For the historical course, see Gorni. Although slighly unresponsive to the ambiguities and tensions in Tasso's writing, Gorni is right in stating that: "Il poeta è ancora tessitore, ma si contenta di ornare una tela non ordita da lui: l'arte sua antica gli è sottratta, e dalle sue mani escono solo 'fregi al ver' di cui egli si affretta a chiedere licenza" (29–30).

Goffredo's real war strategies, offers the poet the occasion to present a pair of "characters" matched according to opposite and complementary principles: one, Argante, is rude and threatening, but genuine; the other, Alete, is diplomatic and smooth-spoken.[8] Tasso's intent is specifically to have the barbarous nobility of one of the poem's future protagonists emerge from the contrast, but here I shall consider the other character.

Alete's moral and psychological characterization ("parlar fecondo e lusinghiero e scorto, / pieghevoli costumi e vario ingegno / al *finger* pronto, a l'*ingannare* accorto: / gran fabro di calunnie, *adorne* in modi / novi, che sono accuse, e paion lodi," 2.58)[9] is the premise of a discourse that hides a message of threatening content behind the flattery of Goffredo ("cominció poscia, e di sua bocca uscieno / più che mel dolci d'eloquenza i fiumi," 2.61).[10] In these two brief quotations reappear, underscored by my emphasis, precisely the two semantic fields inaugurated in the protasis by the textual metaphor ("s'adorno in parte") and the simile of the drinking glass ("i soavi licor"); moreover, Alete's "parlar lusinghiero" bears a disquieting relation to "lusinghier Parnaso."

Let us go forward and look now at a character considerably more important than the obscure Alete, and a liar par excellence, Armida. In canto 4, she arrives at the Christian camp to bring division and jealousy, and in this she plays the traditional role that ancient epics usually assigned to Discord, sent by enemy gods, just as here Armida is sent by Satan. In order to provoke pity and to seduce, the lady recounts her made-up story of persecution, presenting herself as the innocent victim of an uncle greedy for wealth and power. The event, which in its general

---

8. One can capture antiphrastically the character of the man already in the etymology of the word: "A-lete" means without hiding, without simulation. A suggestion for such a choice could have come to Tasso from a text such as Etica Nicomachea, a work very much in circulation in the sixteenth century, in which the term "philalethes" recurs in opposition to simulators of words and actions (1127 a–b).

9. Exalted "by a flowing and feigning and prudent speech, by compliant manners and a shifty nature, ready at pretense, experienced at deception. A great fabricator of slanders, he decks out in novel terms what appear to be praises and are accusations."

10. "[T]hen he began and rivers of eloquence sweeter than honey issued from his mouth."

scheme shows traces of analogous episodes from the romance tradition, refers therefore to that tradition as to a language of deceit.[11] Armida is the instrument of the powerful magus Idraote, who counts no less on her beauty as a woman than on her arts as a witch to draw away troops from the crusader army. In the speech in which he tells her her mission, a wholly Counter-Reformation *raison d'état* is invoked to justify politically the demonical mandate and at the same time to furnish an alibi for the introduction of the amorous element as disturbance of epic action. In my view, the interest in these octaves comes from the extraordinary complexity of their figural fabric:

> Dice: —O diletta mia, che *sotto biondi*
> *capelli e fra sì tenere sembianze*
> *canuto senno e cor virile ascondi,*
> e già ne l'arti mie me stesso avanze,
> gran pensier volgo; e se tu lui secondi,
> seguiteran gli effetti a le speranze.
> *Tessi la tela ch'io ti mostro ordita,*
> di cauto vecchio essecutrice ardita.

> Vanne al campo nemico: ivi s'impieghi
> ogn'arte feminil ch'amore alletti.
> Bagna di pianto e fa' melati i preghi,
> tronca e confondi co' sospiri i detti:
> beltà dolente e miserabil pieghi
> al tuo volere i più ostinati petti.
> *Vela* il soverchio ardir con la vergogna,
> e fa *manto* del vero a la menzogna.[12]

11. One of the most respected historical critics of Tasso's sources, Vincenzo Vivaldi, points to similar narratives in texts such as *Costante*, *Angelica innamorata*, *Palmerino d'Oliva*, and *Amadigi*. See *Sulle fonti*, 1.80. Vivaldi notes that research on chivalric antecedents, refused by Tasso less in intention than in practice, could be just as productive as the typical investigation of classical ties in heroic poems.

12. This simulated discourse contains, however, its own unmasking, since the weaver of deceits presents herself as victim of others' deceits. Alluding to her uncle's doubleness, Armida speaks of a "maligno . . . pensiero interno" hiding "sotto contrario manto" (4.45) and of deceits that he "adorna e tesse" to his own advantage (4.58).

Prendi, s'esser potrà, Goffredo a l'esca
de' dolci sguardi e de' be' detti adorni,
sì ch'a l'uomo invaghito omai rincresca
l'incominciata guerra, e la distorni.
Se ciò non puoi, gli altri più grandi adesca:
menagli in parte ond'alcun mai non torni. —
Poi distingue i consigli; al fin le dice:
—Per la fe', per la patria il tutto lice.— (4.24–26) [13]

The use of the Petrarchan formula of the lady who "sotto biondi capei
[nasconde] canuta mente" [14] functions here as a strategy of covering and
hiding. This is confirmed a while later by the double metaphor of the *velo*
and the *manto*, which are designated as the operative instruments of the
seductress. But the complementary figure of "weaving" is also present
to enrich an already familiar image, a woof to be inserted on a warp that
is already prepared, and which evokes, in turn, the Siren's song foretold
by the "melati preghi" and later crowned by the "pensati inganni" that
Armida "spiega / in suon che di dolcezza i sensi lega" (4.38). The com-
pactness of this rhetorical fabric is the same as that of poetic deceit, and
it insinuates the threat of a dangerous exchange of health and sickness:

Ahi crudo Amor, ch'egualmente n'ancide
l'assenzio e 'l mel che tu fra noi dispensi,

13. "He says: 'O my dear, who under golden hair and outward beauties so delicate keep con-
cealed a manly heart and gray-haired wisdom, and in my arts already outstrip myself, I am
revolving a great plan. And, if you lend it your aid, the results will answer to our hopes.
Weave the web that I show you all laid out, a bold-hearted agent for a cautious old man. //
Go to the enemy camp; there make use of every feminine art that entices to love. Bathe your
entreaties in tears and make them honied; cut off your words and mingle them with sighs.
A grieving and piteous beauty may work the most obdurate breasts to your will. Your over-
much boldness veil with maidenly modesty, and make of the truth a mantle for your lying.
// If it be possible, take Godfrey with the bait of your sweet glances and lovely fashioned
speech, so that the war stirred up may grow wearisome now to a man enamoured, and he
may carry it elsewhere. If that you cannot do, angle for the greatest of the others; lead them
off into a region whence none may ever return.' Then he details his plans; at last he says:
'For the Faith, for the Fatherland, all is permitted.' "

14. Petrarch, 213.3.

e d'ogni tempo egualmente mortali
vengon da te le medicine e i mali! (4.92)[15]

We can easily see that the long segment dedicated to the presence of Armida in the Christian camp (4.28–96; 5.60–85) represents the narrative extension of this figural field. The lady's fascination results from a game of transparencies issuing from her external semblance (the visible covered, the hidden uncovered), an eroticism of veils and mantles meant to awaken the others' desire without satisfying it.[16] Armida's seductive strategy is balanced, in fact, between offer and refusal, stimulus and brake, ostentation and mask. The proteiform variety of her "being," converted into a pure phenomenal succession of "appearances," is explicated according to the occasion and the addressee:

Usa ogn'arte la donna, onde sia colto
ne la sua rete alcun novello amante;
né con tutti, né sempre un stesso volto
serba, ma cangia a tempo atti e sembiante.
Or tien pudica il guardo in sé raccolto,
or lo rivolge cupido e vagante:
la sferza in quegli, il freno adopra in questi,
come lor vede in amar lenti o presti. (4.87)[17]

15. "Ah cruel Love, how equally are we destroyed by the honey and the gall that you dispense to us; and equally fatal come from you at once the sickness and the remedies."

16. "[D]'auro ha la chioma, ed *or dal bianco velo / traluce involta*, or discoperta appare" (94.29); "*Mostra* il bel petto le sue nevi ignude, / onde il foco d'Amor si nutre e desta. / *Parte appar de le mamme acerbe e crude, / parte altrui ne ricopre invida vesta*" (4.31); "Come per acqua o per cristallo intero / *trapassa* il raggio, e no'l divide o parte, / per entro il *chiuso manto* osa il pensiero / sì penetrar ne la vietata parte" (4.32). In *Malpiglio*, the dissimulation of hidden spiritual beauties is predicated as a seductive courtly technique, since a virtue that hides itself, but gives itself fleetingly to the others' gaze, hastens the desire that its treasures be brought to light: "Questo nascondersi nondimeno si può fare con alcuno avedimento, per lo quale la picciola parte che si dimostri genera desiderio di quella che si ricopre, e una certa stima e opinion de gli uomini e del principe medesimo, che dentro si nasconda a un non so che di raro e di singolare e di perfetto" (2.558–59).

17. "The lady uses every art by which any new lover may be caught in her net; nor does she keep the same countenance for all, nor at all times, but changes her looks and acts to suit

What appears to be simple "sprezzatura" (albeit with some ambiguities) in chaste Sofronia, Armida's Christian rival, who "sua beltà non cura," in Armida becomes the art and calculus of "dissimulation" aimed at "dishonest" ends:

> Lodata passa e vagheggiata Armida
> fra le cupide turbe e se n'avede.
> No 'l mostra già, benché in suo cor ne rida
> e ne disegni alte vittorie o prede.   (4.33)[18]

The distinction between outer semblance and inner state between the two women is truly subtle. On the one hand, the haughty virgin Sofronia, who is noticed by everybody, does not notice anybody ("mirata da ciascun passa e non mira") and makes her veil into an instrument of chastity ("nel vel ristretta") rather than of artfulness; on the other hand, Armida does not hide her beauty ("non coprì le sue bellezze e non l'espose") but captures the male eye with her *neglecta venustas*:

> Non sai ben dir s'adorna o se negletta,
> se caso od arte il bel volto compose.
> Di natura, d'Amor, de' cieli amici
> le negligenze sue sono artifici.   (2.18)[19]

In effect, the attitudes of both, as Tasso describes them, correspond to techniques amply codified by the various *artes amatoriae* of the sixteenth century, a sort of subaltern equivalent and feminine declension of the strategies of courtly success based on the homologous values of

---

the moment. Now she keeps her gaze at home shamefast, now sends it abroad wanton and wandering. On these she uses the bridle, on those the whip, as she sees that they are forward or slow in loving."

18. "Praised and desired Armida passes among the lustful troops; and she is aware of it: she gives no sign, though in her heart she smiles and projects great victories and plunders from it."

19. "You do not quite know whether to say she adorns or neglects herself, whether accident or art composed her lovely face. Her negligencies are the artifices of Nature, of Love, of her friendly stars." On Sofronia, see Erspamer 123–25.

grazia and *sprezzatura*.[20] Sofronia's extreme equilibrium is broken in Armida, due to the excess of calculated intention that renders vain every "innocence" in artifice. In this, the contrast between the two women is consistent with the development of mannerist and Counter-Reformation thought that was tilting the compromise toward one of the extremes, already ambiguous in Castiglione, of "sprezzatura" and "simulazione."[21] The discourse of feminine fakery has, among its effects, that of generating other deceitful discourses, which at times displace our attention from the figural thickness of the text to the joints of its structure. Armida's most illustrious victim in this incursion into the Christian camp is, as I have already suggested, Eustazio, Goffredo's younger brother. Entrapped like so many by the lady's beauty and her seductive arts, he does not hesitate to believe her story and would therefore like Goffredo to dedicate himself to helping her by diverting precious forces from the siege. The brief argument between the two of them, based once again on the contrastive effect of their characters—Goffredo as firm and unmovable and Eustazio as fragile to temptations—has profound implications for the diversified strategies of epos and romance. The captain's mistrust coincides with the defense of the mission committed to him—and therefore with the epic linearity of the text—and subordinates digressive adventure to the typical romance structure of deferral.[22] As he will explain after yielding to the decisions of an assembly favorable to Eustazio's requests, his opinion was in fact "non di negare alla donzella / ma di darle *in stagion matura* aita" (5.3). On the other hand, Eustazio, who as head of the "guerrieri di ventura" is less bound to collective obliga-

20. For Patrizi, Betussi's two treatises, *Dialogo amoroso* (1543) and *Il Raverta* (1544) had proposed again "il tema della dissimulazione in una ricca casistica amorosa." Even as early as Piccolomini's *Raffaella* (1539), he writes, one could see "una strategia seduttiva che si appoggia . . . sul principio della 'sprezzatura' (dell'atto di seduzione) e della dissimulazione (dei sentimenti non 'convenienti')" (882–83).

21. For a correction of a somewhat conventional classicism, see Ferroni 138–43. I have been developing some of the issues above in a forthcoming article, "Torquato Tasso in the Age of Dissimulation."

22. See my essay "Il Furioso."

tions, calls on barely believable demands of "cortesia," putting into play "il dover, ch'a dar tenuto / è l'ordin nostro a le donzelle aiuto" (4.80), that is, giving priority to the logic of "romance":

> Ah! non sia ver, per Dio, che si ridica
> in Francia, o dove in pregio è cortesia,
> che si fugga da noi rischio o fatica
> per cagion così giusta e così pia.
> Io per me qui depongo elmo e lorica,
> qui mi cingo la spada, e più non fia
> ch'adopri indegnamente arme o destriero,
> o 'l nome usurpi mai di cavaliero.   (4.81)[23]

The above coincides with a moral delegitimation of the chivalric code, invoked for the purpose of "dissimulation":

> *e con sì adorno inganno*
> *cerca di ricoprir la mente accesa*
> *sotto altro zelo; e gli altri anco d'onore*
> fingon desio quel ch'è desio d'amore.   (5.7)[24]

III

The discourse of deceit is entrusted not only to Armida's great machinations or Eustazio's little hypocrisies, for in the case of Erminia and

23. "Ah, let it not be (for God's sake) that it be reported in France, or wheresoever courtesy is prized, that peril or travail for cause so just and pious is shunned by us. For myself, I lay down here my helmet and cuirass, here I unbuckle my sword, and will no more unworthily manage arms or steed, or ever usurp the name of knight-at-arms."

24. "And with such ornamental fabling seeks to hide under a different zeal his mind inflamed; and the others too pretend desire of honor in that which is desire of love." The courtesy code as organic to a precise narrative genre had in the "romanzo" of Tasso's father still intact positive connotations: "Ch'ei ben sa, che difender le donzelle / da violenza d'uomo iniquo e rio, / di cui son l'arme sol lagrime belle, / officio è di guerrier cortese e pio" (*Amadigi*, 84.39). In Goffredo instead there has been a splitting of the two historically knit values of courtesy and *pietas*.

her innocent deceits (6.88) this discourse is necessary to guarantee the woman's survival within the contradictory condition of "enemy/lover." As we know, Erminia loves Tancredi, whose war slave she once was. Treated courteously at first and then freed, she is forced by her origin and faith to serve the pagan cause. In the classic scene of *teichoscopia* in canto 3, inspired by the famous Homeric model (*Iliad* 3), Erminia points out to King Aladino the most illustrious warriors of the Christian army, as she looks down on them from a high tower. When Tancredi's turn comes, she must mask the true nature of her sentiments before her interlocutor, simulating hatred and a thirst for revenge:

Poi gli dice infingevole, *e nasconde*
sotto il manto de l'odio altro desio:
—Oimè! bene il conosco, ed ho ben donde
fra mille riconoscerlo deggia io,
ché spesso il vidi i campi e le profonde
fosse del sangue empir del popol mio.
Ahi quanto è crudo nel ferire! a piaga
ch'ei faccia, erba non giova od arte maga.
Egli è il prence Tancredi: oh prigioniero
mio fosse un giorno! e no'l vorrei già morto;
vivo il vorrei, perch'in me desse al fero
desio dolce vendetta alcun conforto. —
Così parlava, e de' suoi detti il vero
da chi l'udiva in altro senso è torto;
e fuor n'uscì con le sue voci estreme
misto un sospir che 'ndarno ella già preme.   (3.19–20)[25]

25. "Then she speaks, feigning, and hides beneath the mask of hatred a different passion: 'Ay me, I know him indeed, and indeed I have reason that I ought to recognize him amid a thousand; for often have I seen him fill the fields and the deep ditches with the blood of my people. Ah, how cruel he is in wounding! The wound that he makes no medicine avails, nor magic art. // He is Prince Tancredi: oh, would that he were some day my prisoner! and sure I would not want him dead. I would want him alive, that sweet revenge might render me some comfort for my fierce desire.' So she spoke: and the truth of her speech by him who

The ambiguity of Erminia's discourse, confined to a "mask" that commits violence against her "person," plays on the transliteration of amorous language, the accomplice being that Petrarchan code that intends for "wounds" the amorous kind, and for "prisoner" and "revenge" the skirmishes of the erotic duel.[26] This is one exemplary case among many in a poem where military conflict solicits the activation of an agonistic rhetoric that imprints the language of love (2.34–35).[27]

The extreme stylistic compactness of Tasso's lexicon permits almost no distinction, at least on the surface, between Erminia's "honest dissimulation" ("e nasconde sotto il manto de l'odio / altro desio") and Armida's "dishonest" kind ("fa manto del vero a la menzogna") and that of Eustazio ("e con sì adorno inganno / cerca di ricoprir la mente accesa / sotto altro zelo"). In Erminia's case the reification of the metaphor works with such determination as to impose on the character a rhetoric of action beyond that of language. If dissimulation consists essentially of a "knitting" and a "covering" of the word, the double disguising to which Erminia is later constrained will appear to follow perfectly: first under the lying warrior clothes of Clorinda ("finger mi vuo' Clorinda; e ricoperta / sotto l'imagin sua d'uscir son certa," 6.87), then under coarse country clothes, when, being intercepted while she seeks to aid a wounded Tancredi, she takes refuge in the ancient woods and finds comfort among the shepherds. Her condition as an oppressed and torn woman is demonstrated, as previously when putting on Clorinda's heavy armor ("Co 'l durissimo acciar preme ed offende / il delicato collo

heard her is twisted to another sense. And with her last words issued forth an intermingled sigh that now she represses in vain."

26. One can find also in Petrarch the roots of Erminia's mimic dissimulation, beyond the verbal one: "et così aven che l'animo ciascuna / sua passion sotto 'l contrario manto / ricopre co la vista or chiara or bruna" (102.9–11).

27. Another example of the reification of the amorous language due to its explicit metaliterary conscience can be found in the lament of Olindo condemned to the stake, together with his beloved Sofronia: "Quest'è quel laccio ond'io sperai / teco accoppiarmi in compagnia di vita? / questo è quel foco ch'io credea ch'i cori / ne dovesse infiammar d'eguali ardori? / Altre fiamme, altri nodi Amor promise, / altri ce n'apparecchia iniqua sorte."

e l'aurea chioma, / e la tenera man lo scudo prende, / pur troppo grave e insopportabil soma," 6.92),[28] in the discomfort of an incongruous and unnatural disguise:

> La fanciulla regal di rozze spoglie
> s'ammanta, e cinge al crin ruvido *velo*;
> ma nel moto de gli occhi e de le membra
> non già di boschi abitatrice sembra.
> Non copre abito vil la nobil luce
> e quanto è in lei d'altero e di gentile,
> e fuor la maestà regia *traluce*
> per gli atti ancor de l'esercizio umile. (7.17–18)[29]

The dialectic of disguise is to all effects double: first we note the disguise of the character, who when speaking, dressing, or posing, allows to shine through a nature contrary to what is given on the surface, and shows how much necessity imposes a mask that is not the result of a free choice but of a self-repression painfully suffered. Second, the epic-Christian discourse is itself full of disguises, for the romance digressions that lie beneath false epic appearances are disguised as constriction and "errantry" (Erminia "erró senza consiglio e senza guida," 7.3), either as evasive regression in the ancient chivalric woods or as labored refuge in the pastoral arcadia, a *locus amoenus* removed both from war and from the court, where already the *Aminta*, however, in these same years was verifying the impossibility of the idyll.[30]

---

28. "With hardest steel she oppresses and offends her delicate neck and golden hair; and her tender hand takes up the shield—a burden too heavy and insupportable."

29. "The royal maiden clothes herself in rough garments and binds a rustic kerchief round her hair; but in the movements of her eyes and limbs she appears not always a dweller in the groves. // The peasantish habit does not hide the noble light, and all that there is in her of the proud and generous; and her regal majesty shines forth even through the actions of her humble daily round."

30. See Barberi Squarotti.

IV

The same armor, furtively taken by Erminia, will be laid down by Clorinda in exchange for "rusty and black" arms that foreground the tragic misunderstanding that causes her her death. Once again, therefore, disguise lies at the origin of romance *peripezia*, accepted here in its most anguished meaning of "errore." That the character lives artistically in an extraordinary dialectics of covering/uncovering has been splendidly demonstrated by Fredi Chiappelli; for my part, I have elsewhere underscored the transgressive value, alongside the edifying one, that a similar change of semblances and wrappings has for this character.[31] Here I will add that Clorinda's final and fatal disguise functions both as the dissimulation of an identity (still unknown even to the character herself) and as the liberation of an amorous language that earlier was inhibited by the cuirasses of religious and knightly militancy or, rather, by epic constraints. Only through the misunderstanding of a mask can the contact between the two lovers, their reciprocal recognition, be manifest— and then only in a tragic way and with the edifying purpose that constitutes the necessary alibi for it. Even Clorinda, like her friend Erminia but without being aware of it, lives in the misunderstanding of an unknown condition (that of being Christian) and of a repudiated nature (that of being a woman). This disjuncture is foretold by the miracle of her birth as the white daughter of a black mother, her first, congenital "disguise." Clorinda's mask is importantly not only that of her bogus faith and pagan militancy, but also that of her denial of femininity and eros under virile semblances and military armor (not imposed, as in the case of Erminia, but indeed sought as a function of a "dissimulated" identity):

> Costei gl'ingegni feminili e gli usi
> tutti sprezzò sin da l'età più acerba:
> a i lavori d'Aracne, a l'ago, a i fusi
> inchinar non degnò la man superba.

---

31. Chiappelli describes Clorinda's destiny as "larvale" (56–65). See also Zatti, *L'uniforme*, 137–42.

Fuggì gli abiti molli e i lochi chiusi,
chè ne' campi onestate anco si serba;
armò d'orgoglio il volto, e si compiacque
rigido farlo, e pur rigido piacque.   (2.39)[32]

Another exchange of armor has Rinaldo as its protagonist and is a
no less significant metamorphosis of identity. The young Italian knight,
in line of succession to Dudone, raises his arms against the Norwe-
gian prince Gernando, provoked by his poisonous insinuations, and
kills him. Then, in order not to incur Goffredo's law, he abandons the
Christian camp and seeks glory elsewhere, far from the walls of Jeru-
salem, in free and adventuresome undertakings. In tune with the new
romance world, at a certain point Rinaldo chooses to lay down his cru-
sader arms in order to wear those of an enemy he has killed (14.53). The
exchange of arms, as I noted earlier, is a manifestly symbolic act, since
this new pagan-like identity is a return to the old one, to the condi-
tion of knight errant in which Tasso had celebrated this character in his
youthful romance, Rinaldo. By betraying his Christian mission, Rinaldo
situates himself in the field of error and deviance, whose indices are the
"enemy" emblems and the regression into the romance space of "adven-
ture."[33] In both cases, Clorinda's and Rinaldo's, the ambiguity of the
masks permits the liberation of an "other" dimension with respect to the
heroic-Christian epos: respectively, the amorous and the adventurous.[34]

32. "She from her earliest age altogether disprized the feminine nature and its usages; her
proud hand did not deign to bend to the tasks of Arachne, to the needle, to the spindle. She
avoided soft habits and sheltered places, who yet in the fields preserves her chastity. She ar-
mored her countenance in pride, and it pleased her to keep it severe; and though severe it
was pleasing."

33. The episode where Rinaldo, full of indignation for Goffredo, goes into voluntary exile
from the Christian camp is clearly inspired by the incident that inaugurates the narrative
movement of the Iliad (there, offended by Agamennon, Achilles retires in a tent, thus com-
promising the fortunes of the war). Tasso himself confirms the point in his Lettere poetiche.
It pays to notice, however, that he uses the episode to play on the double registers of the
romance and of the epic codes, thus transforming the rejection of epic authority into ro-
mance, and paganizing the adventures. See Quint 470.

34. Only in one case does the disguise not have painful or dramatic connotations. Such is

Given these premises, the parabola of the "errant" must fatally extinguish itself in Armida's amorous prison. In the poem, the lady is the knowing artifex of transformation and mutation: she is, at once, Circe— who acts on the identity of others (6.86 and 10.66)—and Proteus—who acts on her own identity: "tentò ella mill'arti, e in mille forme / quasi Proteo novel gli apparse inanti," 5.63).³⁵ The magus's operation is an active transformation of reality. But this reality, in a character swept away in an ephemeral game of appearances, is perceived negatively as illusion, inconsistency, and deceit (as in Goffredo's skeptical reflection: "ché nel mondo mutabile e leggiero / costanza è spesso il variar pensiero," 5.3).

Now the Armida of canto 16 plays two opposite roles in the space of a few octaves: that of the seductress who has lost her force as a result of being deceived by love, which she habitually instills in others, and that of the *maga*, whose magic is called into question by a force that, though defeated by a superior power, still tries tenaciously to govern the world of cognitive illusion and sentimental inconstancy. The poet's identification with her (when she is defeated) and with her magical world (which is about to dissolve) corresponds to the lost illusion of arresting the universe's continual metamorphosis, a metamorphosis of which Armida is the emblematic cipher. Her condemnation, on the other hand, is justified by the poet's awareness of the deceit performed against reason and truth.

---

the case of Vafrino, Tancredi's squire, an expert in both Arabic language and customs, who uses a disguise to introduce himself into the Egyptian camp. Here too the name "means" (in Latin "vafer" means cunning, shrewd, sagacious), and the character is lively and adaptable: "uom pronto e destro e sovra i pie' leggiero, / audace sì, ma cautamente audace, / che parla in molte lingue, e varia il noto / suon de la voce e 'l portamento e 'l moto" (18.75). The praise (in Erasmus) and the condemnation (in Calvin) of "vafrities" had divided the sixteenth-century religious world over Nicodemitic dissimulation. See Biondi. On Vafrino as a somewhat anomalous "comic" or "low" type in a heroic poem, see Jenni.

35. On this complementarity, see Rousset 29–30.

V

The traits of Armida in canto 16 are, initially, her usual ones: her *sprezzatura* is studied negligence, which makes appear natural what instead is the fruit of calculation. Thus, Armida "langue per vezzo" (languishes under his caress); in her breast "le peregrine rose" (the stranger roses) are linked "a i nativi gigli" (with native lilies); if at first " 'l crin sparge incomposto al vento estivo," (her hair she looses in disarray to the summery air) she then braids the locks and disciplines "con ordin vago i lor lascivi errori" (into lovely order their wanton wanderings). The new element is that the character finds perfect equivalence in the well-known *aemulatio* of art and nature that characterizes the amorous scenario of canto 16:

> e quel che 'l bello e 'l caro accresce a l'opre,
> l'arte, che tutto fa, nulla si scopre.
> Stimi (sì misto il culto è co'l negletto)
> sol naturali e gli ornamenti e i siti.
> Di natura arte par, che per diletto
> l'imitatrice sua scherzando imiti.
> L'aura, non ch'altro, è de la maga effetto,
> l'aura che rende gli alberi fioriti:
> co' fiori eterni eterno il frutto dura,
> e mentre spunta l'un, l'altro matura. (16.9–10) [36]

The more nature resembles its Edenic origin the more it increases in the onlooker the suspicion of its falsity, of the simplicity that betrays the mask. Since the model of affectation and false naturalness has substituted authentic and primal naturalness in the magic place of the *Libe-*

---

36. "[A]nd (what increases the beauty and price of the work) the art that makes it all is nowhere revealed. // You would judge (so mingled is negligence with care) both the grounds and their improvements only natural. It seems an art of nature, that for her own pleasure playfully imitates her imitator. The very breeze (not to speak of the rest) is the work of the sorceress, the breeze that causes the trees to be in flower: with blossoms eternal eternal lasts the fruit, and while the one buds forth, the other ripens."

rata, the simplicity of these places becomes paradoxically the sign of the presence of magic artifice, and therefore of deception. "Artificio di ogni artificio è metter sommo artificio in alcuna cosa e far che non appaia; e ciò che la rende più bella e cara, per non vi si scorgere affettazione," Guastavini comments in a note on Tasso's passage.[37] Such a comment echoes an ancient and complex tradition.

Ancient because the application of the principle of eloquence dates back at least to the Anonymous of the Sublime: "l'arte infatti è perfetta quando sembra esser natura, e dal canto suo la natura ha realizzato il suo scopo quando contiene in sè dissimulata l'arte" (ch. 22).[38] Complex, because it is situated at the intersection of diverse cultural referents. In fact, naturalness and artifice ("sì misto è 'l culto co 'l negletto") sum up an aesthetic ideal that informs many sixteenth-century artistic theories.[39] They are inspired, that is, by that canon of *sprezzatura* and *grazia* that, transferred to the area of behavioral norms, is the founding rule of the courtier's success: "Però si pò dir quella esser vera arte che non pare esser arte: né più in altro si ha da poner studio, che nel nasconderla: perché se è scoperta, leva in tutto il credito e fa l'omo poco estimato."[40]

It is precisely to Castiglione, the honored master of courtiership, that Tasso will link himself in the *Malpiglio*, where the theme of acquiring grace at court leads to an admired and nostalgic mourning for a golden age in which *sprezzatura* still permitted—even via the crooked path of simulation of "nature"—the expression of the individual virtue. Now instead, feigning is one of the main virtues, he writes, and the courtier's life is a daily trial. Thus one's goal is to defend oneself against the envy of others (of one's equals and of the prince himself), a self-defensive strategy of dissimulation that seeks to hide, more than exalt ("appari il

37. See Guastavini, *Discorsi*. D'Angelo retraces such a tradition along the double register of rhetorical and esoteric doctrines.

38. See Praz 111.

39. On this, see Chiappelli's note in the 1982 edition of Tasso, *Gerusalemme* (632); for the concept, see Monk.

40. Castiglione, 1.26. Mario Equicola's treatise *De natura de Amore* (1525) applied the principle (the art of "ben dire" and the Ovidian technique of seduction) to the lover's eloquence.

cortigiano a occultare piuttosto che apparere"), man's virtues and merits: "[l'uomo di corte] non soltanto nelle dispute, ma in tutte l'azioni della vita dovrebbe contender, cedendo in quella guisa che fanno alcuni esperti lottatori, i quali piegandosi a quella parte dove gli tira l'avversario, con questo pieghevole artificio più facilmente il gettano a terra."[41] It is to Tasso that another Torquato, Accetto, largely makes reference,

41. *Dialoghi*, 561. Dissimulation as a play of mirrors pervades many aspects of the Tassian universe. Even the duelling technique, in which Tasso was a celebrated master throughout the seventeenth century, seems modeled in fact after a game of pretence and simulations that does not substantially differ from Armida's seductive technique. See the first duel between Tancredi and Argante:

Cautamente ciascuno a i colpi move
la destra, a i guardi l'occhio, a i passi il piede;
si reca in atti vari, in guardie nove:
or gira intorno, or cresce inanzi, or cede,
or quivi ferire accenna e poscia altrove,
dove non minacciò ferir si vede,
or di sé discoprire alcuna parte,
e tentar di schernir l'arte con l'arte.

De la spada Tancredi e de lo scudo
mal guardato al pagan dimostra il fianco;
corre egli per ferirlo, e intanto nudo
di riparo si lascia il lato manco.
Tancredi con un colpo il ferro crudo
del nemico ribatte, e lui fere anco;
nè poi, ciò fatto, in ritirarsi tarda,
ma si raccoglie e si ristringe in guarda. (6.42–43)

To remain on the "art of war" subject, some diversions ordered by Goffredo during the siege of Jerusalem confirm this tactical principle of dissimulation: "Machine ed arme poscia ivi più spesse / dimostra ove adoprarle egli men pensa; / e il deluso pagan si riconforta / ch'oppor le vede a la munita porta" (18.55, 62). In *Convivio*, Dante recognizes also the rhetorical figure for dissimulation, taking it probably from Cicero (*De oratore* 2.67.269) which he describes in these terms: "E questa cotale figura in rettorica è molto laudabile, e anco necessaria, cioè quando le parole sono a una persona e la 'ntenzione è un'altra" (3.10.7). To exemplify it, he gives this extraordinary simile which brings us back to the figuration in Tasso: "Ed è simigliante a l'opera di quello savio guerriero che combatte lo castello da uno lato per levare la difesa da l'altro."

more than half a century later in claiming that: often it is more virtuous to dissimulate virtue not with the veil of vice, but by not showing all its rays, as not to offend envy's impaired right and the fear of others ("spesso è virtù sopra virtù il dissimular la virtù, non col *velo* del vizio, ma col non dimostrarne tutti i raggi, per non offender la vista inferma dell'invidia e dell'altrui timore"). His discussion, rediscovered today with great interest after Croce first gave attention to it years ago, offers noteworthy starting-points for an analysis of Armida and her magical realm.[42] Here I am not so much interested in the theoretical and practical justifications of dissimulation (in relation to the courtier's life or to religious life), all the more since Armida's dissimulation is everything but "honest." But two points that Accetto focuses on come close to my concerns. First, Accetto forges a nexus between dissimulation and ostentation. These two attitudes appear opposite and turn out instead to be complementary because the character who constructs a mask in reality hides himself in order better to appear as he wants to appear.[43] Second, Accetto's extension of the concept of the human realm to the natural one makes of dissimulation a key for universal interpretation (with implicit religious reference to a post mortem where all the masks will fall off and the pure and naked truth will triumph — the ideological subtext for the same baroque antithesis of being/appearing):

se pur si considera la natura per tante altre opere di qua giù, si conosce che tutto il bello non è altro che una gentil dissimulazione. Dico il bello de' corpi che stanno soggetti alla mutazione, e veggansi tra questi i fiori e tra' fiori la lor reina; e si troverà che la rosa par bella perchè a prima vista dissimula di esser cosa tanto caduca, e quasi con una semplice superficie di vermiglio fa restar gli occhi in un certo modo persuasi ch'ella sia porpora immortale; ma in breve, come disse Torquato Tasso:

---

42. The first modern edition came in 1928; two years later Croce and Caramella edited the treatise for the volume *Politici*, 143–73.

43. See Rousset 267–76.

"quella non par che desiata inanti
fu da mille donzelle e mille amanti" (16.14)
perché la dissimulazione in lei non può durare. E tanto si può dir
di un volto di rose, anzi di quanto per la terra riluce tra le più belle
schiere d'Amore; e benchè della bellezza mortale sia solito dirsi di
non parer cosa terrena, quando poi si considera il vero, già non è
altro che un cadavero dissimulato dal favor dell'età, che ancor si
sostiene nel riscontro di quelle parti e di que' colori che han da divi-
dersi e cedere alla forza del tempo e della morte." (Ch. 9, "Del bene
che si produce dalla dissimulazione")

Accetto plucks the simile of the rose, bending it to singular signi-
fication, precisely in Armida's garden, where the destiny of the meta-
morphosis of bodies is dissimulated in illusionistic stability, and nature
repeats the rhetorical paradox of a deceit with honest aims. If feminine
seduction is the unscrupulous use of a "proteiform" art of *variatio*, the
dissimulation of which Accetto speaks reduces this plurality to an oxy-
moron, fixes it in the *coincidentia oppositorum*. And in fact it is in Armida
that the two contrasting extremes are linked, the supreme grace of the
lady and the horrid repugnance of the monster. The same very beautiful
creature who fascinated Rinaldo in the garden (canto 16) reappears to
him among the trunks of the enchanted wood (canto 18) in the form of a
frightful giant, Briareus, the last incarnation of Proteus:

Egli alza il ferro, e 'l suo pregar non cura;
ma colei si trasmuta (oh novi mostri!)
sì come avien che d'una altra figura,
trasformando repente, il sogno mostri.
Così ingrossò le membra e tornò oscura
la faccia e vi sparir gli avori e gli ostri;
crebbe in gigante altissimo, e si feo
con cento armate braccia un Briareo. (18.35)[44]

44. "He raises the sword and pays her prayers no heed; but she is transformed (O new mon-
strosities!) even as it happens that out of one shape a dream projects another, suddenly

Consistent with the identification observed earlier between character and nature, the Edenic landscape that was created by her magic art—the only possible perpetuation in the Christian world of the classical locus of the golden age—becomes transformed at Armida's hand. It can survive, in fact, only as dissimulation of an artifice that is quickly demystified: the garden is pure appearance that hides a substance of opposite meaning. When Armida, having abandoned the hope of keeping Rinaldo, dissolves the garden and the palace with just one gesture, not a trace remains of this enchanted realm:

> Come imagin talor d'immensa mole
> forman nubi ne l'aria e poco dura,
> che 'l vento la disperde o solve il sole,
> come sogno se 'n va ch'egro figura,
> così sparver gli alberghi, e restar sole
> l'alpe e l'orror che fece ivi natura.   (16.70)[45]

The Edenic semblances make room for that very horrid nature which beautiful appearances had dissimulated up to now. Significant, I would say, is the shifting from character to landscape carried out here by Tasso with respect to the Ariostan model: thanks to Melissa's ring, Ariosto's Ruggiero unmasks Alcina's identity as a repellent old woman, but the poem does not tell us anything about the nature of the Edenic world the witch had prepared for him (a typical and easily recognizable Renaissance court).[46] In this instance, Ariosto dismantles the mechanism of

---

transmuted. So she magnified her limbs and turned her countenance dark, and the crimson and the ivory vanished away. She grew to a huge giant and became a Briareus with a hundred armed hands."

45. "As sometimes the clouds in the middle air form images of a mighty mass, and last but little time, for the wind disperses them or sun dissolves; as a dream that an invalid fashions goes away; so disappeared the buildings and only remained the mountains and waving shades that Nature created there."

46. Ariosto 7.8–79. A propos of Ariosto, let us remember that he too took up the theme of simulation/dissimulation in two famous prologues: "Quantunque il simular" (4.1–3) and "Oh quante sono incantatrici" (8.1–3). In both cases, he legitimized as "honest" the fiction

allegory. In Tasso, on the other hand, Armida keeps intact her prerogatives of beauty and seduction, but her realm is pure appearance, behind which lies hidden the naked horror of nature, a squalid and sterile desert. In the *Gerusalemme liberata*, thus, the relation of identity between beauty and horror remains quite solid.

Armida's habitual residence is, moreover, situated on the banks of the Dead Sea, where once there arose the damned cities of Sodom and Gomorrah, and it is there that she makes her return after the dissolution of her magical world:

> Al fin giungemmo al loco ove già scese
> fiamma dal cielo in dilatate falde,
> e di natura vendicò l'offese
> sovra le genti in mal oprar sì salde.
> Fu già terra feconda, almo paese,
> or acque son bituminose e calde
> e steril lago: e quanto ei torpe e gira,
> compressa è l'aria e grave il puzzo spira.   (10.61)[47]

The place is therefore a biblical-Dantesque realm of horror surrounding a marvelous castle where the Edenic scene, the *locus amoenus*, is punctually renewed (10.62–64).[48] Both metamorphoses in time, as in the case of the garden, or here contiguity in space, imply an equivalence, a coincidence of opposites, pleasure and horror. Moreover, is not perhaps the

---

used by Bradamante and Ruggiero for self-defense against the professional betrayers Brunello and Alcina.

47. "At last we arrived at the place where flame of old descended from heaven in swollen flakes, and upon a people so hardened in evil-doing avenged their offenses against nature. It was once a fertile land, a prosperous contryside; now the waters are bituminous and warm and the lake sterile; and wherever it twists and winds, the air is thick and breathes a heavy stench."

48. The biblical source is Genesis 19:24 ("Dominus pluit super Sodoman et Gomorrham sulphur et ignem a Domino de caelo"); the Dantesque one is double: "Sovra tutto 'l sabbion, d'un cader lento, / piovean di foco dilatate falde, / come di neve in alpe sanza vento" (*Inferno* 14.28–30) and "I' vedea lei, ma non vedea in essa / mai che le bolle che 'l bollor levava, / e gonfiar tutta, e riseder compressa" (*Inferno* 21.19–21).

demonic space of the wood of Saron the most clamorous overturning of the preceding Edenic scene? Already horrible by nature (13.2–3), it increases its own sinister fascination when its trunks are populated by demons through the enchantments produced by the pagan magus Ismeno. But the wood is not simply the garden's opposite, it is also its redoubling, because it contains the garden in turn (18.18–24); it is its antithesis as well as its equivalent. The art of simulation exalts the intuition of a reality in constant metamorphosis, trapping the elusiveness of mutation in a dialectic of contraries. This multiplicity of "appearances" is fixed in antithesis since Tasso, to his dismay, cannot reduce it to the singularity of "being." Therefore, demonic wood and Edenic garden, infernal monsters and beautiful women, all exist in ambiguous cohabitation.

But also *succhi amari* and *soavi licor* mingle in a single brew. In confirmation of diffidences that Tasso's writing does not succeed in dissimulating, it is in Armida's magic realm that the "fonte del riso" arises, where we are tempted to recognize a sort of upturned mirror of the poetic drinking glass:

> Un fonte sorge in lei che vaghe e monde
> ha l'acque sì che i riguardanti asseta;
> ma dentro a i freddi suoi cristalli asconde
> di tosco estran malvagità secreta,
> ch'un picciol sorso di sue lucide onde
> inebria l'alma tosto e la fa lieta,
> indi a rider uom move, e tanto il riso
> s'avanza alfin ch'ei ne rimane ucciso.   (14.74) [49]

Even this *fonte* is inspired by the dialectic of dissimulation, or of an above and a below, of an outside and an inside, which, far from corresponding to one another, are polarized in the antithesis of the "acque

---

49. "On it wells up a spring that has waters so pure and inviting that it rouses thirst in those who look upon it: but it conceals within its crystal cold the secret malice of a strange venom, for one little draught of its shining waters straightway intoxicates the soul and makes it giddy; then it moves a man to laughter; and in the end his laughing proceeds so far that he lies dead of it."

vaghe e monde" and of the "tosco estran." The beneficent deceit of poetic medicine can be painfully converted into the "malvagità secreta" of a pleasure that kills.[50]

VI

An analysis of Tasso's representation of nature must include a comment on the great poetry of the night, which represents by common judgment one of the poetic vertices of the *Gerusalemme liberata*. The consistent metaphorics that characterize these nocturnals manifest profound connections with the arguments treated thus far. Compare these four descriptions:

"Era la notte, e 'l suo stellato velo / chiaro spiegava e senza nube alcuna" ("It was night, and she spread forth her starry veil in clarity and without a single cloud," 6.103)

"Sorge intanto la notte, e 'l velo nero / per l'aria spiega e l'ampia terra abbraccia" ("Meanwhile Night is rising and spreads her black veil through the air and takes the broad earth in her embrace," 10.78)

"[M]a poi, quando stendendo il fosco manto / la notte in occidente il dì chiudea, / tra duo suoi cavalieri e due matrone / ricovrava in disparte al padiglione" ("But then when night, extending her dark mantle, shut up the daylight in the west, with two of her knights and two maids of honor she took shelter apart in her pavilion," 5.60)

"Ma già distendon l'ombre orrido velo / che di rossi vapor si sparge e tigne . . . votò Pluton gli abissi, e la sua notte / tutta versò da le tartaree grotte" ("But now the shadows spread a horrible veil that is

50. This is exactly what Tasso fears in his mature reflections on poetics so much so that he chose to solve the knot politically: "Però al politico s'appartiene di considerare quale poesia debba esser proibita, e qual diletto, acciochè il piacere, il quale dee essere in vece di quel mele di cui s'unge il vaso quando si dà la medicina a' fanciulli, non facesse effetto di pestifero veleno, o non tenesse occupati gli animi in vana lezione" (*Discorsi*, 67).

sprinkled over and stained with reddened mists . . . Pluto emptied the abyss, and poured forth all his own realm of night from the caverns of Tartarus," 9.15)

In cantos 6.103 and 10.78, the nocturnal veil is pure and joyful transparency, the carrier of a sleep that will be just compensation for the labors of living. But in the two other cases sleep is full of disquiet and torments of desire (5.60) or anguished by the nightmares of a night coming from the realm of Satan (9.15). All four passages contain the "textual" metaphor *velo* and *manto*.[51] We may simply say that we are fully within the code; but why such a constancy of images, almost a figural obsession, a *métaphore obsédante*? Doesn't this metaphor also find its semantic reason in that dialectic, encountered at various levels, of covering and dissimulating, a dialectic of an appearance that hides—repressing or saving, according to the case—a secret being? If the sweetness (but also the deceit) of poetry is expressed in the superimposition of ornaments of the marvelous over the plot of truth, the beauty (but also the deceit) of the world materializes neoplatonically in a *velo* or a *manto* that hide the true nature of things. Beauty and knowledge, seduction and truth seem to be for Tasso in irremediable antithesis: the veil and the cloak that one would want to tear in order to possess the truth, or penetrate for erotic satisfaction (or simply lay down—Accetto *docet* [ch. 23]— in order to render triumphant the authentic value of man) are also the locus of erotic temptation and poetic pleasure: *succhi amari* and *soavi licor* can ambiguously coexist, but they cannot be reconciled, because they dissimulate in harmony a radical oxymoron.

In the moment of greatest triumph of the destructive pagan force— during the drought that strikes the crusader camp, already run through with shudders of sedition—the night, invoked as relief of daylight heat —declares instead its complicity with evil:

51. Both terms are used by Accetto to define dissimulation through a metaphor (chs. 1, 5, 14, 23, 24, 25). In chapter 4 there is perhaps the best image: "non essendo altro il dissimulare che un velo composto di tenebre oneste e di rispetti violenti, da che non si forma il falso, ma si dà qualche riposo al vero, per dimostrarlo a tempo" (42).

Non ha poscia la notte ombre più liete,
ma del caldo del sol paiono impresse,
e di travi di foco e di *comete*
e *d'altri fregi* ardenti il *velo intesse.*
Né pur, misera terra, a la tua sete
son da l'avara luna almen concesse
sue rugiadose stille, e l'erbe e i fiori
bramano indarno i *lor vitali umori.*
Da le notti inquiete il dolce sonno
bandito fugge, e i languidi mortali
lusingando ritrarlo a sé no 'l ponno;
ma pur la sete è il pessimo de' mali,
però che di Giudea l'iniquo donno
con veneni e con *succhi aspri e mortali*
più de l'inferna Stige e d'Acheronte
torbido fece e livido ogni fonte.   (13.57–58)[52]

The night seems to be Satan's gaze: "rosseggian gli occhi, e di veneno infetto / come infausta cometa il guardo splende" (4.7). But allusively evoked by the *succhi aspri e mortali* in significant antithesis with the *vitali umori*, it is the poetic discourse which appears most threatened by the poisoned lymph, the most ambiguous and compromised, by means of the "textual" metaphor, with the temptations of Armida and the horrors of Satan. How much awareness is there in Tasso of this risky *contaminatio?* Textual error, the deceit of the word, shines through in the plot of writing much more painfully than one would be led to suspect at first sight. In effect, in the *Liberata* we find confronted and practiced at its highest de-

52. "No pleasanter thereafter are the shades of night, but they seem minted from the heat of the sun, and her veil interwoven with pillars of fire and comets and such blazing gauds. And to your thirst, O wretched Earth, not even her dewy exhalations are granted by the miserly moon; and grasses and flowers long in vain for their life-giving moisture. // Sweet sleep flees banished from these restless nights; and suffering mortals cannot call it back by any blandishment; but yet the thirst is the worst evil of all, for Judaea's wicked lord made every spring filthy and unwholesome with poisons and secretions more bitter and deadly than hellish Styx and Acheron."

gree of awareness the artifice of all Counter-Reformation poetics, where the bitter juices of instructive purpose and the soft liquors of sensual pleasure, combined in a daring mixture, are justified, but also denied, reciprocally. Poetic language, which by its nature feeds on "ornaments" or pleasant deceits, is called upon contradictorily to serve the purpose of the highest truth, the historic and Christian one.

Nevertheless, the dark night by which Tasso's poetry is ambiguously compromised is also an anxiety for liberation toward the light:

> Notte, che nel profondo oscuro seno
> chiudesti e ne l'oblio fatto sì grande,
> piacciati ch'io ne 'l tragga e 'n bel sereno
> a le future età lo spieghi e mande.
> Viva la fama loro; e tra lor gloria
> splenda del fosco tuo l'alta memoria. (12.54)[53]

Singing here of the fatal encounter between Tancredi and Clorinda, Tasso wishes that darkness, which, cloak-like, encloses the memory of that epic duel ("splenda del fosco tuo l'alta memoria"), might allow it to continue to shine, and let the glory of the two knights live on through his poetry ("viva la fama loro"). Tasso's poetry celebrates at once the truth torn from the darkness, and the darkness that dissimulates this truth, since that instrument of deceit which is the language of the poet is also truth's only way of access.[54]

Translated by Valeria Finucci with Michael Sherberg

Works Cited

Alighieri, Dante. *Il convivio*. Ed. Enzo Quaglio. Florence: Le Monnier, 1964.

——. *La divina commedia: Inferno*. Ed. Charles Singleton. Princeton: Princeton UP, 1970.

Ariosto, Ludovico. *Orlando furioso*. 2 vols. Milan: Garzanti, 1974.

53. "O Night, that would hold enclosed within your deep dark breast and in oblivion exploit so great, please you that I may draw it forth and in the clear serene display it and send it on to future ages. Let their fame survive; and amid their glory a noble memorial of your darkness shine."

54. A somewhat different version of this essay appears in Italian in Zatti, *L'ombra*.

Accetto, Torquato. *Della dissimulazione onesta.* Ed. Silvano Nigro. Genoa: Costa & Nolan, 1983.

——. *Della dissimulazione onesta. Politici e moralisti del Seicento.* Ed. Benedetto Croce and Santino Caramella. Bari: Laterza, 1930. 143–73.

Barberi-Squarotti, Giorgio. "La tragicità dell'Aminta." *Fine dell'idillio: da Dante a Marino.* Genoa: Melangolo, 1978. 139–74.

Biondi, A. "La giustificazione della simulazione nel Cinquecento." *Eresia e riforma nell'Italia del Cinquecento.* Florence: Sansoni, 1974.

Castiglione, Baldassarre. *Il libro del cortegiano.* Ed. Ettore Bonora. Milan: Mursia, 1972.

Chiappelli, Fredi. *Il conoscitore del caos: una 'vis abdita' nel linguaggio tassesco.* Roma: Bulzoni, 1981.

D'Angelo, P. " 'Celare l'arte': per una storia del precetto 'Ars est celare artem.' " *Intersezioni* 6.2 (1986): 321–42.

Erspamer, Francesco. "Il pensiero debole di Torquato Tasso." *La menzogna.* Ed. Francesco Cardini. Florence: Ponte alle Grazie, 1989. 120–36.

Ferroni, Giulio. "Sprezzatura e simulazione." *La corte e il cortegiano.* Vol. 1. Ed. Carlo Ossola. Rome: Bulzoni, 1980.

Gorni, Guglielmo. "La metafora del testo." *Strumenti critici* 38 (1979): 18–32.

Guastavini, Giulio. *Discorsi ed annotazioni sopra la Gerusalemme Liberata di Torquato Tasso.* Pavia: Appresso gli eredi di Gierolamo Bartoli, 1592.

——. *Risposta ad alcune opposizioni fatte alla proposizione e invocazione usata dal Tasso nella Gerusalemme Liberata. Opere,* by Torquato Tasso. Ed. Giovanni Rosini. Pisa: Niccolo Capurro, 1828.

Jenni, Adolfo. "Il realismo borghese nella *Liberata* e il personaggio di Vafrino." *Lettere italiane* 12.4 (1960): 401–13.

Monk, Samuel Holt. "A Grace beyond the Reach of Art." *Journal of the History of Ideas* 5 (1944): 131–50.

Ovid. *Ars Amatoria. Liber 1.* Oxford: Clarendon, 1977.

Patrizi, Giorgio. "Il libro del cortigiano e la trattatistica sul comportamento." *Letteratura italiana. Le forme del testo. La prosa.* Vol. 3, bk. 2. Ed. Alberto Asor Rosa. Turin: Einaudi, 1984.

Petrarca, Francesco. *Petrarch's Lyric Poems.* Ed. and trans. Robert Durling. Cambridge: Harvard UP, 1976.

Praz, Mario. "Il giardino di Armida." *Il giardino dei sensi. Studi sul manierismo e il barocco.* Milan: Mondadori. 1975.

Quint, David. "La barca dell'avventura nell'epica rinascimentale." *Intersezioni* 5.3 (1985): 467–88.

Rousset, Jean. *La letteratura dell'età barocca in Francia: Circe e il Pavone.* Bologna: Mulino, 1985.

Scianatico, Giovanna. "Le Tasse et le Manierisme." *Revue de littérature comparée* 4 (1988): 545–57.

Sozzi, Bartolo. "Il Tasso e il 'Manierismo.' " *Studi Tassiani* 32 (1984): 111–22.

Speroni, Sperone. "Dialogo della Istoria." *Trattatisti del Cinquecento,* Vol. 1. Ed. Mario Pozzi. Milan: Ricciardi, 1978. 725–84.

Tasso, Bernardo. *L'Amadigi di Bernardo Tasso colla vita dell'autore e varie illustrazioni dell'opera.* Bergamo: Lancellotti, 1755.

Tasso, Torquato. *Dialoghi.* Ed. Ezio Raimondi. Firenze: Sansoni, 1958.

———. *Discorsi dell'arte poetica e del poema eroico.* Ed. Luigi Poma. Bari: Laterza, 1964.

———. *Gerusalemme liberata.* Ed. Bartolo Sozzi. Milan: Feltrinelli, 1961.

———. *Gerusalemme liberata.* Ed. Fredi Chiappelli. Milan: Rusconi, 1982.

———. *Jerusalem Delivered.* Trans. Ralph Nash. Detroit: Wayne State UP, 1987.

———. *Lettere poetiche.* Parma: Guanda, 1995.

———. "Il Malpiglio overo de la corte." *Dialoghi.*

Ulivi, Ferruccio. *Il manierismo del Tasso e altri studi.* Florence: Olschki, 1966.

Vivaldi, Vincenzo. *Sulle fonti della Gerusalemme liberata.* Catanzaro: Officina Tip. di G. Calò, 1893.

Weinberg, Bernard, ed. *Trattati di poetica e di retorica del Cinquecento.* Bari: Laterza, 1974.

Zatti, Sergio. "Il Furioso fra epos e romanzo." *Giornale storico della letteratura italiana* 163 (1986): 483–514.

———. *L'ombra del Tasso: epica e romanzo nel Cinquecento.* Milan: Bruno Mondadori, 1996.

———. *L'uniforme cristiano e il multiforme pagano: saggio sulla Gerusalemme Liberata.* Milan: Il Saggiatore, 1983.

Trickster, Textor, Architect, Thief:
Craft and Comedy in *Gerusalemme liberata*

WALTER STEPHENS

In canto 18 of *Gerusalemme liberata*, writing irrupts into the plot of Tasso's highly intertextual poem. Attacked by a falcon, a carrier pigeon takes refuge with Goffredo, who discovers a letter from the Egyptian general Emireno to King Aladino in Jerusalem, announcing the imminent arrival of Muslim reinforcements for the besieged town. As if this adaptation of Homeric bird omens were not already abundantly explicit, Goffredo announces to his assembled lieutenants that the messenger (freighted with overtones of the Holy Spirit) has brought a revelation from divine providence: "—Vedete come il tutto a noi riveli / la providenza del Signor de' cieli" ("See how the providence of Heaven's king can reveal all things to us").[1] This incident inaugurates an extensive series of Homeric imitations that will occupy much of cantos 18 and 19. The progression and tension among these imitations have striking intertextual and metaliterary implications for Tasso's poem and its representation of authorship.

Tasso's Nestor figure, the aged Raimondo, renowned for his aptitude at tactical deception (*bellico frodo*, GL 3.62.5), suggests that a spy be sent to discover the Egyptian plan of attack (GL 18.49ff.). Tancredi nominates his squire, a brave, cautious, polyglot master of disguise named Vafrino, for the mission.

> Venne colui, chiamato; e poi ch'intese
> ciò che Goffredo e 'l suo signor desia,

---

1. *Gerusalemme liberata*, ed. Caretti 18.53 (henceforth cited as GL). Translations of GL by Nash, with occasional modifications in square brackets. Other translations my own unless otherwise attributed.

alzò ridendo il volto ed intraprese
la cura e disse: — Or mi pongo in via.   (GL 18.58)

(He came when summoned; and when he understood what Godfrey
and his master wanted, he lifted up his countenance, smiling, and
undertook the charge, and said: "Already I am on my way.")

Why does Vafrino smile? The ironic smiles of Rinaldo notwithstanding,
the *Liberata* has until this moment excluded comedy.[2]

I. Trickster

Perhaps Vafrino smiles because he is a virtuoso trickster. His smile
may also signal Tasso's own self-congratulatory confidence, for he en-
trusts to Vafrino a long Homeric *imitatio* in which Tancredi's squire rivals
two of Odysseus's trickiest adventures. Vafrino's very name embodies
Tasso's challenge to Homer, for it declares him the quintessential trick-
ster: it is the diminutive of *vafro*, the Italianized form of Latin *vafer*,
which denotes the subtlety, craftiness, and cunning of the trickster.[3]
Tasso scholars have traditionally read Vafrino intertextually, interpreting
his name as a riposte to Trissino's Doletto, a treacherous valet in *Italia
liberata dai Goti*. But as their names indicate, both Doletto and Vafrino are
modeled on Homer's Dolon, a Trojan spy who appears in book 10 of the
Iliad, which is traditionally called the *Doloneia*. Dolon's name is an alle-
gorical substantive reflecting the Greek *dolos* or "trick" and its adjectival
form *dolios*; Trissino's Doletto flaunts a name based on *dolus*, the Latin
cognate of *dolos*, while Vafrino enacts the broader and more suggestive
vafer. Tasso's plot eliminates Trissino from the three-way rivalry, how-
ever, for Vafrino more resembles Dolon than either resembles Doletto.[4]

2. Compare GL 5.12.4 and 5.42.1.

3. The word *vafer* seems to appear in Latin only as an adjective. But the substantive *vafro* did
appear in Italian in Tasso's lifetime. Louise George Clubb has drawn my attention to Decio
Grisignano, *Il vafro: commedia. Rappresentata in Salerno con generale applauso* (Venice: Giacomo
Vincenci, 1585). I have not yet had access to the text.

4. Homer, *Iliad*, book 10 entire, esp. ll. 299–464. Even more than Homer's Dolon, Trissino's

Tasso's challenge to Homer is itself tricky. Although Vafrino is almost magically adept at espionage, Dolon was a *failed* spy who never penetrated the Greek camp. Odysseus, who was engaged on a symmetrically identical mission for the Greek side, immediately detected Dolon, captured him, tricked him into revealing the layout of the Trojan encampment by implicitly promising to release him, and then allowed Diomedes to kill him. As Jenny Strauss Clay observes, Dolon's allegorical name foregrounds his role as foil to Odysseus: "It is ironically appropriate that Odysseus, the man of *doloi* par excellence, should be pitted against an opponent named Dolon. . . . In short, the trickster, Dolon, is outtricked." This irony was not lost on Euripides, or whoever rewrote the *Doloneia* in the tragedy *Rhesus*.[5] Subsequent plot developments in the *Liberata* confirm Vafrino's enactment of Odyssean cunning rather than the failed *doloi* of Dolon. Thanks to Vafrino's espionage, the Egyptian Ormondo, charged with infiltrating the Christian army and assassinating Goffredo, is recognized and killed before he can act.[6]

The notion that Odysseus is the consummate *dolon* of the *Doloneia* was ratified already in the *Odyssey*. "I am Odysseus son of Laertes, known before all men / for the study of crafty designs, and my fame goes up to the heavens."[7] Virgil also identified Odysseus with *dolus* or fraudulent cunning, in Laocoön's famous warning about Greeks bearing gifts, and Ovid and other Latin authors followed suit.[8] Tasso's choice of the name Vafrino to designate an epigone of Odysseus is singularly appropriate,

---

Doletto is a thoroughly negative personage (bk. 22). See 3.119ff. in the edition of London, 1779, esp. 3.125: "Doletto, or ti bisogna oprar l'ingegno" ("Doletto, now you must use your wits"). Editors of Tasso also like to compare Vafrino to Boiardo's trickster Brunello, but this personage differs in function and "character" (or ethical tone) both from Vafrino and from Dolon (Caretti, quoting Ferrari, at GL 18.57.3; Guglielminetti [533] demurs).

5. Clay 117; see the irony in *Rhesus* where Hector exclaims, "You are well named, my crafty Dolon" (Euripedes 4.14).

6. GL 19.62–65, 86–88; 20.44–46.

7. *Odyssey* 9.19–20; see Segal 131–32; Pucci 185–87.

8. "[U]lla putatis dona carere dolis Danaum? Sic notus Ulixes?" (*Æneid* 2.43–44); cf. *Metamorphoses* 13.1–398.

for sixteenth-century humanists made *vafer* Odysseus's characteristic epithet: Ravisius Textor called him *callidus et vafer*, Robert Estienne *vafer consilio*, Josse Bade *Graecorum omnium vaferrimus*, and Erasmus *callidus, astutus, et vafer*.[9] When Tasso wrote *Gerusalemme conquistata*, he tacitly admitted the relation between his trickster and the Homeric Odysseus by turning Vafrino's exploits into a slavish imitation of the *Doloneia*, complete with a hapless Dolon-figure for Vafrino to kill during his mission.[10]

II. Textor

Homer amplifies the defeat of Dolon by making him a shameless boaster. Vafrino courts disaster by inflating Dolon's vaunts, and declaring that he will discover the most intimate thoughts of the enemy leader. Yet despite the hyperbole, Vafrino succeeds fully, and learns every detail of the enemy plan. Tasso's Homeric trickster lore thus signals the reader that, like the providential carrier-pigeon, Vafrino bears knowledge more characteristic of a god or an author than of an ordinary character or *actant*. Indeed, Fredi Chiappelli observed that Vafrino lays claim to insight in phraseology that recalls God's omniscient glance into the souls of the crusaders:

> "Quanta e qual sia quell'oste, e ciò che pensi
> il duce loro, a voi ridir prometto:
> vantomi in lui *scoprir gli intimi sensi*
> e i secreti pensier trargli del petto."[11]

("I promise to tell you how many is that host, and of what quality, and what their captain is thinking; I make it my boast to *discover his inmost feelings* and to extract from his breast his secret thoughts.")

Vafrino's explicit claim to quasi-authorial omniscience and the Homeric intertext of his role are reminiscent of Odysseus's prowess as storyteller,

---

9. Defaux ch. 3, esp. pp. 59, 60, 66, 67, 132, 159 n. 20, 162 n. 44, 162–63 n. 46.

10. *Gerusalemme conquistata* 16.67–87 (henceforth GC).

11. GL 18.59.1–4; emphasis added. See Chiappelli's note, p. 740.

including his friendly rivalry with Alkinoös's bard Demodokos. But Tasso will reinforce the metaliterary aspect of Vafrino's exploits by a continual series of references to cloth, clothing, and weaving. These references prepare for the intricate "tissue" of puns and other allusions to the etymological identity of texts and textiles that Tasso weaves when, with the help of Erminia, Vafrino learns the full extent of the Egyptian plans. Textile allusions begin the moment Vafrino is introduced, with a play on *tendere*:

> Venne colui, chiamato; e poi ch'*intese*
> ciò che Goffredo e 'l suo signor desia,
> alzò ridendo il volto ed intraprese
> la cura e disse: —Or mi pongo in via.
> Tosto sarò dove quel campo *tese*
> le *tende* avrà, non conosciuta spia.
>
> (GL 18.58.1–6; emphasis added)

(He came when summoned; and when he *understood* what Godfrey and his master wanted, he lifted up his countenance, smiling, and undertook the charge, and said: "Already I am on my way. Soon I shall be where that camp will have *spread* its *tents*, a spy unrecognized.")

Vafrino's smile is perhaps our signal to enjoy the exhilarating convergence of plot, intertext, and metaliterary allusion.

The textile references intensify and become explicitly metaliterary at the moment Vafrino begins to make good his boast of stealing the Egyptian general's inmost thoughts:

> Di qua di là sollecito s'aggira
> per le vie, per le piazze e per le *tende.*
> I guerrier, i destrier, l'arme rimira,
> l'arti e gli ordini osserva e i nomi apprende.
> Né di ciò pago, a maggior cose aspira:
> spia gli occulti disegni e parte *intende.*
> Tanto s'*avolge,* e così destro e piano,
> ch'adito s'apre al padiglion soprano.

Vede, mirando qui, sdruscita *tela*,
ond'ha varco la voce, onde si scerne,
che là proprio risponde ove son de la
stanza regal le ritirate interne,
sì che i secreti del signor mal cela
ad uom ch'ascolti da le parti esterne.
Vafrin vi guata e par ch'ad altro *intenda*,
come sia cura sua conciar la *tenda*.   (GL 19.60–61)

Hither and thither he wanders observantly among the streets, the parade grounds and the *tents*. He watches the soldiers, the horses, the weaponry, observes their disciplines and formations, and learns the names of things. Not satisfied with that, he aspires to greater things: he spies out their hidden designs and partially [*understands*] them. He so *insinuates* himself, and is so dexterous and smooth, that an entrance is opened to the chief pavilion.

Looking about him here, he sees a torn *canvas* from whence a voice is issuing by which he can make out that right there are the inner retreats of the royal chamber, so that the master's secrets are ill concealed from a man who might be listening from the outside. Vafrine pries about there, and appears to be *intent* on something else, as if it were his business to mend the *tent*.

Tasso evokes a figurative sense of the term *tela* (fabric), which in his time related weaving to plots and conspiracies.[12] Vafrino's voyeuristic gesture complements and glosses the written message borne by the carrier pigeon, but his peering and listening through the rift in a textile are already explicitly textual and authorial, as the lexical recalls of his initial boast imply. He is an inscribed poet figure whose metaliterary function is precisely to "conciar la tenda," to discover and eliminate those gaps in *tessitura* that threaten the desired outcome of Tasso's *testo*.[13]

12. E.g., Bruno 142: "ordir qualche tela verso di Bonifacio" ("to weave some web to catch Bonifacio"). See also Tommaseo/Bellini 6:50.

13. In *Discorsi del poema eroico* (Scritti 222), Tasso refers to the *favola* or plot as *testura*. For analogous uses of *tessere* and its derivatives, see Scritti 6, 28, 186, 187, 212, 222, 226, 228. See also

Like the letter-bearing bird, he is a providential figure whose actions are determined by authorial foresight into plot, rather than by stylistic embellishment or chance. The phrase "conciare la tenda" actually echoes the so-called *lettere poetiche* Tasso wrote to his committee of revisors: there, *conciare* and its derivatives are his preferred terminology for emendations of all sorts made to the text of his poem.[14]

III. Architect

Vafrino represents the point where all the valences of trickery converge with all the valences of authorship. He is an inscribed surrogate author or "stage manager," whose function is to ensure the desirable unfolding of the plot. Northrop Frye named this function *architectus*, recalling the tricky slave in Plautus who functions as a master builder of deceit or *architecton doli*.[15] The Egyptian plot to assassinate Goffredo will be carried out by means of textile disguise, with counterfeit uniforms and insignia that should render the assassins indistinguishable from Goffredo's own guard; thus, Vafrino's consummate, author-like deceitfulness provides the only solution to the breakdown of plot expectations threatened by the disruption of heraldic signs.

The metaliterary character of Vafrino's role is further inscribed as parody, both intertextually, in his emulation of Odysseus, and intratextually as well, when he mimics the coarse rivalry of Armida's suitors Tisaferno and Adrasto (GL 19.67ff.). The first requirement of both parody and espionage is self-effacement, an extreme mobility or instability of identity. Vafrino's task is all the easier since Tasso postulates no stable,

---

tessuto, tessere, tessitura, testura, tela, tramare, ordire, intreccio, intrecciare, in Tommaseo/Bellini, as likewise, the pair *intrico/intrigo (intricare/intrigare),* where the former is to be construed literally, and the latter figuratively.

14. See especially the noun *conciere* (e.g., Tasso, *Lettere* 1.78).

15. On the *dolon* as *architectus* in comedy, see Frye 173, 174, 197. Plautus's Palaestrio in *Miles Gloriosus* is referred to as *architectus* by another servant (246). See also Salingar 118. The best treatment of tricksters in classical and Renaissance comedy is Salingar, chs. 3–5 (pp. 76–242). Also of interest is Beecher.

independent identity for him, and recounts nothing about him except his service to Tancredi. Like Odysseus, Vafrino is a "Nobody" because he can be anybody, "an Egyptian from Memphis or a Phoenician from Tyre" (GL 18.60). Odysseus's claim to be No-Man is a pun (outis/mêtis) that "associates the abandonment of heroic identity with the guile" or mêtis, a precondition of dolos, that characterizes Odysseus.[16] If Vafrino the arch-parodist is an avatar of Odysseus, Odysseus's own ability to change radically is thematically guaranteed in the Odyssey by the figure of Proteus. Homer refers to Proteus's shape-changing skill as "tricky," and this trickiness is emblematic of those qualities the Odyssey valorizes, and which Odysseus most fully enacts by withholding his identity and by continually assuming new ones.[17] By assimilating him to Odysseus, Tasso makes Vafrino fulfill the Protean freedom from properties and propriety that the elder Pico attributes to the ideal man (Pico 106).

Vafrino's Odyssean changeability enhances his air of a poet: in the Odyssey (11.363–66) and in Plato's Republic the reprehensible poet possesses all the mimetic powers of the consummate trickster. The "bad" Platonic poet is a virtuoso mime, a trickster who can imitate anything and anyone because he displays (and perhaps has) no essence or identity of his own.[18] As actor or mime, the trickster further emphasizes the theatricality or contrivedness of the metaliterary dimension he oversees. In these roles as poet and actor, the trickster represents the author as archetype of the magician, a master of illusion and, possibly, of reality itself; one thinks of Bruno and Buffalmacco in the Decameron, of the fictionalized Brunelleschi (a literal architect) in the Novella del Grasso legnaiuolo. Norman O. Brown traced these implications to the Homeric world, showing that "the word [dolos], which in the classical period

---

16. Odyssey 9.366–67, 401–14. See Segal 138; Pucci 183n.; Winkler 144–45.

17. Brown 19. See also Salingar 94 (on shape-changing), 112 (trickster as shape-changer and "go-between in several senses"). Pucci remarks (86–87) that disguise is Odysseus, since he is always in it.

18. GL 18.57.2–60.8; Stephens, "Mimesis" 1984: 239; Segal 138; Salingar 103 (on Plato and mimesis as magic), 104 ("The trickster-hero is a projection of the 'ingenious' poet").

meant trickery, in archaic Greek carries implications of magic."[19] Certainly there is a shamanistic dimension to the *Doloneia*, where the animal-skin costumes of the actors bestow or symbolize paranormal and non-human attributes (Clay 118). Thus it is fully appropriate for Vafrino to ride a horse reminiscent of Rabicano, the magical steed who, in Boiardo and Ariosto, was so swift that he left no footprints in the sand.[20]

IV. Thief

An intertextual reading of Vafrino invites further conclusions about Tasso's reading and appropriation of Homer, his representation of authorship, and thence about intentionality within the *Liberata*.[21] If Tasso's trickster behaves like an author, the author himself performs *doloi*—especially thefts—worthy of Odysseus himself. Like Odysseus or a comedic tricky slave, Tasso becomes a consummate *bricoleur*, constructing his plots (storylines and conspiracies) from materials "found" and appropriated.

Yet the homologies traced between Vafrino and his author are themselves deceptive so long as they do not account for the presence of Erminia. When the narrating voice abandoned Erminia in canto 7, she was an apprentice poet, inscribing her woes on a forest of trees. Though she was locked in a Petrarchan circuit of celebratory self-pity at that time, she returns in canto 19 as a paradigm of authority and authoriality.[22] She sees through the disguise of Vafrino, recognizes him, and barters the information he needs in exchange for another chance to attract Tancredi's notice. Henceforth, Vafrino's mastery and control of Erminia is only ap-

---

19. Brown 18–19. The connection is not impressionistic, according to Brown, who notes, "The words connoting magical action in the classical period are derived from roots whose original meaning is just as close to the notion of trickery as it is to that of magic" (18).

20. GL 18.60.7–8; *Orlando furioso* 15.40 entire and passim.

21. On Tasso and Homer, see Stephens, "Reading Tasso."

22. Migiel notes (67) that Erminia is the only character in GL who "entrusts his or her story to the written word."

parent, and his occultation of her vital contribution to his intelligence gathering is perhaps only an extension of the secrecy she demands as she attends privately to Tancredi.[23] There is a strong sense in which Erminia hijacks Vafrino, for she both defeats him in his role as Odyssean military spy, and then restores that role. To do this, she recasts him as a parodic Odysseus, a trickster valet straight out of Renaissance *commedia erudita*.

Because he is Odyssean and Protean, Vafrino is a compulsive mimic, and Erminia exploits his one moment of excess. When his attempts to learn the crucial details of the Egyptian assassination plot have been momentarily thwarted, his response is hypermimetic: hoping to learn something from the *donzelle* surrounding Armida, he parodies, "quasi per gioco" ("as if in jest") the fanfaronades of Adrasto and Tisaferno: "Anch'io / vorrei d'alcuna bella esser campione" ("I too would like to be the champion of some beauty," GL 19.78). In so doing, he slides into a form of self-parody, but also, like a stage valet in Renaissance comedy, he becomes a parodic Odysseus. The fact that Vafrino's actions have previously retraced those of *dolios Odysseus* is already a prime qualification for comedic role-play, since tricky slaves in ancient comedy prided themselves on being *dolosi* and often compared themselves explicitly to "wily Odysseus." [24] Moreover, it was common in Tasso's time to identify the *Odyssey* as the archetype of comedic plot, as Erasmus did in his adage *Ilias malorum:* "the learned opine that the plots of tragedies were taken from the *Iliad*, just as those of comedies were taken from the *Odyssey*." [25] The burlesque of noble courtship is a characteristic routine of the

---

23. GL 19.119–27, esp. 119.3–4 ("Vafrino a la donzella, e non discoto [da Tancredi], / ritrova albergo assai chiuso e secreto"; "Vafrine finds for the lady—and not far off—a shelter close [to Tancredi] and secret"). Cf. Migiel 70.

24. Salingar 117, 119. Cf. Palaestrio in *Miles Gloriosus* 2.2.197–98: "dum consulo / quid agam, quem dolum doloso contra conservo parem" (Plautus 140).

25. "[I]n Iliade Homerica nullum mali genus non recensetur. Unde ex hac docti putant Tragoediarum argumenta fuisse sumpta, sicut ex Odyssea Comoediarum" (quoted by De- faux 62–63). The persistent figure of the crafty servant makes my opposition of comedy and tragedy preferable in this context to the opposition between epic and romance familiar in scholarship on the *Liberata*.

comedic aspiring Odysseus. When Vafrino mimics Tisaferno and Adrasto's courtship of Armida, he enacts a stock scenario much like that in Ariosto's *Lena*, where the *vafro* Corbolo makes obscene advances to the eponymous procuress while mediating his master's courtship of the timid heroine. Likewise, in *Intrichi d'amore*, the one comedy attributed to Tasso, the valet Magagna's lewd engagement to the procuress Bianchetta parodically consummates a vertiginous outbreak of decorous betrothals that has engulfed all but two of the nobler characters. As parodist and *eiron*, the comedic *vafro* performs a fundamentally metaliterary function, because hypermimesis is a form of infinite regression: Ariosto's Corbolo openly compares himself to the *servi callidi* of Roman comedy, but it was already a commonplace for those same Roman stage servants to compare themselves to stage servants.[26]

Vafrino's moment of mimetic excess destroys his invisibility by giving him a stereotypical theatricality and casting him in a generically recognizable role. The comedic convention is troped as character or personality when Vafrino lowers his guard and smiles a second time, and the gesture reveals his identity to Erminia.[27] Erminia is a connoisseur

---

26. E.g., Plautus 142.

27. Both Ferrari (243) and Guglielminetti (569) note that Erminia's recognition of Vafrino's telltale *atto nativo* (GL 19.79) recalls Saladino's recognition of Messer Torello in *Decameron* 10.9.53. The echo seems plausible: Branca says of Torello's smile that it is a "a means of recognition [*agnizione*] of which there is no trace in Boccaccio's antecedents or in the medieval and early modern short story [la *novellistica*] in general" (*Decameron* 1218 n.). Guglielminetti concludes that this resemblance corroborates his contention (533) that Vafrino "has nothing to do with Homer's Dolon," and is "not an epic product but, so to speak, of a Boccaccian alloy." Guglielminetti is apparently referring to Boccaccian trickster figures like Maso del Saggio, Bruno, and Buffalmacco (569). Neither Guglielminetti nor Branca appears to have noticed the strong parallels between the novella of Messer Torello and the *Odyssey*: recognitions, the importance of hospitality, the suitors, the wife's determined fidelity, the husband's surprise last-minute return, and so on. Saladin serves the same role for Torello as Alkinoös did for Odysseus, while a magical flying bed not only works like the Phaeacian ship that returned the sleeping Odysseus to Ithaka, but also recalls the importance of Odysseus's marriage-bed. Above all, this is an *Odyssey* with a happy ending for all its characters: no one dies and the would-be second husband renounces his claim on "Penelope." Whether Boc-

of disguise and convention, and this talent makes her the consummate author surrogate of the *Liberata*. She steals the scene from Vafrino by appropriating the terms he has offered, not to her, but to another *donzella* (GL 19.77–79), and claiming him as her champion. But no sooner has she hijacked Vafrino's comedic scene than she replaces him firmly within his more heroic Odyssean role. In so doing, she appropriates a still more powerful role for herself, a role for which the poem has long prepared her. When she declares "Riconosciuto / ho te, Vafrin: e tu me conoscer déi" ("I have recognized you, Vafrine; you ought to know me," GL 19.80), she reenacts the exploit of the only Homeric character who ever claimed to have penetrated Odysseus's disguises. In book 4 of the *Odyssey*, Helen recounts how Odysseus infiltrated Troy shortly before its fall:

He flagellated himself with degrading strokes, then threw on
a worthless sheet about his shoulders. He looked like a servant.
So he crept into the wide-wayed city of the men he was fighting,
disguising himself in the likeness of somebody else, a beggar,
one who was unlike himself
                                          . . . and they all
were taken in. I alone recognized him even in this form,
and I questioned him.   (*Odyssey* 4.243–51)

In fact, Erminia outdoes her Homeric model. Helen confessed that Odysseus "in his craftiness eluded me" and succeeded at his mission: she relates that "after striking many Trojans down with the thin bronze / edge, he went back to the Argives and brought back much information." [28]

The more thoroughly Vafrino retreats into his Odyssean role, the more completely Erminia defeats him. He vainly attempts Odysseus's most

caccio could have intended or Tasso consciously recognized the Odyssean themes in Messer Torello's tale is beside the point: the fact is that Boccaccio's novella is narratologically *Odysseyesque*, rather than being of a typically Boccaccian "alloy."

28. *Odyssey* 4.257–58; Helen claims that she had to swear not to reveal Odysseus's identity until he was safely returned to the Achaean camp in order to induce him to reveal "all the purpose of the Achaians" (4.253–56).

characteristic trick, by telling Erminia the sort of fictional autobiography that Homeric scholars call a Cretan tale (e.g., Clay 124–26). Yet Erminia wins the bluffing match and constrains Vafrino to take her with him. Henceforth Vafrino must play a double role: his price for displaying Odyssean military cunning is to serve Erminia as a comedic tricky valet, mediating the erotic reunion of a feckless hero and a beautiful *innamorata*. By rewriting Vafrino's role as comedy, Erminia quite literally steals the show. In fact, she steals Vafrino himself: if not from the epic plot, then from his exclusive allegiance to epic roles and to Tancredi. She reveals that Vafrino was once her loyal confidant; even now he owes himself her *fedele*, and henceforth, he is as much her valet as Tancredi's squire (GL 19.96, 90). Her interactions with Vafrino lock the two of them and Tancredi into something resembling what Louise George Clubb (6–14) calls a theatergram, a stereotyped configuration of actantial roles and vectors of plot.

V. *Vafra*

In the space between Vafrino's two smiles, Tasso's poem modulates from the revelation of God's providence, with all its epic and tragic implications, to comedy, the art form that celebrates purely human providence in all its gritty amorality. Erminia's shift from fecklessness to enterprise resembles nothing so much as the career of certain heroines in Renaissance comedy, for all of whom Lelia of Gl'*ingannati* may stand as archetype. Lelia disguises herself as a boy and becomes her beloved's valet, in order to maximize her control over the plotting—as both storyline and conspiracy—of her own career as *innamorata*. From this condensation of two originally separate roles emerges a new character stereotype of the *vafra*, who mediates her own love affairs under an assumed male identity. Erminia declares herself incapable of fraud (GL 19.89), but this declaration only applies to her epic role as the enslaved seamstress forced to create the disguises of Goffredo's would-be assassins. In fact, she has long been a *vafra* (however incompetent) in love. She described her first attempt to rejoin Tancredi (while disguised as Clorinda the male-impersonator) as an "innocent fraud" inspired by Love and overseen by Fortune, and this conjunction of forces is the arch-paradigm of Renaissance comedy.[29] Once Erminia appropriates Vafrino, she is able to repudiate her role as incompetent *vafra* (*errante ancella*, wandering maiden, GL 19.101), while maintaining its manipulative advantages.

This play with comedic stereotypes, far more than characterological considerations, stimulates those readers who have debated the *vexata quaestio* whether Tancredi will ever repay Erminia's love.[30] Renaissance comedy is notably indifferent to characterological individuation, and so to the extent that Erminia's story follows theatrical plot paradigms, one might plausibly forecast her eventual success. Indeed, if Erminia's future with Tancredi can be discussed at all, it is only in terms of such paradigms, not in terms of characterization. One might equally well forecast Erminia's success by reading Tancredi from the standpoint of his place in the situations that Erminia and Vafrino construct. To return to the example of Gl'ingannati, Lelia's perseverance does not so much inspire love in her beloved as provoke an almost rational conversion. From the perspective of Renaissance comedy, one could predict a similar conversion on Tancredi's part. Reading backward in light of comedic conventions, one might even interpret Vafrino as a projection or emanation of Tancredi, since Tancredi sends him on the mission that "fortuitously" recovers Erminia. Leo Salingar remarks that the *vafro* of Roman New Comedy "is no more than an instrument. He is set to solve a problem for someone else."[31] Hence, like Tancredi's earlier pursuit of Erminia when she was disguised in the armor of Clorinda,

---

29. GL 19.89 and 6.88. Note the matching rhyme schemes (*modo/frodo* and *modi/frodi*, respectively). "[T]he trickster in New Comedy is nearly always lucky. . . . [H]e depends upon Fortune for his complete success as a rule. . . . But on the other hand, the wheel never completes its turn in New Comedy without the help of a deceiver, whether an impudent slave or a free citizen who keeps something of the buffoon or trickster in him" (Salingar 157).

30. See Corrigan, Murtaugh, Migiel.

31. Salingar 107; Frye concurs (197): "The helpful fairy, the grateful dead man, the wonderful servant who has just the qualities the hero needs in a crisis, are all folktale commonplaces. They are romantic intensifications of the comic tricky slave, the author's *architectus*."

his volunteering of Vafrino's services in the epic cause could be read tendentiously as Tancredi's unconscious search for Erminia. Vafrino, whose name reveals him as an antonomasia, personifies just the craftiness and heat that the inert, melancholy Tancredi lacks.[32] At the same time, Vafrino's mission is the symmetrically reversed, successful repetition of Erminia's earlier attempt at reunion: whereas she knowingly sent her own squire to infiltrate the Christian camp and find Tancredi,[33] the latter unwittingly sends Vafrino to infiltrate the camp where Erminia resides. At any rate, Erminia's unmasking and appropriation of Vafrino, her first appearance in the poem since the contretemps precipitated by her own unsuccessful disguise, gives her a control over Tancredi that succeeds precisely—and only—to the extent that it resembles comedic paradigms of erotic reunion.

Thus, the question of Erminia's "destiny" is best posed in terms of a tension between plot conventions or paradigms and mimetic effects or characterization. The expectations of a "happy ending" provoked by intradiegetic symmetries and the typically comedic patterns of love intrigue counterpose the sheer amount of space and speech devoted to Tancredi's obsession with Clorinda. Other typically theatrical elements, like the doubling of Erminia and Clorinda, or the cryptosexual rivalry of Tancredi and Argante, could be invoked on the side of a "happy ending," yet without resolving the tension. No recourse to character psychology or Tasso's declared intentions for the poem can decide the question either way.[34]

---

32. Even Callimaco Guadagni of Machiavelli's *Mandragola*, one of the craftiest of *giovani* in *commedia erudita*, is beset by melancholy and depends on the parasite Ligurio to overcome it.

33. GL 6.98–100. This nameless personage otherwise has exactly the same minimal attributes as Vafrino; he is a squire (a term that would be inappropriate, except for the fact that Erminia is momentarily in armor) and faithful: *un suo fedel scudiero; lo scudiero fedel; "o mio fedele"; quel leale* (GL 90.4; 91.1; 99.1; 100.7).

34. Corrigan maintained that evidence internal to the *Liberata* demonstrated Erminia would ultimately marry Tancredi. Attempting to read the Erminia subplot against a theory of romance, Murtaugh reached the same conclusion. Migiel (64) correctly warns that, as a text, "[t]he poem in no way sanctions a happy end for Erminia."

VI. Architecta

What remains after such debate is the sheer textuality of Erminia's return to prominence. In theatrical comedy, the *doloi* or tricks of the crafty servant figure the *doloi* of the author's solutions to a narrative impasse. Indeed, Northrop Frye (173-74) proposed the theatrical crafty servant as the quintessential *architectus* or surrogate author. But while Vafrino begins his career as the *architectus* of "Tasso," the implicit author or narrating voice of an epic poem, within the text he is subordinated to the unmistakably authorial powers of Erminia. She, too, is an *architecta*, but it is not at all clear that she is "Tasso's" *architecta*. Although "the author" exploits her desire for erotic reunion in order to advance the epic plot, it is Erminia who transforms Vafrino into a comedic go-between. Despite her appearance of meekness and timidity, it is Erminia's resistance that makes her interesting to readers, and some of that resistance is directed at "Tasso," her author.

Erminia's ambivalent relation to authorship is inherent in the thoroughness with which she imitates Helen of Troy. In terms of overt ideologies, both Helen and Erminia are the consummate outsiders; as character, each is an "enemy" wherever she goes, having chosen an allegiance to which she was not born. Indeed, Erminia's name seems to hint at her solitude and isolation.[35] But this otherness and isolation is precisely the sign of the author, and both Helen and Erminia rival their authors at a very basic textual level. While her emulation of Helen in the unmasking of Vafrino has escaped notice, many critics have recognized that the poem introduces her through an imitation of Helen's *teichoskopia*, the scene in book 3 of the *Iliad* where Helen stands on the walls of Troy and identifies the leaders of the Achaean army for Priam.[36] In each heroine's

35. Cf. *ermo, eremo, eremita*, and GL 19.98: "pur in parte fuggimmi *erma* e lontana; / e colà vissi in *solitaria cella*, / cittadina de' boschi e pastorella" ("but I fled to a distant and lonely region and there lived in *solitary* cell, a shepherdess and citizen of the woods").

36. *Iliad* 3; GL 6. "[T]he scene that became known as the *teichoskopia*, the viewing from the wall, in which Helen for the first time identifies the chief Achaian leaders for the benefit of Priam (this after nine years of conflict!)" (Else 168). Tasso of course corrects this famous

teichoskopia, her voice alternates with that of the poet in such a fashion that by instructing her adoptive king she prefigures—rather than repeating—the author's instruction of his reader or listener.[37]

In both cases, the heroine assumes authorial powers by taking over the function of herald, the inscribed connoisseur of heroic identity and prowess. As Norman O. Brown observes, the herald was "the ceremonial expert in the rituals that center around the royal palace," and hence, aside from a bard or other singer, the inscribed figure most available to stand in for the Homeric poet. As much as any poet, the archaic herald depended upon his exact knowledge of the identities and prerogatives of warriors in order to maintain ceremonial order.[38] Because he was *porte-parole* and mediator of differences, the archaic herald was also the archetypal trickster figure, as Odysseus demonstrates. In *Iliad* 2 he appropriates the role of herald and functions as both trickster (intradiegetically, "in the story") and *architectus* (at the metaliterary level). He prevents the Achaeans' desertion by taking Agamemnon's scepter (the herald's badge of office), marshaling the army back to assembly, and defeating the eloquent demagogue Thersites. Dolon, the eponymous victim of Odysseus's craftiness in the *Iliad*, is also introduced as the only son of a herald.[39] Helen's role as inscribed poet in *Iliad* 3 depends on the the-

---

Homeric gaffe by having Erminia's *teichoskopia* take place as the Christians approach Jerusalem for the first time.

37. The best treatment of Erminia's interaction with the narrator is in Martinelli 43–49, esp. 48: "Erminia is at once spectator and actor, author and personage, and this referential duplicity finds correspondance on the stylistic level in the ambiguities of her discourse."

38. Brown 26–32. Quotation from p. 27. Curiously, Brown does not examine the figures of Odysseus or Helen at all as heralds or tricksters.

39. On Odysseus as herald, see *Iliad* 2.169–277; 9.158–59, 299, 312–13. When Odysseus takes Agamemnon's scepter, he first throws aside his cloak, "which was caught up / by Eurybates the herald of Ithaka who followed him" (2.183–84). Athena, who delegates this heraldic duty to Odysseus, then stands beside him "in the likeness of a herald" once he completes it (2.280). Thersites rivals Odysseus with his "endless speech," and Odysseus calls him "fluent orator" (2.212, 246). On Dolon, *Iliad* 10.314–17, esp. 314–15: "But there was one among the Trojans, Dolon, Eumedes' / son, the sacred herald's. . . ."

matic continuum bard/herald/trickster even more than does Odysseus's role in the previous book of the poem, a feat that jibes with her status as the one Homeric character capable of besting Odysseus's trickiness.[40] Erminia's imitation of that feat leads to a far more explicit victory over Vafrino, Tasso's anointed *architectus*, than Helen achieved over Odysseus.

VII. Textrix

Like Vafrino, Erminia demonstrates her relation to authority and authorship through her manipulation of textiles. Although Tasso's allusive exploration of textile textuality begins when Vafrino first boasts of his powers, the allusions do not become explicit until Erminia reveals the true extent of the Egyptian conspiracy, when she "unfolds a tissue of deceit."

> . . . ei le disse: —Or di' come a la vita
> del pio Goffredo altri l'insidie *tende*. —
> Allor colei [Erminia] de la congiura *ordita*
> l'iniqua *tela* a lui [Vafrino] *dispiega e stende*.[41]

(He said to her: "Now tell how this man is *spreading* his [snares] for the life of worthy Godfrey." Then she *unfolds* and *ravels out* for him the wicked *web* of the *planned* conspiracy.)

The renewed pun on *tela* (textile and conspiracy) finally ratifies the textuality of Vafrino's exploits—but only by subordinating him to Erminia,

40. In *Odyssey* 4.265–89 Menelaus recounts how Helen almost defeated Odysseus's stratagem of the Trojan horse. In her husband's anecdote, Helen figures as a trickster-ventriloquist, counterfeiting the voices of Achaean wives in order to lure out their husbands. Whereas she had compared herself favorably with Odysseus in her own anecdote, Menelaus compares Odysseus favorably to *her*, hinting at her equality or possible superiority. See further in Winkler, 140–41.

41. GL 19.86.3–6. As the italics indicate, *tendere* (*agguati, insidie, trappole*) (to set ambushes, snares, traps) forms part of the same complex of associations that embraces *tessere* and *tramare*.

who guards her most important revelations until he has removed her from the Egyptian camp.

Erminia is Tasso's most explicit poet figure, as well as his most powerful, because she so thoroughly imitates Helen. Helen is Homer's archweaver, and this skill makes her perhaps the consummate poet figure among all Homeric mortals: she is introduced in the *Iliad* as weaver and narrator even before she speaks as herald. When Iris arrives to summon her to the ramparts for her *teichoskopia*, Helen is already weaving a tapestry depicting the Trojan War, and exploiting her privileged information to memorialize the struggle for possession of herself (*Iliad* 3.121–28). Her knowledge of the besieging troops is thus both authoritative and *authorial*. When Tasso rewrote canto 3 of the *Liberata* as canto 7 of the *Conquistata*, he tacitly admitted how closely Erminia imitates the authorial functions Helen possesses in *Iliad* 3. When Erminia (now recast as "Nicea") is called to the ramparts,

> . . . la trovâr che doppia e larga tela
> d'aureo e serico stame ella tessea.
> Subito a quel chiamar si veste e vela,
> qual ninfa in vista, o qual terrena dèa,
> lasciando l'opre in cui le guerre antiche
> e de' turchi ha conteste aspre fatiche.
> (GC 7.36.3–8)

(They found her weaving a double and wide web of gold and silken threads. At their call she dresses and veils herself quickly, looking like some nymph or terrestrial goddess; and she leaves the works in which she has interwoven the ancient wars with the harsh travails of the Turks.)

Tasso clinches the dependence of Erminia/Nicea on Helen in the "contextual" (*con-tessere*) parallel between "ancient wars" and those of the modern Turks. Nicea's project is "double" because it is intertextual: she is weaving Helen's story as well as her own.[42] The *Conquistata*'s descent

---

42. Cf. *Iliad* 3.125–28: "[Iris] came on Helen in the chamber; she was weaving a great web, / a red folding robe, and working into it the numerous struggles / of Trojans, breakers of

into slavishness in this passage indicates just how thoroughly Erminia already imitated Helen as arch-*architecta* and arch-*textrix* in the *Liberata*.[43] Moreover, the *Conquistata* inscribes and prefigures its own intertextuality in a textile "pre-text" that mimics Helen's woven narrative of the Trojan War. A wondrous tent, woven by a "maestro accorto" ("skillful master") ekphrastically relates the *antefatti* of the tale that Tasso's narrator will recount.[44] Tasso's emphasis on male authorship here is highly problematic: because he attributes a Helenesque textile narrative to a male *maestro*, Helen's residual presence constantly menaces the integrity of Tasso's authorial voice.

This female threat is substantial. Within the Homeric paradigm to which Tasso adheres, women are weavers, and this skill is related to their one means of self-defense, verbal deviousness or *dolos*.[45] But it also figures their status as artists, as mistresses (or masters!) of *techné*. In Homer, even Penelope (the more obvious characterological prototype of Erminia) is tricky, and expresses her trickiness precisely through her artistic prowess, by weaving and unweaving the supposed shroud of her father-in-law. As feminist critics point out, Homer's Penelope is not the passive prize of patriarchal cliché. She takes an active role in reconstituting her marriage, and the shroud of Laertes, the putative, but absent and impotent master of her household, figures her tenuous but tenacious control over that "unraveling" household. As Penelope tells the disguised Odysseus, "These men try to hasten the marriage. I weave

---

horses, and bronze-armoured Achaians, / struggles that they endured for her sake at the hands of the war-god."

43. Remember that Homeric trickiness also catalyzes another descent into slavishness in the *Conquistata*, the addition of Vafrino's Dolon-like victim.

44. GC 2.92–3.52. The fact that Erminia imitates Helen's "text" while the Tassian narrative explicitly traces itself to a "source" woven by a male *textor* exemplifies the dynamic complained of by Joplin.

45. Segal 134. Conversely, Clorinda's epic ethos, plain speaking, and male-gendered identity figure her repudiation of "Arachne's works." See GL 2.39.1–4, where "ingegni femminili" ("feminine . . . [arts]") recall the Greek *techné*, which encompasses weaving, magic, and trickery (Brown 22). Note also that Hercules among the "meonie ancelle" ("Maeonian serving maids," GL 16.3) holds the emblems of "Arachne's works." See further in Miller.

my own wiles."[46] And indeed she was always "tricky" and prized on account of it—the *Odyssey* implies that her trickiness makes her worthy of Odysseus, and her personal manservant, whom she brought from her father's home to Odysseus's, is allegorically named Dolios.[47]

Helen's weaving is even more intimately "enmeshed" with her story than Penelope's. The conventionally feminine and inherently tricky or technical act of weaving empowers Helen to appropriate the male-gendered function of herald during her *teichoskopia* or view from the walls of Troy, thus prefiguring and rivaling the Homeric narrator. All these roles Helen bequeathes to Erminia. Erminia's first task in Tasso's poem is mimicking Helen's appropriation of heraldic and bardic knowledge. As in the *Iliad*, this use of the displaced female ostensibly serves the epic plot by describing the heroes of "our side" as they appear to the enemy. Yet Erminia's task as herald is even more showily textual than Helen's; in order to identify the armored Christian knights for Aladino and the reader, she must decode their heraldic signs to recall their physical characteristics (GL 3.17.7–8, 37.5ff., 58.5ff.). The more emphatic textuality of Erminia's heraldic moment presages her trickier and more rebellious

---

46. "Penelope is a master-weaver, and weaving is an appropriate image for the work of the epic poet [of the *Odyssey*,] who specializes not in recitals of heroic battle but the plotting and counter-plotting of a household in conflict. The weaving in question is not just any old dry goods but specifically tricky and clever designing of interdependent tensions, the warp and woof of crossed purposes and inimical motives. Athena helps Odysseus 'weave a *mêtis*,' a cunning plan to restore himself to his house (13.386), and when he feels the events are closing around him he wonders whether some god is 'weaving a deceit' to entrap him (5.356). Penelope, of course, literally weaves a deceit in the form of Laertes' shroud, but she also 'winds up balls of tricks,' *dolous tolupeuô* (19.137), using the word for winding yarn. If weaving is a good metaphor for plotting and the *Odyssey* is preeminent in such plotting, then it is all the easier to see not only Odysseus but Penelope too as a figure of the poet, quietly working behind the scenes" (Winkler 155–56; see also Foley 89–91, Segal 134–36).

47. *Odyssey* 19.137; cf. 2.93ff., 24.125ff. See Segal 134. Penelope refers to the servant Dolios as "my own servant, whom my father gave me to have" when she married Odysseus, and she sees him as mediating her access to male trickery: "let someone . . . summon the old man Dolios, / . . . so that he may / go with speed to Laertes and sit beside him and tell him / all, and perhaps he, weaving out the design in his heart, / may go outside" (*Odyssey* 4.735–41).

authorial future, beginning with her "double-cross" of Emireno, when he forces her to design the assassins' fake crusader insignia (GL 19.87–89), and ending with her appropriation of Vafrino. The fact that heraldic and bardic lore was conventionally reserved for males accounts for the transgressive impression both heroines create, whether ethically as "characters," or narratologically as *actants* who momentarily step outside the plot and rival the narrator. But Erminia is more actively transgressive. Her desire for reunion and matrimony with Tancredi threatens to subvert her utility as *architecta* or authorial problemsolver in the *Liberata*, both because she mimics Helen's appropriation of authorial functions, and even more because she redefines Vafrino's roles in her pursuit of a happy ending.

VIII. The Queen of the Happy Ending

Erminia's entire actantial career, rather than one or two scattered moments, is modeled on that of Helen. That systematic dependence is the ultimate though half-hidden cause of readers' fascination with the question whether Erminia will marry Tancredi. Most of her biographers have seen that Erminia was introduced through an imitation of Helen's *teichoskopia*, but none of them appears to have noticed that the imitation does not end when Erminia finishes identifying the Christian heroes for Aladino. Tasso resumes the imitation when Erminia observes the duel of Tancredi and Argante (GL 6.55.5ff.), so that after three intervening cantos the poem deepens the personal significance of her *teichoskopia*. In the *Iliad*, the public or epic significance of Helen's identification of the Achaean heroes is, from her point of view, incidental. She has a personal and erotic motivation for coming to the walls: to witness the duel between Menelaus and Paris, that is, between her legitimate husband and her paramour. Erminia does not fully recall this emotional context until her second *teichoskopia*, when she observes Tancredi and Argante's duel: her fearful solicitude for Tancredi's safety, and her dread of the religious and political obligation to use her healing arts on Argante rather than Tancredi, mimic and simplify Helen's ambivalent reactions to the duel of her two mates. Erminia's three entrances in Tasso's poem thus expand on Helen's entrances into the *Iliad* and the *Odyssey*, respectively: a *teichoskopia* that hypothesizes an erotic reunion, and an encounter with a trickster whom the heroine interprets as the ideal mediator for that reunion.

Furthermore, because Tasso combined Odysseus's two spying missions to stage the meeting of Erminia and Vafrino, he invites a closer scrutiny of the way Helen contests and revises the Iliadic value system. In her anecdote Helen completely disrupts Odysseus's Iliadic epic ethos by putting him in a situation that is militarily untenable. She claims that after recognizing and unmasking him, she bathed, anointed, and reclothed him before allowing him to continue his mission (*Odyssey* 4.252–58); yet such hospitality would have nullified his disguise and compromised both his mission and his safety. Whether or not one perceives her anecdote as a lie, it is absurd from the epic—that is, military—standpoint of the *Iliad* (Winkler 141).

Helen's words do not indicate that she misunderstands the military and strategic nature of Odysseus's task. Rather, her anecdote seems to address other needs that are uniquely hers. In the first place, it establishes her superior cunning and subtlety, for no other mortal claims to recognize Odysseus in disguise (Winkler 140–41). Secondly, Helen's interest in narrative—her own and others'—has one focus, that of the happy ending. In the *Odyssey* (4.259–64), Helen claims that when she met Odysseus in disguise, she was repentant and homesick.[48] Not only is Helen's anecdote an anti-*Iliad*, her personality in the *Odyssey* is practically unrecognizable to a reader coming from the *Iliad*. She narrates her meeting with Odysseus from the perspective of a happy ending, for she is now once more ensconced in Menelaus's household, as his implausibly contented and esteemed wife. Seeing her in her own household, one might doubt whether the Trojan War had ever happened. Moreover, Helen is narrating to Telemachus, and thus her story functions both to

---

48. In the *Iliad* she vehemently expresses the same sentiments to Paris after he has forfeited the duel with Menelaus (3.426–36)

congratulate herself for having recognized Telemachus's resemblance to Odysseus, and to reassure him against despairing of reunion with his father. Helen implicitly presents her anecdote of unmasking Odysseus as the foreshadowing of two happy endings, her own return to Menelaus's household, and Odysseus's homecoming to Ithaka.

Her viewpoint is infectious, of course: however silly her anecdote may be in Iliadic terms, it makes perfect sense in the context of her concern with happy endings, and the narrator of the *Odyssey* employs it to foreshadow the poem's own happy ending, its contestation of Iliadic tragedy. This is an effect of narratology, not of character: the *Odyssey* as a whole vindicates the themes of Helen's tale in the elementary narrative tension whereby her recognition, testing, and adorning of Odysseus in Troy prefigure Penelope's cagey though courtly response to him when he returns to Ithaka in disguise. Like the *Odyssey* as a whole, and indeed logically prior to it, Helen revindicates—against verisimilitude and her own character—the values of domesticity, return, and reconciliation against the epic and tragic ethos of separation and loss. Whether Helen actually bathed and primped Odysseus is beside the point, for her story redefines him. Against the whole weight of the *Iliad*, Helen makes Odysseus's homecoming humanly plausible for the first time in the *Odyssey*.

Tasso identifies the two heroines through episodic imitation despite their differences in character, for he is less interested in Helen's self-described inconstancy or Erminia's timidity than in their shared trickiness, and in the challenge their suggestive *techné* poses to the epic narrator. By derailing Vafrino's imitation of the Iliadic *Doloneia* and making him repeat Helen's domestication of Odysseus, Erminia performs a textual and generic revision similar to Helen's, but even more radical, since the Helen of the *Odyssey* never challenges its ethos, but only that of the *Iliad*. The discontinuities between the comedic and tragic Homeric subtexts of Vafrino's career seem to foreshadow the clash of mimetic and diegetic expectations that muddles the destiny of Tancredi and Erminia. Her happy ending is no more verisimilar than Helen's own, and Tasso's suspension of it may even be partially a reaction against the inverisimilitude of Helen's return to domestic contentment. And yet

Erminia's mimetically implausible dream gives her considerable power over the narrative, to the point that she can contest the authority of the poet himself.

IX. Auctrix

The idea of a "character" contesting the authority of the agent who writes her is absurd: Erminia is nothing more than the recurrent intersection of proper name, intertextual recall, and certain characteristic expressions of unfulfilled desire. Yet it will not do to maintain that all Erminia's powers within and over the text devolve upon her legitimately from the omnipotent hand of "Tasso" (or Tasso). Tasso's fascination with Helen in her function as Homer's dominant inscribed author-figure must have been considerable, for it seems clear that he modeled Erminia on Helen's consummate skill at authorial roles, as *vafra*, *architecta*, and *textrix*. Tasso's desire to be an author is in some sense a desire to appropriate and "tame" Helen, perhaps somehow to "redeem" her through the figure of Erminia. Thereby, he creates a new problem: how to redeem the function of poet (the Foucaultian author-function) from the competition Erminia represents. Erminia's preoccupations infiltrate and contaminate the very narrating voice of *Gerusalemme liberata*, in ways that are hidden and tricky.

Erminia's challenge begins from an absurdity. In mimetic or characterological terms, her imitation of Helen observing the duel of Menelaus and Paris makes no sense: Tancredi and Argante are emphatically not fighting for possession of Erminia in the way that Menelaus and Paris fought over Helen. But just as Helen did in her story of unmasking Odysseus, Erminia interprets her experience from a private and sentimental perspective, rather than a public, political, and epic viewpoint. From her point of view, the duel *is* over possession of her, and that interpretation infiltrates the narration of the poem even before the duel takes place. When Erminia identifies the Christian troops for Aladino in canto 3, the alternation of her voice with that of the narrator creates an elaborately elusive fugue that expands the erotic triangle of *Iliad* 3

(Paris / Helen / Menelaus) into a tetragon of desire, which explores the hypothetical pairings between Erminia, her alter ego Clorinda, Tancredi, and Argante. This figure is outlined by metonymy, through the sheer physical proximity of the four proper names, and is glossed by the asides of Erminia and the narrator. Later, in canto 6, Erminia acts out the script implied by these pairings, when she rejects her presumed duty to tend the wounds of Argante, dresses in the armor of Clorinda, seeks out Tancredi, and is mistaken by him for Clorinda. Henceforth, throughout the *Liberata*, the four personages' interactions lock them into a configuration of two interfacing relational triangles that repeats the allusive pairings of Erminia's *teichoskopia*. This schema of interactantial relations resembles the theatergram of love intrigues that typifies entwined double plots in tragedy and comedy.[49]

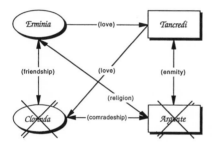

Our attention to these relations is determined entirely by the force of Erminia's desire, which is expressed textually through precise reenactments of Helen's preoccupation with reunion. Argante and Clorinda are inseparable, but they are no more "in love" than Tancredi and Argante were aware of dueling for the hand of Erminia. Their comradeship is readable as repressed or unacknowledged eros only within the

49. Neither Corrigan, Murtaugh, nor Migiel discusses the presence of Argante, though Jovine (38) and Guglielminetti (66–67, 154–55) do. On the double plot in Italian comedy, see Salingar 175–242, esp. 186–87. "In an Italian double plot, the events in each plot are so arranged as to interfere causally with those in the other, and the actions on the stage follow a strictly temporal sequence, so that each plot can react on the other at exactly the right moment" (Salingar 223).

tension of their relations to Erminia and Tancredi. Erminia's desire for him highlights and overdetermines vectors of expectation that are created by nothing more than shifting configurations of physical proximity among herself and the other three personages. This is particularly true of the situational symmetries between her search for Tancredi in cantos 6 and 7 and her encounter with Vafrino in canto 19, between Tancredi's nighttime pursuit of her in Clorinda's armor and his nocturnal duel with Clorinda (cantos 6, 7, and 12), and between the outcomes of Tancredi's duels with Clorinda and Argante (GL 12.70, 19.28). But Erminia's desires also inflect the presentation of Clorinda and Argante's habitual companionship, particularly in canto 12, when they reenact the exploits of the Virgilian lovers Nisus and Euryalus. The result is that Erminia's desire diffuses throughout the text, becoming what I have elsewhere called a "desire of the text." [50]

In characterological terms, Erminia is an unlikely Helen figure. But Tasso was clearly less interested in Helen's self-confessed inconstancy than in her trickiness, which the Homeric texts present as authorial and authoritative roles: *vafra, architecta, textrix*. In fact, Tasso's imitative *agon* with Homer takes place largely through the attempt to appropriate and tame Helen in the figure of Erminia. Yet Erminia is no more tractable with her author than with Tancredi or Vafrino. Her craft makes her the single most valuable *architecta* for the epic plot, but she exacts a price, for the force of her desire permeates the Tassian narrator's choreography of Tancredi, Clorinda, and Argante. Her command "prepara il guiderdone" ("make ready the fee," GL 19.114) appears directed at him as well as at Tancredi. By refusing to grant that *guiderdone* explicitly, the narrator reluctantly acknowledges Erminia's problematic power over the text, and attempts to circumvent it.

---

50. Stephens, "St. Paul," 173; see also Eco 64, 66, and Stephens, "Reading Tasso," 296–97. Argante and Clorinda are repeatedly described as *coppia* and *consorti* by the narrator and characters in canto 12 (stanzas 7, 11, 15, 44), terms that evoke the couples Olindo and Sofronia and Gildippe and Odoardo (cf. GL 1.56.7, 20.98.4–6, 20.35.7). And the layered rivalry of Argante and Tancredi in canto 19.3–5 is mediated by the memory of Clorinda as *donna* (lady) rather than warrior.

In fact, much of the Tassian poet's attempt to constitute his own poetic authority takes place through rivalry with Erminia, as though she were a predecessor poet, rather than his own creation. That paradoxical rivalry derives from the thoroughness with which Erminia emulates and outdoes the figure of Helen. The Tassian poet presents himself as an epigone of Erminia and Helen in the very exordium of the poem by claiming the role of *textor*, begging his muse's pardon for weaving ornaments into the epic truth of his tale (GL 1.2). A stanza later, he presents himself as a Lucretian trickster-physician of souls, masking bitter medicine with sweet syrups.[51] The narrator's chosen roles as poet and physician are conspicuously combined within the plot by Goffredo's medic Erotimo, whose allegorical name suggests the ideal balance between *Amore (eros)* and *Onore (timé)* that both Erminia and the Tassian narrator seek. Yet Erotimo fails at both roles: having abandoned poetry for medicine, he stands by impotently as an angel heals Goffredo. Conversely, Erminia succeeds in her role as *medica* by becoming a poet when, lacking precisely the herb the angel brought to Erotimo, she restores Tancredi to life with nothing but the *note potenti e maghe* of her song.[52] This is Erminia's final homage and challenge to Helen as poet physician: before narrating her encounter with Odysseus, Helen mixed a literal potion to counteract the heartache her tale might cause her husband and guests.[53] At the same time, Erminia's song is a potent challenge to the Lucretian ideal of the Tassian poet, for it both revives and appropriates Tancredi. Her command of silence and promise of enlightenment carry an authority that the Tassian narrator never reserves for himself. And she fulfills his ideal

51. Commentators unanimously agree in seeing GL 1.3.5–8 as an echo of Lucretius 1.936–42.

52. "Charms . . . powerful and magical," GL 19.113.3–4. On Erminia's powers, see also 6.67 entire. Both passages assimilate her to Goffredo's poet-medic Erotimo (GL 11.70), as well as to the narrating voice (GL 1.3 entire).

53. "Into the wine of which they were drinking she cast a medicine / of heartsease, free of gall, to make one forget all sorrows. . . . / Now when she had put the medicine in, and told them to pour it, / taking up the story again she began to speak to them: '. . . [L]isten / to me and be entertained. What I will tell you is plausible'" (*Odyssey* 4.220–39).

of an innocent fraud, a good fraud that gives *salute: da l'inganno suo vita riceve* (GL 6.88; 19.114; 1.3: "from his deception [he] receives life").

Erminia is Tasso's most powerful poet figure, and her unruly presence is a challenge the poet himself cannot entirely overcome. Tasso's other Homeric poet figures are less problematic. Even Armida can be defeated by textual means: her Circean skills at metamorphosis, weaving frauds, and magical *carmi* are neutralized by a long modulation that exploits the Petrarchan common term between "pagan" love magic and the Christian ideal of Mary as perfectly submissive female, or *ancella* (Stephens, "St. Paul," 193–99). But Erminia's challenge remains, and the poet's refusal to end her story is an act of resistance rather than mastery. As I noted earlier, Erminia's authoritative return in canto 19 was preceded by an apprenticeship as solitary Petrarchan lyricist in canto 7. Petrarchism was one of a few acceptable outlets for female poetic aspiration in Tasso's time, but it was also the authoritative paradigm for self-construction through poetry. The poet himself is a reconstructed Petrarchan, as countless echoes and verbatim quotes attest in the *Liberata*. Erminia is the author's principal competitor, and the text's very refusal to grant her an explicit "happy ending" is an ironic index of the thoroughness with which she exercises the powers and prerogatives proper to her author. His domestication of Armida is sudden enough to disturb many readers, but he can only tame Erminia, if at all, by accepting the terms that she dictates.

Tasso's challenge to Homer is in large measure a project to dominate the figure of Helen, but the project can never completely succeed, precisely because Erminia successfully challenges Helen as inscribed author. The cunning with which Tasso camouflages Erminia's dependence on Helen, eliding Helen's personality while maintaining her metaliterary trickiness, backfires by making Erminia an even more deceptive Helen. Erminia's plangent rhetoric of helplessness disguises her actantial resemblance to Helen and captures the romantic imagination of readers, and so it masks the force with which intertextual dynamics actually determine our forecast of her erotic "destiny." Erminia's quietly defiant appropriation of her beloved is perhaps a figure for her theft of the whole

Tassian "show," and for the thoroughness with which she insinuates comedic paradigms into the epic.

Works Cited

Ariosto, Ludovico. *La Lena. Il teatro italiano*, Pt. 2: *La commedia del Cinquecento*. Ed. Guido Davico Bonino. 3 vols. Turin: Einaudi, 1977–78. 1: 151–232.

———. *Orlando furioso*. Ed. Lanfranco Caretti. Turin: Einaudi, 1971.

Battaglia, Salvatore, gen. ed. *Grande dizionario della lingua italiana*. 17 vols. issued. Turin: UTET, 1961–.

Beecher, Donald A. "Intriguers and Trickster: The Manifestations of an Archetype in the Comedy of the Renaissance." *Comparative Critical Approaches to Renaissance Comedy*. Ed. Donald Beecher and Massimo Ciavolella. Ottawa, Ont.: Dovehouse Editions Canada, 1986. 53–72.

Boccaccio, Giovanni. *Decameron*. Ed. Vittore Branca. Turin: Einaudi, 1980.

Brown, Norman O. *Hermes the Thief: The Evolution of a Myth*. 1947. Reprint. New York: Vintage Books, 1969.

Bruno, Giordano. *Candelaio. Il teatro italiano*, Pt. 2: *La commedia del Cinquecento*. Ed. Guido Davico Bonino. 3 vols. Turin: Einaudi, 1977–78. 3:133–92.

Clay, Jenny Strauss. "Odysseus: Name and Helmet." *Homer's The Odyssey*. Ed. Harold Bloom. New York: Chelsea House, 1988. 103–26.

Clubb, Louise George. *Italian Drama in Shakespeare's Time*. New Haven: Yale UP, 1989.

Corrigan, Beatrice. "Erminia and Tancredi: The Happy Ending." *Italica* 40 (1963): 325–33.

Defaux, Gérard. *Le Curieux, le glorieux et la sagesse du monde dans la première moitié du XVIe siècle: l'exemple de Panurge (Ulysse, Démosthène, Empédocle)*. French Forum Monographs, no. 34. Lexington, Ky.: French Forum, 1982.

Eco, Umberto. *Interpretation and Overinterpretation*. Ed. Stefan Collini. Cambridge: Cambridge UP, 1992.

Else, Gerald F. *Plato and Aristotle on Poetry*. Ed. Peter Burian. Chapel Hill: U of North Carolina P, 1986.

Euripides. *Rhesus*. Trans. Richmond Lattimore. *The Complete Greek Tragedies: Euripides*. New York: Washington Square Press, 1968. 4: 6–51.

Foley, Helene P. " 'Reverse Similes' and Sex Roles in the *Odyssey*." *Homer's The Odyssey*. Ed. Harold Bloom. New York: Chelsea House, 1988. 87–101.

Foucault, Michel. "What Is an Author?" *Textual Strategies: Perspectives in Post-Structuralist Criticism*. Ed. Josué V. Harari. Ithaca: Cornell UP, 1979. 141–60.

Frye, Northrop. *Anatomy of Criticism: Four Essays*. 1957. Reprint. Princeton: Princeton UP, 1971.

Homer. *The Iliad*. Trans. Richmond Lattimore. 1951. Reprint. Chicago: U of Chicago P, 1970.

———. *The Odyssey.* Trans. Richmond Lattimore. New York: Harper Torchbooks, 1968.

Intronati di Siena, Accademia degli. *Gl'ingannati. Il teatro italiano,* Pt. 2: *La commedia del Cinquecento.* Ed. Guido Davico Bonino. 3 vols. Turin: Einaudi, 1977–78. 2.87–183.

Joplin, Patricia Klindienst. "The Voice of the Shuttle Is Ours." 1984. Reprint. *Rape and Representation.* Ed. Lynn A. Higgins and Brenda R. Silver. New York: Columbia UP, 1991. 35–63.

Jovine, Francesco. *La licenza del fingere: note per una lettura della "Liberata."* Rome: Bulzoni, 1980.

Lucretius (Titus Lucretius Carus). *De rerum natura.* Trans. W. H. D. Rouse. Rev. Martin Ferguson Smith. Loeb Classical Library. London: Heinemann, 1982.

Machiavelli, Niccolò. *Mandragola. Il teatro italiano,* Pt. 2: *La commedia del Cinquecento.* Ed. Guido Davico Bonino. 3 vols. Turin: Einaudi, 1977–78. 1:89–150.

Manetti, Antonio di Tuccio (attr.). *La novella del Grasso legnaiuolo. Novelle del Quattrocento.* Ed. Aldo Borlenghi. Milan: Rizzoli, 1962. 337–89.

Martinelli, Alessandro. *La demiurgia della scrittura poetica: Gerusalemme liberata.* Florence: Olschki, 1983.

Migiel, Marilyn. "Tasso's Erminia: Telling an Alternate Story." *Italica* 64 (1987): 62–75.

Miller, Nancy K. "Arachnologies: The Woman, the Text, and the Critic." *The Poetics of Gender.* Ed. Nancy K. Miller. New York: Columbia UP, 1986. 270–95.

Murtaugh, Kristin Olson. "Erminia Delivered: Notes on Tasso and Romance." *Quaderni d'Italianistica* 3.1 (1982): 12–23.

Ovid (Publius Ovidius Naso). *Metamorphoseon.* Ed. B. A. van Proosdij. Leiden: E. J. Brill, 1968.

Pico della Mirandola, Giovanni. *Oratio de Hominis Dignitate, Heptaplus, De Ente et Uno.* Ed. Eugenio Garin. Florence: Vallecchi, 1942.

Plautus, Titus Maccius. *Miles Gloriosus. Plautus: With an English Translation.* Trans. Paul Nixon. 5 vols. Loeb Classical Library. London, Heinemann; Cambridge, Mass., Harvard UP, 1916–1977. 3: 120–285.

Pucci, Pietro. *Odysseus Polutropos: Intertextual Readings in the Odyssey and the Iliad.* Ithaca: Cornell UP, 1987.

Salingar, Leo. *Shakespeare and the Traditions of Comedy.* Cambridge: Cambridge UP, 1974.

Segal, Charles. "*Kleos* and Its Ironies in the *Odyssey.*" *Homer's The Odyssey.* Ed. Harold Bloom. New York: Chelsea House, 1988. 127–49.

Stephens, Walter. "Mimesis, Mediation and Counterfeit." *Mimesis in Contemporary Theory: An Interdisciplinary Approach,* Vol. 1: *The Literary and Philosophical Debate.* Ed. Mihai Spariosu. Philadelphia: John Benjamins, 1984. 238–75.

———. "Reading Tasso Reading Vergil Reading Homer: An Archeology of Andromache." *Comparative Literature Studies* 32.2 (1995): 296–319.

———. "Saint Paul Among the Amazons: Gender and Authority in *Gerusalemme liberata.*" *Discourses of Authority in Medieval and Renaissance Literature.* Ed. Kevin Brownlee and Walter Stephens. Hanover, N.H.: UP of New England, 1989. 169–200.

Tasso, Torquato. *Gerusalemme conquistata*. Ed. Luigi Bonfigli. 2 vols. Bari: Laterza, 1934.

———. *Gerusalemme liberata*. Ed. Lanfranco Caretti. Turin: Einaudi, 1971.

———. *Gerusalemme liberata*. Ed. Fredi Chiappelli. Milan: Rusconi, 1982.

———. *Gerusalemme liberata*. Ed. Severino Ferrari. Rev. Pietro Papini. 1917. Reprint. Florence: Sansoni, 1970.

———. *Gerusalemme liberata*. Ed. Marziano Guglielminetti. 2 vols. 1974. Reprint. Milan: Garzanti, 1982.

———. *Gerusalemme liberata*. Vol. 3 of *Opere*. Ed. Bruno Maier. 5 vols. Milan: Rizzoli, 1963–65.

———. *Intrichi d'amore*. Ed. Enrico Malato. Rome: Salerno Editrice, 1976.

———. *Jerusalem Delivered*. Trans. Ralph Nash. Detroit: Wayne State UP, 1987.

———. *Le lettere di Torquato Tasso, disposte per ordine di tempo*. Ed. Cesare Guasti. 5 vols. Florence: Le Monnier, 1852–55.

———. *Scritti sull'arte poetica*. Ed. Ettore Mazzali. 1959. Reprint. Turin: Einaudi, 1977.

Tommaseo, Niccolò, and Bernardo Bellini. *Dizionario della lingua italiana*. 1874. Reprint. 6 vols. Turin: UTET, 1929.

Trissino, Giovan Giorgio. *Italia liberata dai Goti*. 3 vols. London [i.e., Livorno]: Giovanni Tommaso Masi, 1779.

Virgil (Publius Vergilius Maro). *P. Vergilii Maronis Opera*. Ed. R. A. B. Mynors. Oxford: Clarendon, 1968.

Winkler, John J. "Penelope's Cunning and Homer's." *The Constraints of Desire: The Anthropology of Sex and Gender in Ancient Greece*. By John J. Winkler. London: Routledge, 1990. 129–61.

"Un così valoroso cavalliero":
Knightly Honor and Artistic Representation
in Orlando furioso, Canto 26

KATHERINE HOFFMAN

Insofar as the *Orlando furioso* with its breakneck succession of episodes can be said to have lulls, canto 26 is one of them. One of several cantos in which the plot is sustained and embroidered, it includes no major narrative beginnings, turning points, or endings. Canto 26's main distinction is its allegorical art passage, the description of a mysterious fountain whose sculptures represent sixteenth-century monarchs battling a monster symbolizing avarice. But apart from this still center, in which the knights sit down and rest between bouts of furious activity, the narrative streams through, disregarding the boundaries of the canto. Looked at thematically, however, canto 26 displays a clear unity organized around the fountain scene, forming in effect a complete miniature discourse on one of the *Furioso*'s main themes, knightly honor. This theme is associated particularly with Ruggiero, whose preoccupation with honor's conflicting dictates is the main stumbling block in the epic plot line of his union with Bradamante and founding of the Este dynasty.[1]

The discourse of canto 26 defines honor by showing it in conflict with avarice. The canto's structure is simple: after a two-stanza exordium, the honorable, knightly rescue of Viviane and Malagigi from the Maganzesi in the first part (stanzas 3–29) contrasts with the extremely unchivalrous

I gratefully acknowledge many helpful suggestions I received from Virginia Green, Michael Hakkenberg, and Michael Heller, who were kind enough to read drafts of this article. And I am especially indebted to Albert Ascoli, who presided over several metamorphoses of what began as a paper for an independant study.

1. On the play between epic closure and romance digressiveness in the *Furioso*, see especially Giamatti, "Headlong Horses" 270, 298–307; Parker 40–53; Ascoli 363–64; and Zatti 9–14.

and avaricious brawl over horses and armor in the last half of the canto (stanzas 54–137). These two episodes are divided by a passage in which a relief sculpture shows honor, in the form of a group of knights, allegorically defeating avarice, in the form of a monster. But beneath its calm, celebratory surface, the allegory of the fountain passage complicates the surrounding discourse by placing the canto's discussion of individual honor and avarice in a broader perspective that is at once both historical and aesthetic. This dual perspective explicitly relates the theme of honor to the sixteenth-century Italian court culture out of which the poem itself originates. On the one hand, the knights allegorically battling avarice represent the rulers of Europe, circa 1516–32: what does canto 26's story of honor and avarice among fictitious knights imply about the real-life leaders of Ariosto's own day? On the other hand, these rulers also represent the poet's patron class, whose honor is the subject of his verses: what do honor and avarice mean in the relationship between poet and patron?[2]

I will demonstrate that as a thematic unit centered on the fountain passage, canto 26 creates a complex moral economy between individual honor and avarice that is developed in the action surrounding Ruggiero in the rest of the canto. Defining honor in opposition to avarice makes self-denial fundamental to the concept of honor being developed in the canto. Looking first at the juxtaposition of the beginning and ending battle scenes, and then at the effects of the central fountain passage, I will argue that the discourse of canto 26 demonstrates how problematic the relation between selfless honor and greedy avarice is on all three levels: the moral, the political, and the artistic. Morally, as the two contrasting battle episodes demonstrate, the problem is the impossibility

2. The use of allegory in the *Furioso* has mostly been discussed in relation to the episode of Alcina's island in cantos 6–7 and that of the moon in cantos 34–35. On the allegorical aspect of these episodes, see especially Ascoli 124, 264–71, and Kennedy. For a view of Ariosto's poetics, apparently apart from overtly allegorical passages like these, as actively resisting allegorical interpretation, see Javitch. Javitch sees allegorical interpretation as inherently reductive; in my view, however, the importance of allegory is that it foregrounds the whole issue of interpretation.

of honorable knights keeping their motives clear of selfish pride and acquisitiveness. Politically, as the fountain allegory and its interpretation show, the problem is that knightly honor becomes a polite fiction, an ideological cover, for imperial power politics. And the canto's exploration of these two levels leads to the artistic problem of representing powerful patrons critically in a poem when the artistic means of production are implicated in the moral ambiguities of those politics. They are implicated both because the artist must navigate, and participate in, the politics of the court to gain an audience for his work, and because his dependence on the patron compromises his claim to objective analysis of the political and moral issues the poem raises. The play of honor and avarice in the two long narrative sections of the canto is reflected in the allegorical ecphrasis of the central, descriptive fountain passage, leading ultimately to the question of how to read its celebration of the nobility who are simultaneously the political leaders of Ariosto's day and the patrons who make it possible to publish poems such as the Furioso.

I. The Dance of Chivalry

Canto 26 begins by introducing a complex view of honor in the short exordium, which, as often happens in the Furioso, sets up an interpretive framework for the entire canto.[3] Contrasting the love of honor with the love of riches, the exordium relates this distinction in turn to the familiar theme of the superiority of a past golden age to decadent modern times:

> Cortesi donne ebbe l'antiqua etade,
> che le virtú, non le richezze, amaro:
> al tempo nostro si ritrovan rade
> a cui, piú del guadagno, altro sia caro.
> Ma quelle che per lor vera bontade
> non seguon de le piú lo stile avaro,
> vivendo, degne son d'esser contente;
> gloriose e immortal poi che fian spente.

3. For Ariosto's use of exordia, see Durling 132–38.

Degna d'eterna laude è Bradamante
che non amò tesor, non amò impero,
ma la virtú, ma l'animo prestante,
ma l'alta gentilezza di Ruggiero;
e meritò che ben le fosse amante
un cosí valoroso cavalliero,
e per piacere a lei facesse cose
nei secoli avenir miracolose   (26.1-2).[4]

(In days of old there used to be courteous ladies who prized
virtue above wealth. In our own day it is hard to find a woman for
whom things other than gain are important. But those who, out of
true goodness, avoid the common style of greed, it is they who de-
serve to enjoy happiness in their lifetime and immortal glory after
their death.

So Bradamante is worthy of eternal praise, who loved not wealth
or power, but simply Ruggiero, for his martial valor and his emi-
nence of heart and breeding. She merited so valorous a knight for
her suitor; she merited that to please her he performed exploits in
future times deemed miraculous.)

These stanzas set up categories of value by unpacking the various mean-
ings of the Italian concept of *valore*. The positive values of "l'antiqua
etade" ("days of old")—*virtú* in the positive sense, the Roman moral
quality of manliness—are contrasted with the degraded values of "il
tempo nostro" ("our own day"), in which moral value has become eco-
nomic value. In the second stanza of this opening, Bradamante is the
shining example of the virtuous ladies of yore just described in the first
stanza. Loving Ruggiero not out of selfishness or for material gain, but
for his honor, she deserves his love in return; and insofar as she draws
it, causes him to do the great deeds he does "per piacere a lei" ("to

---

4. Quotations from the *Furioso* are taken from the Lanfranco Caretti edition of the poem,
3rd edition (Einaudi, 1966). Translations are from Guido Waldman's version of the poem
(Oxford, 1974).

please her"). Indeed, so great is the power of this love that it inspires deeds which seem "miracolose"—incredible in ordinary human terms. The selfless love of honor instead of the selfish love of riches is "vera bontade," true goodness, and those who practice it deserve happiness in this life and a glorious immortality after they die. The miraculousness of Ruggiero's deeds is the measure of the moral integrity of their love.

The exordium thus defines honor in contrast to avarice, as a quality that transcends it and, in fact, takes over its vocabulary. To most modern ladies of "il tempo nostro," the measure of something's value would be how expensive, or "caro," it is; but the rare virtuous lady is the one "a cui . . . altro sia caro" ("to whom . . . other things are dear"; emphasis mine). In the same way, in the second stanza, Bradamante's love of Ruggiero's heroic qualities makes her deserve love in return from this "valoroso cavalliero" ("valorous knight"); his "valore" in this context is both his knightly valor—which consists of his "virtù," his "anima prestante," and his "alta gentilezza"—and also his virtue or worth, which has nothing to do with the kind measured in material riches or power. Their relationship demonstrates the love and honor of "l'antiqua etade," the golden age before human language and relations were tainted with monetary concerns. In the rest of the canto, the distinction between moral valor and material value will be shown to pervade the realm of history.

The first part of the canto, immediately following the exordium, presents an example of the sort of "virtú" and "alta gentilezza" that Bradamante loves in Ruggiero. Having saved Ricciardetto in the preceding canto, Ruggiero has set out with him and Aldigiero on a noble mission to rescue their kinsmen, Viviane and Malagigi, from being sold to their murderous enemies, the Maganzesi. Along the way they meet Marfisa, who foregoes her customary challenge to join their honorable enterprise. Once they reach the plain where the Moors are handing the brothers over to the Maganzesi, they attack, Ruggiero and Marfisa perform great deeds, and both forces are routed. The knights then free the captives, take possession of the abandoned ransom, and retire to a well-earned rest at the fountain nearby. The whole episode is a classic adventure of knightly honor in action. The honorable motives of Ruggiero and the other knights — rescuing kinsmen and the kinsmen of friends — contrast to the greedy and despicable ones of the Moors, who see Viviane and Malagigi merely as commodities to be turned into gold (10.6), and the Maganzesi, who are happy to receive their enemies bound and incapable of defending themselves. The courtly encounter with Marfisa strengthens the contrast between the knights' adherence to the human bonds of courtesy, and their opponents' greed for gold and revenge. The formal, elegant, and rather verbose tone in which the episode is recounted reinforces this contrast. It includes elaborate asides by the speaker to explain the situation to the reader, thus courteously honoring the human bond between poet and reader as well — as, for example, when Marfisa first appears on the scene:

> Parmi veder ch'alcun saper desia
> il nome di costui, che quivi giunto
> a Ruggiero e a' compagni si offeria
> compagno d'arme al periglioso punto.   (8.1–4)

(It looks to me that some of you would like to know the name of this man who was offering to join Ruggiero and his comrades-in-arms at this perilous juncture.)

When the knights meet in the forest, they address each other as courtly knights should, with formulaic challenges and responses. No courtesy is omitted; they even jest to show their insouciance at the coming battle, in which four of them will fight two large forces. Marfisa compares the battle to a "festa," a party, and Ruggiero picks up the joke:

> Gl'invitati ancora
> non ci son tutti, e manca una gran parte.
> Gran ballo s'apparecchia di fare ora.   (11.1–3)

(The guests are not all here yet; a good number are still missing. We have a grand ball in preparation here.)

And when the Maganzesi arrive, they are "presso a cominciar la danza" ("ready to begin the dance"). The dance is a figure that formalizes and aestheticizes the chivalrous order that the knights are acting out, and the style of the passage as well as the behavior of the knights conforms to this order.

This courtly order among the episode's heroes contrasts with the immediate chaos and confusion that overcome the Moors and the Maganzesi as soon as they are attacked. The confusion results from more than just terror at the might of Marfisa and Ruggiero; there is another, unforeseen factor,

> Di qui nacque un error tra gli assaliti,
> che lor causò lor ultima ruina. (15.1–2)

(This gave rise to an illusion among those assaulted—an illusion that ultimately caused their ruin.)

The two armies, seeing their leaders killed but not knowing the origin of the attack, naturally enough assume each other to have turned traitor (after all, one army is Christian and the other is Moorish), and start to fight among themselves. This little comment is slipped in just before we go on to hear of the amazing prowess of Ruggiero and Marfisa; yet it is this error as much as their strength that causes ("causò") the ultimate ruin of the two armies. The courtly values that Ruggiero and his companions shared with Marfisa turned her from a potential enemy to a friend by allowing them to trust one another. But the selfish and materialistic values of the Moors and the Maganzesi keep them from acting together, even in their common interest. They are left open to the united attack of their enemies, unwitting abettors of their own downfall. Thus the rescue episode displays a pattern which lines up Ruggiero and his friends with orderly, chivalrous courtesy based on human consideration, while the Moors and Maganzesi display a chaotic selfishness, materiality, and greed.

There is, however, a note of qualification. So great is the prowess of Ruggiero and Marfisa that they take on a mythic status in each other's eyes, and compare each other to Hector, Mars, and Bellona. But in the rush of hyperbole and epic similes the speaker stops to admit that it all sounds rather incredible. Marfisa's admiration for Ruggiero becomes more and more inflated until the speaker breaks off in something like embarrassment:

> e se non che pur dubito che manche
> credenza al ver c'ha faccia di menzogna,
> di piú direi; ma di men dir bisogna.   (22.6–8)[5]

(and were I not anxious lest truth, wearing the mask of falsehood, be denied belief, I would go further—but I had bettter understate the facts.)

In the face of the reader's probable disbelief, the speaker turns, as he has before, to the authority of Archbishop Turpin:

> Il buon Turpin, che sa che dice il vero,
> e lascia creder poi quel ch'a l'uom piace,
> narra mirabil cose di Ruggiero,
> ch'udendolo, il direste voi mendace.   (23.1–4)

(Our good Turpin, who knew he told the truth but let men believe what they would, attributes marvels to Ruggiero, though you might call him a liar if you heard him.)

This is one of many joking references to Turpin throughout the poem. Ruggiero's deeds are incredible—literally "cose / nei secoli avenir miracolose" ("exploits in future times deemed miraculous"), for we of this later day have a hard time believing them. Either times have degenerated so much that we can no longer conceive of such prowess, or we are fools to believe these historians, Ariosto and Turpin alike. Playfully deflating its own hyperbole, the passage reminds us, in effect, that this is literature, not life, we are witnessing—an artifice that lets men believe what they will. It's as we like it.

---

5. "Ver c'ha faccia di menzogna" ("truth with a lying face") is a direct quote from Dante's description of Geryon (*Inferno* 16.124). For a discussion of Ariosto's debt to Dante in his representation of the truth-speaking powers of poetry, see Ascoli 252–54.

There is no attempt to reconcile these contradictory possibilities; the contradiction is simply presented, calling attention to the artifice being exercised in setting up the ideal of courtly honor in this episode, the artificial conflation of the classical ideal of a golden age and the medieval ideal of courtly honor, and the problems of interpretation that such artifices engender. This theme of artifice and interpretation will be picked up later in the canto. But even if it is presented with a wink, the ideal of courtly honor is affirmed as well as defined in the rescue episode as a whole, for its alternative, as shown in the behavior of the Moors and the Maganzesi, is a chaotic rapaciousness that is morally reprehensible, and ultimately self-destructive.

II. Honor into Avarice

The second and greater part of the canto's action, the lengthy contention between the four rescuers and two other knights, shows just how self-destructive the lack of true honor can be. After their battle, the knights rest at the fountain and admire its sculptures, but their interlude is broken off by the appearance of Ippalca, with news of Rodomonte's theft of the horse Bradamante had sent to Ruggiero. Once again it is time for a knightly adventure; but this time, the same knights who moved with the group precision of a courtly dance ensemble through the rescue episode gradually fall apart into a pack of squabbling individuals who resemble the chaos-prone Moors and Maganzesi rather than the heroic rescuers. The second episode of the canto in effect deconstructs the first one, showing us a side of the Christian knights which corresponds to the greed of "il tempo nostro" ("our own day") rather than to the courtly honor of "l'antiqua etade" ("days of old").

We follow the progress of this transformation in our epic hero, Ruggiero. He starts out by making sure that he is the one who will help Ippalca, while hiding his true motive for wanting to do so from Bradamante's kinsmen because he does not want them to realize his liaison with her. Ricciardetto, who would normally be the one to avenge the slight to his sister, defers to Ruggiero's desire to undertake the adventure alone because of the service Ruggiero has just performed in freeing

186 KATHERINE HOFFMAN

his cousins. We are still in the territory of courteous formulas, but an unchivalrous deceptiveness now lurks behind them; Ruggiero is beset by the quandary that plagues him throughout the *Furioso*, pulled in different directions by his loyalty to Bradamante and his sense of his knightly honor. Once they have set off together, Ippalca tells him the full story of Rodomonte's challenge, and his rage swells:

> vede che biasmo e *dishonor* gli fia,
> se tôrlo a Rodomonte non s'affretta,
> e sopra lui non fa degna vendetta.
>
> (65.6–8; emphasis mine)

(it would be to his shame and discredit if he did not hasten to retrieve him from Rodomonte and wreak suitable vengeance upon the thief.)

The concept of honor has already undergone a metamorphosis here. Ruggiero feels dishonored for three reasons: the stolen horse is his, Bradamante sent it to him, and Rodomonte took it to spite him. Of the three, only one has to do with his love for his lady; the other two pertain to his horse and the challenge to his name. Instead of originating in a principled love and obligation to others, as in the exordium and the rescue episode, honor here has as much to do with personal considerations as with justice, and the personal considerations are two-thirds egotistical pride. Ruggiero's personal honor attaches not only to his behavior, but to his horse and to his name. A challenge to his name is in effect equated with the theft of his horse, both prized possessions deeply involved with his honor. When it comes to his own sense of identity as a knight, honor is a possession as much as an ethical program.

This ethical dimension is emphasized when Ruggiero immediately comes upon a fork in the road; the longer route leads gently over the plain, while the shorter is rough and mountainous. At this point we might recall the last time we saw Ruggiero faced with a choice of paths.[6] On Alcina's island (6.60), even though he had been warned by Astolfo to

6. For Ariosto's use of the *topos* of the crossroads and the figure of Hercules in relation to Ruggiero and the *Furioso* as a whole, see Saccone 210–19 and Ascoli 52–70.

take the rough, mountainous road to Logistilla, Ruggiero allowed himself to be detoured along the smooth level path to Alcina's castle, with disastrous results. In that encounter, too, Ruggiero was dealing with allegorical representations of avarice (Erifilla and her monster offspring and followers). In the island episode, the plot was carefully designed to strike at Ruggiero's pride in his knightly prowess. Alcina's handmaidens, simply by appearing, chased away the monsters he was having such difficulty vanquishing; his resulting humiliation (6.70) made him "content" to ignore Astolfo's advice and go with them down the smooth road. His manipulation by means of his pride was completed when, along the way, the maidens offered him the sop of defeating Erifilla, the figure of Avarice itself. He was encouraged to strike her down, but deterred from actually killing her. This hollow victory allowed Ruggiero to maintain a sense of himself as a valorous knight, when in fact it demonstrated his enslavement, through his pride, to Alcina and the principle of sensual satisfaction she represented. He became her "valoroso" knight, valuable to her, that is, for material (sensual) reasons, not for his honor and moral integrity; and he accepted this debased standard for himself by deluding himself that the two kinds of "valore" were one and the same.[7]

The reuse of the crossroads *topos* at this point in canto 26 serves to emphasize how Ruggiero, in his rage, has slipped back into the state of egotistical delusion that made him vulnerable to Alcina twenty cantos earlier. He has regressed from conceiving of honor as the service of a just cause in the rescue episode (easy enough to do when there is no pressing personal stake in the cause) to conceiving of it as pride in his own prowess and reputation, and the accoutrements that accompany and symbolize them; physical prowess has become a means of asserting his personal worth, rather than a manifestation of its intrinsic existence. And in his pride Ruggiero ceases to be heroic, and becomes subject to chance and luck, just as the Moors and the Maganzesi were in the rescue scene. As if to illustrate this, the trope of the divided road is turned on

7. For some suggestive extended readings of the Alcina episode, see Giamatti, *Earthly Paradise*, 142–64, and Ascoli 121–246.

its head and emptied of its usual moral meaning: by taking the shorter road, Ruggiero and Ippalca miss Rodomonte going the other way on the longer one, and they are forced to track their prey back along the rejected road to the very fountain from which they started out. The faster way to Ruggiero's goal would have been the longer road, but the fastest way of all would have been to stay put. There is no way for Ruggiero to have known this; the laws of chance have taken over what was a moral trope, turning his perfectly reasonable shortcut into the longest cut possible.

With the entry of Rodomonte and Mandricardo into the action, we reach the midpoint of the canto. The entire remainder is taken up by an ignominious brawl among Rodomonte, Ruggiero, Mandricardo, and Marfisa. The two pagan knights, having made a truce in their fight over Doralice when they heard that Agramante needed their help, come with her to the fountain and find Ricciardetto, Aldigiero, Viviane, Malagigi, and Marfisa, who has donned woman's clothing. Mandricardo immediately devises a scheme to acquire Marfisa for Rodomonte, so that he himself can keep Doralice.[8] He challenges the knights, and rapidly downs all four of them. But when he comes to claim Marfisa, she reveals herself to be a knight, too; they fight; and, since each wears enchanted armor, it ends in a draw. Rodomonte stops their fruitless combat by suggesting that Marfisa join them in helping Agramante and the pagan cause, and she gladly agrees. At this point Ruggiero returns, and challenges Rodomonte. The fighting starts all over again, only worse; at issue are Ruggiero's horse, which Rodomonte refuses to give up, and the arms and insignia of Hector, symbolic of imperial Trojan heritage, which both Ruggiero and Mandricardo claim the sole right to wear. Ruggiero challenges Rodomonte; Mandricardo challenges Ruggiero; Ruggiero fights Rodomonte; Mandricardo fights Ruggiero; Marfisa fights Mandricardo again; Rodomonte fights Ruggiero again; Ruggiero fights Mandricardo

8. Marfisa's proposed role as a currency of exchange between male knights, and her challenge of it, raise the issue of the "valore" of women in the poem. Gender issues have been highlighted in some excellent recent criticism of the *Furioso*, centering mainly on the figures of Bradamante and Angelica; see Benson, Finucci, and both articles by Shemek.

again; Rodomonte fights Ricciardetto. There is every reason to believe that this series of duels will go on forever when Malagigi brings it to an abrupt halt by enchanting Doralice's palfrey so that it runs away with her, drawing Rodomonte and Mandricardo in hot pursuit. The result is a deafening silence.

But although Rodomonte and Mandricardo have brought most of the contention with them, and seem to take it away with them when they leave, they are not solely responsible for the brawl. As we have seen, Ruggiero's detour with Ippalca, characterized by his burgeoning pride and rage, has in fact led up to it. And the scene reinforces this connection in its vocabulary. Mandricardo, treating Marfisa as an object to be acquired by force, offends the honorable conception of love, replacing it with an economic one:

> sí come Amor si regga a questa guisa,
> che vender la sua donna o permutarla
> possa l'amante, né a ragion s'attrista,
> se quando una ne perde, una n'acquista (70.5–8).[9]

(as though Love could thus be ruled, so that a lover could sell or swap his lady, and have no reason to be sad if, on losing one lady, he acquired another!)

But love is more than just part of the subject-matter of the stanzas in which Mandricardo tries to carry out his scheme. Viviane unhorsed falls "all'erbe e ai fiori . . . in braccio" ("in the soft embrace of meadow-

---

9. On the proposed exchange of Marfisa for Doralice, as well as the speaker's outrage over it, see Zatti 98–99. He argues that Mandricardo's proposal strikes at an ideological nexus of the *Furioso*, since it questions the whole ideal of coutly love which sends Orlando mad and makes Zerbino and Isabella tragic heroes: "la spregiudicatezza del cavaliere pagano riflette una luce ambigua non solo sul negativo della follia di Orlando, ma anche sul positivo della sublime devozione di Zerbino, procedenti da una medesima matrice ideale" ("the pagan knight's broadmindedness casts an ambiguous light not only on the negative spectacle of Orlando's madness, but on the positive spectacle of Zerbino's sublime devotion, since both proceed from the same ideal," 99; translation mine).

grass and flowers"; 74.4); Aldigiero falls similarly "tra fiori e erbe," and, wounded, is described as having "rosso sul'arme, e pallido nel volto" ("crimson on his armor and pallor in his face," 76.8). The language of the scene itself evokes the flowery landscape and traditional colors of courtly love poetry. Mandricardo is destroying the ideal of courtly love as he downs the four knights, and the ideal is connected precisely, as the exordium showed, with the love of honor. Even Marfisa is only able to fight Mandricardo to a draw; with his magic armor and Orlando's sword, he is invincible. Ruggiero's love for Bradamante is part of his motive for wanting revenge on Rodomonte, but it is his own honor, not hers, that he feels has been so grieviously slighted. Once Mandricardo has symbolically overthrown the basis of courtly honor in unselfish love, the field is open for the endless squabbling to follow, which only Mala- gigi's supernatural intervention can stop.

Another aspect of the scene's vocabulary also reinforces the Christian knights' degeneration. In stanza 77, Ricciardetto falls to Mandricardo, but "non già per suo fallo" ("not by his own fault"): he would have proved his worth better "se fosse stato pari alla bilancia," had he been Mandricardo's equal or had equal luck. Had Rodomonte not intervened in stanza 84, Mandricardo and Marfisa could have fought for days: "tutto quel giorno e l'altro appresso ancora" ("all that day and the next one as well"). Similarly, when Rodomonte behaves in an uncharacteristically Job-like way and refrains from fighting Ruggiero, we are told he would do the same even if he had Ruggiero completely in his power; normally he would travel miles for such a contest, but on this occasion, with Agra- mante so much in need of him, he would refuse the chance to fight even Achilles. Meanwhile Ruggiero gives Mandricardo such a blow that

> partito
> quel colpo gli avria il capo, come un torso,
> se Ruggier Balisarda avesse avuta,
> o Mandricardo in capo altra barbuta. (126.5–8)

(that blow would have split open his head like a stalk, had he had Balisarda, or had Mandricardo been wearing a different helmet.)

Finally, Ricciardetto would have fared ill at Rodomonte's hands had Malagigi not intervened to stop the brawl. The episode is filled with "would haves" and "could haves"—conditional verbs which constantly remind us that under different circumstances, things would have turned out differently. We have left the realm of chivalrous moral convention and entered one of luck and circumstance, which is also the realm— as we saw with the Moors and the Maganzesi earlier in the canto—of self-defeating chaos. Within this realm, the one who prevails (however momentarily) is the one with enchanted armor or a special sword. Ruggiero and his companions have jettisoned all pretense that their honor consists in helping others and are simply fighting for their own personal prestige. The more they isolate their individual honor as a purely personal quality, the more it contradicts itself: it becomes a moral imperative which can only be fulfilled by physical force and by lucky chance.

This paradox is manifest in the way the knights' identities melt together as the scene progresses. Viviane, Malagigi, Aldigiero, and Ricciardetto fall indistinguishably one after the other to Mandricardo's lance. When Mandricardo comes to claim Marfisa, he cites common usage as his claim to her: "che di ragion di guerra così s'usa" ("the custom of war must be observed"). She, however, cites the same rule to defy him, since she belongs to no knight but herself. When they run at each other and both fall, he curses the sky and the elements, she curses Heaven. Both are cursing their bad luck, but both are wearing enchanted armor which protects them at the same time that it frustrates their ability to attack each other. The harder they fight against each other, the more they are the same. And as the brawl continues, counterchallenge follows challenge, counterattack follows attack, and each knight claims what the other has until there is literally nothing to choose among them. The irony is of course that the things for which they are fighting are badges of identity, signs that designate the bearer as being unique and a hero.[10]

10. Discussing the even more extreme continuation of this brawl in canto 27, Donato highlights the same themes I have been stressing, of identity, difference, and the objects of desire: "Since the objects that generate quarrels matter little and for any practical purpose

Both Mandricardo and Ruggiero claim the distinguished valor and heritage that the arms of Hector symbolize, both Ruggiero and Rodomonte the distinguishing advantage of a horse like Frontino. Yet in contending for these mobile evidences of particularity, they only become more and more alike, while their personal honor becomes indistinguishable from childish egotism and pride. For these greedy knights, instead of something that inspires chivalrous action, honor has become a commodity that one acquires. Honor has become a form of avarice.

The two-part narrative action of canto 26, then, presents us with two pictures of knightly honor: a definitive, ideal one, associated with a golden age and presented as an orderly relation among people which is both moral and aesthetic; and a degenerate version of this ideal, the parody of heroism found in the brawl scene, in which moral valor has been reduced to the physical value of swords and armor and horses. But what are we to make, finally, of this juxtaposition? Canto 26's exordium would have us believe that the ideal of honor was the norm in the golden age, only to degenerate in "our time"; but when was this golden age? Bradamante and Ruggiero are given as the examples of golden-age love and honor, yet the same knights, and especially Ruggiero, who displayed mythic heroism based on moral superiority in the rescue episode effortlessly match the rage, pride, and moral blindness of their foes by the canto's end. The *Furioso*'s action ostensibly takes place in the new golden age of the founding of the Este dynasty, yet in the second episode of the canto the very founder of the dynasty is the prime example of modern degeneracy. How far back do we have to go for the golden age? [11]

---

are interchangeable, every quarrel is identical to any other and there is absolutely no possible way of establishing an order within the quarrels themselves except through the drawing of lots—that is to say, by establishing from the very beginning purely arbitrary differences where there is [really] nothing but identity" (41).

11. This sense of nostalgia might usefully be related to Quint's discussion in *Epic and Empire* of the death of the epic, even as it was experiencing a last revival, in the Renaissance. According to Quint, the epic's "nostalgic visions of aristocratic autonomy" were ceasing to be relevent in a world where "the nobility . . . found their traditional role and their identity

This is precisely the question addressed by the descriptive passage that divides the canto. To Ruggiero and his friends, stanzas 30–53 are an interlude of well-earned rest after an arduous fight; the relief sculpture on the fountain is only added entertainment, just as the *Furioso* itself is an entertainment for the Este court and the nobles of Italy in their moments of leisure. But the subject matter of the relief is more than just entertainment; it picks up the themes of the exordium, illustrating the moral struggle of honor against avarice that Ruggiero has just won and is about to lose in the following action. In the exordium, it was not only love of riches that stood opposed to honor: Bradamante "non amò tesor, non amò impero" ("loved not wealth or power"). This broader definition of avarice is taken up in the fountain passage, which thus enlarges the scale of the canto's discussion. At the same time that the fountain sculptures allegorize the struggle between honor and avarice, they prophesy the glory of sixteenth-century Europe; the allegory and the prophecy invite the reader to step back and consider the discussion of honor and avarice in terms of their actual operation in history. The individual knightly honor and avarice embodied in Ruggiero's adventures is seen in the context of political behavior.

In the fountain relief, avarice is represented as an emblematic beast reminiscent of Erifilla on Alcina's island, wreaking havoc in the courts of sixteenth-century Europe. The beast is fought and defeated by the great Renaissance monarchs Francis I, Maximilian of Austria, Charles V, and Henry VIII, along with Pope Leo X; but like Erifilla, though it is defeated, it is not eliminated. Avarice preys upon both the Christian and the pagan nobility: "a re, a signori, a principi, a satrapi" ("kings and barons, princes and satraps"; 32.4). But its worst damage is done at the papal court at Rome. The kings and the pope are presented as its natural

undermined both from below, in competition with a newly powerful mercantile bourgeoisie, and from above, as their role and identity were absorbed as instruments in the war machinery of modern absolutist monarchy" (10).

enemies; it is a corruption that must be rooted out of a healthy society from the top down, in typical Renaissance hierarchical fashion. Yet when the beast is finally subdued, the freed nobles who troop to the victory celebration are few: "Parea del mondo ogni timor rimosso" ("it appeared that the world was freed of every terror"), but "nobil gente accorrea, non però molta" ("nobles hastened up—however, not many"; 36.5.7). The story is thus a commentary on sixteenth-century European society and on society and human nature in general.

Curiously enough, however, this story is told twice during the fountain interlude. First it is told by the brief inscriptions and the poem's description of the allegorical figures, which were so artfully carved that but for the lack of voices they seem to the viewers to be alive. The allegory shows all fortresses, castles, and cities falling to the beast, who overruns more and more territory until it has overtaken the entire world: "tutta / e Francia e Italia e Inghilterra, / l'Europa e l'Asia, e al fin tutta la terra" ("all of France and Italy and England, Europe and Asia, and in the end all the world"; 31.6–8). Thus its influence is described in terms of conquering power; the avaricious behavior of the nations is their warlike contention and territorial greed. But it doesn't stop there; at its extreme, Avarice takes over the entire cosmos:

> Par che agli onor divini anco s'estenda,
> e sia adorata da la gente sciocca,
> e che le chiave s'arroghi d'avere
> del cielo e de l'abisso in suo potere.   (33.5–8)

(It seemed he was even acceding to divine honors and being worshipped by the mindless rabble; and that he had arrogated to himself the custody of the keys to heaven and hell.)

Taking over the keys of Saint Peter, Avarice has invaded the papacy as well as the temporal world; the pope, selling clerical honors and moral sanctions to enrich himself materially, is adored for his splendor by the credulous folk to whom he is supposed to be ministering. The allegorical correction for this state of affairs shows the kings and the pope throwing off their avaricious ways in stylized victory over the beast: Francis I and Maximilian wound each of its sides with their swords, Charles V stabs its throat with his lance, and Henry VIII gores its breast with his dart, while Leo X holds it by the ears.

Malagigi's interpretation of this allegory gives the figures the voice they lack, telling the story a second time, but with major additions. First he adds an explanation of the fountain's origin: Merlin created it in King Arthur's time to prophecy future glory, and yet the great deeds of the future will be necessary only because avarice will have spread so pervasively. Malagigi also adds an account of the beast's own origins to the depiction of the fountain's creation. It came into the world from hell

> a quel tempo che fur fatti
> alle campagne i termini, e fu il pondo
> trovato e la misura, e scritti i patti. (40.2–4)

(at the time when lands were assigned boundaries, when weights and measures were established, and pacts written.)

Avarice, having come into the world along with the measures and rules that govern both internal and external social relations, is inextricable from civilization, from national and political self-consciousness, and from the rules that govern them. The coming of Avarice marks the end of the golden age when harmony was the natural state of affairs, there were no nations, and laws and measures were therefore unnecessary.

We have come full circle to "l'antiqua etade" ("days of old") again. But at this point the true golden age, the age when avarice was unknown, has been pushed back into an irretrievable past: before the age of Ruggiero and Bradamante and Charlemagne, which seems a golden age to the sixteenth-century nobility; before even the age of Arthur and Merlin, the golden age to which the characters of the Furioso, in turn, look back; back into an age before boundaries between territories, weights and measures, or pacts among nations. That is, it is beyond the reach of imaginable history, and even of the founding myths that are appropriated as history. Once appropriated, such myths lose their "golden age" quality because there is always a further golden past from which they, too, derive their values.[12] By showing the world of the poem as part of an infinite progression of golden age myths, Ariosto points out the interpretive constructedness of history: each age looks back to the illusion of a historical golden age, a real connection with its founding myth. This critique of idealized, mythic history discredits the entire dynastic structure of history that the poem is supposed to be celebrating. There is a sense here that the old view of history was losing its value in explaining current events—the same conviction which was leading Machiavelli and Guicciardini to write history in new ways during Ariosto's lifetime.

The grouping of rulers who fight Avarice reinforces this sense of historical constructedness. In the final, 1532 version, the group's membership telescopes the time period over which the poem appeared, for example mixing the Emperor Maximilian, who died in 1519, with his successor Charles V. In *La strategia delle varianti* Alberto Casadei traces the way that, in passages like these, Ariosto typically added new historical figures and events without erasing the earlier, outdated ones in the successive editions of the *Furioso*, thus achieving an "atemporal" effect, which is emphasized even more in canto 26 by a shift in verb tense from imperfect to present between the 1521 and 1532 editions (Casadei 50). This collapsing of contemporary history into one scene emphasizes a sense of continuity behind the political changes which occurred between 1516 and 1532, even as it registers them.

The idea that modern times have degenerated from an ideal past is not jettisoned completely, however; the situation has worsened as history has proceeded. Malagigi explains that in their own time, avarice has managed to overwhelm only the common folk, but that by the time of the prophesied future (that is to say, in the present of the *Furioso*'s sixteenth-

---

12. For a good general overview of the golden age myth, see Levin. Defining the golden age as "a nostalgic statement of man's orientation in time, an attempt at transcending the limits of history" (xv), he maintains that "the growth of historical consciousness in the sixteenth and seventeenth centuries encouraged a mood of lateness," which led to a resurgence of nostalgia for an ideal past (148).

century readers) the monster will have conquered the nobility as well, and things will be so bad that all the world will beg them to vanquish it. Malagigi has put the sculpture's depiction of Avarice's gradual conquest into a historical context that points directly to the moral responsibility of the *Furioso*'s Este readers.

In his interpretation of the sculpture, Malagigi further emphasizes the beast's connection with the mythical dawn of civilization by comparing it to the Python of Ovid's *Metamorphoses* (1.438–44), the great snake which was one of the first creatures to result from the union of earth and water when the world was made. In Ovid, Apollo is only able to kill the Python with great difficulty, by shooting it with the arrows he has used hitherto only to kill animals for food; civilization begins when the animal within man is subdued for the good of the collectivity, and when hunger is no longer the greatest enemy of humankind. Like Erifilla and the allegorical beast, the Python is hard to kill, but unlike them it finally is done away with. But while Ovid's Python is subdued to make civilization possible, avarice in the fountain story comes along *with* civilization — including the pacts that define honorable relations among nations. Avarice arises with national self-consciousness, honor, and responsibility, and seems therefore to be involved in their very essence. History, in this sense, is the history of avarice's destructive progress through the world. This view corresponds to what Felix Gilbert has called the Boethian view of history common in the Middle Ages—that in the fallen world, Providence looks exactly like Fortune (Gilbert 218). But where is the controlling Providence that gives the medieval and humanist historian a sense of a world beyond the human realm of fortune? Of what does the honor of these conquerors of the beast Avarice consist?

In the allegory, Francis I conquers avarice by crossing the Alps and capturing Milan. The invasion described in this passage is that of 1515, which was launched by the newly crowned king in revenge for the French defeat at Novara two years earlier.[13] The allegory assumes that Francis I's

---

13. The French avoided the trap laid at Monginevro by Prospero Colonna ("chi all'incontro avrà occupato il monte" ["who shall have invaded the mountains from the other side"];

just reign will replace the corrupt, avaricious one that defied him, yet no mention is made of his generosity or justice, as we might expect. Instead Malagigi emphasizes Francis I's splendor:

> quando in splendor real, quando nel resto
> di virtú farà molti parer manchi,
> che già parver compiuti; come cede
> tosto ogn'altro splendor, che'l sol si vede.   (43.5–8)

(regal in splendor, a paragon of every virtue, he shall expose the shortcomings of many who had seemed perfect—just as every light is diminished the moment the sun appears.)

Exploiting the familiar etymological ambivalence between moral virtue and physical strength in "virtú," Malagigi presents the king's royal splendor as his chief virtue, the only one mentioned separately and by name. The four rulers and the pope of this passage were famous in the early sixteenth century for their liberality, especially Maximilian and Henry VIII, and like all Renaissance princes they led lives of private luxury and ostentatious public display. But in the context of this passage, their splendor is not a generous, but a conquering one. Thus Francis I's heroic qualities put him on the level of Caesar, Hannibal, and Alexander, the great conquerors of antiquity: his "eccellenze" include

> l'animo del gran Cesar, la prudenza
> di chi mostrolla a Transimeno e a Trebbia,
> con la fortuna d'Alessandro, senza
> cui saria fumo ogni disegno, e nebbia.   (47.3–6)

(the courage of great Caesar, judgment such as Hannibal showed at Trasimene and Trebbia, and the fortune of Alexander, without which every scheme must be but smoke and mist.)

---

defeated the Swiss mercenaries at Marignano ("l'Elvezio spezzerà" ["shall devastate the Swiss"]); and captured Milan ("espugnerà il castel" ["shall capture the castle"]): stanzas 44–45.

In stanza 44, the reference to Francis I's recent (in 1516) ascension to the throne, "non ferma ancor ben la corona in fronte" ("his crown not yet firmly on his brow"), emphasizes his need to secure his power and that of France as much as the "giusto . . . e generoso sdegno" ("righteous and noble anger") that the speaker piously attributes to him in the next breath. The figurative level of the allegory's meaning, in this historicizing explanation of it, keeps collapsing into the literal one; the metaphor of conquest keeps pointing not to a moral process that is *like* conquest, but to actual conquest. Francis's honor is based not on his virtues, but on his conquering power.

The entire stanza immediately following the description of the battle reinforces the comparison between Francis and the conquerors of classical times by lingering on the conquering power of his sword:

> Sopra ogn'altr'arme, ad espugnarlo, molto
> piú gli varrà quella onorata spada.   (46.1–2)

(To conquer it, one weapon will be worth far more to him than any other: his honored sword.)

Symbol either of violent conquest or of just retribution, Francis I's honored sword draws together and inextricably connects his valor, his splendor, and his conquering might. The corruption of the Milanese court, symbolized by the beast, resides presumably in the greed of its rulers, who rule badly because they rule only for themselves. Yet we have found no assurance in the passage's presentation of him that the leader of the antiavarice league has motives that are any less self-serving. Instead the implication is that they have directly to do with his desire for personal power and the desire of France as a nation to rule in Italy—in a word, *impero*.[14] Honor and avarice are the measure of national as well as personal

14. Casadei differs from this reading of Francis I, placing the emphasis in the comparison on the virtues, rather than on imperial status of the classical rulers. Thus he sees Francis being made a type of the ideal Renaissance knight. Casadei argues that the imperial comparison is not made until the 1532 *Furioso* and the imagery it adds surrounding Charles V, who is set up as political conqueror in contrast to Francis's ideal knight. This is part of his

relations, and they threaten to become confused on the national level in the same way that they do (as in the brawl scene) on the personal one. In 1516 when the first *Furioso* appeared, Francis I had recently ascended the throne and, with the invasion of 1515, was the new Machiavellian hero on the scene. By 1532, Francis had been decisively defeated, and Charles, now emperor and newly crowned by Pope Leo's successor, had consolidated his power and was in firm control of northern Italy. Yet despite the revisions between 1516 and 1532, Francis remains the active hero of the fountain allegory; the knightly hero and the imperial conqueror are melded together, reinforcing the collapse of political honor into avarice.

Thus Malagigi's version of the allegory represents the rulers, especially Francis I, as demonstrating something very like the avarice they are supposed to be fighting—but on a national scale. The description of the sculpture that precedes Malagigi's interpretation allows room for a good, honorable kind of *impero* that opposes and can vanquish the avaricious conquering power the beast displays. Malagigi's interpretation, however, relegates this optimistic view of societal, national honor to a golden age which is by definition irretrievable; throughout history, and increasingly so, *impero* has been the tool of avarice, not honor. Malagigi has introduced a sense of history into the allegory, which, when examined, raises the persistent possibility that the "historical" connections between present acts and a past golden age are wishful constructs, idealizations that contradict reality. Ruggiero and Bradamante are supposed to represent a golden age of the Este dynasty, yet Ruggiero himself must look either back to an unimaginable time before history, or forward by prophecy to the very future that is looking back to him, for a golden age. History and human experience admit no golden-age moral certainty; the

---

larger thesis that the local, Este-oriented politics of the 1516 *Furioso* are broadened to a more comprehensive view of Italian peninsular politics by the 1532 edition (Casadei 51–57). The added stanzas (50–52) in the later edition, which add many more Italian nobles of the 1520s to the list of those applauding Avarice's defeat, confirm his contention that the politics of the poem broadened in its successive editions, but in my view Casadei downplays too much the imperial imagery surrounding Francis I.

moral superiority of courtly honor is literally out of date. When the historical past is conceived of in mythic terms as a golden age, the history ends up corrupting the myth instead of the myth purifying the history. The myth loses its moral fixity and becomes hopelessly enmeshed in the moral ambiguities of human experience.

In the end, then, Malagigi's interpretation has the effect of teasing out the ambiguities that were latent in the allegory and highlighting the difference between the moral ideal of a providential history the allegory holds up, and a narrower, sharper perspective on the historical events to which it refers. In war-torn northern Italy of the early sixteenth century, it would be hard to see the "conquering sword" as merely a metaphor. The French invasions of Italy, starting in 1494, were by the early sixteenth century recognized as inaugurating an era of war, international interference in Italian affairs, and dizzying political reversals that made the last half of the Quattrocento seem in contrast, ironically, itself a golden age of stability and prosperity (see especially Gundersheimer 225–77, Durling 138–40, Gilbert 203–70, Pocock 114–55). Since 1494, Ferrara had passed repeatedly into and out of alliance with France and Rome and Venice, buffeted like all the Italian states by political forces it could not control. In the fountain allegory, Francis I is the heroic scourge of the beast Avarice, a conqueror who is motivated by justice, not greed; but the passage as a whole emphasizes the distance between this idealization and the practical concerns of power politics and war. And in fact, the dedication to national self-aggrandizement and the greed for power which motivate these practical concerns are exactly the characteristics represented by the allegorical beast. Read in this light, then, the seeming encomium of Francis I can be seen as a piece of mocking sarcasm. By describing the French king as the ideal of generous, disinterested international diplomacy, the passage only emphasizes how much the French seemed in retrospect to have been a dreadful incarnation of the destructive greed the beast represents. Beast and pursuers are one, just as Ruggiero and his friends degenerated into the image of their former enemies.

At the same time, however, that this allegory read ironically deplores the French invasions and the general political situation in sixteenth-century Italy, it can be read straightforwardly as a castigation of the Italian city-states. In this view, their greedy strife, reminiscent of the Christian-pagan brawl that ends the canto, was not only intensified by the invasions from the north but occasioned them in the first place. These periodic invasions (which became commonplace in the Cinquecento, with Italy a battleground for the great struggle between the Valois and the Hapsburgs) were seen as a chastening scourge, culminating in 1527 with the ignominious sack of Rome by uncontrollable mercenaries. The beast Avarice, if it represents the pride and greed of the Italian states, got a severe beating from the northern invasions—even if the invaders were hardly the ideal chivalrous figures depicted in the fountain allegory. The French could be seen as having performed some of the function, in Italy, of the allegorical heroes.

But if the fountain passage suggests a resemblance, under the idealized facade, between the allegory's heroic rulers and the squabbling knights in the canto's narrative action, the parallel works the other way too. Honor in the fountain allegory is, at least in theory, directed toward the righting of social wrongs—the corruption of church and state because of the greed of those who run them. But avarice is so pervasive in society and in human nature in these times, according to the allegory, that those who celebrate its downfall

> eran pochi verso gl'infiniti
> ch'ella v'avea chi morti e che feriti. (53.7–8)

(were few compared with the countless number that the monster had slain or wounded)

This emphasis on the need to fight avarice as a social ill only reminds us that the knights in canto 26's action are ignoring their social responsibilities (to fight for their kings) in their pursuit of personal ends. The obvious parallel to this state of affairs in the poem as a whole is Orlando's desertion of Charlemagne to pursue Angelica. Malagigi makes this point about social responsibility, however, just before the knights demonstrate in the ensuing episode that they have missed it completely. The fountain allegory and the brawl, from this perspective, reflect back and forth upon each other: the rulers of sixteenth-century Europe are unlike their idealized pictures on the fountain in exactly the same way that the enraged Ruggiero charging alternately at Rodomonte and Mandricardo is the complete opposite of the chivalrous hero of the rescue episode. The moral degeneration traced on the individual level in the narrative sections of canto 26 mirrors the moral problems with sixteenth-century politics traced in the fountain episode. All of these heroes, like Orlando, have left off fighting for their common cause, leaving their moral duty languishing in their preoccupation with personal concerns.

The example of Orlando, in fact, underlies the whole canto, and underlines the connection between the knights of the poem and their sixteenth-century counterparts. Like Orlando, the knights Mandricardo, Rodomonte, and Marfisa immediately drop all thought of Agramante and the siege of Paris the moment their honor is questioned; Ruggiero submerges his ultimate Christian duty to Bradamante in his rage over his horse and arms; and the other knights are inevitably drawn into the whirlpool of ever-renewed challenge and attack. But it goes even further than that; as the brawl continues, they all come closer and closer to a state of *furor* which is reminiscent of Orlando's madness, witnessed only three cantos earlier in Canto 23. Underneath his staunch refusal, at first, to fight Ruggiero, Rodomonte hides a burning rage, "tanto a quel punto sotte le faville / le fiamme avea del suo *furor* sopite" ("so well had he doused the flames of his wrathful temper to a mere glow," 95.5–6; emphasis mine). When Mandricardo challenges Ruggiero's right to wear Hector's arms,

> Come ben riscaldato àrrido legno
> a piccol soffio subito s'accende,
> cosí s'avampa di Ruggier lo sdegno. (103.1–3)

(As a piece of dry tinder, warmed through, will catch fire at the slightest puff, so Ruggiero's fury blazed up.)

Against the rising wrath of the three knights, Marfisa's efforts to conciliate the growing conflict are as futile as those of a peasant trying to stave off the flood and save his fields (no fruitful intercourse here). Ruggiero and Rodomonte, prefiguring their final battle in Canto 46, attack each other like beasts: "come cinghial, . . . come il lione . . . tolto su le corna / dal bue" ("like a boar, like a lion who has been tossed by a bull"). And Ruggiero storms about Rodomonte like a tempest. Thus their madness, like Orlando's, is a loss of humanity as well as identity; like Orlando, they have become raging animals, forces of nature. The beast Avarice is one more manifestation of the frustrated desire to possess that drove Orlando mad, and thus it is no accident that the canto ends with Doralice fleeing in a way that makes her resemble Angelica in canto 1.[15] The movement of Doralice at the end of canto 26 also contrasts with the faithful fixity of Bradamante at the canto's opening, just as Bradamante's love of honor in another contrasts with the self-seeking prestige-grubbing of the brawlers. Yet apart from her idealized portrayal in this canto, Bradamante spends the greater part of the poem wandering out in search of Ruggiero; the ideal of stationary faith turns so easily into the movement of desire. Their pursuit of personal honor, at its extreme, brings them to the same impasse as the pursuit of desire—the endless chase after the ever-receding object. At the end of the canto, Rodomonte and Mandricardo are chasing Doralice, while Ruggiero and Marfisa are chasing Rodomonte and Mandricardo; the chase of desire and the chase of personal honor are the same chase, and this fruitless, ongoing chase is the very stuff of history.

IV. Literary Honor and Avarice in the Furioso

There is a further similarity between the *furor* of Orlando and that of the canto 26 knights. Malagigi mounts the spell that ends the brawl "sol

15. Zatti also makes the connection between canto 26 and Orlando's madness (98). Zatti argues that these characters' madness mediates the poem's critique of a dogmatic and rigid adhesion to both the courtly code of ideal chivalric behavior and the Petrarchan literary code of sublime love.

con parole" ("only with words"). His voice prompts another; the spell, causing the horse to jump and run, makes Doralice scream, and her voice is the only thing that can rouse Rodomonte and Mandricardo from their rage. If language is the feature that separates humanity from animals, it is appropriate that it should be a verbal magic which is able to bring the self-perpetuating brawl to an end. Malagigi plays an interesting role in his control over the action at this decisive moment. His verbal magic, along with his magical powers of interpretation in the fountain scene, display a power with words that mirrors that of his own poet-creator, Ariosto, the creator of the verbal magic that is the *Furioso*. But although Malagigi's spell is Ariosto's instrument for changing the course of the canto's action, it does not resolve the conflict. Instead it simply moves the story to another part of the forest: the squabbling of these knights over their horses and arms continues, with even more complications, through canto 27 and beyond. What Malagigi's spell does is to set a horse in motion, recollecting the original flight of Angelica, which not only began the poem's action in canto 1, but also established the runaway horse and the pursuit of desire as the quintessential emblem of Ariosto's narrative technique.[16] Malagigi's spell ending the brawl highlights the fact that the poem's narrative is after all a verbal creation of Ariosto's, perpetuated or terminated at the artist's will.

Similarly, the fountain itself, even in the description that precedes Malagigi's interpretation, is a verbal creation of the poet Ariosto, who has added it to the series of supposedly Merlin-built fountains created "sol con parole" by his predecessor Boiardo in the *Innamorato*. The knights' request that Malagigi explain the fountain's allegory to them highlights art as the carrier of multiple meanings, a construct that must be interpreted. Their initial reaction to the fountain, naive enjoyment, also points the way to a more sophisiticated interpretive response by the knowledgeable reader, who by this time in the poem has certainly

16. The seminal analysis of frustrated desire as a major thematic and structural principle of the *Furioso* is of course by Donato. The imagery of horses and reining is explored in detail by Giamatti, "Headlong Horses," 292–304 and Ascoli 376–93.

picked up the cues of moral meanings behind the poem's actions and descriptions. Finally, the contemporary historical content of the fountain's supposed prophecies also raises the whole question of the *Furioso*'s celebratory poetic project. Looking back at the exordium, we can see that Ariosto has linked the theme of honor to that of literary art from the very beginning of the canto. In stanza 1, honor's opposite is described in quasi-literary terms as "lo *stile* avaro" ("style of greed")—not only as avarice itself, but as a style; and the principal way that ladies who do not follow the style of greed can become "gloriose e immortal" ("glorious and immortal") after death is through the sort of artistic celebration which the poem, throughout its length and in the very next lines, performs for Bradamante. The suggestion is that to the opposing moral styles for ladies' behavior there correspond opposing literary styles; behind the greedy ladies of "il tempo nostro" ("our own day") we discern the shadows of the greedy poets of today who flatter their patrons for gain regardless of their real virtue or sinfulness. This questioning of the poet's motives is a recurrent theme of the *Furioso*, culminating in the allegory of fame on the moon in canto 35 (35.1–30) and in the exordium to canto 36 (36.1–10). The canto 26 exordium of course aligns itself with the virtuous few who follow the old style of praising only "vera bontade" ("true goodness"), with the second stanza presented as a prime example. In fact, the second stanza includes an idealized rendition of the *Furioso*'s whole dynastic element, including the love of Bradamante for the valorous Ruggiero and the many "cose / nei secoli avenir miracolose" ("exploits in future times deemed miraculous") that they do and that befall them. The exordium as a whole, then, both defines the moral discussion to come in the canto, and suggests a self-conscious link between the problem of honor and avarice and the *Furioso*'s own poetic enterprise.

This view of the poem as verbal creation collapses the sculpted figures together with Malagigi's explanation, and in fact with the narrative surrounding the fountain episode, into one verbal construct; the sculptures themselves are only linguistic constructs in Ariosto's game of building upon and surpassing Boiardo and his other literary predecessors. The point of view represented by the poet and his stand-in, Malagigi—as interpreter, spell-worker, creator—might seem at first one of power, from which we could for a moment gain perspective on the confusing, continuous process by which honor and avarice, greed and desire succeed each other.[17] But how effective is this magic? Doralice's wordless scream echoes the howls of the mad Orlando, who lost the power of language along with his sanity, just as Rodomonte's and Mandricardo's pursuit of her echoes Orlando's of Angelica. If the runaway horse figures the runaway passion that eludes moral and rational control,[18] then the passions of anger and pride have only been replaced by the passion of desire, and the poet implicates himself (as he has in the Turpin passage and many others throughout the poem) in the uncontrolled blindness of passion.

Of course, balancing every runaway horse in the *Furioso*, as A. Bartlett Giamatti pointed out, is the unforgettable image of the hippogriff curbed and ridden by Astolfo ("Headlong Horses" 300). Giamatti traces the way that this classical image of moral and rational control over the passions has by the Renaissance, in the literary epic, also become an image of aesthetic control.[19] But at the end of canto 26 the knights are

17. Durling's analysis of the poet-persona's control of the narrative in the *Furioso* (114–32) has been reinforced by many, including Donato, Parker, and Zatti; Giamatti makes one of the strongest cases for it in "Headlong Horses." Astolfo's control of the hippogriff and detachment single him out, in Giamatti's view, as a stand-in for the poet. While Giamatti may overstate the case—by underemphasizing both the irony with which Astolfo's career is presented and the balancing metaphors in the poem which emphasize moral action rather than detached control—it is clear that Astolfo and parallel figures such as Malagigi are used to raise the issue of the effect of the medium of poetry on its message in key places throughout the poem.

18. As it does in the exordium to canto 11 (11.1–2), just at the point when Ruggiero, in his eagerness to ravish the naked Angelica, has speedily forgotten every moral lesson he learned from Logistilla, and is about to lose the hippogriff.

19. Via Dante; according to Giamatti, in the *Commedia* the aesthetic and the moral are united in the imagery of curbing" ("Headlong Horses," 270), and it passes this imagery down to its descendants in the Renaissance epic. Ascoli, however, sets Giamatti's positive reading against Donato's negative interpretation of the hippogriff representing the impossibility, by its very grotesqueness, of such a union (Donato 58), in order to raise the possibility that Ariosto is using this imagery ironically (Ascoli 248).

all galloping off after each other, completely out of control. Any knight who was "in se raccolto" ("self-possessed") in the rescue episode is now "di se tolto" ("out of control") in the brawl (Ariosto's terms, highlighted by Giamatti); and they have all passed from one state to the other without comprehension. Any understanding of the connection comes from viewing these experiences, not living them. In just such a way, the plight of Viviane and Malagigi in the first part of the canto did not touch Ruggiero personally, and his and Marfisa's emotional detachment went along with their mythical heroism. Once they have a personal stake in what is happening, and especially it seems when their pride is involved, they descend inevitably to the world of real human experience, where motives are mixed and moral absolutes become façades behind which to hide the more unsavory ones.

This realm of mixed motives extends to include the poem itself and its author. Far from being merely a disinterested observer, Ariosto has a direct personal stake in the reception of his poem, his literary reputation, and the operations of power at the Este court, which extend to the arena of artistic patronage and production. His checkered career with Ippolito and Alfonso gave him frequent cause for bitterness (Catalano 439–454, 533–34, 538–39, 555; Gardner 118–29, 158–64, 178–84, 233). The Este are notably absent from the fountain's potentially scathing political analysis (there is a brief mention of "due Erculi, due Ippoliti" among the nobles who cheer Francis I's victory) — for very clear reasons, given the way that the beast and its pursuers tend to merge. This moral analysis of the current political scene, too dangerously critical to make directly to one's patrons, can be made more safely on the level of humanity and general international politics, while at the same time it can apply to the general conditions of northern Italian society.[20] By leaving the Este patrons out of the analysis, the passage allows them

20. The only Italian states specifically mentioned are those who were enemies of Ferrara and the French. The particular drubbing that Rome receives may be due to a combination of Ferrara's increasing rebelliousness against the tradition of papal control, the time-honored tradition of criticizing clerical corruption, and Ariosto's personal disappointment in the lack of expected patronage from Leo X.

to participate in its moral outrage at Italy's desolation without having to acknowledge their own part in it. The Este were at the height of their power in the first half of the Cinquecento; this canto demonstrates—by what it leaves unsaid as well as by what it hints at and shows directly— exactly how precarious the dependence of artists like Ariosto on their patrons' princely favor was. It shows the dark side of what Lauro Martines calls art's "alliance with power" in the Italian Renaissance (Martines 241–71). In Ferrara, Boiardo's *Innamorato* has given way to Ariosto's *Furioso*, which only continues the chase after both generous patronage and a stable point from which meaning can be reliably constructed, and moral values applied to experience.

Canto 26 thus invites two seemingly conflicting readings: a celebratory interpretation which seems to correspond to the heroic, chivalrous order of the "danza" ("dance") in "l'antiqua etade" ("days of old") represented by Ruggiero and Marfisa in the rescue episode, and which underlies the prophecy of a providential dynastic history; and another more critical interpretation whose negative name is "lo stile avaro" ("style of greed"), which corresponds to "il tempo nostro" ("our own day") and appears as a corrupt and debased version of the first, and which leads us to a sense of history as merely opportunistic human action.[21] As we saw in the exordium, "lo stile avaro" is that of those who flatter for gain. And yet taken as a whole, while canto 26 has shown the impossibility

---

21. My reading here may be compared to that of Zatti, who traces the way that the *Furioso* consistently questions the "cortese-cavalleresco" value-system that it is based upon and tries to validate. See especially Zatti ch. 4, 91–111. Comparing Ariosto's and Machiavelli's analysis of ideals subject to fortune, Zatti contends that in the *Furioso*, "più che la presenza di due codici moral-comportamentali a confronto, si registra qui la contraddizione interna a un modello classicheggiante di umanistica misura e di idealità cavalleresca, che tuttavia non ha la forza di generare una consapevole alternativa, limitandosi così a farsi specchio delle sue lacune e delle sue 'disarmonie' " ("more than the presence of two moral-behavioral codes in confrontation, we find registered here the internal contradictions of a classicizing model of humanistic measure and chivalric ideals; which all the same does not have the force to generate a conscious alternative, limiting itself to holding up a mirror to its own limitations and 'disharmonies,' " 100; translation mine).

of the ideal, heroic style in the real world of overwhelming human passions, it does not play flattering sycophant to the Este patrons either. Instead, Ariosto treads a thin line between the two styles. He cannot simply praise the worthy, for as the fountain scene and the brawl amply show, the patrons and all they represent are not simply (or even mainly) worthy; but neither does he simply flatter them at the expense of all moral integrity. His critique of his patrons is indirect, yet it is there, and it is scathing. The art of the *Furioso* in this canto self-consciously inhabits the gap between an impossible (but worthy) ideal and a reprehensible (but recalcitrant) reality, between values and experience, between old and new senses of history—using the former in each case to criticize the latter and the latter to show the insufficiency of the former. The fountain scene, the silent allegory in conjunction with Malagigi's deconstructing interpretation of it, enlarges the scale of this dialectical critique beyond the question of personal morality to include the question of national morality, and finally, of aesthetic morality as well.

Works Cited

Ariosto, Ludovico. *Orlando furioso.* Ed. Lanfranco Caretti. Torino: Einaudi, 1966.

———. *Orlando furioso.* Trans. Guido Waldman. Oxford: Oxford UP, 1974. Rpt. 1991.

Ascoli, Albert Russell. *Ariosto's Bitter Harmony: Crisis and Evasion in the Italian Renaissance.* Princeton: Princeton UP, 1987.

Benson, Pamela. *The Invention of Renaissance Woman.* University Park: Pennsylvania State UP, 1992.

Bruscagli, Riccardo. *Stagioni della civiltà estense.* Pisa: Nistri-Lischi, 1983.

Casadei, Alberto. *La strategia delle varianti: Le correzioni storiche del terzo Furioso.* Lucca: Pacini Fazzi, 1988.

Catalano, Michele. *Vita di Ludovico Ariosto.* 2 vols. Biblioteca dell' "Archivium Romanicum." Vols. 15–16. Ed. G. Bertoni. Florence: Olschki, 1930–31.

Donato, Eugenio. "Per selve e boscherecci labirinti: Desire and Narrative Structure in Ariosto's Orlando Furioso." *Literary Theory / Renaissance Texts.* Ed. Patricia Parker and David Quint. Baltimore: Johns Hopkins UP, 1986. 33–62.

Durling, Robert. *The Figure of the Poet in Renaissance Epic.* Cambridge, Mass.: Harvard UP, 1965.

Finucci, Valeria. *The Lady Vanishes: Subjectivity and Representation in Castiglione and Ariosto.* Stanford: Stanford UP, 1992.

Gardner, Edmund G. *The King of Court Poets: A Study of the Work, Life and Times of Ludovico Ariosto.* New York: Greenwood, 1906, rpt. 1968.

Giamatti, A. Bartlett. *The Earthly Paradise and the Renaissance Epic.* Princeton: Princeton UP, 1966.

——. "Headlong Horses, Headless Horsemen: An Essay on the Chivalric Romances of Pulci, Boiardo, and Ariosto." *Italian Literature: Roots and Branches.* Ed. K. Atchity and G. Rimanelli. New Haven: Yale UP, 1976.

Gilbert, Felix. *Machaivelli and Guicciardini: Politics and History in Sixteenth-century Florence.* Princeton: Princeton UP, 1965.

Gundersheimer, Werner. *Ferrara: The Style of a Renaissance Despotism.* Princeton: Princeton UP, 1973.

Javitch, Daniel. "Rescuing Ovid from the Allegorizers: The Liberation of Angelica, Furioso X." *Ariosto 1974 in America.* Ed. A. Scaglione. Ravenna: Longo, 1976. 85–98.

Kennedy, William. "Ariosto's Ironic Allegory." *Modern Language Notes* 88 (1973): 44–67.

Levin, Harry. *The Myth of the Golden Age in the Renaissance.* Bloomington: Indiana UP, 1969.

Martines, Lauro. *Power and Imagination: City-States in Renaissance Italy.* New York: Random House/Vintage, 1979.

Parker, Patricia. *Inescapable Romance: Studies in the Poetics of a Mode.* Princeton: Princeton UP, 1979.

Pocock, J.G.A. *The Machiavellian Moment: Florentine Political Thought and the Atlantic Republican Tradition.* Princeton: Princeton UP, 1975.

Quint, David. *Epic and Empire: Politics and Generic Form from Virgil to Milton.* Princeton: Princeton UP, 1993.

Shemek, Deanna. "Of Women, Knights, Arms, and Love: The Querelle des Femmes in Ariosto's Poem." *Modern Language Notes* 104 (1989): 68–97.

——. "That Elusive Object of Desire: Angelica in the *Orlando Furioso.*" *Annali d'italianistica* 7 (1989): 116–41.

Saccone, Eduardo. "Prospettive sull'ultimo Ariosto." *Modern Language Notes* 98 (1983): 55–69.

——. *Il soggetto del Furioso e altri saggi tra Quattro e Cinquecento.* Napoli: Liguori, 1974.

Zatti, Sergio. *Il Furioso fra epos e romanzo.* Lucca: Pacini Fazzi, 1990.

III
ACTING OUT FANTASIES

The Masquerade of Masculinity:
Astolfo and Jocondo in Orlando furioso,
Canto 28

VALERIA FINUCCI

"Mirror, mirror on the wall,
Who's the fairest of them all?"
—J. Grimm, "Snow White"

"Madamina, il catalogo è questo
Delle belle che amò il padron mio,
Un catalogo egli è che ho fatt'io,
Osservate, leggete con me."
—L. Ponte, *Don Giovanni*

Stories are written to be read. So what do we make of an author who urges his readers to skip the very tale he is proposing for their attention? "Donne, e voi che le donne avete in pregio," Ludovico Ariosto pleads in *Orlando furioso* (1532),

> per Dio, non date a questa istoria orecchia,
> a questa che l'ostier dire in dispregio
> e in vostra infamia e biasmo s'apparecchia; ...
> ... Lasciate questo canto, che senza esso
> può star l'istoria e non sarà men chiara.   (1–2)

("Ladies—and ladies' devotees—by all means disregard this tale which the innkeeper is preparing to relate to the disparagement, to the ignominy and censure of your sex. . . . Skip this canto: it is not essential—my story is no less clear without it.")[1]

---

1. Numbers refer to octave. Unless otherwise noted, all citations are from canto 28 (English translation by Waldman).

To be sure, such modesty is often employed as a device: in *Metamorphoses* 10, Ovid uses the same tactics before he embarks on the story of Mirrha:

> Terrible my tale will be!
> Away, daughters! Away, parents! Away!
> Or, if my singing charms you, hold this tale
> In disbelief; suppose the deed not done;
> Or, with belief, believe the punishment.

Ovid had some ethical reasons for his warning, since Mirrha's tale is one of incest and unlawful daughterly desire. But what Ariosto is planning to retell, almost two-thirds of the way through his chivalric romance, is a bawdy story of male sexual prowess, one that his readers would hardly find culturally demanding or difficult to condone. In fact, he did not even invent his subject matter, for this novella had been widely circulated in print, under the title "Historia del re di Pavia."[2] That Ariosto included this authorial disclaimer for reasons of morality appears unlikely.

Could this repudiation then constitute a rhetorical ruse, one that Ariosto—often accused of being logorrheic—might have invented to tantalize his readers? First published in 1516 in forty cantos (slightly revised in 1521), the *Furioso* had six additional cantos and hundreds of new stanzas added at the time of the now standard 1532 edition. The convoluted plot of love and war, which constitutes the main thrust of the work, is spiced here and there with set pieces from the novella tradition. Some of these pieces are ribald, others are not; but salaciousness is not usually a trigger for authorial restraint in the *Furioso*. It may well be that Ariosto knew that the best way to catch his readers' attention was to advise them

---

2. See Beer, 239 and 255, n. 86. Ariosto's novella constitutes the core of Giovanni Sercambi's "De ingenio mulieris adultera," and displays an array of Boccaccian elements that the audience of the time might have easily recalled. For connections with Boccaccio, see Rajna, 436–55; and Barbirato, 331. Barbirato retraces points in common with the *Decameron*'s stories of King Agilulf, 3.2; Madonna Filippa, 6.7; and Pinuccio, 9.6. This story also bears an intriguing resemblance to the frame story of *One Thousand and One Nights*, where Shahryar and his brother decide to have the women they enjoyed during the night killed at dawn. To avoid such an outcome Scheherazade spins her one thousand and one tales. See Scaglione.

to pass over what he was writing. One has simply to recall how successful, narratively speaking, this and other frustrating interruptions of action in the text are to realize that he knows how to create suspense in preparation for a climactic ending.[3]

To take Ariosto at his word—and his argument makes him an advocate of women's rights *ante literam*—the tale of King Astolfo and of the nobleman Jocondo is not worth reading because women do not fare well in it. Ariosto then rushes to offer the one reason he is constrained to include such a story in his *Furioso*: it is there for its historicity, because the piece comes to him from his master, Turpino, whose (questionable) authority guarantees the "truthfulness" of his other sources, at least in matters of war. Finding the novella politically incorrect for his mixed audience, Ariosto distances himself from its ostensible narrator, an innkeeper. This narrator, however—himself a new historicist *ante literam*—knows how to avoid being dismissed: his story is true, he claims, and his source is the nobleman Gian Francesco Valerio, a historical figure of Ariosto's time.[4] Whether the novella recounts actual events or not is beside the point, for even at his most cogent moments Ariosto is unreliable; as for the innkeeper, he may be giving his story about women's inconstancy and sexual hunger a mysogynistic spin because he needs to entertain an irascible knight, the Saracen Rodomonte. Rodomonte has hated women ever since he was scorned by his fiancée, Doralice; he had seized the occasion for a lengthy, vituperative curse on the female sex just a few octaves earlier (27.117–21).

Before offering my own hypothesis on Ariosto's motives for his disclaimer, let me summarize the novella. In two key details Ariosto revises the tale of the Lombard king who travels from country to country following his discovery of the queen's infidelity: he adds the theme of King Astolfo's handsomeness and accompanying narcissism, which seems out of place in an account of men cuckolded by women, and he shrinks

---

3. For a reading of this rhetorical tactic, see Javitch, "*Cantus interruptus*."
4. In the 1516 and 1521 versions of *Orlando furioso* there is an octave in which the innkeeper asserts that his story is true. See the Ermini edition of the text, 2.26, 75.

the entourage of traveling companions to one, Jocondo. The story be-
gins with the presentation of Astolfo as the most handsome man in the
world: "fu ne la giovinezza sua sì bello, / che mai poch'altri giunsero a
quel segno" ("[he] was so handsome in his youth that seldom had any-
one matched him for beauty," 4). When, in this masculine version of the
"Snow White" fairy tale, the king is told that there is a better looking
man than himself residing in Rome, he summons the rival, Jocondo, to
his court to see if the claim is true. He is warned, however, that his invi-
tation may be refused, for this knight is too much in love with his wife
ever to leave her. Eventually Jocondo undertakes the journey to Lom-
bardy, but he has immediate reasons to regret this decision: turning
back to retrieve a neck chain given him by his wife as a good-bye present
and pledge of faithfulness, he finds her in bed with a stable boy. Need-
less to say, by the time he arrives in Lombardy his vaunted beauty is lost.
It takes some time for Jocondo to discover a way out of his melancholic
moroseness and become once more true to his name. The occasion that
affords him this recovery is the chance witnessing through a hole in
the wall of King Astolfo's wife, dallying with a dwarf. Feeling equal or
even superior to the king now, for at least his own wife had the decency
to choose a better-looking man with whom to commit adultery, he di-
vulges the matter to Astolfo. Since the king had promised not to harm
the queen, no matter what was revealed about her, the two men decide to
take their anger elsewhere.[5] They leave Lombardy on a winding journey
across Europe with the avowed purpose of inflicting on one thousand
men what has been inflicted on themselves. This task turns out to be
easy, since no woman resists their sexual advances, whether because of
their handsomeness or because of the money they generously bestow.

Pleasure soon disappears from this arrangement, however, because
the repetitive nature of their enterprise and the need to continuously
exercise their prowess make a chore of what started out as a sexual

5. On a similar story of wife's betrayal, that of Anselmo being told of his wife's unfaithful-
ness in cantos 42–43, the reaction is more primitive: Anselmo decides to kill her, although
eventually he changes his mind.

adventure: when every desire is satisfied, what is the point of desiring more? To curtail this useless libidinal expenditure, the two friends resort to a new arrangement. They buy a young Spanish woman, Fiammetta, from her father and pledge to share her sexually on an equal basis on the understanding that a woman may remain faithful if two men, rather than one, take turns in satisfying her sexually.[6] But even this movement from polygyny to polyandry proves inadequate, failing as it does to take into account female agency: one night Fiammetta, exercising for the first time her desire to desire, to give the story a female-friendly reading—or, to give it a mysogynistic one, letting her own sexual hunger dictate her actions, as do all the women in our story—allows a former acquaintance, a Greek, to make love to her while she lies in bed between her two owners. Astolfo and Jocondo will take no more: acknowledging that women have minds and sexual needs of their own, they choose monogamy and return to their wives. "Così fan tutte!"

No wonder that this novella, with its abundance of erotic offerings, touched a nerve in people's imagination. Among the many set pieces of the *Furioso*, the story of Astolfo and Jocondo was the most successful from the very beginning: influential imitations were written not only in Italy but also in France (by La Fontaine) and Spain (by Cervantes and the picaresque writers); even today it is considered perhaps the best novella of the sixteenth century.[7] True, better than the main storyline, the novellas could nonchalantly offer some sexual *frisson* or give a polemical reading of gender frictions, thanks in part to their "disposable" nature: for, since the protagonists were not the main ones, Ariosto could eliminate—with no apparent damage to the structure of his work—whatever proved too controversial during readings at court. But I would prefer to link the success of this story to the obsession with erotica that swept

6. Unfortunately, even though Astolfo and Jocondo's sexual record is nothing short of outstanding (including the Spanish girl Fiammetta and their wives, they seduce one thousand and three women), they are still unable to match the record set by Don Giovanni, who reached the same number in Spain alone ("e in Spagna son già mille e tre").

7. See, for example, Guglielminetti 14. On Ariosto's novellas, with references to Boccaccio and Boiardo, see Franceschetti.

Italy during the first half of the sixteenth century and reached its apex in the middle 1520s. The publication of Pietro Aretino's *I sedici modi (The Sixteen Ways)*, which coupled Giulio Romano's illustrations of human sexual acrobatics and the "divino" Aretino's verbal nimbleness, took place in 1524; and painfully hilarious treatises on the goodness of prostitution, such as Aretino's *Ragionamenti* (1534), come out of the same obsession.[8] Titian's *Venus of Urbino*, the great masterpiece of erotic painting (1538), was still to be executed of course, yet its commission, made years earlier, was fostered by the contemporary interest in the representation of the nude and eroticized body. Voyeuristic and virtuosistic sex, in short—narrated, versified, played, or illustrated—sold.

The moral of the Astolfo and Jocondo story is that it is pointless for men to try to keep up with the desires of sex-crazed females.[9] By renouncing all women in the end, our two men seem to suggest that the reason for cuckoldry is not that men are insufficiently potent, but that they somehow have been caught up in a definition of manhood that is linked, wrongly (as can be expected), to women's needs. No matter how often virility is staged, it must be endlessly restaged, they discover, when maleness is tied to a genital sexuality that requires women's faithfulness for confirmation of its adequacy. In this sense, the "wise" knight Rinaldo, with Orlando, the most powerful Christian paladin, is right, unlike our two men, in refusing to learn whether his wife has been faithful:

> Ben sarebbe folle
> chi quel che non vorria trovar, cercasse.
> Mia donna è donna, ed ogni donna è molle:
> lascian star mia credenza come stasse. (43.6)

---

8. Another contemporary case of illustrated erotic scenes is Jacopo Caraglio's *The Loves of the God*, which, like Aretino's *Modi*, used an apparatus of verses. On "Venus" and eroticism in art, see Pardo and Ginzburg.

9. Barbirato argues that while men leave women for love in the *Furioso*, women leave men because they are moody (Doralice), oversexed (Gabrina), or greedy (Argia) (345–47). In short, women are incapable of true love and keep their own interests in mind at all times.

(He would be an utter fool who sought for what he had no wish to find. My wife is a woman, and every woman is pliant. Let my faith remain undisturbed.)

Whatever Rinaldo's preference, the story of Astolfo and Jocondo was understood and rewritten by a host of writers throughout Europe as the two men's Don Juanesque revenge for their wives' infidelity; the fact that the king and his companion break faith with the one thousand other women in the process never became a point of interest. Ariosto, as I mentioned, urges his readers to skip over this story because it disparages women. But I would like to propose a different reason for his disclaimer. What I read in canto 28 is not so much a sustained reflection on the perils for men of female sexuality but rather the perplexing working through of the notion that masculinity may be other than what it is made to stand for in culture, and that virility — notwithstanding the satyriasis displayed — does not per se guarantee male power. That this insight is embedded in the most unlikely setting for the questioning of masculinity, given the collection of "manly" acts recorded in the story, may be less strange than it appears, for this chivalric epic probes, after all, the tattered illusions and phantasmic progresses of romances of old. And what a success the *Furioso* was at it: the text was an incredibly popular one, read, sung, recited, memorized, even staged throughout most of the sixteenth century, and with sales handily surpassing those of the Bible.[10]

As I read it, Ariosto portrays man in the Astolfo and Jocondo story as just as feminized and narcissistically centered on physical attributes as woman can be in traditional culture. In short, masculinity is a construct, a masquerade, a display, a performance, just like femininity.[11] It

10. For an account of the spectacular success of the *Furioso*, see Javitch, *Proclaiming a Classic*, ch. 1; and Beer. Although Matteo Maria Boiardo's *Orlando innamorato*, of which the *Furioso* is a "continuation," was technically the first book published in Italian to reach beyond the rich and educated, only the *Furioso* sold by the thousands. For a reading of gender in the *Furioso*, see Finucci, *The Lady Vanishes*; see also Shemek, Benson, and McLucas.

11. For femininity as a masquerade, see Lacan, "The Meaning of the Phallus," 85, and Rivière. For a companion piece to this essay, see my study of the masquerade of femininity

has often been said that the sixteenth century was obsessed with the notion of female promiscuity and the consequences that the lack of chastity among females had for men.[12] By juxtaposing a plot centered on men's revenge for this penchant in women, a revenge that requires the display of some forms of macho masculine sexuality, with a characterization of maleness that is constructed as shifting, Ariosto underscores the neurosis behind the cultural construction of masculinity as the defining trait of what a man is. I do not intend to link effeminacy directly with a discourse on homoeroticism, because for me effeminacy is central to any discourse on sexuality, be it heterosexual or homosexual. This is especially true when we focus on a period in which new, ideologically inflected definitions of male subjectivity were being explored and when what constituted socially legible homosexual behavior is different from our contemporary view.[13] At the same time, I do not read effeminacy as a sure sign of disorder and demise of the Law of the Father. A feminized, or potentially unstable, masculinity should perhaps not be pathologized in an era in which male homosocial ties clearly had their place within

("The Female Masquerade") as I see it played out in Ariosto's Dalinda and Gabrina episodes. In that essay I read the masquerade of femininity following Freud, Lacan, Rivière, and Irigaray, as well as Mary Ann Doane and Sue-Ellen Case.

12. Though this concern is reflected in many stories of the *Furioso*, the compulsive examination of sexual indiscretions and paranoid fears of cuckoldry better fits, I think, another genre—theater—and is associated with such names as Machiavelli, Bibbiena, and Aretino, as well as Ariosto.

13. Valerie Traub has argued for such delinking in the context of Shakesperean drama (136). See also the essays in Goldberg. In the popular view, Lombards were the people who most practiced and exported the crime of sodomy, as the Englishman, Sir Edward Coke, complained: "*Bugeria* is an Italian word, . . . and it was complained of in parliament, that the Lumbards brought into the realm the shameful sin of sodomy, that it is not to be named, as there it is said." See *The Third Part of the Institutes of the Laws in England* (London, 1797) and Cohen 188. In the *Decameron*, Boccaccio makes the protagonist of his only transparently homosexual story (5.1), Pietro, a man from Lombardy. But also keep in mind that, for Germans, sodomizers were specifically Florentines, not Lombards. See Roche. Many in Europe, on the other hand, considered Venice the "depraved" city par excellence of the period, given its close ties to the East and its reception of unorthodox customs. See Ruggiero.

a heterosocial/sexual symbolic. My tools in examining this story come mostly from psychoanalysis, because Freudian, and, to a lesser extent, Lacanian analyses allow me more fully, I hope, to probe the inner life of characters offered as ambiguous and to concentrate on their confused articulations of identity.

Don Juan–style sexual gratification has dependably come across in culture as manly. But does the possession of hundreds of women make men heterosexual in their choice of object? More to the point, are our two fetishists of the penis, Astolfo and Jocondo, more masculine because they dispense their sexual favors widely? Lacan suggests that this is hardly so: "virile display in the human being itself appears as feminine" ("The Meaning of the Phallus," 85). In the early modern period, too, excessive sexual expenditure was linked to emasculation, because overconcentration on sexual, bodily matters showed lack of manly restraint and practicality, and thus made man resemble woman. A case in point is that of Antony, whose love for Cleopatra rendered him womanish in Shakespeare's play. Medical treatises of the time stressed the same principle: moderation made a man manly; too much or too little sex was unhealthy, turned the individual morose, was detrimental to the brain, and could lead to an early death.[14] Erotic manuals tended to emphasize the quality, variety, originality, and theatricality of the heterosexual encounter, not repetition.[15]

Ariosto has Astolfo and Jocondo start their debauching errantry not because they are sexually unfulfilled or wanton themselves but because they want to cuckold other men for the sake of reestablishing some sexual "worth" for themselves after their respective conjugal betrayals. Thus their motive for hypersexuality is political. The mistake of conflating penis and phallus, however, makes these two friends forget where

---

14. Most medieval or early modern doctors, from Isidore to Guainerius and from Della Porta to Parè, had something to say on sexuality and the way to express it, help it, and regulate it. The field of critical studies on the subject is wide. See, for example, Jacquart and Thomasset, and Laqueur.

15. See, for example, Aretino.

power lies; their journey toward the consolations of romance turns out to be full of pitfalls, founded as it is on the vagaries of sex: not sex as suicide, as in the case of Callimaco in Niccolò Machiavelli's comic play *La Mandragola*, but sex as social competition. Astolfo and Jocondo's search is also misplaced because their aim is to recoup a loss brought upon them by their wives. But this loss exists only in their unconscious—their sexual misadventure at home undermined their feelings of wholeness and narcissistic omnipotence—because they never truly possessed what they now mourn as lost.

This journey into sexual one-upmanship reveals more homoerotic frisson than heterosexual curiosity, a fact that is evident not only when Astolfo and Jocondo competitively share more or less the same women in sequence, but also when they perversely require one female to lie in bed between them, in a triangulation of desire à la Girard, so that each is present when the other is sexually engaged.[16] Their agenda is homosocial rather than sexual; it is directed at men and addresses male fears about sexual inadequacy. But it has nothing to do with women, whose only task is to provide the body. In this sense I would like to revise the formulation posited originally by Eve Sedgwick in which homosociality is presented to prevent homosexuality. In my view, this homosocial state of being does not necessarily exclude homoeroticism. Thus the apparently heterosexual triangle with Fiammetta somehow enacts the Freudian insight that in triangular situations a man can sublimate his feelings for another man by claiming that he does not love him, for she is the one who ostensibly does.

Central to this male/male sharing is the circulation and exchange of women, who are bought, used, and then released for further sexual consumption. No actual female face or name is supplied to the reader in this story, apart from Fiammetta's, since the point for Astolfo and Jocondo is not to think of any woman as a subject, but to act out an exhibitionistic need to be seen by other men as manly through the possession of their anonymous wives. Hypermasculinity is a masquerade theatrically staged

16. Of Girard, see *Deceit*.

for the sake of other men; what drives our two companions is after all collectomania, not erotomania. As Irigaray argues, "reigning everywhere, although prohibited in practice, hom(m)osexuality is played out through the bodies of women, matter, or sign, and heterosexuality has been up to now just an alibi for the smooth workings of man's relation with himself, of relations among men" (172). Even the two men's final settling on the prostitute Fiammetta confirms that the prostitute has worth precisely because she has been used, that is, she has been thoroughly objectified and rendered passively available.[17] As the narrator explains, Fiammetta is chosen because it is easy to have her, for she provides the "furnace" in which to satisfy unproblematic sexual needs:

> Pigliano la fanciulla, e piacer n'hanno
> or l'un or l'altro in caritade e in pace,
> come a vicenda i mantici che danno,
> or l'uno or l'altro fiato alla fornace.   (54)

([they] took their pleasure with her in turns, in peace and charity, like two bellows each blowing alternately upon the furnace.)[18]

The ambiguous masculinity of Astolfo and Jocondo is not all that undermines the prevalent reading of this story as one of male hyperbolic sexual prowess, for Ariosto adds a trait to his characterization of the two men that does not usually sit well with hypermanhood: male beauty. If beauty is what turns women into objects of desire, why would an author strip men of their customary position of power as subjects and emphasize a physical attribute that turns them into objects? And why write so fulsomely of male beauty in a story in which women seem to be taken

---

17. "The more it [the body] has served," Irigaray writes, "the more it is worth. Not because its natural assets have been put to use their way, but, on the contrary, because its nature has been 'used up', and has become once again no more than a vehicle for relations among men" (186).

18. On the choice of Fiammetta because of the "comodità" she offers, see Barberi-Squarotti, 41.

the least by the handsomeness of their counterparts? But here is how Astolfo is introduced by the innkeeper:

> Bello era, ed a ciascun così parea:
> ma di molto egli ancor più si tenea.
> Non stimava egli tanto per l'altezza
> del grado suo, d'avere ognun minore;
> né tanto, che di genti e di ricchezza,
> di tutti i re vicini era il maggiore;
> quanto che di presenza e di bellezza
> avea per tutto 'l mondo il primo onore.   (5)

(Yes, he was handsome, and everyone recognized it, but he was far and away his own greatest admirer for this. He valued less the eminence of his station, which set him over everybody else; or the magnitude of his wealth and nation, which made him greater than all the neighbouring kings; what he valued most of all was the pre-eminence he enjoyed throughout the world for his beautiful physique.)

Now, although the issue of male handsomeness has not been tackled with the frequency with which female beauty has been on a variety of fronts, Vitruvian parameters of ideal proportions did indeed center on the male body. Unlike female beauty which was associated with ornaments, following a more or less standard Petrarchan catalogue of parts, male beauty was linked to measurements. Moreover, given that beauty is the good of all exertions on the part, say, of the visual artist, and culturally and biologically the male body was considered more functionally perfect than the female, the artist, it was thought, could realize the perfect idea of beauty precisely by representing the male body.[19] Even treatises dedicated solely to women, such as Agnolo Firenzuola's *On the Beauty of Women* (1541), made clear that female and male beauty are com-

19. See, for example, how Benedetto Varchi works through this concept in Michelangelo's art, both visual and poetic, in *Il libro della beltà e della grazia* (published in the 1540s but written earlier).

plementary: every woman should have something of the male in her and vice versa.

For Neoplatonics, male handsomeness was of course a visualization of inner virtues: good external features were thought to reflect an internal moral goodness, or, as Bembo states in Castiglione's *Il libro del cortegiano*, the handsome are good ("e li belli boni," 4.58).[20] In this sense, Astolfo would, by virtue of being handsome, be a better king than most, and Jocondo, a good nobleman. But such is hardly the case: Astolfo gives little thought to political matters and even leaves his kingdom unattended for reasons that are hardly pressing; and Jocondo proves incapable of or uninterested in improving his father's fortune: "la roba di che 'l padre il lasciò erede, / nè mai cresciuta avea nè minuita" ("the inheritance bequeathed him by his father had neither grown nor shrunk in value," 9). Both men, in fact, although born into a position of wealth, power, and authority, are described as emasculated on these fronts; their masculinity in this respect is given as problematic, as if to parallel some hypothesized disarray of the paternal function. Politically speaking, the two men would then reflect the historical failure of contemporary Italian princes and dukes to further a nation-building process, a goal that eluded Italy for centuries to come. This inability, Machiavelli teaches, had its roots in the opportunism, disinterest, and narcissism of those in charge: real-life, mindless, self-centered Astolfo figures.

Let me note that the politics of spectatorship are not necessarily the same when handsome men, rather than women, are displayed. Astolfo might have been a worthy subject for a painting by Apelles and Zeuxis, the narrator emphasizes. But the women that Zeuxis painted had their individualities canceled out in the representation, because Zeuxis seized whatever parts of five female bodies he saw as perfect and painted them to reflect his idea of a single beautiful woman as his mind constructed her.[21] Here, by contrast, Astolfo is presented as in control of his representation. He lavishly praises the parts of his own body that are well

20. On this connection, see Haywood, 131.

21. For a reading of the Zeuxis story in these terms, see Castiglione's *Cortegiano* (1528),

formed: "essendosi lodato / or del bel viso or de la bella mano" ([he] "often flattered himself, one moment on his beautiful face, the next, on his exquisite hand," 6). And he presents himself to his courtier Fausto as sure of his superior body: "avendolo un giorno domandato / se mai veduto avea, presso e lontano, altro uom di forma così ben composto" ("he asked Fausto whether he had ever, anywhere, set eyes on a man as well built as himself," 4–5). Jocondo too, for his part, knows what he needs to improve his physical goods and acts on this knowledge, as when he orders rich clothes for himself before leaving Rome to meet Astolfo: "vesti fe' far per comparire adorno, / che talor cresce una beltà un bel manto" ([he] "ordered new clothing, to make his appearance suitably dressed—for a handsome cloak will enhance a man's looks," 12).[22] Emphasis on handsomeness then is empowering and not objectifying when one is in charge of the representation.[23] In no instance, however, no matter how much masculinity is deessentialized, is the handsome male body directly appreciated by another man, for heterosexual boundaries must remain in place at all costs. Any unrepressed form of erotic contemplation would inevitably be understood as homosexually voyeuristic. Fausto, for one, although he listens politely, is unimpressed by Astolfo's body.

Of course, if beauty does not make men powerless, it makes them womanish. Interestingly, the feminization of men does not entail here,

---

book 1, section 52. See also Finucci, *The Lady Vanishes*, ch. 2. According to Pliny, Zeuxis's women were chosen following an intriguing scheme: first the most handsome men of Croton were identified, then their sisters were chosen. Thus male beauty prefigured and confirmed female beauty. I would like to thank Mary Pardo for reminding me of this connection.

22. More than today, clothing stood for status and class in the sixteenth century. Sumptuous display was not necessarily linked to effeminacy, if done with taste and no garish excess. In the *Cortegiano*, for example, Castiglione spends considerable time examining the appropriate color, shape, and material of clothes befitting sophisticated courtiers on the rise.

23. Note, in this context, Laura Mulvey's insights on pleasure in looking, where the visual representation of men stands for castration: "according to the principles of ruling ideology and the psychical structures that back it up, the male figure cannot bear the burden of sexual objectification" (20).

as is often the case, the masculinization of women, because the narrative's motor is erotics and not power. Femininity is cast as disruptive and at odds with social relations no matter who embodies it, woman or man. When men are represented as feminized, the apprehension that this gender-related anxiety generates is displaced onto the other sex, and the result is the representation of women as out of control, devouring. Such a movement is clearly mapped in our tale. Women do not simply make love: their erotic pursuits make them betray their well-endowed husbands, choose lewd men, and forget all laws of decency and status-connected self-restraint. Jocondo's wife is unwilling to wait more than an hour after her husband's departure to betray him; the queen gives herself to a dwarf even after he rebuffs her. The two women's lovemaking is shown to have animal connotations: the first lover chosen is dirty; the second, grotesquely shortened. By contrast, Fiammetta is cast as less of a threat to the two men than their wives because she is unmarried and functions as a servant. Once it is settled that she will be equally shared, the level of erotic competition between the two men diminishes, since she will—by contract—betray, but only with the other person in the triangle.

Another instance of problematic characterization of masculinity in this novella can be seen in the rendering of the two men's narcissism, again a feature at odds in a story that apparently means to poke fun at women.[24] In "On Narcissism," Freud hypothesizes that the route toward outgrowing narcissism is through outgrowing one's self-centeredness and loving another. Men give up their narcissism with time but women, he argues, often retain it. The men in our story have clearly not followed the path outlined above, despite their age. Astolfo and Jocondo have a specular relationship, in that each identifies with the other by desiring the same object. A characteristic of the narcissist is, notoriously, an exhibitionistic desire to be admired. Such is the case of Astolfo. He constitutes his own love object and, although married, not only loves himself

---

24. Elizabeth Bellamy has called narcissism "the dominant neurosis of the Furioso" (87). For a study of female narcissism in the Furioso, see Finucci, The Lady Vanishes, ch. 4.

alone, but even solicits admiration from his subjects—until he is told that there is another man as handsome as he. Rather than try to eliminate his rival, like the queen in "Snow White," he decides to check out the competition. His desire to see his purported double is partly a desire to dominate the other by the superiority of his physical attributes and partly a desire to recognize himself in the other. When he gets reassured that Jocondo is not superior to him in beauty, he begins to "love" him because the other, handsome and of the same sex, constitutes his mirrored image.[25]

Although seemingly less narcissistically self-centered than Astolfo, Jocondo displays many of the same traits. I have already remarked on his desire for sartorial style. His love for his wife is narcissistic in that he finds gratification in seeing himself exclusively loved, in reflecting himself in the eye of another from whom he dreads to be separated. He is so fused with her that he neglects his chivalric obligation to obey the king's command without question or delay. Like Astolfo, he sees the other not as his alter ego but as his alterity. His wife functions more as a mother for him than the queen does for Astolfo, in that separation from her, because she is necessary for his selfhood and socialization, can only bring self-fragmentation and loss. This is why his narcissistic wound at discovering himself cuckolded is not only deeper than Astolfo's, but gets inscribed in his face, which loses its appeal:

> e la faccia, che dianzi era sì bella,
> si cangia sì, che più non sembra quella.
>
> Par che gli occhi se ascondin ne la testa;
> cresciuto il naso par nel viso scarno;
> de la beltà sì poca gli ne resta,
> che ne potrà far paragone indarno. (26–27)

(his face, once so handsome, changed beyond recognition. His eyes seemed to have sunk into his head, his nose seemed bigger on his gaunt face; so little remained of his good looks that there was no further point in matching him with others.)

25. On the mirroring of the subject onto the object, see Borch-Jacobsen 86.

The loss of facial beauty is a mask of hysteria, for disfigurement, Freud argues, can be the physical equivalent of "a slap in the face" ("Medusa's Head").

Refusing to take vengeance first, Jocondo runs away from home, falls into melancholia, and withdraws from company, until he discovers the queen's betrayal of her husband. In making Astolfo catch his wife in *flagrante delicto*, Jocondo finds himself vindicated, since the king is his superior and the queen shows herself to be anything but queenly in her sexual life. Having abjected the 'mother' (the queen is a mother figure par excellence), he can now fully identify with an ideal phallic image, a substitutive paternal ego in the person of the king; Astolfo helps him regain a sense of fullness of the self.[26] Interestingly Jocondo recovers his beauty then and there:

> Allegro torna e grasso e rubicondo,
> che sembra un cherubin del paradiso;
> che 'l re, il fratello, e tutta la famiglia
> di tal mutazion si maraviglia.   (39)

(He became happy again, filled out, took on colour, looked once more like a cherub from paradise—a transformation which astonished his brother and the king and the entire household.)

Such a turn of events, however, brings no end to the hysteria, which, in mimetic sympathy, now infects Astolfo. Hysteria appears in the figural rendering of the two men as constantly phallicized figures, their journey reduced to a series of erections as they give spur, through fantasies of omnipotence, to their narcissistic rage for having been "diminished":

> Travestiti cercaro Italia, Francia,
> le terre de' Fiamminghi e de l'Inglesi;
> e quante ne vedean di bella guancia,
> trovavan tutte ai prieghi lor cortesi.
> Davano, e dato loro era la mancia;

26. See Kristeva for this movement from the abjected mother to the imaginary father (41–42).

e spesso rimetteano i denari spesi.
Da loro pregate foro molte, e foro
anch'altretante che pregaron loro.   (48)

("In disguise they scoured Italy, France, Flanders, and England,
and as many fair-cheeked ladies as they saw, they found responsive
to their prayers. They would give money, and they would receive
payments—indeed often they recovered their disbursements. Many
ladies received their addresses, and as many more made advances
to them.)

Hysteria is evident in their choice of Fiammetta as a psychotic defence
against their fear of being sexually upstaged by the other, so that she
is made to exist as a welcoming vagina in a *ménage à trois*, on duty at
all hours:

sempre in mezzo a duo la notte giaccio
e meco or l'uno or l'altro si trastulla,
e sempre a l'un di lor mi trovo in braccio.   (61)

(I always sleep between the two of them. There is always one or the
other making love to me—I'm always in the arms of one of them.)

That Ariosto makes Fiammetta throw the arrangement over in the end,
allowing her to cast off a masochistic acceptance of the erotics of power
in favor of a parodic sexual *presa di coscienza*, testifies not so much to the
fact that where there is a will there is a way but that the stakes of Astolfo
and Jocondo's picaresque search have become paranoiac.

It is not by chance that all this lovemaking is sterile. Neither the two
wives nor any of the one thousand women Astolfo and Jocondo make
love to ever gets pregnant. One could conclude that in tandem with their
characterization as effeminate, the two men are constructed as unable
to father. But this is the case only in the final, 1532, version of the *Furioso*,
and the revision is significant. In the first and second editions, the nar-
rator gave Astolfo a son; in fact, the story starts by naming Astolfo the

father of the man who is king of Lombardy at the time when the story is being told: "Astolfo Re di Longobardi: quello / che costui che regna hor tenne per padre"("Astolfo, king of the Lombards, the one who was the father of the present king," 26.4; my translation). This reference is eliminated in the third version, where the king is introduced not as a father but as a brother—of a monk—also without issue, from whom he inherited the kingdom: "Astolfo, re de' Longobardi, quello / a cui lasciò il fratel monaco il regno" ("Astolfo, the King of the Lombards who was left his kingdom by his monastic brother," 4). The choice is telling, for in removing the anxiety over reproduction that fueled many of these early modern stories of cuckoldry, Ariosto is able not only to explore at length and with intriguing results the vagaries of a phallic desire separated from a patriarchal injunction to secure name and property through generation; he is also able to present the work of emulation/competition between men as disruptive when it leaves no space for sublimation.

Making a series of women bear the weight of the two men's loss of self does not lead to a solution; repetition, if necessary to control feelings of bereavement or to restage lack as a way of mastering it, hardly solves their original problem or brings them closure. No matter how much the mother seems to be abjected, she returns to haunt the two men; trying to figure out what she desires—and why she does not desire them—Astolfo and Jocondo can only scatter their environment with female bodies. Still, it is only through compulsive repetition that they can rehearse the momentous scenes that eventually drew both away from their homes. And that these scenes are traumatic is onomastically suggested by the only woman named in the story, Fiammetta. Such a name could be easily read as Ariosto's literary nod to the master of the Italian novella, Boccaccio, who made of "Fiammetta" a household name. But I would like to suggest another, less obvious meaning for it: Fiammetta as "little flame." Jean Laplanche has argued that fire is a figure that paradigmatically allows the subject to perceive a traumatic event (Problématiques, 3.194–96). In the Furioso, more than standing as a flame of passion, Fiammetta stands, diminutively, as the emblem of a trauma that will not be healed.

Let us take the case of Jocondo first. This knight seems at the beginning of the story to have a well-adjusted, heterosexual libido. But his object libido is redirected toward the ego (ego libido) following two traumatic scenes of seduction: of his wife and of the queen. Both scenes play all three of the original fantasies described by Laplanche and Pontalis: the primal scene, the seduction, and castration ("Fantasy"). These scenes are fantasies in that they are framed (the first by a veil, the second by a tiny hole in the wall) and oedipal in their figuration. Jocondo is the "child" in both the first scene, through identification with the stable boy (" 'l ragazzo," 36) making love to an older woman, and in the second, through identification with a dwarf (a shorter man, and thus in fantasy a younger man), making love to the queen.[27] The difference in the second scene is that in the movement from mother to Mother, female sexual desire has been made grotesque: the queen not only makes love to an inferior being but is insatiable and irreverent: "non si fa festa giorno" ("they had no rest-day," 37). Moreover, if in the first scene Jocondo is the unwilling and startled onlooker, in the second he is in control and thus reenacts, and tries to master in the repetition, the original trauma of castration.

Both scenes have something *unheimlich* about them. In the first scene Jocondo is returning home in a hurry to retrieve the necklace given him by his wife, which he had left under the pillow. Seeing his wife asleep on the conjugal bed with a servant in postcoital *somnolentia*, he experiences a sort of Medusan castration and cannot react:

> La cortina levò senza far motto,
> e vide quel che men veder credea:
> che la sua casta e fedel moglie, sotto
> la coltre, in braccio a un giovene giacea. . . .
> S'attonito restasse e malcontento,
> meglio è pensarlo e farne fede altrui,
> ch'esserne mai per far l'esperimento
> che con suo gran dolor ne fe' costui.
> Da lo sdegno assalito, ebbe talento

27. For a Freudian examination of the primal scene, see "Infantile Neurosis."

di trar la spada e uccidergli ambedui:
ma da l'amor che porta, al suo dispetto,
all'ingrata moglier, gli fu interdetto.
. . . Quanto potè più tacito uscì fuore,
scese le scale, e rimontò a cavallo.   (21–23)

("He lifted the curtains without a word—and was no little surprised
by what he saw: his chaste and loyal wife under the covers in a young
man's arms! . . . Was he dumbstruck and dismayed? You had better
take another's word for this than undergo the experience at first
hand, as did Jocondo to his great chagrin. In a fit of fury he made
to draw his sword and slay the pair of them; what stopped him was
the love which despite himself he bore his thankless wife. . . . So he
crept out of the room as silently as he could, descended the stairs,
[and] mounted his horse.)

The reaction that is not staged, the scream that does not come out,
shows that Jocondo is unable to separate himself as yet from his too
close other and embrace the law.[28] No wonder that he plunges into mel-
ancholia. The innkeeper implicates his male listeners in his retelling,
just as much as the author implicates his male readers, by deflecting
paranoia on them as well: better to be told about such a fact than to ex-
perience it, better to hear than to see.

In the second scene, of the queen and her dwarf, Jocondo cannot be-
lieve the strange spectacle ("sì strano spettacolo," 39) that is taking
place, and has to look at it again and again, for at first he thinks he is
dreaming. This salacious, voyeuristic look provokes in him a feeling of
disgust.[29] The dwarf, in his grotesquely shortened form and hunchback

28. As Žižek puts it, "the silent scream attests to the subject's clinging to enjoyment, to
his/her unreadiness to exchange enjoyment" (i.e., the object which gives body to it) for the
Other, for the Law, for the paternal metaphor" (118). Jocondo will stage his reaction later in
the form of copulation with the one thousand other women.
29. The ability to override disgust is precisely what for Freud promotes scopophilia in the
pervert: "this pleasure in looking (scopophilia) becomes a perversion (a) if it is restricted

shape, moreover, is a figure of both castration and the uncanny ("uno sgrignuto mostro e contrafatto," 35; "vil sergente," 42; "il bruttissimo omiciuolo," 43). This time Jocondo's reaction is voiced and vindictive, for misery loves company; by calling Astolfo to witness his own debasement and thus somehow symbolically castrating him, he finds a way out of his self-imposed quarantine, recovers a sense of selfhood, and becomes a man of the world.

Astolfo at first has the identical reaction that Jocondo had in seeing his wife's adultery: he is unable to take in all this ocular proof at once. In his case, too, the scream cannot be voiced:

> Se parve al re vituperoso l'atto,
> lo crederete ben, senza ch'io 'l giuri.
> Ne fu per arrabbiar, per venir matto;
> ne fu per dar del capo in tutti i muri;
> fu per gridar, fu per non stare al patto:
> ma forza è che la bocca al fin si turi.   (44)

(That this struck the king as outrageous you will accept without my having to swear to it. He was ready to explode, to run amuck; he was ready to ram his head against every wall, to scream; he was ready to break his oath. But in the end he had perforce to plug his mouth.)

But then, unlike Jocondo, who gets stuck in melancholia as a response to narcissistic injury, Astolfo proceeds straight to mania, and the picaresque journey begins.

What follows, in its outer search for revenge on other men and its inner search for a woman—a mother—who will not betray, is predicated on fantasy. In fantasy, individuals can identify across gender and even with inanimate elements in the scene of fantasy. Astolfo can thus identify with Jocondo, and vice versa, and possess through him and with him any woman, also available to the other, but whose enjoyment can be magnified by seeing another person desiring her. Each can identify with

---

exclusively to the genitals or (b) if it is connected with the overriding of disgust (as in the case of voyeurs)"("Three Essays," 157).

all women in their being able, at least as they are imagined, to be utterly possessed and passive. Given the desire to be observed while copulating, as in the arrangement with Fiammetta, each can identify also with the men who took their place in their wives' beds. Each can identify with Fiammetta as well and fantasize being loved/possessed by an object of homoerotic desire without actually acting out this fantasy. Finally, each can identify with the whole scene and repeat ad infinitum his own primal scene with the other as the silent onlooker. But although Astolfo or Jocondo can assume at will both a feminine and a masculine position, as subject each can only look on, excluded. Knowledge brings powerlessness.

This hysterical doubling/mutual emulation is in any case difficult to hold down. If doubling, in its link to castration anxiety, is beneficial because it allows the individual to cancel the female threat by getting reassurance through the image of the other as the same ("E perchè [dicea il re] vo' che mi spiaccia / aver più te ch'un altro in compagnia? ["Why—exclaimed the king—should I object to sharing a woman with you more than with another?"], 50),[30] it can on the other hand give rise to hostility, because the quasi-similar other is too similar.[31] Such a feeling does not necessarily arise out of a competition for the same object, nor is the result of wanting to act out the same desire. Freud notes, for example, that normal jealousy can be many times "experienced bisexually," that is, the jealous subject wishes to be in the place not only of the rival but also of the beloved.[32] Thus identification across gender can be sustained by jealousy just as it is by fantasy.

The way out of narcissistic rage, mimetic repetition, and duplicate selfhood presents itself when Astolfo and Jocondo recognize that they do not know what the other desires and that no woman can be wholly

30. According to Freud, the "double was originally an insurance against the destruction of the ego. . . . This invention of doubling as a preservation against extinction has its counterpart in the language of dreams, which is fond of representing castration by a doubling or multiplication of the genital symbol" ("The Uncanny," 240).

31. In Fineman's words, emulation is "that paradoxical labor of envy that seeks to find difference in imitation" (74).

32. See Freud, "Certain Neurotic Mechanisms." On jealousy, see also Maus.

owned. Had they been willing to learn from Fiammetta's choice, or had they asked themselves "What does woman want?" rather than putting their conceits on center stage, they would have understood that what matters for women in sex is neither repetition nor at least two men per night, but perhaps the chance to decide for themselves. Outwitting her two lovers, Fiammetta got herself not so much a man who did not "dismount once all night long" ("scender non ne vuol per tutta notte," 64), as Ariosto puts it, but the one she wanted. True, the grammatical referent for "non ne vuol" is the Greek lover rather than Fiammetta, and thus his desire rather than hers may once more be represented. Yet Fiammetta had reassured him earlier of the extent of her desire ("Credi (dicea) che men di te nol bramo" ["I want this no less than you do"], 60), and also had to be, at the very least, inventive and precise in her directions to him, for the location in bed where she was lying was crucial to their sexual satisfaction:

> Il Greco, sì come ella gli disegna,
>
> . . .
>
> va brancolando infin che 'l letto trova:
> e di là dove gli altri avean le piante,
> tacito si cacciò col capo inante.
>   Fra l'una e l'altra gamba di Fiammetta,
> che supina giacea, diritto venne;
> e quando le fu a par, l'abbracciò stretta,
> e sopra lei sin presso al dì si tenne. (62–64)

(the boy, following her instructions, . . . groped his way till he found the bed—into which, at the point where the sleepers had their feet, he quietly intruded head first. He slipped between the legs of Fiammetta, who was lying on her back, and slid her up until they were face to face, when he hugged her tightly. He straddled her till daybreak.)

It is at this point, filled with a veritable sexual nausea, that Astolfo and Jocondo remove themselves from active heterosexual desire altogether and start to live where they have always wanted: in fantasy. The sudden end of their erotic quest and their return home, the resolution of the "errore"/"errare" paradigm, does not constitute for me a smart, bourgeois choice, as has been argued; I read it as a way to cancel out the other by remaining involved in the narcissistic story of selves as ideal selves.[33] In doing so Ariosto's characters can disavow difference. Still, their choice does mark a change. True, nothing has changed in the domestic situation that made the two men leave their wives in the first place; moreover, desire has not been erased, nor has concupiscence been conquered. But what has changed is that women have been removed from the equation. They are eliminated, not to erase the trauma, but because they in a sense were in the equation under false pretenses, for they never existed per se. The one thousand and three women were always and only, to take it once more from Lacan, "symptoms" of men's subjectivity.[34]

To be sure, the two friends could have found a degree of pleasure in shifting to some form of feminine masochism after they were apprised of Fiammetta's adventure with her Greek lover. Or they might have responded with melancholic withdrawal, as Jocondo did following his wife's betrayal. But by now their errantry has become shabby, and the women they share are of lower and lower social status. So they opt to show their phallic power by marking the successful exorcism of their fears with a Gargantuan, hysteric, orgasmic laughter:

Poi scoppiaro ugualmente in tanto riso,
che con la bocca aperta e gli occhi chiusi,
potendo a pena il fiato aver del petto,
a dietro si lasciar cader sul letto.

33. Zatti reads in the story not bourgeois morals, but a wisdom-bound madness ("un giocondo errore," 50). For Gareffi, the conclusion of the novella shows that while men tell stories, women make them ("Rimangono gli uomini a raccontarsi le storie, le donne le fanno," 91).

34. Interesting, in this context, is the observation made by Franceschetti that there is one element of the traditional novella completely absent in Ariosto, that of the "beffa," in which women show—through their wit, cunning, or savoir faire—the stupidity and gullibility of their mates (835–36).

> ... ebbon tanto riso, che dolere
> se ne sentiano il petto, e pianger gli occhi.   (71–72)

(Then they burst into fits of laughter, their mouths open and their eyes shut till, practically breathless, they fell backwards onto the bed. . . . [T]hey had laughed so much that their ribs ached and their eyes streamed.)

This also puts an end to their adventures in the never-never land of unbound sexual gratifications; before leaving, they allow Fiammetta to wed her lover and thus sanction the institutionalization of desire through marriage, the end of romance through an astute reading of the economics of loving.

At home, Astolfo and Jocondo will be, as before, and as they like it, once more alone and on center stage. Surprisingly, at the very moment in which they decline to judge, and let themselves be judged, as manly men, they are rendered as fully masculinized, for their masculinity is tied now not to sex—the flesh after all cannot signify, Lacan teaches—but to the power of the phallus. In the final version of this tale Ariosto omits an octave, present in the two earlier editions, that refers to a son born from the union between the queen and the dwarf and aptly named Strange Desire ("Stranodesiderio"). This name was later shortened into "Desire" to avoid improper allusions to the queen's sexual tastes.[35] Had he kept this bastard son in the text, Ariosto would have left Astolfo still living through the story of his sexual and oedipal demise, still trapped in the tensions and pleasures of the family romance. By deleting the illegitimate son, Ariosto brings the novella full circle, for we are told that neither Jocondo nor Astolfo will let themselves now be contaminated anew by their wives' aberrancies: "di ch'affanno mai più non si pigliaro," (74) ("who never occasioned them another moment's distress"). Erotic politics are pushed aside to make room for gender politics. There is no

---

35. "Il Re il primo figliuol che poi gli nacque / nomo a battesmo Stranodesiderio / ma poi crescendo Strano se gli tacque / che pel nano alla madre era improperio" (2.26.75). We do not know whether the child was a dwarf like his father.

doubt that, once back in power, the king and the knight will restart their love affair with the mirror.

So what does this story tell us about the representation of masculinity in *Orlando furioso* and the chivalric romance, and about gender relations in the sixteenth century in general? Should the reader skip the canto because women are portrayed dismissively, as Ariosto suggests, or because men are represented as masquerading masculinity, even when they aggressively test its most praised attribute, virility? Is there a real difference, all things considered, between the kind of manhood impersonated by Count Orlando, whose desire thrives on postponement until he realizes that he has arrived too late at his dreamed sexual banquet and goes mad, and the kind of manhood impersonated by Astolfo and Jocondo, whose desires are gratified to the point of disenchantment? In both cases what constitutes masculinity is very much at stake; if, as the Saracen knight Mandricardo hints, the end of Orlando's search for love leads him to a metaphoric self-castration ("E dicea ch'imitato avea il castore, / il qual si strappa i genitali sui" ["The count had imitated the beaver, he explained, who rips off his genitals"], 27, 57), then Astolfo and Jocondo's return to reality neither brings them closer to understanding the secret of women nor makes them better equipped to put an end to their self-mystification. In any case, whether in Orlando's world of romance or in the cynical, commodified realm of Astolfo and Jocondo, the confrontation with otherness leaves women out of the equation. But while for Orlando the endless search for armor or for Angelica is a postoedipal longing for a lost or perhaps never fully developed selfhood, for Astolfo and Jocondo, I would argue, the search for a mother who will not betray them is a search for a preoedipal, primal, Edenic world, uncontaminated by the confrontations and the urgencies of the symbolic. Thus, for Orlando the end of his story in the *Furioso* means his return to, and total embrace of, the paternal order, while for Astolfo and Jocondo the end of their search is a reimmersion in the narcissism with which their story started out, the return to sameness.

The trials of masculinity in Ariosto show how incomplete the articulations of identity—masculine as well as feminine—were in the period in which he wrote, and how deeply the emergent definitions of what was private and what was public influenced the social construction of gender. The boundaries between normal, normative, and deviant behavior were in many ways just as permeable in the secularized world of Ariosto testing the illusions of a bygone era of romance adventures, as they are in our postmodern times. In the end, if gender is, in the Lacanian sense, a masquerade, a form of fetishistic transvestism, then the labyrinthine, ironic narrative of the *Furioso* clearly lends itself to an examination of undecidability. For here identity is mimicry, and fantasy—or its extreme, madness—is endlessly employed to protect impassioned and neurotic characters from a death drive that demands attention but allows delays now and then, *petites mortes* indeed.

Even the authorial feint at the beginning, Ariosto's plea to his readers not to pay attention to him because the social conventions he is representing are not his credo but belong to a spurious father, Master Turpino —who has throughout been unable to signify any truth—can be understood as a request to take the story lightly, to read its surface and not its depth, to laugh at women, no matter how reproachable the business may be, because it is too dangerous—or too bewildering—to laugh at men.

Works Cited

Aretino, Pietro, *Sonetti lussuriosi (i modi) e dubbi amorosi.* Milan: Newton, 1993.

Ariosto, Ludovico. *Orlando furioso.* Ed. Filippo Ermini. 3 vols. Rome: Società Filologica Romana, 1911.

——. *Orlando furioso.* Ed. Marcello Turchi. Milan: Garzanti, 1978.

——. *Orlando furioso.* Trans. Guido Waldman. Oxford: Oxford UP, 1983.

Barberi-Squarotti, Giorgio. *Prospettive sul Furioso.* Turin: Tirrenia, 1988.

Barbirato, Giorgio. "Elementi decameroniani in alcune novelle ariostesche." *Studi sul Boccaccio* 16 (1987): 329–60.

Beer, Marina. *Romanzi di cavalleria: Il Furioso e il romanzo italiano del primo cinquecento.* Rome: Bulzoni, 1987.

Bellamy, Elizabeth. *Translations of Power: Narcissism and the Unconscious in Epic History.* Ithaca: Cornell UP, 1992.

Benson, Pamela. *The Invention of the Renaissance Woman.* University Park: Penn State UP, 1992.

Boccaccio, Giovanni, *The Decameron.* Trans. Guido Waldman. Oxford: Oxford UP, 1993.

Borch-Jacobsen, Mikkel. *The Freudian Subject*. Trans. Catherine Porter. Stanford: Stanford UP, 1988.

Castiglione, Baldassarre. *Il libro del cortegiano*. Ed. Ettore Bonora. Milano: Mursia, 1984.

Cohen, Ed. "Legislating the Norm: From Sodomy to Gross Indecency." *South Atlantic Quarterly* 88.1 (1989): 181–217.

Fineman, Joel. "Fratricide and Cuckoldry: Shakespeare's Doubles." *Representing Shakespeare: New Psychoanalytic Essays*. Ed. Murray Schwartz and Coppélia Kahn. Baltimore: Johns Hopkins UP, 1980. 70–109.

Finucci, Valeria. "The Female Masquerade: Ariosto and the Game of Desire." *Desire in the Renaissance: Psychoanalysis and Literature*. Ed. Valeria Finucci and Regina Schwartz. Princeton: Princeton UP, 1994. 65–88.

———. *The Lady Vanishes: Subjectivity and Representation in Castiglione and Ariosto*. Stanford: Stanford UP, 1992.

Firenzuola, Agnolo. *On the Beauty of Women*. Trans. and ed. Konrad Eisenbichler and Jacqueline Murray. Philadelphia: U of Pennsylvania P, 1992.

Franceschetti, Antonio. "La novella nei poemi del Boiardo e dell'Ariosto." *La novella italiana: Atti del convegno di Caprarola 14–24 sett. 1988*. Ed. Enrico Malato. Rome: Salerno Ed., 1989. 805–41.

Freud, Sigmund. "Certain Neurotic Mechanisms in Jealousy, Paranoia, and Homosexuality." *Collected Papers*. New York: Basic Books, 1959. 2:232–40.

———. "From the History of an Infantile Neurosis." *Collected Papers*. 5:473–607.

———. "Medusa's Head." *The Standard Edition of the Complete Psychological Works of Sigmund Freud*. Trans. and ed. James Strachey. 24 vols. London: Hogarth, 1953–74 [hereafter SE]. 18 (1955): 273–74.

———. "On Narcissism: An Introduction." SE 14 (1957): 69–102.

———. "Three Essays on the Theory of Sexuality." SE 7 (1953): 122–243.

———. "The Uncanny." SE 17 (1955): 219–52.

Gareffi, Andrea. *Figure dell'immaginario nell'Orlando Furioso*. Rome: Bulzoni, 1984.

Haywood, Eric "Would You Believe It? A Tall Story from Ariosto." *Italian Storytellers: Essays on Italian Narrative Literature*. Ed. Eric Haywood and Cormac O'Cuilleanain. Dublin: Irish Academy P, 1989. 113–49.

Ginzburg, Carlo. "Tiziano, Ovidio e i codici della figurazione erotica nel '500." *Tiziano e Venezia: Atti del convegno internazionale di studi*. Ed. Carlo Ginzburg et al. Vicenza: Neri Pozza, 1980. 125–35.

Girard, René. *Deceit, Desire and the Novel: Self and Other in Literary Structure*. Trans. Y. Freccero. Baltimore: Johns Hopkins UP, 1965.

Goldberg, Jonathan, ed. *Queering the Renaissance*. Durham, N.C.: Duke UP, 1994.

Guglielminetti, Marziano. "Introduzione." *Novellieri del Cinquecento*. Ed. Marziano Guglielminetti. Milan: Ricciardi, 1972.

Irigaray, Luce. *This Sex Which Is Not One.* Trans. Catherine Porter. Ithaca: Cornell UP, 1985.

Jacquart, Danielle, and Claude Thomasset. *Sexuality and Medicine in the Middle Ages.* Trans. Matthew Adamson. Princeton: Princeton UP, 1988.

Javitch, Daniel. "*Cantus Interruptus* in the *Orlando Furioso*," *Modern Language Notes* 95 (1980): 66–80.

———. *Proclaiming a Classic: The Canonization of the Orlando Furioso.* Princeton: Princeton UP, 1991.

Kristeva, Julia. *Tales of Love.* Trans. Leon Roudiez. New York: Columbia UP, 1987.

Lacan, Jacques. "The Meaning of the Phallus." Ed. Juliet Mitchell and Jacqueline Rose. *Female Sexuality: Jacques Lacan and the Ecole Freudienne.* New York: Norton, 1982. 74–85.

———. *Les Ecrits techniques de Freud. Book I of Le Seminaire.* Paris: Seul, 1975.

Laplanche, Jean. *Problématiques.* 4 vols. Paris: Presses Universitaires de France, 1980–81.

Laplanche, Jean, and Pontalis, Jean-Bertrande. "Fantasy and the Origins of Sexuality." *Formations of Fantasy.* Ed. Victor Burgin, James Donald, and Cora Kaplan. London: Methuen, 1986. 5–34.

Laqueur, Thomas. *Making Sex: Body and Gender from the Greeks to Freud.* Cambridge, Mass.: Harvard UP, 1990.

McLucas, John. "Ariosto and the Androgyne: Symmetries of Sex in the *Orlando Furioso*." Diss. Yale University, 1983.

Maus, Katharine. "Horns of Silence: Jealousy, Gender and Spectatorship in English Renaissance Drama." *English Literary History* 54 (1987): 561–83.

Mulvey, Laura. *Visual and Other Pleasures.* Bloomington: Indiana UP, 1989.

Ovid. *Metamorphoses.* Trans. A. D. Melville. Oxford: Oxford UP, 1986.

Pardo, Mary. "Artifice as Seduction in Titian." *Sexuality and Gender in Early Modern Europe. Institutions, Texts, Images.* Ed. James Grantham Turner. Cambridge: Cambridge UP, 1993. 55–89.

Rajna, Pio. *Le fonti dell' Orlando Furioso.* Florence: Sansoni, 1900.

Rivière, Joan. "Womanliness as a Masquerade." *Formations of Fantasy.* Ed. Victor Burgin, James Donald, and Cora Kaplan. London: Methuen, 1986. 35–44.

Roche, Michael. *Forbidden Friendships: Homosexuality and Male Culture in Renaissance Florence.* New York: Oxford UP, 1996.

Ruggiero, Guido. *The Boundaries of Eros: Sex Crime and Sexuality in Renaissance Venice.* New York: Oxford UP, 1985.

Scaglione, Aldo. "Shahryar, Giocondo, Koterviky: Three Versions of the Motif of the Faithless Woman." *Oriens* 11 (1958): 151–61.

Sedgwick, Eve. *Between Men: English Literature and Male Homosocial Desire.* New York: Columbia UP, 1985.

Shemek, Deanna. "Of Women, Knights, Arms, and Love: The *Querelle des Femmes* in Ariosto's Poem." *Modern Language Notes* 104 (1989): 68–97.

Traub, Valerie. *Desire and Anxiety: Circulations of Desire in Shakespearean Drama*. New York: Routledge, 1992.

Zatti, Sergio. *Il Furioso fra epos e romanzo*. Lucca: Pacini Fazzi, 1990.

Žižek, Slavoj. *Enjoy Your Symptom: Jacques Lacan in Hollywood and Out*. New York: Routledge, 1992.

Romance as Role Model:
Early Female Performances
of *Orlando furioso*
and *Gerusalemme liberata*

ERIC NICHOLSON

The streets of Mantua, July 1566: a fight breaks out between retainers of the prince Cesare Gonzaga and a group of professional actors. Two of the latter nearly die in the fray, which an eyewitness describes as one of the most violent brawls he had ever seen. The same individual, Antonio Ceruto, also writes that the men's lives were saved by none other than the actress Flaminia "Romana," who accomplished such wonderful feats with her stone-throwing as to make her a true "Marfisa." From this account, it would appear that Flaminia was the leader of her acting company in more ways than one.[1]

The plot thickens: this same woman, one of the first in history to make acting her profession, would return to Mantua the following year to extend her performance of heroines from the *Orlando furioso*. The Gonzaga court secretary, Luigi Rogna, reports that on July 4, 1567, at least half the city of Mantua thronged to see la Flaminia on stage. He notes that she was highly praised

---

1. The exact date of Antonio Ceruto's letter is July 24, 1566. Ceruto, a jurisconsul and minor poet, wrote an entire series of journalistic letters from Mantua to the Gonzaga residence at Casale. The letter is now kept at the Archivio di Stato di Mantova (Archivio Gonzaga, Busta F.II.8.2575). The relevant original text runs as follows: "alle 22 hore nel accompagnar alla sepoltura mio fratello al carmine, si stacchi una delle maggiori questioni, che mai m'habbia veduto, per il numero grandissimo dell' armi men[d]ate; la quale era tra li comedianti et quelli del Signor Cesare Illustrissimo, et la Flaminia fece con gli sassi cose stupende, al pari d'una Marfisa, et se lei non era senza dubio, ne ne riniaverrano [*sic*] morti. Un paro [pareggio?] di loro: perchè la cosa passò meglio che non si credeva, et con poco sangue" (f. 1r of letter).

for certain laments that she spoke in a tragedy performed by her company, taken from that story by Ariosto which tells of Marganorre. The bride, played by Flaminia, atop the body of her first husband, killed only a short time before on stage, for her revenge gave her new bridegroom, Marganorre's son, poison to drink after having drunk it herself, whereupon the one and the other died on the dead body. Afterwards, the father, who for these deeds wished to kill all the women, was stoned by the women, and died.[2]

Rogna goes on to confirm that la Flaminia's audiences, indeed her fans, "extolled her genius," and Ceruto records that they would shout out "Io sono della parte di Flaminia" ("I'm on the side of Flaminia").[3] These documents thus emphatically convey the versatile star quality of this actress, who had gone from playing a fictional woman warrior in an actual street riot to performing the noble suicidal bride Drusilla in an indoor theatrical production.

While no evidence has been found to confirm whether or not Flaminia promoted an off-stage image of herself as a living Marfisa, it is thus clear that she was perceived as such. By virtue of her leadership of her troupe, it is equally certain that she had assumed a public and professional identity usually reserved for the men of her time: her

2. Rogna's original letter, dated July 6, 1567, is also kept at the Archivio di Stato di Mantova (Archivio Gonzaga, Busta F.II.8.2577). The relevant text runs as follows: "Non hieri l'altro la Flaminia era comendata per certi lamenti che fece in una tragedia che recitorno dalla sua banda, cavata da quella novella dell'Ariosto, che tratta di quel Marganorre, al figliuolo sposo del quale, la sposa, ch'era la Flaminia, sopra il corpo del primo suo sposo, poco dianzi amazzato in scena, per vendetta diede a bere il veleno dopo haverne bevuto anch'essa, onde 'l'uno et l'altro morì sopra il corpo, et il padre, che perciò voleva uccidere tutte le donne, fu dalle donne lapidato et morto." This account, along with other texts on the theatrical "concorso" between the companies of Flaminia and Vincenza Armani (including a performance by the former of "la tragedia di Didone mutata in Tragicommedia" on July 1), are reprinted in Alessandro d'Ancona, *Le origini del teatro italiano*, vol. 2 (Turin: Loescher, 1891), 449–54.
3. Rogna's "estolle l'ingegno" observation appears in the same letter of July 6, while Ceruto's comment is taken from a letter dated July 9 (Archivio di Stato di Mantova, Archivio Gonzaga F.II.8.2577.38v).

position alone would have associated Flaminia with Ariosto's "valorose donne." Moreover, as the director-manager or "capocomico," she would most likely have selected and organized her company's dramatic repertoire. Not a male director but Flaminia herself chose to adapt and perform the Marganorre episode from canto 37 of *Orlando furioso*.[4] Such a choice shows how this and other late-sixteenth-century actresses self-consciously revised and theatrically transformed material from chivalric romance through reading, rewriting, and stage performance. Like the dismounted Marfisa of canto 36, who resorts to kicks, wrestling, and fisticuffs, Flaminia Romana displays her combative prowess even in degraded circumstances: in the street and out of costume, she impresses her audience as someone heroic, larger than life. A year later, she impresses these same audiences even more, and with an ironic twist: rather than playing Marfisa, the woman who vanquishes Marganorre, she plays Drusilla, the woman who inspires this tyrant's extreme misogyny. The act of lapidation, which Flaminia may have deliberately highlighted to recall her off-stage exploit, is displaced into the hands of other performers. The star of the show thus demonstrates her protean virtuosity, switching from streetfighter to heroic and suicidal revenger.

I will return to this early female adaptation of Ariosto's work, to analyze more fully the multiple ways in which it stages gender roles. For now, however, I want to situate the process of adapting chivalric romance to the Italian professional stage within a culture that both revered and reviled that upstart, often unruly figure, the actress. Daniel Javitch has demonstrated how the *Furioso* quickly gained enormous popularity through all sectors of Italian society: he cites such contemporary ob-

---

4. There is the possibility that Flaminia did not invent the adaptation: Leone de' Sommi, a playwright, dramatic theorist, director, and impresario who was prominent in both the Jewish and theatrical communities of 1560s Mantua, wrote a play entitled *Drusilla* (the text has not survived). However, de' Sommi was more closely allied with Flaminia's rival, Vincenza Armani, and would more likely have been writing material for this second actress. On de' Sommi's life, work, and dramatic theory, see Leone de' Sommi, *Quattro dialoghi in materia di rappresentazioni sceniche*, edited by Ferruccio Marotti (Milan: Polifilo, 1968), especially pp. xv–xvi.

ervers as Francesco Caburacci, who wrote that the poem was "pregiata dalle Donne, tenuta cara da i dotti, cantata da gl'indotti" ("prized by the women, held dear by the learned, and sung by the unlearned") and Giuseppe Malatesta, who in his dialogue *Della nuova poesia* (1589) noted that Ariosto's work was continually recited in city and country, academy and hovel, not only by professors and students but also "inculte villanelle" ("uneducated peasant women") and "rozze pastorelle" ("crude shepherdesses") (Javitch 11–14). On many occasions, these recitations were sung, extending the lyric origins of the *ottava rima* form itself (Brown 201–2). Curiously, Javitch's detailed study omits any mention of sixteenth-century dramatizations of the *Furioso*, the logical, almost inevitable extension of oral recitations of the text for a public that was both semiliterate and theatrically attuned. Prized by both "crude shepherdesses" and refined court ladies, the *Furioso* had an avid female audience, and by the 1560s if not earlier, women were also actively staging as well as rewriting the work. As famous, widely admired, and even glamorous artists in their own right, traveling from one city to the next, these actresses were themselves taking on some of the characteristics of their fictional role models: to some extent, their own lives imitated art. Their unorthodox activity bears comparison to the more literary projects of such women as Moderata Fonte, who, as Valeria Finucci has suggestively shown, imparted subjectivity to the female characters of chivalric romance (Finucci, "La scrittura epico-cavalleresca").

To publish a revision of popular romance/epic was one matter. To perform it live, however, was another. While female performers could count on the enthusiasm of their audiences to see Marfisa, Ruggiero, Bradamante, Drusilla, Orlando, and the especially popular Angelica in action, they also had to contend with influential opponents of their very profession. On the one hand, a living, speaking, moving embodiment of a woman warrior could arouse excitement and fascination, as attested by Leone de' Sommi's praise of Flaminia Romana's great rival, Vincenza Armani:

> ma tutto questo di ch'io scrivo, e canto,
> è nulla, al paragon del divin raggio

> ch'ella ne scopre, avolta in viril manto,
> co'l parlare improviso, accorto, e saggio.   (90)

(But all this of which I write and sing, is nothing, in comparison with the divine light that she shines forth, at times in manly guise, with her spontaneous, apt, and wise speaking.)

Writing in 1570, soon after Armani's untimely death by poisoning, De Sommi also commemorates the star's protean talent in playing both the "vaga donna d'Amore accesa" and the "guerriera armata." On the other hand, compelling theatrical transvestism provoked furious attacks, most notably from spokesmen for Counter-Reformation morality. A follower of the generally antitheatrical Carlo Borromeo wrote to the archbishop of Milan in 1570 to express outrage at "infamous actors, who perform on stage all manner of lascivious, libidinous acts, women dressing as boys and boys as women." [5] A few years later, Borromeo's close friend Gabriello Paleotti, archbishop of Bologna, published a tract against theatrical shows in which he specifically condemns "queste donne commedianti" ["these women actors"] for seducing gentlemen admirers and depriving them of their family fortunes (Taviani 39). Such a critique echoes early moralistic commentators on the *Furioso*, who glossed Orlando's and Ruggiero's pursuit of Angelica as a warning to men against exaggerated amorous desire (Javitch 33–37). It also accords with Borromeo's own extremely revealing distinction between the effects of merely reading "libri osceni," and those of actually attending live theatrical performances: "But how much more penetrates into the soul that which the eyes behold than that which one reads in books of that sort! How much more seriously does the live speaking voice harm the minds of adolescents than does the mute voice, printed in books!" (Taviani, *Commedia dell'arte*, 33).[6]

---

5. The letter is cited by d'Ancona, *Le origini*, vol. 2, 179–80: "intanto a rinfiammare lo zelo di San Carlo venivano lagnanze e lagrime di devoti. Un tale scrivevagli scandalizzandosi degli 'infami istrioni, che rappresentano in la loro scena tutte le lascivie, tutte le libidini, vestendosi le donne da maschio, e i ragazzi da donna.' "

6. Borromeo's original text, from a homily given on July 17, 1583, runs as follows: "Ma quanto più penetra nell'anima ciò che gli occhi vedono di ciò che si può leggere in libri di

The actresses' most daring act was thus to give their audiences what they most desired and yet most feared: the living incarnation of the wondrous, alluring, and virile figures of chivalric romance. A man who heard and saw flesh-and-blood women performing powerful female characters would thus lose the security of private reading, or of textual censorship: the acting out of heroic and erotic fantasies caused a live, direct confrontation with the exciting but also disturbing effects of such fantasies.

What were some of these effects? For one, the experience of a female performer's power to enchant her viewers and listeners in a way that simultaneously evoked fictional charmers like Alcina and Armida and the real-life figure of the enticing but widely vilified prostitute. When at the court of Mantua in 1592 a "concerto di donne" sang Claudio Monteverdi's Third Book of Madrigals, they performed adaptations of Armida's impassioned outbursts against the departing Rinaldo ("Vattene pur crudel," *Gerusalemme liberata* 16.59), and in the process inspired pity and admiration from their listeners (Pirotta 279–81). The power of the sorceress's lament, more easily contained and diminished within the pages of Tasso's poem, spilled out to seduce a live audience. Moreover, with their lute accompaniment and ornate costumes, these female singers of erotic madrigals also recalled contemporary "cortigiane" or "sumtuose meretrize" ("sumptuous prostitutes") who for decades had made visual, poetic, and musical entertainments part of their trade (Rosenthal 6–7; Ruggiero 38–48).

No matter how much the partly or even fully professional singer might try to distance herself from women who sold their sexual favors, she thus risked censure and scandal for her potentially disruptive impact on ordered patriarchal society. In 1589 the star soprano Tarquinia Molza was dismissed from service at the court of Ferrara for her love affair with the composer Giaches Wert. Already a widow of forty-one when she had become one of the *dame d'onore* of Lucrezia, duchess of Ferrara in 1583, she had also been the object of Tasso's admiration, and the re-

<hr>

quel genere! Quanto più gravemente la viva voce ferisce le menti degli adoloscenti di quanto non la faccia morta, stampata nei libri!"

cipient of his laudatory verses. A poet as well as a charismatic speaker, Molza was the most admired of the four leading female singers at the Este court, and it was she who sang the soprano part of Armida in Wert's highly wrought, vocally spectacular setting of *Gerusalemme liberata* 16.40–48 (reordered so that the most passionate of the stanzas, number 40, beginning "Forsennata gridava," becomes the climactic one of the madrigal; Einstein, 569–71). Tasso's epic, at one of its most romantic, even melodramatic moments—the split between Rinaldo and Armida— here enters the realm of live female musical performance, and in doing so the abject woman ironically gains the power to enchant and enthrall her male listeners, including the composer himself. Molza and her colleagues in the Ferrarese professional "concerto di donne" of the 1580s were indeed an alluring center of court social and artistic life, since they sang for two to six hours, every afternoon, in the duchess's own apartments. Their infatuated observers called them "angels from paradise," women who "astonished" the eye with their beauty and the ear with their musical virtuosity (Newcomb, *Madrigal*, vol. 1, 68, 269, 271).

In a sense, Armida had found, at least until real-life scandal became too sensational, a new home and purpose in the bodies and voices of the female singers who impersonated her. Still, this home remained a precarious one, since the status of these innovative professional women, if not marginal, was certainly ambivalent. In an important article, Anthony Newcomb observes "that the ladies owed their positions in court primarily to their gifts as musicians, that their positions were of great honor and prestige, and that the question was a novel and delicate one" (Newcomb, "Courtesans," 95). While Tarquinia Molza was expressly recruited by the madrigal-loving Duke Alfonso II, and like her colleague Laura Peverara paid the handsome salary of 300 scudi per year, she and the *concerto di donne* suffered the envy and detraction of those who complained that to gain favor at Ferrara "one needs to know how to sing." Less negatively, the same generous patron who promoted them could also exploit them for the sake of gaining political prestige (Newcomb, "Courtesans," 96–99). Finally, there remained the often unjustified but still widely held identification of musical women as sexually dangerous and morally suspect courtesans, along with the stereotypes of women's intellectual and artistic inferiority. Such attitudes can be seen in Pietro Aretino's writings on and of prostitution, in conservative humanist publications against educating girls in music ("a thing for thoughtless and frivolous women"), in Pope Sixtus V's 1588 ban against women appearing in public theaters (Bowers 135–39), and in the comments of Duke Guglielmo Gonzaga of Mantua, who upon hearing

> the music of these ladies, while it was expected that His Excellency would praise them to the heavens, he burst out so loudly that all the ladies and duchesses present could hear him, "women are quite something: indeed, I would rather be an ass than a woman." Whereupon he rose from his place, and made everyone else do the same, since the singing had stopped.[7]

Even in the cultivated atmosphere of the courts, then, misogynist hostility could interrupt female performance and thus spoil the party. This repressive tendency parallels the containment and conversion of such disruptive, threatening figures as Clorinda and Armida in Tasso's own work.

II

Before assessing the conflicted response to Tasso's chivalric romance/ epic in Claudio Monteverdi's compositions and noted female performances of them, I want to return to the question of the *Furioso*, as both literary and theatrical text. If Tasso's material lends itself to musical, declamatory, dramatically concentrated, and emotionally intense adaptation, Ariosto's by contrast inspires scripts and performances that are

7. The duke's sarcastic remarks were recorded in a letter by the Florentine Orazio Urbani to the Medici court, dated May 15, 1581 (Archivio di Stato, Firenze; Archivio Mediceo, f. 2900). They are reprinted in Anthony Newcomb, *The Madrigal at Ferrara*, vol. 1, 261: "havendo con gran' ceremonia fatto udire a questa eccellenza la Musica di queste Dame, mentre aspettava ch'ella dovesse esaltarle al Cielo ella proruppe dicendo forte di modo che fu sentito e dalle Dame e dalle Duchesse che erano presenti, Gran' cosa son le Donne; in effetto io vorrei esser innanzi un Asino che una Donna, e con questo si levò e fece levar ogni altro perchè si desse fine al cantare."

by turns tragic and comic, serious and ironic, spectacular and grotesque. Although both the *Liberata* and the *Furioso* would furnish plots for later *opere liriche*, the first proves less congenial than the second to the heterogeneous, playful, and often female-centered productions of the early "commedia dell'arte."

Aptly enough, one of the female characters from the *Orlando furioso* whom early *commedia* actresses frequently portrayed was the exotic, alluring, and elusive princess Angelica. Dubbed by modern critics as "that elusive object of desire" (Shemek), and "a symbol of the erotics of scarcity" (Parker), Angelica possesses qualities ideally suited for the leading female performer, or *prima donna*. Her very name, for one, suggests the heavenly status which male admirers commonly attributed to such women as Vincenza Armani and Vittoria Piissimi, the latter of whom was called not only "la bella maga d'amore," ("the beauteous sorceress of love") but also "divina Vittoria, che fa metamorfosi di se stessa in scena" ("divine Vittoria, who metamorphosizes herself on the stage") (Garzoni 814). Secondly, Angelica prefigures stage divas through a crucial erotic *contrapposto*: while she is constantly the object of a desiring spectator's gaze, she is never physically attainable by that spectator. Like a star actress, she can be seen and admired but not touched: to attain her would be to nullify her role in provoking male competition and mimetic desire (Donato). Ariosto, not coincidentally an accomplished comic playwright, explicitly defines Angelica's powers of self-display and self-withholding as both semidivine and theatrical (Wiggins 172): in canto 1, when she comes out of the "dark and blind bush" to appear before her ardent pursuer Sacripante, "fa di se bella et *improvvisa mostra,* | come di selva o fuor d'ombroso speco | Diana in *scena* o Citerea si mostra*" ("made a lovely and *sudden spectacle, showing* herself like Citerea, or Diana *on a stage,* come forth from a wood or shady grove," OF 1.52.2–4; emphasis mine). Deanna Shemek has astutely demonstrated how Sacripante's reaction of ocular "gaudio" and "stupor," likened to that of a mother reunited with her son, accentuates both Angelica's "feminine role-playing" and the Saracen knight's own desire for Imaginary plenitude of the Lacanian kind (Shemek 126).

We can extend this reading, however, to include more direct attention to the context of the stage. Upon emerging from the shade, Angelica tells her spectator: "Pace sia teco; / teco difenda Dio la fama nostra" ("peace be with you; God defend with you our fame," (1.52.5–6). Combined with the terms "improvvisa," "mostra," and "scena," the scriptural echoes associate her with the messenger angels of the *sacre rappresentazioni* (Italian Renaissance sacred plays), and in typically Ariostean fashion complicate the almost simultaneous neoclassical theatrical references to the goddesses of love and chastity. For a late Renaissance actress, who often traveled from town to town and won the hearts of male onlookers, the implications would have been clear: she had a role model in the wandering Angelica, a universally desired, gazed-at object but also self-transforming and performing subject.

The perils of Angelica, moreover, gave actresses the chance to display their tragic and declamatory talents. The Milanese fans of the early seventeenth-century star Orsola Posmoni Cecchini (stage name Flaminia) praised her moving performance of the princess of Catai in the *Pazzia d'Orlando* (Taviani, "Un vivo contrasto," 64–65; Posmoni was also disparagingly called a "Marfisa bizarra" by a rival acting company [Ferrone, *Comici*, vol. I, 82]). At the same time, however, the actress playing Angelica could have been called upon to engage in comical routines. Such is the evidence offered by a remarkable unpublished manuscript of "La gran pazzia di Orlando, opera reale," the first of almost two hundred illustrated *scenari* in the collection of "Scenari più scelti di istrioni," also known as the "Raccolta Corsiniana" (ca. 1625–50). Though this anonymous text may be an amateur enthusiast's concoction rather than an actual play script, it at least emulates the practices of a professional theatrical company: if not the work of the actors and playwrights themselves, it at least offers some idea of the scenes and characters they played.[8] Pride of place is given to the adaptation of the *Furioso*, and the

---

8. Zorzi (206–7) asserts that the Corsiniana manuscript "é probabilmente lo zibaldone piu vicino a un certo tipo di professionismo; ma é un professionismo anch'esso di natura ambigua, perchè non sappiamo se si tratti di una ritrascrizione semplificata (la raccolta appar-

manuscript's authors employed a highly skilled artist to paint a watercolor frontispiece to the work. In the illustration's foreground, a large male nude, presumably Orlando, uproots a large palm tree, while in the middle ground, two warriors engage in combat not far from Ferraù, seen fishing for his lost helmet while the ghost of Argalia emerges from the waters. Rather unexpectedly, the background features a carefully drawn two-story inn, where an exotically clad female figure, presumably Angelica, encounters of all people Pantalone, the Zanni Trappolino, and Dottore Graziano! Three prominent figures or "masks" of the *commedia all'improvviso* thus invade the narrative territory of the *Furioso*, and become the dramatic companions of its most sought-after female character. This mingling of princess and clowns is in keeping with the aesthetic of the early commedia dell'arte, which deliberately played off the elegant against the grotesque, the restrained against the excessive, the romantic against the ridiculous (Taviani, "Un vivo contrasto"). Instead of a "fresca stanza fra l'ombre" ("fresh room amidst the shade"), Angelica in this comic theatrical version finds man-made shelter, managed by a trio of clowns. The play's second scene explains the watercolor vignette, introducing Graziano, Pantalone, and Trappolino as "hosti del buono allogiamento, et guadagno in quanto" ("hosts of a good lodging, by which they make good profit") to whom Angelica, "fuggendo Rinaldo, discorre le suoi innamorati, e volersi nascondere; loro la salutano, sentendo venir genti si ritirano" ("fleeing Rinaldo, tells them about her lovers, and wishes to hide herself; they greet her, and hearing people arrive, they retire") (Raccolta Corsiniana, 3r). At this point, it is unclear whether Angelica enters the inn with her zany hosts, for at the end of act 1 she reappears, now with her cruel abductors who tie her to the rocks, leaving her to lamentations before Ruggiero enters to save her from the Orc. In this adaptation, Ruggiero kills the beast, while Angelica, according to the stage direction, "fa la burla con l'anello" ("does the trick with the ring").

---

tenne al Cardinale Maurizio di Savoia) per un uso della scena o per conservazione documentaria."

This dramatization of the *Furioso* would thus allow the actress playing Angelica to showcase her ability to deliver serious, emotionally charged monologue. Following the "trick with the ring," however, it would also require her to use her comedic talents, since in act 2 she arrives with the wounded Medoro, but only enters the "hostaria" after having performed "lazzi con li buffoni" (Raccolta Corsiniana, 3v). Unfortunately, the manuscript does not specify what these gags or "lazzi" were, but regardless of their exact form, they would have entailed some measure of physical, probably slapstick clowning on the part of the *prima donna*. With the abrupt switch from tragic lament to comic byplay, the actress's own versatile performance would aptly convey the mutability of Angelica. When she next appears in this *scenario*, she negotiates with the *buffoni*, who desire at least monetary reward for their help in curing Medoro; she then expresses her own desire to return to Catai to be crowned. Before leaving the stage, however, the two young lovers "scriveno in molti luoghi Angelica e Medoro" ("write in many places the names Angelica and Medoro"), thus causing Orlando to go mad. The New Comedy term of "commodità," which appears in Medoro's poem inscribed at the entrance of the grotto (23.108), describes not only Ariosto's Angelica but also the dramatic style of this adaptation, which retails a combination of broad comedy and romance.[9] Again, the sequence of comedic, heroic, and romantic motifs dramatizes the almost infinite variety of the heavenly romance princess, the dazzling spectacle who can make herself invisible, the desired object who becomes desiring subject, the experienced woman who in canto 1 is characterized as promiscuous and in canto 19 as a virgin. Such doubleness and elusiveness would thus apply even more palpably to the sixteenth-century actress, protean in her moral status, theatrical talents, performance of gender, and relationship to her audience.

While Angelica offered an especially apt role model for the first professional actresses' performances on stage, other female characters of the

9. I am indebted to Dennis Looney for this observation [in an oral response given to a lecture version of this chapter].

Furioso provided inspiration for these women's self-presentation off the stage. As I noted above, a leading lady such as Flaminia Romana, capable of conspicuous public violence, invited association with the woman warrior Marfisa. If the testimony of Tommaso Garzoni is to be believed, actresses dressed in armor and brandishing swords would often lead their traveling companies into town, inviting the citizens to attend their next performance (Garzoni, in Marotti and Romei 14). Occasionally, women were even born or at least baptized into performing Ariostean archetypes. Although they were not professional actresses, two of the most cultured and graceful dancers at the court of Alfonso II were the Duke's first cousins, christened with the names Bradamante and Marfisa d'Este (Newcomb, Madrigal, 16–17).

By the late sixteenth century, then, female characters were leaping off the pages of chivalric romance: not the least of these was Issabella, the resolutely chaste lover of Zerbino. A common enough Christian name, it nonetheless evokes specific, deliberate ties with the Furioso heroine in the case of Isabella Andreini (1562–1604), the most famous, widely published, and enthusiastically admired actress of her time. In contrast to many of her professional colleagues, Andreini promoted a public image of herself as not only a "prima donna innamorata," but as the chaste and devoted wife of her husband Francesco. "Alma Venus, sed casta," an anonymous author of a poem in her honor calls her, associating her with erotic divinity but also with the beautiful "paragon di continenza" of the Furioso. According to Tasso, this real-life Isabella— or "Bella d'Asia," as he anagramatically dubs her—epitomized love and beauty, and inspired her audience to adore, chastely, her incomparable image: "Felici l'alme, e fortunate i cori, / ove con lettre d'oro Amor s'imprima / nell'immagine vostra, e in cui s'adori" ("Happy the souls, and fortunate the hearts, where with letters of gold Love stamps himself, in your image, and wherein he is adored," Taviani, "Bella"). Like her fictional role model, Isabella Andreini wanders through the world, and provokes love in others, but reserves herself for one man only. As her own writings attest (Fragmenti, 157–58), she knew the Furioso quite well, and may have consciously sought to fulfill the divine prophecy made upon her namesake's martyrdom in canto 29:

Per l'avvenir vo' che ciascuna ch'aggia
il nome tuo, sia di sublime ingegno,
e sia bella, gentil, cortese e saggia,
e di vera onestade arrivi al segno:
onde materia agli scrittori caggia
di celebrare il nome inclito e degno;
tal che Parnasso, Pindo ed Elicone
sempre Issabella, Issabella risuone. (39.29)

("For the future I desire that every woman who bears thy name, be
of sublime talent, and beautiful, kind, courtly, and wise, and at-
tain the very sign of true honesty: whence would come matter for
writers to celebrate the worthy, renowned name; so that Parnassus,
Pindus, and Helicon always would resound 'Issabella, Issabella!' ").

When Andreini herself writes of love, in her pastoral play *Mirtilla*
(1588), in her unpublished poems to Christina of Lorraine in 1589, in
her *Rime* (1601) and *Lettere* (1607), she frequently portrays women as the
more constant sex, praises her addressees for their beauty and chastity,
and characterizes men as gullible, fickle, and prone to infatuation with
all sorts of women, including actresses. As a performer, Andreini most
often played the young woman in love, who through her wit, patience,
perseverance, willingness to disguise herself, skill at manipulating ser-
vants and outsmarting fathers—in short, by doing whatever it takes
—almost always wins the man of her desires. Isabella's associations
with beauty, chastity, boldness, and rhetorical virtuosity may have even
reached England, to find expression in the eponymous heroine of Shake-
speare's *Measure for Measure* (1604). In the "Gran Pazzia di Orlando,"
however, she does not meet any *buffoni*, nor a happy end, and instead
plays the martyr to Rodomonte's villain.

III

Ariosto's other notable witness for female chastity, Drusilla, deceives
her male aggressor in an even more performative way than Isabella, and
as such appropriately takes center stage in one of the first and best docu-

mented female performances of the *Furioso*. As described at the beginning of this chapter, on July 4, 1567, in Mantua, Flaminia Romana led her troupe in a highly praised adaptation of the Marganorre episode from Canto 37 of the *Furioso*. This version appears to have revised the original climactic assassination of the woman-hating tyrant from a forced leap off a tower to a stoning by the avenging women of his realm (in the *Furioso*, the lapidation occurs a few stanzas before his death). I now want to consider not only how but why Flaminia would choose to stage this particular episode. Clearly, the revenge tragedy plot and lengthy tirades of Drusilla offer vividly dramatic material for performance. A close look at the poetic source, however, suggests that gender matters specifically informed Flaminia's intertextual project.

First, canto 37 is the *Furioso*'s most extensive treatment of the pathology of misogyny. To revenge his sons' love-provoked deaths, Marganorre separates his female and male subjects, slits the throats of women escorted by armed knights, and cuts the dresses of unaccompanied women so as to expose their pudenda. Marganorre's cruel law enacts an extreme case of castration anxiety, as he exposes the women's supposedly terrifying lack of the phallus: appropriately, his law that isolates women and tries to make them objects of shame and ridicule is inscribed on a "colonna in piazza" (Finucci, *Lady Vanishes*, 166–68). The canto begins, moreover, with a lengthy encomium of "valorose donne," including that "altro sole" Vittoria Colonna. Ariosto proceeds to recount yet another heroic *impresa* carried out by the valorous Marfisa and Bradamante, but for an actress/director, the praise of famous women writers and artists would have been a stimulus to undertake a noteworthy theatrical venture. Not, however, in the role of the woman warrior, for the leading female character of the Marganorre episode is Drusilla, the woman whom the tyrant's son Tanacro abuses by killing her husband and then seeking her hand in marriage. To achieve her revenge, Drusilla pretends to love her would-be bridegroom, and does so in a carefully theatrical way. She makes her face simulate peace, and shows herself "tutta lieta, e finge / di queste nozze aver sommo disio" ("entirely happy, and she pretends to have the utmost desire to perform these wedding rites," 37.61).

To convince Tanacro of her readiness to marry him, Drusilla adorns and paints herself more than other women: she literally gets herself into make-up and costume for her part as the passive, decorative bride. Inventing a story about the wedding customs of her country, and giving instructions to Tanacro, her old serving-woman, and a priest, she also acts as playwright and director. Finally, she prepares the climactic scene, at the tomb which she had built for her dead husband, herself "di gemme ornata e di leggiadre gonne" ("adorned with gems, and diaphanous skirts," 37.68). The holy office is sung, and then, before an audience of "tutti, uomini e donne," she drinks the poisoned chalice, and maintains a "viso giocondo" as she hands it to her unsuspecting victim (37.68–69). At this point, however, she drops the mask of the happy bride, and expresses her true vindictive passion in both action and words:

> Or quivi il dolce stile e mansueto
> in lei si cangia e quella gran bonaccia.
> Lo spinge a dietro, e gli ne fa divieto,
> e par ch'arda negli occhi e ne la faccia,
> e con voce terribile e incomposta
> gli grida:—Traditor, da me ti scosta! (37.70)

("Now the sweet and gentle style changes in her, and that most pleasing air. She pushes him back, and forbids him, and it seems that she burns in her eyes, her face, and with a terrible, savage voice she cries: Traitor, by me may thou be ruined!")

She continues her tirade for another four stanzas, overwhelming the speechless and then lifeless Tanacro, and with a smile on her face, ends her speech "insieme con la vita" ("together with her life"). In short, she shows herself to be a virtuoso performer. It thus would be a logical choice for a *prima donna* like Flaminia Romana to portray such an impressive and overtly theatrical character. To some degree the actress plays herself, and as she redoubles the process of masking and unmasking feminine roles for a male audience, she alters the comic exposure of female masquerade that Ariosto develops but contains within the "carte" of his book. If, as Valeria Finucci proposes, the cross-dressed, bigen-dered Marfisa pays a severe narrative price for performing such exposure on the page (Finucci, "Female Masquerade," 80–81), the Marfisa-like Flaminia-as-Drusilla becomes a hero by enacting it on the stage. The live performance of this episode entertained its spectators, but it also may have challenged them. For in this case, they saw a woman in a variety of guises, who performs the masquerade of femininity only to undo it, and who revises Ariosto by directing her company to kill Marganorre before he can kill any of the women: in this female revision, the misogynist's law and disorder is not at all enforced, let alone written.

IV

To conclude by contrast, prominent female singers of the *Gerusalemme liberata* apparently enchanted their male listeners, but often with the effect of counteracting the theatrical and emotive impact of the voice with the pathetic, ultimately subordinate quality of the female character. The *concerto di donne* of Mantua for whom Monteverdi composed much of his third book of madrigals in 1592 rivaled their Ferrarese counter-part in leading much of the court's cultural life. When they performed the setting for Armida's impassioned "Vattene pur, crudel," with its leap of a minor sixth on the third word that dramatically bursts forth from the preceding repeated notes (Tomlinson 69–70), they would have cap-tured their listeners' attention, and perhaps their hearts. In dramatic terms, however, they quickly retreated, since the content of their lyric expressed the defeat of a powerful woman, and the conditions of their lyric performance prevented their full transformation into such a charac-ter. In other words, their only partially realized dramatization restricted the potential impact of Armida's frantic, spirited harangue, which in any case signals her yielding to the demands of the Christian warriors' (and Tasso's) epic project. Moreover, these singers were not stars, with their own "diva" status and cult following: they can be contrasted with Virginia Ramponi (stage name Florinda), the wife of Isabella Andreini's actor-playwright son Giovan Battista, who in 1608 enthralled her audiences and moved them to tears with her last-minute, understudy, and bravura singing of Monteverdi's "Lamento d'Arianna" (Fenlon 275–80). Like the same composer's favorite soprano Adriana Basile, the strong-willed Ramponi enjoyed an international reputation, and both her on-stage and offstage magnetism compensated for the grieving female abjection she portrayed, if only to a limited degree.[10]

Revealingly, Monteverdi would later compose an *intermedio* or early "mini-opera" based on another episode of female subjugation from the *Liberata*, namely *Il combattimento di Tancredi e Clorinda* (1624). In the original, Tasso has Clorinda disguise herself not only as a male warrior but also as an unidentified one, the better to ambush the Christians outside the walls of Jerusalem. Having set fire to the enemy's mobile wooden tower, she attempts to run back inside the city walls, but is locked out and then overtaken by the mounted Tancredi. Although the narration dominates, a brief dramatic dialogue follows between the two combatants, neither of whom recognizes the other: like an androgynous actress, the

10. For a thorough and illuminating commentary on the career and public images of Virginia Ramponi, see Ferrone, *Attori mercanti corsari*, 234–62. Ferrone notes how Ramponi, like her mother-in-law, Isabella Andreini, specialized in multiple disguises and rapid changes of identity, including the roles of mad shepherdess (*la Centaura*), Turkish slave boy (*lo Schiavetto*), beautiful lady in erotic love with her own reflection (*l'Amor nello specchio*), and penitent Magdalene (*la Maddalena*). He also posits (246) that the Venetian painter Domenico Fetti portrayed her as an "attrice ideale" in his paintings of Ariadne and Mary Magdalene, the first of which (dated 1611–13) may commemorate her famous 1608 performance of Monteverdi's *Lamento d'Arianna*.

Ramponi's readiness to defend her own fame and disparage that of others comes across in a letter she wrote from Turin on August 4, 1609, to Duke Ferdinando Gonzaga, in which she declares: "saprà poi Vostra Illustrissima com'io ho gettato a terra ogni trofeo eretto dalla Signora Flaminia [Orsola Posmoni Cecchini], e tanto se l'è slungato il naso, quanto l'o haveva superbo alzato; ella è odiata da tutto Torino, per la sua alterigia, et frenesia nell'amor di Cintio" (Archivio di Stato, Mantova; Archivio Gonzaga Autografi, Busta 10, f. 57r). For further documentation of the bitter rivalry between the Compagnia dei Fedeli (the Andreini's and their troupe) and that of the Accesi (Pier Maria Cecchini, his wife, Orsola Posmoni, and their troupe) during the summer of 1609, see Ferrone, ed., *Comici dell'Arte*, vol. 1, 81–94, and 231–38.

biologically indeterminate Clorinda escapes easy identification (Migiel 98). Clorinda turns to face her pursuer, shouting "O tu, che porte / che corri sí?" ("O thou, what art thou bringing, running with so fast?") He responds "E guerra e morte" ("both war and death") and she echoes back "Guerra e morte avrai" (GL 12.52–53). Their encounter, as Tasso specifies, is an explicitly dramatic one: "Degne d'un chiaro sol, degne d'un pieno / teatro, opre sarian si memorande" ("worthy of the bright sun, worthy of a full theatre, deeds thus to be remembered," (12.54).

After a detailed, onomatopoeic description of the sound and fury of their fighting, a pause with more dialogue follows, before the fatal moment arrives "che'l viver di Clorinda al suo fin deve" ("that must end the life of Clorinda," 12.64). Tasso imparts full dramatic pathos to her death, as she breathes her final words with a "spirto di fé, di carità, di speme" ["spirit of faith, of charity, and of hope"], seeking forgiveness and Christian baptism: "Amico, hai vinto: io ti perdon . . . perdona / tu ancora" ("Friend, thou hast won: I forgive thee . . . may thou also forgive me," 12.65–66). Tancredi, his helmet now filled with fresh water for the "grande ufficio e pio" ("great pious office") raises Clorinda's visor and makes the terrifying anagnoresis that renders him "senza / e voce e moto. Ahi vista! Ahi conoscenza!" ("without voice and motion. Ah the sight! Ah the recognition!" 12.67). This became one of the most famous lines of the entire epic, though quoted out of the context of Tancredi's narcissistically driven slaughter of Clorinda, the white Ethiopian androgyne who is his own "double self" (Bellamy 184). For her part, the virgin woman warrior receives the baptism, and thus does not truly die, but goes to heaven as a reborn Christian: "in atto di morir lieto e vivace, dir parea: "S'apre il cielo; io vado in pace" ("in the act of dying thus happy and lively, she seemed to say: "if heaven will open itself, I go in peace," 12.68).

Monteverdi clearly appreciated the full theatrical potential of this sequence in the *Liberata*, combining as it does violent heroic conflict, tragic romance, and religious conversion drama. For the text of his adaptation, he preserved most of stanzas 52 through 68, with some omissions and variations: for example, a fourfold repetition of "che d'armi," to stress the clang of the mounted Tancredi's armor, and even more significantly, the sung delivery, "soavissimo," of Clorinda's final "vado in pace" facial expression. The music of this closing passage, "lento" and then "sfumando," with a delayed cadence on the word "pace," vividly imitates the quiet, pacified state of the dying Clorinda (Maniates 478). Monteverdi omits Tancredi's lament, and thus puts the climactic theatrical focus on the female character's beatific passing, made all the more striking by the singer's fully armored transvestite costume. In his preface to the published version of the work, the composer explains that it was first performed in 1624 before "all the nobility" of Venice at the palace of his patron, Girolamo Mocenigo, "for an evening's entertainment at Carnival time," with Tancredi and Clorinda costumed in swords and armor, the former entering on a "cavallo Mariano" (probably a hobby horse). The two performers enacted the combat with vivid movements and gestures, dramatically accompanying the text as sung by a one-man chorus. Suddenly interrupting a series of conventional madrigals, Il combattimento sprang upon its audience without warning, and introduced them to Monteverdi's newly invented and highly theatrical stile concitato, with its insistent, often rapid-fire rhythms, some in triple time to imitate the galloping of a horse (the "motto del cavallo"), and its use of tremolo and pizzicato for the strings, to underscore the warriors' sword-blows. With such carefully and mimetically crafted agitation, Monteverdi aimed to render grand passions in music so as to complement the contemporary actor's and actress's emotionally charged performances: he himself marked the breakthrough by describing his work, à la Ariosto, as a "song of a kind never heard or seen before" (Pirrotta 288–89, Whenham 243–45).

The stile concitato, then, demonstrated how orchestra and costumed, choreographed singers could work together to maximize the dramatic and emotional potential of a poetic text. As elsewhere in his work for theatrical performance, Monteverdi's innovations point the way toward the baroque, total art form known as opera: indeed, the composer's own Orfeo (1607) and L'incoronazione di Poppea (1642) can be defined as two of the first full-scale European operas. As Susan McClary has proposed, the powerful female characters in these and other Monteverdi productions practice a complex musical rhetoric of "seduction and lament" that at once supports and questions patriarchal authority (McClary 48–52). Moreover, the fact that women were now singing and acting their own provocative roles gave special urgency to their potential critiques of the traditional gender hierarchy. This trend would continue in early operatic performance, at least through the first half of the seventeenth century. That the *Gerusalemme liberata* played its own crucial part in this process is hardly coincidental. Tasso's work features poetic eloquence, highly dramatic moments of conflict, and concentrated emotional expression, especially in its portrayal of love and women. Such elements appear in Armida's sudden desperation at losing both her love and power, in Clorinda's transformation from man-conquering infidel virago to man-conquered lady of Christian virtue, and then in actual live performances of these characters by female *virtuosae*. I italicize this last word to mark the complex masculinizing of women who sang and acted in public, who could play both the manly warrior and the abject heroine, who like Clorinda possess *virtù* but by this same token are morally suspect, for being something other than unified, subordinate female subjects (or objects!) (Schiesari 76–79). As if to contain the possible threat to gender morals posed by the charismatic diva, Monteverdi and his contemporaries had them sing the laments of the abandoned Ariadne, the futile rage of the betrayed Armida, the dying utterance of the vanquished Clorinda. In 1627, Monteverdi wrote a now lost sequel to Il *combattimento*, entitled *Armida*, and the same character would be the subject of numerous musical adaptations during the eighteenth and nineteenth centuries, including one for the 1637 wedding of Grand Duke Ferdinando II de' Medici and Vittoria d'Urbino that culminated with the siege and destruction of the enchantress's castle by the allegorical character "Amor Pudico" (Fabbri 266–67, Solerti 203–10). To some if not a great degree, these female performances enacted the passive-aggressive fantasy of admiring the theatrically spectacular rise and fall of a powerful woman, who pays the price for loving not wisely but too unconventionally. As Catherine Clément has eloquently argued, the pattern of exalting beautiful, doomed heroines only to undo them is at the heart of opera: this seductive art form thus encourages heterosexual men to feel pity, fear, and self-affirmation, and women and homosexual men to identify with and even adore the female victim/martyr/diva (Clément, Koestenbaum). For her part, Tasso's and then Monteverdi's dying Clorinda is rewarded with a blissful final vision of heavenly peace. She is denied, however, the revenging victories of a Marfisa or even a Drusilla, much less the comical escape of a clown-assisted Angelica. Rarely being authors, company directors, and protean, self-performing actresses, the female opera singers of the next two centuries could only faintly follow the lead of a Flaminia Romana or Isabella Andreini. By her own initiative, the latter, a flesh-and-blood but larger than life Isabella, had turned her Ariostan role model into a famous international superstar.

Works Cited

Andreini, Isabella. "Alla Serenissima Madama Cristiana de Loreno . . ." Manuscript copy. Magliabecchi Classe 7, 15: "Poesia." Biblioteca Nazionale di Firenze, Florence.

———. *Fragmenti di alcune scritture.* Venice: Combi, 1625.

———. *Lettere.* Venice: Zaltieri, 1607.

———. *Mirtilla.* Verona: Sebastiano dalle Donne, 1588.

———. *Rime.* Milan: Bordone, 1601.

Ariosto, Lodovico. *Orlando furioso.* Ed. Marcello Turchi. 2 vols. Milan: Garzanti, 1982.

Bellamy, Elizabeth J. *Translations of Power: Narcissism and the Unconscious in Epic History.* Ithaca: Cornell UP, 1992.

Bowers, Jane. "The Emergence of Women Composers in Italy, 1566–1700." *Women Making Music: The Western Art Tradition, 1150–1950.* Ed. Jane Bowers and Judith Tick. Urbana: U of Illinois P, 1986. 116–67.

Brown, Howard M. "Genre, Harmony, and Rhetoric in the Late Sixteenth Century Italian Madrigal." *Renaissance Culture in Context.* Ed. Jean R. Brink and William Gentrup. Aldershot: Scholar Press, 1993. 198–225.

Clément, Catherine. *Opera, or the Undoing of Women.* Trans. Betsy Wing. Minneapolis: U of Minnesota P, 1988.

D'Ancona, Alessandro. *Origini del teatro italiano.* 2 vols. Torino: Loescher, 1891.

Donato, Eugenio. " 'Per selve e boscherecci labirinti': Desire and Narrative Structure in Ariosto's Orlando Furioso." *Literary Theory/Renaissance Texts.* Ed. Patricia Parker and David Quint. Baltimore: Johns Hopkins UP, 1986. 33–62.

Einstein, Alfred. *The Italian Madrigal.* 3 vols. Princeton: Princeton UP, 1949.

Fenlon, Iain. "The Mantuan Stage Works." *The New Monteverdi Companion*. Ed. Denis Arnold and Nigel Fortune. London: Faber & Faber, 1985. 251–87.

Ferrone, Siro. *Attori mercanti corsari: la commedia dell'arte in Europa tra Cinque e Seicento*. Turin: Einaudi, 1993.

——, ed. *Comici dell'Arte: Corrispondenze*. 2 vols. Florence: Le Lettere, 1993.

Finucci, Valeria. "The Female Masquerade: Ariosto and the Game of Desire." *Desire in the Renaissance: Psychoanalysis and Literature*. Ed. Valeria Finucci and Regina Schwartz. Princeton: Princeton UP, 1994. 61–90.

——. *The Lady Vanishes: Subjectivity and Representation in Castiglione and Ariosto*. Stanford: Stanford UP, 1992.

——. "La scrittura epico-cavalleresca al femminile: Moderata Fonte e *Tredici canti del Floridoro*." *Annali d'Italianistica* 12 (1994): 203–31.

Garzoni, Tommaso. *La piazza universale di tutte le professioni*. Venice, 1585.

Javitch, Daniel. *Proclaiming a Classic: The Canonization of Orlando Furioso*. Princeton: Princeton UP, 1991.

Johnson-Haddad, Miranda. " 'Like the Moon It Renews Itself': The Female Body as Text in Dante, Ariosto, and Tasso." *Stanford Italian Review* II (1992): 203–15.

Koestenbaum, Wayne. *The Queen's Throat*. New York: Knopf, 1993.

McClary, Susan. *Feminine Endings: Music, Gender, and Sexuality*. Minneapolis: U of Minnesota P, 1991.

Maniates, Maria Rika. *Mannerism in Italian Music and Culture, 1530–1630*. Chapel Hill: U of North Carolina P, 1979.

Marotti, Ferruccio, and Giovanna Romei. *La commedia dell'arte e la società barocca: la professione del teatro*. Rome: Bulzoni, 1991.

Migiel, Marilyn. "Clorinda's Fathers." *Stanford Italian Review* 10 (1991): 93–121.

Monteverdi, Claudio. *Il combattimento di Tancredi e Clorinda*. Ed. Alceo Toni. Milan: Carisch, 1936.

Newcomb, Anthony. "Courtesans, Muses, or Musicians? Professional Women Musicians in Sixteenth-Century Italy." *Women Making Music: The Western Art Tradition, 1150–1950*. Ed. Jane Bowers and Judith Tick. Urbana: U of Illinois P, 1986. 90–115.

——. *The Madrigal at Ferrara, 1579–1597*. 2 vols. Princeton: Princeton UP, 1980.

Parker, Patricia. *Inescapable Romance: Studies in the Poetics of a Mode*. Princeton: Princeton UP, 1979.

Pirrotta, Nino. *Music and Culture in Italy from the Middle Ages to the Baroque*. Cambridge, Mass.: Harvard UP, 1984.

"Raccolta Corsiniana" ("Scenari più scelti di istrioni"). Manuscript copy. Coll.45.6.5–6. Biblioteca Corsiniana, Rome.

Rosenthal, Margaret F. *The Honest Courtesan: Veronica Franco, Citizen and Writer in Sixteenth-Century Venice*. Chicago: U of Chicago P, 1992.

Ruggiero, Guido. *Binding Passions: Tales of Magic, Marriage, and Power at the End of the Renaissance.* Oxford: Oxford UP, 1993.

Schiesari, Juliana. "In Praise of Virtuous Women? For a Genealogy of Gender Morals in Renaissance Italy." *Annali d'Italianistica* 7 (1989): 66–87.

Shemek, Deanna. "That Elusive Object of Desire: Angelica in the *Orlando Furioso.*" *Annali d'Italianistica* 7 (1989): 116–41.

Solerti, Angelo. *Musica, ballo e drammatica alla corte medicea dal 1600 al 1637.* Florence: Bemporad, 1905.

Sommi, Leone de'. *Quattro dialoghi in materia di rappresentazioni sceniche.* Ed. Ferruccio Marotti. Milan: Polifilo, 1968.

Stevens, Denis, ed. *The Letters of Claudio Monteverdi.* Cambridge: Cambridge UP, 1980.

Tasso, Torquato. *Gerusalemme liberata.* Ed. Lanfranco Caretti. Turin: Einaudi, 1993.

Taviani, Ferdinando. "Bella d'Asia: Torquato Tasso, gli attori, e l'immortalità." *Paragone: Letteratura* 408–10 (1984): 3–76.

——. *La commedia dell'arte e la società barocca. La fascinazione del teatro.* Rome: Bulzoni, 1969.

——. "Un vivo contrasto: seminario su attrici e attori della commedia dell'arte." *Teatro e Storia* 1 (1986): 25–75.

Taviani, Ferdinando, and Mirella Schino. *Il segreto della commedia dell'arte.* Florence: Casa Usher, 1982.

Tessari, Roberto. *Commedia dell'arte: la maschera e l'ombra.* Milan: Mursia, 1981.

Tomlinson, Gary. *Monteverdi and the End of the Renaissance.* Berkeley: U of California P, 1987.

Whenham, John. "The Later Madrigals and Madrigal-Books." *The New Monteverdi Companion.* Ed. Denis Arnold and Nigel Fortune. London: Faber & Faber, 1985. 216–47.

Wiggins, Peter DeSa. *Figures in Ariosto's Tapestry: Character and Design in the Orlando Furioso.* Baltimore: Johns Hopkins UP, 1986.

Zorzi, Ludovico. *L'attore, la commedia, il drammaturgo.* Turin: Einaudi, 1990.

For quotations from Ariosto's *Orlando Furioso* (OF), I have used the edition by Marcello Turchi. For Tasso's *Gerusalemme liberata* (GL), I have used the edition by Lanfranco Caretti. As with all other Italian texts cited in this chapter, any translations are my own.

"Dal rogo alle nozze":
Tasso's Sofronia as Martyr Manqué

NAOMI YAVNEH

Del succo de' fiori nati alla campagna le api ne fanno soave mele e le aragni ne cavano mortifero veneno.

(From the same wildflowers the bees produce sweet honey and the spiders extract mortal venom.) — Gabriel Paleotti, *Discorso intorno alle imagini sacre e profane*

At the beginning of canto 2 of Tasso's *Gerusalemme liberata*, the formerly Christian sorcerer, Ismeno, advises the king of Jerusalem to steal an image of the Virgin Mary from a subterranean chapel, and to place it in his own mosque. Whether through theft or miraculous intervention, however, the "casto imago" disappears. Yet one veiled virgin replaces another: when the king declares he will kill all the Christians unless the image is restored, a beautiful woman comes before him, claiming to be the culprit. By her appearance as well as her actions, Sofronia is linked to the icon, in the exemplarity essential both to martyrdom and post-Tridentine discourse regarding images. In Sofronia, image and imitation, representation and exemplar are conflated, for if her form imitates that of the holy simulacrum, her conduct is modeled on that of the Virgin represented thereby, as well as on that of the virgin martyrs for whom Mary is a typological figure.

This episode, so focused on the question of images and their powers, is highly suggestive in the context of Counter-Reformation treatises on the status of images, a debate with which the self-consciously Catholic poet would no doubt have been concerned. But it also has important implications for a consideration of the function of women in Tasso's Christian epic. For if Sofronia's noble behavior is nothing short of saintly, the description thereof nevertheless evokes many of the ambiguities central to hagiographic narrative—most notably, the androgynous power and chaste eros of the virgin martyrs. Moreover, Sofronia's martyrdom is ultimately averted when she is rescued by the seemingly pagan Clorinda, herself an ambiguous figure, whose own history with regard to images (which we and she discover ten cantos later) is significant both for a consideration of Sofronia's story and for her own deathbed conversion.

Countering Protestant claims which equated the worship of images with idolatry, Tridentine theologians insisted upon the representative quality of images, which make visible what is invisible, and reaffirmed their threefold salutary effects: images instruct, they spark the memory, and they excite the emotions. As the twenty-fifth session of the Council of Trent, *De invocatione, veneratione et reliquis sanctorum, et sacris imaginibus* (held December 3 and 4, 1563) affirmed, images serve not only to show honor to God and his saints, but to instruct the ignorant, and to move both the illiterate and the learned alike to imitation of saintly conduct. The seventeenth-century artist and theologian Giovanni Ottonelli, rearticulating the main issues addressed by sixteenth-century apologists, writes, "l'immagine vedute sono molto potenti per espugnar la rocca degli humani affetti, e per eccitare gli animi all'operatione della virtù, e alla fuga del vitio" (images viewed are very potent in conquering the cliffs of human sentiment, and for exciting souls toward virtuous action and away from vice, 50). Images serve an exemplary function, then; in the words of the Council, they are important,

> not only because the people are thereby reminded of the benefits and gifts bestowed by Christ, but also because through the saints the miracles of God and salutary examples are set before the eyes of the faithful, so that they [the faithful] may give God thanks for those things, may fashion their own life and conduct in imitation of the saints, and be moved to adore and love God. (Schroeder 216)

More than worshipping God for his miracles and adoring his saints for their righteousness and piety, if the goal of all Christians is to live in imi-

tatio cristi, the imitation of Christ, the Catholic is to become an image himself, fashioning himself in emulation of Christ's saints, models in their own lives of the Supreme Exemplar.

But significantly, reaffirming the doctrine of the Medieval Council of Nicea that "no divinity or virtue is believed to be in [images] by reason of which they are to be worshipped, that no petitions can be addressed to them, and that no trust is to be placed in images, as was done of old by the Gentiles who placed their hope in idols" (Schroeder 216), the council and its apologists insist that images are only representative, functioning almost as mnemonic devices to remind the devout of the true objects of *laetria* (God), *hyperdulia* (the Virgin), and *dulia* (the saints). The Catholics rejected Protestant reforms by reasserting the necessity of images in the church, not as objects of worship in and of themselves, but as visible simulacra of their exemplary "prototypes":

> the honour which is shown them [images] is referred to the objects (*prototypa*) which they represent, so that through our images which we kiss, and before which we uncover our heads and prostrate ourselves, we adore Christ and venerate the saints whose likenesses they are. (Schroeder 216)

Ottonelli explains the Christian doctrine that an image comprises three parts: "la materia" (the material), "la forma impressa" (the form impressed upon it), and finally the image itself, "che rappresenta un'altra cosa, di cui tiene la simiglianza, e prende il nome" (which represents another thing, from which it takes its appearance and name, 77). It is this third part alone which should be venerated,

> nella quale l'occhio della nostra mente mira la persona del santo, non secondo l'essere, che ha in se stesso, ma secondo l'essere rappresentato con la similitudine di se stesso, espresso nell'immagine, a cui però dar puossi l'honore, che si deve alla persona. (77)

> (in which our mind's eye sees the person of the saint, not in his own being, but in the being represented with his own appearance,

expressed in the image, to which, therefore, we may pay the honor which we owe to the person.)

The distinction between the saint him- or herself and the representation is thus maintained: while the image renders visible what is invisible, the image is only worthy of honor by virtue of *resemblance*, not *substance*. The *materia* itself is innocent, and it is for this reason, according to Gabriel Paleotti, author of one of the most important post-Tridentine treatises, that the same image "partorirà più differenze" (will give birth to several meanings; vol. 2, 172). The cardinal offers as an example the metal serpent created by Moses in Numbers 21: "ad alcuni era in loco di cosa sacra, ed altri in vece d'idolo" (some held it a sacred thing, some an idol). Paleotti continues, "onde noi veggiamo che ancor del succo de' fiori nati alla campagna le api ne fanno soave mele e le aragni ne cavano mortifero veneno" (whence we see that from the same wildflowers the bees produce sweet honey, and the spiders extract mortal venom; 172). The source of idolatry, then, is not the image itself, but what we do with it; the image which Moses was instructed to make by the same God whose commandments forbade graven images was not an idol but rather a reminder of the power of God to heal. Its destructive source lay in the unwillingness or inability of its observers to make the hermeneutic leap from creation to Creator. As the biblical episode and Paleotti's metaphor suggest, the choice is quite simply between life and death — a contrast confirmed by the New Testament's typological analogy between the raising up of the brazen serpent and of the Son of Man. But this insistence on the necessity of both faith and interpretation points up the inherent danger of such representations (a menace with which both the post-Tridentine theologians and Tasso himself were aware): if the salutary effect of the image, as Paleotti's metaphor emphasizes, is dependent on the spiritual state and the active will of the Christian, who, like a bee, takes the raw substance and transforms it into something new, then no matter how piously constructed, any Christian image may become an idol.

It is precisely this idolatrous inability to recognize the crucial distinction between "essere" and "essere rappresentato," to make the interpretive leap between substance and resemblance, that Ismeno, who "confonde le due leggi a sè mal note" (confuses the two laws he ill understands; 2.2.4), demonstrates when he misappropriates an image from his former religion, Christianity, attempting to place it in the service of his new, opposing faith; a faith which, ironically—out of its own inability to see that distinction—rejects all images. Ismeno's confusion of religions is dramatized by his actions: placed in the mosque of the infidel, the "casto imago" becomes an idol in Christian as well as the overly literal Islamic terms.

But if Ismeno's misuse of the image demonstrates his ignorance and impiety as both Christian and Muslim, Clorinda's paradoxical request that the Christian pair be freed in return for her own future service to the pagan army displays not only a better understanding of the religion in which she was raised, but a proleptic comprehension of the faith into which, we will learn ten cantos later, she was born, will be baptized, and will die. Correcting the advisor's ecumenical blasphemy, Clorinda recognizes the image as an idol in Muslim and Christian terms:

> Fu de le nostre leggi irriverenza
> quell'opra far che persuase il mago:
> chè non convien ne' nostri tèmpi a nui
> gl'idoli avere, e men gl'idoli altrui.   (2.50.5–8)

(It was irreverence to our laws to do the work which the wizard persuaded you to, because it's improper for us to have our own idols in our temples, much less the idols of others.)

Giving the lie to Sofronia (and transforming her, as we shall see, from Bride of Christ to bride of Olindo) and uniquely among the pagans, the *donna guerriera* demonstrates her piety by attributing the disappearance of the image not to any human but to God (whom in stanza 51 she acknowledges as Macon), an attribution which the poet himself—in that uncharacteristically and therefore suggestively ambiguous explanation of the image's disappearance—has already underscored as the most pious of choices:

O fu di man fedele opra furtiva,

o pur il Ciel qui sua potenza adopra,

che di Colei ch'è sua regina e diva

sdegna che loco vil l'imagin copra:

ch'incerta fama è ancor se ciò s'ascriva

ad arte umana od a mirabil opra;

ben è pietà che, la pietade e 'l zelo

uman cedendo, autor se 'n creda il Cielo.   (2.9)

(Either it was the secret work of the hand of one of the faithful, or indeed Heaven exercises here its power, because it scorns that a vile place should conceal the image of Her who is its queen and goddess. So that Fame is uncertain still whether that act be ascribed to human handywork or to miraculous agency. It is good religion that, giving up the claims of human piety and zeal, heaven be thought agent.)

But if the disappearance of the Virgin from the mosque illustrates both the miraculous powers of images and Reform Catholicism's emphasis on their representative similitude, the episode also demonstrates the exemplary importance of saints and their representations. As stated earlier, one veiled virgin replaces another: hearing that the king plans to kill all the Christians of Jerusalem unless the image is returned, the beautiful virgin Sofronia, chastely veiled but fearless, claims to have burned the icon:

Vergine era fra lor di già matura

verginità, d'alti pensieri e regi,

d'alta beltà; ma sua beltà non cura,

o tanto sol quant'onestà se 'n fregi.

È il suo pregio maggior che tra le mura

d'angusta casa asconde i suoi gran pregi,

e de' vagheggiatori ella s'invola

a le lodi, a gli sguardi, inculta e sola.   (2.14)

A virgin there was among the Christians, of mature maidenhood, of lofty and queenly thoughts, of lofty beauty; but she cares nothing for her beauty or only so far as it may adorn her chastity. Her greatest merit is that she hides her great merits within the walls of a narrow house, and steals away from the praises and glances of admirers alone and unsolicited.

If Sofronia physically resembles the "casto imago" which has disappeared, her behavior is modeled on that of the exemplar of chastity the image represents. The apparent oxymoron of "matura verginità" recalls the Virgin Mother, in Dante's words "umile e alta più che creatura," the Queen of Heaven exalted not only by her beauty, but by her humble obedience. Significantly, this second virgin, hiding her merits within narrow walls, evokes the tropes of the intensely erotic *Song of Songs* that traditionally figure the Virgin as *hortus conclusus* (garden enclosed) or *turris eburnea* (tower of ivory). But if Sofronia is thus iconographically linked to the Blessed Virgin, her actions recall those of the virgin martyrs, whose life stories enjoyed a resurgence of popularity in the aftermath of the Counter-Reformation.

Martyrdom was singularly compelling to Cinquecento Catholics as well as to Protestants. Not only were the catacombs, with their depictions of the early Christian martyrs newly revealed,[1] but the discovery of the "New" World, with its myriad souls to be claimed, followed by the rise of Protestantism, created a new generation of martyrs. The novitiate of the newly founded Jesuit order, for example, devoted to education and the propagation of the faith, were trained to expect and welcome martyrdom as an opportunity both to serve and to imitate Christ,[2] and the

1. The smaller and relatively simple catacombs of Saint Sebastian, on the Appian Way, were already the object of nocturnal pilgrimages by a select group of priests (Cardinal Borromeo, for example) when in 1578 the Catacombs of Priscilla were discovered, revealing to the fascinated city "subterranean Rome." See Baronius's *Annales* and the discussion in Male, 119ff.

2. The *Imago primi saeculi*, published in Antwerp in 1640 to commemorate the first centenary of the society, exhorts its members to embrace their particular vocation: "[Saint Bernard said] "It is in vain that I am a Christian, if I don't follow Christ. It is in vain that we are Jesuits, if we do not follow Jesus. We deserve to be called deserters, if we do not respond to the great name which we profess. For the name of Jesus, injury and calumny await us; for him, prison, chains and death itself accompanied by the most cruel sufferings, menace us. I

simultaneous representation of both early Christian and contemporary martyrdom—in devotional volumes, histories and even the walls of their churches—served to contextualize contemporary suffering, placing the most recent atrocities in an historic continuum with the traditional.[3] But militant missionaries were not the only martyrs celebrated; equally venerated were the young, beautiful women who had sacrificed themselves to protect the virginity vowed to Christ the Bridegroom, and the histories of these chaste exemplars were repeated in numerous images and hagiographic compendia. The virgin martyrs offered a moral rather than anagogical exemplarity as they came to represent the individual struggle against concupiscence, for if the sinner might never face the infidel in England or Japan, he or she daily confronted the desires of the flesh. As a form of physical subjugation and sanctification, then, chastity was the complement to martyrdom.

The earliest authority for the superiority of celibacy was Jesus himself, who encouraged his followers to make themselves as eunuchs for the Kingdom of Heaven, and while marriage was permitted in the early church (cf. Paul, "it is better to marry than to burn"), the sanctity of bodily purity is extolled throughout the patristic tradition. But in the equation of holiness with wholeness, women especially are exhorted to renounce earthly pleasures and the life of the body defiled by Eve's sin.

The church's particular concern with female chastity reflects the historical fact that it is the virginity of its brides upon which patriarchal culture depends.[4] But if the protection and disposal of a girl's virginity

---

speak to men who daily suffer these struggles for the health of souls. What will we do, companions in arms? Will we retreat? Soldiers, will we abandon our leader? We must imitate our emperor: It is in vain that we are Jesuits, if we do not follow Jesus" (525; my translation).

3. Such diachronicity was a means of legitimation for both Catholics and Protestants, who staked claim to the same early Christian martyrs.

4. Examining the implications of rape for the virgins of late Renaissance Rome, Elizabeth Cohen argues virginity's value "as a metaphor for control, a mark both of the family's ability to protect and discipline its members and of the girl's success in restraining herself;" in other words, virginity was a sign of familial and individual honor, and accordingly, the unmarried girl's "loss of virginity, whether voluntary or involuntary, signified both shame and

had economic and dynastic implications, the choice of a life of celibacy could in fact offer her some measure of power which she might otherwise lack.[5] After Trent, the autonomy of religious communities for women was greatly reduced,[6] but even so, the convent continued to offer a life of contemplation, of intellectual and spiritual fulfillment, and freedom from the pain—often mortal—of repeated childbearing.[7]

This choice of freedom was given a theological twist by the tradition associating the female with the dangers of sexuality. All women sinned in Eve, but just as Mary is the "Second Eve" whose humility redeems her forbearer's fault, so the imitation of Mary's virginity assures a woman a

---

a measure of escape from the control on which the family constructed its collective self-esteem" (172–73). Discussing sex crimes in Renaissance Venice, Guido Ruggiero points out that the perpetrators in rape cases where the victim was a patrician virgin of marriageable age were both prosecuted and punished much more vigorously than when the victim was married or of a lower class. Both Ruggiero and Cohen provide evidence that victims were often willing to marry their attackers since the crimes against them had rendered these women otherwise unmarriageable.

5. Of the early Christian period, Elaine Pagels comments, "For women . . . celibacy sometimes offered immediate rewards on earth, as well as eventual rewards in heaven. . . . [W]omen who 'renounced the world'—whether wealthy and aristocratic . . . or women without means . . . —thereby claimed the opportunity to travel, to devote themselves to intellectual and spiritual pursuits, to found institutions, and to direct them" (96). Regarding the medieval period, Kathryn Gravdal remarks that "for some medieval audiences virginity was a positive sexual category. It represented the choice to remain outside male desire and the refusal to circulate as an object of male possession. To refuse to go to the marriage market is, in the Middle Ages, one path to female autonomy, however limited and narrow" (27). See also Salisbury passim.

6. After the Council of Trent, female orders were subject to much greater supervision by the bishops, but there was an increased interest in convents not only for converted prostitutes but also for "unfortunate women" such as the "malmaritate" and "zitelle" who had nowhere to go. See Cohen 1982 and 1989.

7. Obviously not all women joined the convent seeking a life of contemplation. Women were often forced to enter convents due to the insufficiency of their dowries. Moreover, the church reaped financial rewards from these women, who brought to the convent the dowries too small to attract an acceptable husband.

higher degree of sanctity. If woman is the cause of the Fall, the wicked temptress who leads Adam to temptation and sin, a rejection of sexuality —the product of sin—reduces her postlapsarian penalties. The virgin cannot suffer the pains of childbirth, and the fasting and ascetism that usually accompany her chaste behavior often result in amenorrhea.[8] The integrity of the virgin body endows it with the purity requisite to holiness: the Virgin Mary, model for all virgins, is the "garden enclosed," the "fountain sealed," the "spring shut up" of *Song of Songs* in the highly sensual typology itself designed to tame the eroticism of Solomon's poetry.

Paradoxically, the virginity celebrated by the church as the most valued state of womanhood denies the very nature of a woman's biology, a rejection reflected in the theology of chastity. Paul states in the Epistle to the Galatians, "There is neither Jew nor Greek, there is neither bond nor free, there is neither male nor female: for ye are all one in Christ Jesus" (3:28). This genderless society is glossed by the church Fathers not only as a denial of female sexuality, but of being female. Jerome, for example, a fierce advocate of virginity,[9] declares in his commentary on Ephesians, "As long as a woman is for birth and children, she is different from man as body is from soul. But when she wishes to serve Christ more than the world, then she will cease to be a woman, and will be called man" (Jerome, *Comm. in Epist. and Ephes.*, III. v; qtd. in Warner 73). Similarly, Ambrose writes,

> She who does not believe is a woman and should be designated by the name of her sex, whereas she who believes progresses to perfect manhood, to the measure of the adulthood of Christ. She then dispenses with the name of her sex, the seductiveness of youth, the garrulousness of old age. (bk. 10; qtd. in Warner 372.)

8. For discussions of the relationship between female holiness, and fasting and amenorrhea, see Bynum.

9. See, for example, Jerome's twenty-second letter, "To Eustochium," in which he argues the virtues of chastity. Marriage, he claims, is tolerable only because more virgins are thereby produced.

Yet despite the masculinizing effects of chastity, virginity itself is the source of a spiritual sensuality that surpasses earthly pleasures. In erotically charged language, Jerome urges Eustochium to embrace the Bridegroom alone, as she seals herself off from the rest of the world:

Semper te cubiculi tui secreta custodiant, semper tecum sponsus ludat intrinsecus. Oras: loqueris ad sponsum; legis: ille tibi loquitur, et, cum te somus oppresserit, veniet post parietem et mittet manum suam per forament et tanget ventrem tuum et tremefacta consurges et dices, "Vulnerata caritatis ego sum," et rursus ab eo audies: "Hortus conclusus soror mea sponsa. . . ."

(Always allow the privacy of your own room to protect you: always let the Bridegroom play with you within. You pray: You speak to the Bridegroom. You read: He speaks to you, and when sleep overtakes you, he will come from behind and put his hand through the hole of the door, and touch your heart, and trembling, you shall rise and say, "I am wounded by love," and back from him you hear, "A garden enclosed is my sister, my spouse.") (Jerome 108. My translation.)

Once again, the echo of *Song of Songs* and the attendant iconographic recall of the Virgin Mary underscore the paradoxical erotics of chastity that is a central feature of the lives of the virgin martyrs.

The sexual inversion described by both Paul and the church Fathers is a hagiographic commonplace: virginity grants the martyr "masculine strength" to withstand the myriad torments heaped upon her seemingly frail body. Yet despite the insistence of the Fathers on the defeminizing and even desexualizing nature of virginity, the sexual aspect of these narratives is a very striking feature. As Kathryn Gravdal notes in a study of rape in medieval saints' lives, "hagiography affords a sanctioned space in which eroticism can flourish, and in which male voyeurism becomes licit, if not advocated."[10]

10. Gravdal 24. She continues: "The representation of seduction or assault opens a licit space that permits the audience to enjoy sexual language and contemplate the naked female body."

The life of the virgin martyr follows a general pattern: a beautiful maiden, usually "noble of birth, but even nobler of virtue," has vowed herself to Christ. When she refuses to marry a pagan, she is denounced as a Christian, and terrible suffering is inflicted upon her—to no avail, for she withstands fire, the rack, boiling lead, and other tortures without fear or damage. Yet although the hagiographic sine qua non is of course the maintenance of virginity despite repeated assaults, the martyrs are consistently stripped of their clothing and thus visually violated, while actual sexual penetration is deflected into violent acts such as stabbing or even, as with Agatha, mastectomy. Juliana is broken on a wheel until her marrow spurts out, Saint Ofitha beheaded and Apollonia's teeth pulled out. When Lucia, through God's grace, becomes so heavy that she cannot be moved to a brothel,[11] she is bathed in urine, until finally a knife is thrust into her throat. No form of violation is objectionable, as long as the martyr's virginity remains intact, for a ruptured maidenhead is the one wound Christ cannot heal.[12]

Despite the biblical and patristic insistence upon the androgynizing or even masculinizing effects of virginity, chastity in these "Lives" is constructed as a rejection of earthly marriage in favor of spiritual and sensual union with a superior Bridegroom whose attributes, as described by Saint Agnes in a sixteenth-century Tuscan *vita*, include "nobile gene-

---

11. The attempt to corrupt the virgin by bringing her to a brothel is a hagiographic commonplace. Tertullian maintains in his apologia that, "[b]y condemning the Christian maid rather to the lewd youth than to the lion, you have acknowledged that a stain of purity is more dreaded by us than any torments or death." If these tales suggest that virginity gives a woman unnatural strength, they also implicitly support the assertion that a woman cannot be raped without her consent, for if Agnes or Agatha could remain chaste in a house of prostitution, surely other women can remain chaste outside of one. Cf. Augustine, who asserts that a despoiled virgin is no longer worthy of the convent, because she must have had some pleasure in the act.

12. Cf. Ambrose: to lose one's virginity is to deface the work of the Creator. According to Augustine, even if a woman is raped, she is less pure—she is of an ambiguous state, neither virgin nor wife. Hence we find nuns such as Ebba, who literally deface themselves (cut off lips or noses) in order to prevent rape. See Schulenberg.

ratione, ornata bellezza, abundanti ricchezze, insuperabil fortezza e potenza, eccellente amore" (noble birth, superior beauty, abundant wealth, unsurpassed power and strength, and excellent love). The patroness of bodily purity continues of her chosen "amatore," "his love is chastity, his touch is sanctity and virginity." No form of physical violation is possible against Christ's chosen bride, for when Agnes is dragged to a brothel and stripped naked, "el Signore prestò alli capili suoi tanta densità ch'era molto più coperta con li capelli che con le vestimenta" (the Lord gave her hair so much thickness that she was much more covered by her hair than by her clothing; *Vita*, 57–57v.); when the girl is thrown on a funeral pyre, even the flames part, refusing to burn her. But Agnes, in a citation from pseudo-Ambrose suggestive for our discussion, "went to the place of execution more cheerfully than others go to their wedding," and while the gathered crowd weeps, she happily accepts a knife in the throat in the displaced penetration common to martyrologies. "Et in tal modo," the narrative concludes, "lo sposo candido e rubicondo Christo Iesu la consacrò a se in sposa e martire" (and in this way, the candid and beautiful Jesus Christ consecrated her to himself as his bride and martyr).

Returning to Tasso, we find that Sofronia's story evokes the displaced sexuality of the traditional saint's life. Once she claims to have stolen and burned the sacred icon, the living virgin is put to fire as well:[13]

13. Sofronia's model is not only the virgin martyrs of hagiography, but the "casto imago" she replaces, itself a virgin:

> ... impaziente
> il re se 'n corse a la magion di Dio,
> e sforzò i sacerdoti, e irreverente
> il casto simulacro indi rapio;
> e portollo a quel tempio ove sovente
> s'irrita il Ciel co 'l folle culto e rio.
> Nel profan loco e su la sacra imago
> susurrò poi le sue bestemmie il mago.   (2.7)

(Impatient, the king ran to the house of God, and forced the priests, and irreverent he ravished away from there the chaste image. And he took it to that temple where often Heaven is angered by a foolish and sinful rite. Then in that profane place and over the holy image the sorcerer muttered his blasphemies.)

Presa è la bella donna, e 'ncrudelito
il re la danna entr'un incendio a morte.
Già 'l velo e 'l casto manto a lei rapito,
stringon le molli braccia aspre ritorte.
Ella si tace, e in lei non sbigottito,
ma pur commosso alquanto è il petto forte;
e smarrisce il bel volto in un colore
che non è pallidezza, ma candore.   (2.26)

(Already she is ravished of her veil and chaste mantle, and her soft
arms are restrained by cruel bonds. She is quiet, and not dismayed
but rather moved, however courageous is her breast; and her beau-
tiful face is blanched by a color which is not palor, but candor.)

Just as Agnes "went to the place of execution more cheerfully than others
go to their wedding," Sofronia—wept by Christians and pagans alike—
remains unmoved, facing her torture with the courage and strength
shared by epic heroes and virgin martyrs. But the description, even as it
reminds us of her "petto forte," underscores Sofronia's beauty and vul-
nerability through the juxtaposition of contrasts ("bella donna" versus
" 'incrudelito . . . re," "molli braccia" versus "aspre ritorte"). As she is
ravished of her veil and chaste mantle, twice the reader is reminded of
Sofronia's beauty ("bella donna," "bel volto") and her color, while repre-
senting the candor of innocence rather than the pallor of fear, is never-
theless the white skin extolled in sixteenth-century treatises on beauty.[14]

This ambiguity, even ambivalence, in Sofronia's appearance is note-
worthy from her first entrance into the poem, as numerous critics have
discussed:[15]

Like the virgin martyr placed in a brothel, the simulacrum is brought to a profane place and
subjected to "bestemmie." This virgin isn't required to sacrifice to idols (as in the tale of
Saint Agnes, for example); rather, she is the idol. But just as Agnes stands firm, so, too, does
this image—which disappears.

14. See, for example, Federigo Luigi da Udine and Agnolo Firenzuola. Also see the discus-
sion in Yavneh.

15. See, for example, Hampton, McLucas, Migiel, and Yavneh.

La vergine tra 'l vulgo uscì soletta,
non coprì sue bellezze, e non l'espose,
raccolse gli occhi, andò nel vel ristretta,
con ischive maniere e generose.
Non sai ben dir s'adorna o se negletta,
se caso od arte il bel volto compose.
Di natura, d'Amor, de' cieli amici
le negligenze sue sono artifici.   (2.18; my emphasis)

(The virgin went forth alone among the crowd; she neither exposed
nor concealed her beauties. She lowered her eyes, she walked along
wrapped in her veil, with manners modest and spirited. You do not
quite know whether to say she adorns or neglects herself, whether
accident or art composed her lovely face. Her neglects are the arti-
fices of Nature, of Love, of her friendly stars.)

The genuine yet ambiguous artlessness of Sofronia, neither covering nor
exposing herself, will be placed in high relief two cantos later by Ar-
mida's bravura *sprezzatura* before the Christian army,[16] when, feigning
modesty, the temptress presents herself as a Petrarchan beauty.[17] Ar-
mida's hyperbolic version throws the ambiguities of the earlier virgin's
conduct and her "magnanima menzogna" into high relief: Sofronia's
ambiguous appearance—which piety demands we read as negligence—
becomes art in the self-presentation of the equally mendacious tempt-
ress four cantos later, lying to the leader of the opposing army and faith.
Yet Sofronia's authentic *vaghezza* attracts *vagheggiatori* as well, even as she
"steals away from their glances." Moreover, the direct second-person
address to the reader ("Non sai ben dir"), evoking the similarly equivo-
cal description of the disappearance of the image which Sofronia's body
replaces (O fu di man fedele opra furtiva, o pur il Ciel qui sua potenza
adopra), underscores the true ambiguity of her appearance, even as it

16. "Parte appar de le mamme acerbe e crude,/ parte altrui ne ricopre invida vesta" ("Part
appears of her unripe, firm breasts, part is covered by her envious dress," 4.31.3–4).
17. See Yavneh.

activates the imagination, forcing a visualization later recalled by Armida's breasts in their envious dress.

But even within Sofronia's "plot," someone seeks to give her a different meaning, to transform hagiography into romance. While Sofronia's beloved is Christ, her lover is the Christian Olindo, who has long admired the beautiful virgin from afar, and now seeks to die in her place by claiming that *he* is the culprit.

Olindo's urge to self-martyrdom is heroic, but prompted by the wrong sentiments. Whereas Sofronia seeks to emulate Christ by redeeming the Christians, Olindo desires only to save his unknowing beloved; indeed, his description of his alleged nocturnal quest for the image through "inaccesibil vie" (2.29.4) is suggestive of the sexual violation similarly displaced in the saints' lives. Sofronia's words resist this usurpation of her narrative, emphasizing her masculine fortitude and self-sufficiency:

> Non son io dunque senza te possente
> a sostener ciò che d'un uom può l'ira?
> Ho petto anch'io, ch'ad una morte crede
> di bastar solo, e compagni non chiede.   (2.30.5–8)

("Am I then unable without you to bear what the wrath of a man can do? I, too, have a heart that thinks itself alone sufficient for one death, and asks for no companions.")

Since neither will renounce the claim of having stolen the icon, both Sofronia and her lover are condemned to death. That their presence together on the pyre literalizes and parodies standard lyrical tropes of the flames of love, is underscored both by the romance nature of the episode's literary sources in Heliodorus's *Ethiopica* and Boccaccio's *Decameron*[18] as well as by Olindo's hyperliteralized laments:

18. In *Decameron* 5.6, the lovers are bound together as a direct result of their passion: they have been caught naked together in bed. The use of a novella from the *Decameron's* fifth day (when "si ragiona di ciò che ad alcuno amante, dopo alcuni fieri o sventurati accidenti, felicemente avvenisse" [the subject is what happily befalls someone in love after various

"Quest'è dunque quel laccio ond'io sperai
teco accoppiarmi in compagnia di vita?
questo è quel foco ch'io credea ch'i cori
ne dovesse infiammar d'eguali ardori?
. . .
Piacemi almen, poich'in sì strane guise
morir pur dei, del rogo esser consorte,
se del letto non fui. . . .
　　O fortunati miei dolci martiri!
s'impetrarò che giunto seno a seno
l'anima mia ne la tua bocca io spiri;
e venendo tu meco a un tempo meno,
in me fuor mandi gli ultimi sospiri."　(2.32–35)[19]

("Is this then the knot with which I hoped to yoke myself in lifelong company with you? Is this the fire that I thought should inflame our hearts with equal ardor? . . . At least it gives me pleasure [since in such strange fashion you too must die] to be your consort in the funeral pyre, even if I have not been consort in your bed. . . . Oh my fortunate torments, if, breast joined to breast, my soul should expire upon your mouth; and you at the same time fainting away with me breathe forth your last sighs over me.")

Later in the poem, the effeminacy of the hero Rinaldo will be emphasized as he lies in Armida's lap:

S'inchina, e i dolci baci ella sovente
liba or da gli occhi e da le labra or sugge,
ed in quel punto ei sospirar si sente

---

cruel and unfortunate occurrences]) weights the narrative in Olindo's favor, suggesting the direction its conclusion will take. On Tasso's use of Heliodorus, see Stephens.

19. In an early draft of the poem, the couple was placed on the flames tied face to face. Tasso, concerned that the scene might be overly erotic, changed their position to "tergo al tergo, e 'l volto ascoso al volto" (back to back, and face hidden from face) (2.32). Olindo's words, however, do not seem to recognize this shift.

> profondo si che pensi: "Or l'alma fugge
> e 'n lei trapassa peregrina." (16.19)

(She leans down and now from his eyes repeatedly drinks in sweet
kisses, and now sucks them from his lips. And at the same moment
he is heard to sigh so profoundly that you would think, "Now his
soul is leaving him and makes a pilgrimage into her.")

Rinaldo's behavior in canto 16 is modeled on the parodically exem-
plary depictions of both Antony and Hercules, emasculated by infatua-
tion, found on the walls of Armida's garden. But unlike the pagan Ar-
mida, who distracts Rinaldo from his duty to God and captain, Sofronia
corrects her idolatrous admirer, providing an explication of Christian
martyrdom. A true mediatrix, Sofronia counters and corrects Olindo's
literalistic romance reading of their encounter by literally redirecting her
lover's gaze toward heaven:

> "Amico, altri pensieri, altri lamenti,
> per più alta cagione il tempo chiede.
> Chè non pensi a tue colpe? e non rammenti
> qual Dio prometta a i buoni ampia mercede?
> Soffri in suo nome, e fian dolci i tormenti,
> e lieta aspira a la superna sede.
> Mira 'l ciel com'è bello, e mira il sole
> ch'a se par che n'inviti e ne console." (2.36)

("Friend, the moment calls for other thoughts, other laments, for
a much higher cause. Why don't you think upon your sins, and re-
member what ample reward God promises the righteous? Suffer in
his name; let the torments be sweet, and joyously aspire to the high
seat. Look at the heavens, how beautiful they are, and look at the
sun, which seems to invite and console you.)

But Sofronia is not permitted her martyrdom. In the episode's resolu-
tion, Sofronia's masculinity is supplanted by Clorinda's, for the saint's
life is given a romance ending: Sofronia becomes the bride not of Christ,
but of Olindo:

> Va dal rogo a le nozze. . . .
>
> [Olindo] volse con lei morire: ella non schiva,
>
> poi che seco non muor, che seco viva.   (2.53.7–8)

([Olindo] goes from the pyre to his nuptials. . . . He wanted to die with her: she does not scorn, when he does not die with her, to live with him.)

This seemingly felicitous conclusion points up an ambivalence in the otherwise uplifting episode. On the funeral pyre, as in the life of Saint Agnes, the female has greater spiritual strength than the male. In the *imitatio christi* which is the quintessence of martyrdom, Sofronia is not afraid to sacrifice herself for Christ and his people. Indeed, it is precisely the virgin's *fortezza* that moves the *donna guerriera* to rescue her:

> Mira che l'una tace, e l'altro geme,
>
> e più vigor mostra il men forte sesso.
>
> Pianger lui vede . . .
>
> e tacer lei con gli occhi al ciel sì fisa
>
> ch'anzi 'l morir par di qua giù divisa.
>
>   Clorinda intenerissi, e si condolse
>
> d'ambeduo loro e lagrimonne alquanto.
>
> Pur maggior sente il duol per chi non duolse,
>
> più la move il silenzio e meno il pianto.   (2.42–43)

(She sees that one is silent and the other groans, and the weaker sex shows the greater strength. She sees him weep . . . and that [the woman] remains silent, with her eyes so fixed on the heavens that she seems before death to be separated from down here. Clorinda waxed tender and felt sorrow for them both, and wept for them a bit. Yet she feels greater sorrow for the one that sorrowed not; silence moves her more and complaining less.)

Although the virgin martyr's body may be exposed and even penetrated (cf. Agatha, Lucia), she remains powerful as long as that one crucial orifice remains intact: virginity, like the beauty of the temptress, is a source of strength, and thus, paradoxically, a potential threat to the Christian order, in which man is to be "the head of the woman, as Christ is of the Church."[20] I have argued elsewhere that Armida's conversion at the conclusion of the poem, with its obvious echo of the Virgin Mary's submissive response at the Annunciation, serves to grant the previously errant temptress a Christian teleology more in keeping with the overarching values of Tasso's orthodoxy, both reaffirming Christianity's sexual hierarchy and reemphasizing the dangers of the temptress's former reification. Similarly, Sofronia's union with Olindo not only underscores the sacrament of marriage by which two bodies become one soul (a spiritualization of their literal binding on the pyre), it restores the Christian status quo, reaffirming the Pauline male-female hierarchy which her "masculine strength" had threatened to undermine.[21]

The arrival of Clorinda evokes a new and less threatening martyrology, for if Sofronia has rejected Olindo's entreaties to let him die in her place, the arrival of the successful knight on horseback effects Sofronia's transformation from virgin martyr to damsel in distress. We are no longer in the life of Saint Agnes, but that of Saint George, who rescues the only daughter of the king, sacrificed to the dragon then ravaging the kingdom. The virgin's actions in the hagiographical narrative have a particular resonance for Sofronia: she pleads with the knight to save himself, leaving her to die alone. "Brave knight, make haste to save thyself, lest thou likewise come to naught! Suffice it that I die!"[22] Saint George saves not only the virgin but her people, body and soul, for they are all converted to Christianity. In Tasso's poem, Sofronia has already

---

20. Cf. Ephesians 5:22–24: "Wives, be subject to your husbands as to the Lord; for the man is the head of the woman, just as Christ also is the head of the church. Christ is, indeed, the Saviour of the body; but just as the church is subject to Christ, so must women be to their husbands in everything." See also, for example, I Corinthians 11:7: "man is the image of God and the mirror of his glory, whereas woman reflects the glory of man."

21. Cf. Colossians 3:18: "Wives, be subject to your husbands; that is your Christian duty."

22. The echo of the life of Saint George can also be viewed as a commentary on Olindo, who is willing to die in the virgin's place, but who—unlike both George and his imitator, Clorinda—is unable to save her.

saved her people from imminent danger; it is left to the pagan warrior to save their savior.

Yet Clorinda—the white child of black parents, a Christian raised as a pagan, a *donna guerriera* with no marital aspirations—appears an odd casting choice as the Saint George who restores the Christian status quo; Sofronia is saved by a figure yet more masculine than herself. The significance of both Saint George and Sofronia for Clorinda will not be made clear until ten cantos later, when the warrior will discover that her own birth narrative, like Sofronia's almost-martyrdom, hinges on the miraculous powers of images for the truly devout, as well as on the personal protection of the male saint whom she resembles in both appearance and action.

As we and she discover in canto 12, Clorinda's own physiognomy provides the supreme example of how an image "partorirà più differenze." After spending her pregnancy gazing in devotion at an image of Saint George rescuing a Petrarchan virgin from a fierce dragon, the chaste and piously Christian queen of Ethiopia, locked in a tower by her sexually jealous husband, gives birth to a white child. Like the image of the virgin which disappears in canto 2, this living version of the queen's devotional image will engender different readings for different people, even as she takes on the qualities of all the "devote[d] figure[s]" of the "pietosa istoria" (12.23). Although Clorinda's mother recognizes the daughter's whiteness as the sign of her own piety, she is also cognizant that to the jealous Senapo—himself like the dragon—Clorinda's physiognomy will be a monstrous portent[23] of his wife's infidelity. Meanwhile, Clorinda may look like the virgin in the image, but, as stated above, she assumes the attributes of Saint George, disdaining "womanly arts" to arm herself, and even rescuing a white virgin, bound not to a dragon but a young man. Finally, the *donna guerriera* is the dragon as well, "monstrous" to those who, like Ismeno and the king of Jerusalem, do not understand how to read images both as the white daughter of a black family and as a woman—however virtuous—living as a knight.

23. Cf. Migiel, on the pun of "monstro" as both monster and demonstration or sign.

But if Clorinda's rejection of the womanly arts links her to Sofronia's transgressive actions, her baptism and death, like the latter's marriage, likewise restore the status quo. If Sofronia, transformed from virile virgin protagonist to damsel in distress, is denied the martyr's death which is "the climactic episode in the hagiographic text" (Gravdal 21), Clorinda has it for her. Not only is her death in the service of Christ (Tancredi is, after all, slaying the best of the pagan warriors), but it is only at her death that she accepts Christianity, as the submissiveness of her conversion underscores: "se rubella / in vita fu, [Dio] la vuole in morte ancella" ("If in life she was a rebel, God wants her to be a handmaiden in death," 2.65.7–8).

As Clorinda is baptized and dies, her appearance recalls not only the "bianca . . . bel volto" and "gote vermiglia" of the properly Petrarchan virgin depicted in her mother's chamber, but also the beautiful, white but never otherwise described Sofronia; here is the genuine "pallidezza" which in Sofronia is "candore":

> D'un bel pallore ha il bianco volto asperso,
> come a' gigli sarian miste viole.   (12.69)

(Her fair face is overspread with a lovely pallor, as would be lilies mixed with violets.)

Even her eyes are fixed on heaven—"gli occhi al cielo affisa"—as Sofronia had urged Olindo in her own aborted martyrdom.[24] But as Walter Stephens has remarked, that word "pallore" also recalls the face of Clorinda's black mother, fainting at the sight of her white child: "e di palida morte si dipinse" (Stephens 77). In Stephens's fascinating reading, "the black woman's pallor assimilates her both to the white damsel represented in her painting and to her pallid daughter, both as 'candid' infant and as dead woman in the distant future" (77).

24. Sofronia directs Olindo's eyes toward the sun, which both invites and consoles: ("Mira il sole / ch'a se par che n'inviti e ne console" 2.36). As Clorinda fixes her eyes on heaven, "in lei converso / sembra per la pietate il cielo e il sole" ("it seems that the sun and the heavens are bent toward her for pity," 12.69).

The line's resonance, however, goes beyond Tasso's poem, for it is an epic allusion—and one which reminds us of images in a different, but suggestive, context. In book 8 of the *Aeneid*, Vulcan's shield proffers a prediction of Aeneas's future which is a review of the historical *Aeneid*'s recent past; more significantly for our discussion, the ekphrastic description is of an image that provides a gloss to the previous events of the poem. For it is only after reading the visual representation of the battle of Actium that the reader finally comprehends the full meaning of the threat that Dido earlier posed to Aeneas and to the empire. In an exact echo of the line which depicts Dido preparing her pyre in book 4, Cleopatra is described as "pale with approaching death" (*pallida morte futura*): the fate that Aeneas has so narrowly averted is that of Antony, who aligned himself with the Egyptian Cleopatra against Rome, thereby excluding himself from the empire and from history.

The recall of Dido, and her historic counterpart, Cleopatra, functions as both a reminder and a correction: as with Sofronia, whose ambiguous appearance we considered above, the sign of the queen of Ethiopia's piety (her white daughter) can be misread, thereby linking both women to these famously transgressive women of classical epic and empire. Yet Clorinda's beautiful, pallid death, like that of her mother and like Sofronia's marriage, reminds the reader that, however powerful she may be, the true end of Christian womanhood is passivity and grace. Just as Armida at the poem's conclusion will signal her conversion from temptress to handmaiden with her direct quotation of the Virgin Mary's words at the Annunciation ("Ecco l'ancilla tua," she declares to Rinaldo), Clorinda's transformation from "rubella" to "ancella" announces that the ultimate exemplar, the woman behind the white virgin, is always the Virgin herself.

Works Cited

Ambrose, Saint, Bishop of Milan. *Expositio evangelii secundum Lucam*. Tornholti: Brepols, 1957.

Bynum, Carolyn Walker. *Holy Feast and Holy Fast*. Berkeley: U of California P, 1987.

Cohen, Elizabeth. "No Longer Virgins." *Refiguring Women: Perspectives on Gender and the Italian Renaissance*. Ed. Marilyn Migiel and Juliana Schiesari. Ithaca: Cornell UP, 1991.

Cohen, Sherill. "Asylums for Women in Counter-Reformation Italy." *Women in Reformation and Counter-Reformation Europe: Public and Private Worlds*. Ed. Sherrin Marshall. Bloomington: Indiana UP, 1989. 166–188.

———. "Convertite e malmaritate: donne, 'irregolari' e ordini religiosi nella Firenze rinascimentale," *Memoria* 5 (1982): 46–69.

Firenzuola, Agnolo. *Dialogo delle bellezze delle donne*. Milano: Società Tipografica de' Classici Italiani, 1802.

Gravdal, Kathryn. *Ravishing Maidens: Writing Rape in Medieval French Literature and Law*. Philadelphia: U of Pennsylvania P, 1991.

Hampton, Timothy. *Writing from History*. Ithaca: Cornell UP, 1990.

Imago primi saeculi. Antwerp, 1640.

Jerome, Saint. *Select Letters of St. Jerome*. Trans. F. A. Wright. Cambridge, Mass.: Harvard UP, 1980.

Luigi da Udine, Federigo. *Il libro della bella donna*. Venice, 1543. Reprinted in Zonta, *Trattati del Cinquecento sulla donna*. Bari: Laterza, 1913.

McLucas, John. "Clorinda and Her Echoes." *Stanford Italian Review* 10 (1991): 81–92.

Male, Emile. *L'Art religieux de la fin du XVIe siècle, du XVIIe siècle et du XVIIIe siècle: Etude sur l'iconographie après le Concile de Trente*. Paris: Libraire Armand Colin, 1951.

Migiel, Marilyn. "Clorinda's Fathers." *Stanford Italian Review* 10 (1991): 93–121.

Ottonelli, Giovanni Domenico. *Trattato della pittura, scultura, uso et abuso loro. Composto da un teologo e da un pittore. Per offerirlo a' Signori Accademici del disegno di Fiorenza e d'altre Città Christiane*. Florence, 1652.

Pagels, Elaine. *Adam, Eve, and the Serpent*. New York: Random House, 1988.

Paleotti, Gabriel. *Discorso intorno alle imagini sacre e profane*. Bologna, 1582. Reprinted in *Trattati d'arte del Cinquecento: fra manierismo e controriforma*, ed. Paola Barocchi. Vol. 2. Bari: Laterza, 1961.

Ruggiero, Guido. *The Boundaries of Eros: Sex Crime and Sexuality in Renaissance Venice*. New York: Oxford University Press, 1985.

Salisbury, Joyce E. *Church Fathers, Independent Virgins*. New York: Verso, 1991.

Schroeder, Rev. H.J., O.P. *Canons and Decrees of the Council of Trent*. Orig. text with English trans. London: Herder Press, 1941.

Schulenberg, Jane Tibbetts. "The Heroics of Virginity: Brides of Christ and Sacrificial Mutilation." *Women in the Middle Ages and the Renaissance*. Ed. Mary Beth Rose. Syracuse: Syracuse UP, 1986. 30–72.

Stephens, Walter. "Tasso's Heliodorus and the World of Romance." *The Search for the Ancient Novel*. Ed. James Tatum. Baltimore: Johns Hopkins UP, 1994, 67–87.

Tasso, Torquato. *Gerusalemme liberata*. Ed. Anna Maria Carini. Milan: Feltrinelli, 1961.

———. *Jerusalem Delivered*. Trans. Ralph Nash. Detroit: Wayne State UP, 1987.

Vita de tutti i santi. Florence, 1561.

Warner, Marina. *Alone of All Her Sex: The Myth and the Cult of the Virgin Mary*. New York: Pocket Books, 1976.

Yavneh, Naomi. "The Ambiguity of Beauty in Tasso and Petrarch." *Sexuality and Gender in Early Modern Europe: Institutions, texts, images*. Ed. James Grantham Turner. Cambridge: Cambridge UP, 1993. 133–57.

For quotations from Tasso's *Gerusalemme liberata* I have used the edition by A. M. Carini and the translation by R. Nash (modified at times).

Writing beyond the Querelle:
Gender and History in Orlando furioso

CONSTANCE JORDAN

This essay will argue that Ariosto's epic takes the woman question beyond the limits set by contemporary treatments of the *querelle des femmes* and engages issues discussed in the ampler confines of Renaissance philosophical thought. These issues relate to the construction of gender, but they also escape containment by or within the praise/blame discourse of the *querelle* to become implicated in debates on morality, politics, and the market. They are consistently brought into focus in episodes that illustrate a reading of history. The woman question in the *Orlando furioso* is not only a matter to be understood in light of Renaissance custom and social practice, but also as the basis of a historiographical norm, as a point of departure in a way of reading history.

We should begin by noting that the terms of the *querelle* hardly begin to cover the literature on the nature of woman current in sixteenth-century Europe.[1] Its greater part consists of treatises on domestic government that describe the duties and privileges of women as well as men, and outright defenses of women that apologize for the sex and attack misogyny. Both kinds of literature display strategies of argument that refer to natural law, sex, and gender, and the role of the female and the feminine in history. But unlike treatises on domestic government, defenses of women attempted to invalidate the idea that woman was naturally the subject of man, and to deny that divine will had instituted relations between man and woman as those between a superior and his

1. For an assessment of the *querelle des femmes* in the Furioso, see especially Tomalin, Shemek, Benson. For a recent criticism of readings of the poem in light of the *querelle*, see Bellamy, "Alcina's."

subordinate.[2] The attack on elements of divine law that were thought to sustain patriarchy was relatively circumscribed by what readings of scripture could be made to suggest. By contrast, the attack on natural law opened a much larger field of inquiry. Its most obvious reference was to history. Once historical exceptions to the rule of female inferiority and subservience to the male were recognized as not only common but bound up with culturally specific interests, natural law mandating the subjection of women could be denounced as an invention of those who had an interest in preserving such an arrangement. Where natural law notions of society had mandated adherence to hierarchical arrangements of authority and power in relation to sex and gender, Renaissance defenses of women pointed to the variability, and hence also to the conventionality of practices governing relations of gender as they were instituted by custom and positive law.

I think it is not too much to claim that sixteenth-century prowoman argument depended on new readings of history. Its writers urged their readers to look again at what passed for historical record, to notice its inconsistencies, its ambiguities, its professions of faith in the divinely ordained destiny of one or another people as opposed to its representation of evidence supporting or denying the operation of such a providence.[3] Of course, to problematize the reading of history was not a goal for early feminists alone; it is rather that prowoman argument found its proper place in the literature of skepticism that sought to revise canonical ways of thinking about human beings and society.

2. For a survey of this literature, see Jordan, *Renaissance Feminism*; for the humanist context of Renaissance attitudes to women, see Maclean. A recent study on the nature of woman in early modern England provides useful information on Renaissance opinion in general; see Sommerville.

3. Prowoman argument often took the form of a catalogue of women famous for participating in public life. Boccaccio's essentially ironic treatment in his *De mulieribus claris* provided such writers as Christine de Pisan, writing *Le Livre de la cité des dames*, with a pretext for a revisionary reading of this material. For an analysis of de Pisan in light of Boccaccio and contemporary opinion, see Quilligan. For Boccaccio's text, see Jordan, "Boccaccio's In-famous Women."

The simplest criticism of the so-called natural law of woman's sub-jection was directed at the concept of gender as wholly consistent with biological sex. Gender was rather represented as a cultural not a natural phenomenon, and hence as largely (although not entirely) independent of physiological determinants. Gendered behavior was regarded as fluid and considered as if it were constructed along a spectrum of possibilities that allowed everyone, whether male or female, a prospective latitude of masculine or feminine behaviors, to be adapted to particular cir-cumstances. True, instances of androgyny cited by defenders of women usually celebrated the virile woman while they ignored the feminine man. Eventually, however, feminist discourse evolved a rich typology of gender in which conventional expressions of a positive virility, such as courage and justice, could be contrasted with others of a negative kind, such as brutality and cruelty; and expressions of a positive femininity, such as clemency and temperance (specifically linked to chastity), could be compared with such conventionally feminine vices as vanity and gar-rulousness.

This kind of symbolic androgyny also affected the idea of agency in the woman as well as in a man who had to function in offices of subordination. Religious and philosophical orthodoxy had taken its cue from Aristotle's biology. There, woman was depicted primarily as nur-turant, a merely passive vessel in which were nurtured the homuncular seeds of the man. In their social role, women were comparably secon-dary, suited only to take orders from men who were judged to be natu-rally authoritative. Aristotle had asserted that woman's intelligence and discourse were formless and inchoate unless shaped by man's direction, a claim Erasmus was to repeat (Jordan, *Feminism*, 29–34, 60–64). Femi-nist apologists, appealing to history to contradict this essentialism, saw a need for what might be called a new anthropology, a different set of figures by which to tell stories of birth, maturity, and senescence, and to describe human generation and historical regeneration in ways more attuned to the part woman played in these processes. In her study of the female in pre-Socratic antiquity, Page du Bois sketches the fea-tures of such an anthropology, some elements of which I think survived in the culture of Renaissance Europe.[4] These elements contribute to figurations of the female agency and are registered in Ariosto's poem.

We can begin by asking why Ariosto gave a woman character, Bradamante, the most important and imposing visions of history. Three episodes are obviously relevant: Bradamante's descent into Merlin's tomb, her visit to the castle on the Rocca di Tristano (an addition to the 1532 edition of the poem), and the celebration of her marriage by the loan of the Emperor Constantine's prize tent, a work of art woven by the Trojan prophetess, Cassandra. On or in each of these structures—tomb, castle, and tent—is inscribed a history that is also a prophecy. In effect, they make Ariosto's poem an instance of repeated metalepsis: the period in which Charlemagne's paladins are described as establishing his empire is represented as if it expressed the origins and the end of Este power, and a future in which Italy would triumph over her enemies. Although Bradamante's vision in Merlin's tomb shows her the future of only the Este dynasty, she is the character for whom an interest in the course of Italian history is understood to be the most fervent in the poem. As the surviving parent of the first Este family, she is the poem's principal reader of history, uniquely positioned to assess its meanings. As a whole, these visions reveal different aspects of her place in that history. Merlin's tomb is the site of archaic and classical images of the woman as virgin and mother; it shows the nature of kinship, of race or *gens*, and it institutes woman as the basis of dynastic integrity. The castle on the Rocca di Tristano illustrates the capacity of woman to behave symbolically as androgyne: her double gendering affects social practice through her interpretation of custom and law. At stake at the castle are the means by which culture is continuously made and remade. And finally, the manner in which Cassandra's tent features in Bradamante's wedding conveys the nature of the woman's role as wife. Its status at the ceremony—neither a gift nor a conventional loan for which interest is charged but rather an item borrowed without charge and virtually without term (for less than twenty-four hours), Cassandra's tent celebrates Bradamante's spe-

4. See du Bois, esp. 39–64, 86–109.

cial privilege. Unlike the bride who is conventionally traded on the aristocratic marriage market, Bradamante is neither objectified as a gift exchanged between men, nor valued according to the fluctuating prices of a market.[5] As the vehicle for a notion of marriage that is at once orthodox and revolutionary, governed by conscience and dismissive of the customs governing the traffic in nubile women, Cassandra's tent provides a critique of property as it affected the lives of women in the sixteenth-century Italian family.[6] In the primitive *oikos* instituted by the union of Bradamante and Ruggiero is shadowed an idealized domestic economy in which both male and female share value and agency, attributes comprised in what Ariosto calls "valor." What all three structures have in common is the representation of ideas of a generativity that depends on female and feminine as well as male and masculine "valor."

Ariosto expresses Bradamante's agency and value in images that invite analysis of her generative functions. The Aristotelian argument against having wives in common, as Plato had recommended, stressed that women should belong to men so that fathers could recognize their own children. Translated into social practice, this dictum required that nubile women be constantly under surveillance. Bradamante's masculine status as *cavalliera* obviously jeopardizes her feminine status as virgin, as normatively and conservatively domestic, as one who preserves and does not

5. In a comprehensive and nuanced account of relations between concepts of value as fixed by code or fluctuating in instances of exchange within the world of the poem, Sergio Zatti distinguishes Bradamante as a character who refuses to put a price on Ruggiero, that is, to exchange him for another entity. Zatti suggests that a comparable inflexibility frequently results—in other cases—in disaster; in general, he claims, the poem demonstrates the virtue of negotiation. Bradamante's example is therefore unique; at the same time, it unifies the otherwise disparate themes of the poem: "La contraddizione di Bradamante è in questo senso l'ossimoro di tutto il poema, dilaniato fra ideale e empiria, utopia e pragmatismo, uno e molteplice: quell'ossimoro che il Carne-Ross fa consistere nel 'to celebrate at one and the same time the beauty of an inconstant universe and the virtues of the constant heart'" (104–5).

6. For a study of some aspects of this family life, see Klapisch-Zuber; Kuehn, esp. 197–257. See also Chojnacki. For a discussion of the rhetorical shaping of economic determinants in Leon Battista Alberti's *Della famiglia*, see Freccero.

consume property. In the episodes illustrating her relation to tomb, castle, and tent, the desire that propels her out across the epic landscape of Europe and leads her to these structures is matched by a countervailing power that allows her to resist passion, ambition, and the appeal of material wealth.

Merlin's Tomb

The prelude to Bradamante's descent into Merlin's tomb is that oddly silent encounter she has with Sacripante in canto 1. Here her virility is both established and defined. She appears as "un uom gagliardo e fiero," and yet she knows that the rules of chivalric encounter do not require any unnecessary violence: having unhorsed her opponent, she rides away, "stimando aver assai."[7] The fact that an innocuous rebuke to one who tried to rape her satisfies her wish for revenge is intended, I think, to convey her commitment to *mesure*, the virtue of temperance desired by all heroes of romance. But she has yet to be fully tested. While she can forego the chivalric satisfaction of punishing Sacripante severely, by wounding or even killing him, it is unclear that she would be as temperate in an encounter with Ruggiero, whom she passionately desires (as we know from her history in Boiardo's poem). Her career will be shaped by continuous challenges to her ability to moderate desire, to renounce absolute conquest, and to insist on agency.

Bradamante's desire is first understood as a dangerous yet protected attribute when, spurred to free Ruggiero from the control of his guardian (the magician Atlante), and indifferent to her "onore" and duty to protect Marseille, she follows Pinabello's journey through a "selva oscura" to the "pietra dura" of a mountain peak into whose stony recesses she tumbles (2.68, 70). Her fall is paradoxically both a form of chastisement and a sign of encouragement. The danger of taking a Petrarchan journey for love is clear. But despite and in an inverted sense because of its obvious risks, it also traces a way to love. As Peter Marinelli has pointed

7. Ariosto 1.60, 64.

out, Bradamante's passage through the wilderness duplicates the conditions of Ruggiero's youth as Boiardo tells it; as Ruggiero must transcend by a Christian civility the effects of the infidel "loci selvaggi" in which he has grown up,[8] so must Bradamante's desire be disciplined by the hardness of wilderness and its reversals. The image of the rocky tomb recalls the fate of Astyanax, Ruggiero's ancestor, who hid in a sepulcher under a great stone to avoid capture, but also, more allusively, the generative stones of Hellenic and especially Theban autochthony which were regarded ambiguously as both fruitful and hard or virginal (du Bois 86–97). For Bradamante, the fall from desire and into stone—sterile, incapable of generation, and therefore an image of death—is the pretext for her "generosità." The apparent thwarting of her erotic will, "voglia," provides paradoxically the situation in which she learns that it will be favored (3.9, 16, 19).

The idea that mortality is the condition of generativity is obviously Virgilian; in the *Orlando furioso*, it is illustrated by Ruggiero's career. As long as he is Atlante's prisoner, he will be prevented from both marriage and a violent, premature death, events that appear to be deeply implicated in each other inasmuch as generation implies mortality. It is more dramatically manifest in Ariosto's feminized transumption of Virgil's descent into the underworld. To see the future and fulfill his destiny, Aeneas had to dismiss desire (*Aeneid* 4.340–47); Bradamante, by contrast, accomplishes both because she embraces desire. But from canto 3 on—that is, in action taking place after her descent into Merlin's tomb—her desire is tempered, its expressions inflected according to the conditions in which she finds herself. She acquires and deploys constructively the qualities of hardness and wildness that were so prominently features of her earlier Petrarchan journey of error and errancy. Her military exploits are manifestations of her amorous *castità*; they protract her quest for Ruggiero but they also permit it. Later, in the presence of Ruggiero, her love is qualified by an overtly countervailing resistance. Having freed him from his third place of confinement, Atlante's second palace of

8. Marinelli 63–64.

pleasure, she tempers her desire for him in light of their unpropitious circumstances. Her virtue enables her to exert the kind of control she had earlier displayed before Sacripante: "lei non vuol sempre aver dura e selvaggia," although for the time being she must be just that (22.34). This moment of intransigeance looks forward to its positive inversion, her "rocklike" resistance to any husband but Ruggiero in cantos 44 and 45.

The masculine aspect of Bradamante's character is matched by a corresponding femininity in some of her male descendants who appear in her vision of history. Feminist apology celebrated virtues conventionally gendered as feminine or required of the female: mercy, loyalty or devotion, and honesty; in short, qualities necessary in the exercise of temperance. Bradamante's descendent Ugo exercises a patriotic courage, "patrio valor," but with just cause, "giusta cagione" (3.27); another, Azzo, is more a friend of "cortesia" than "guerre" (29); Obizzo and his companions form a group, "bello and amichevol," in which Alberto is notable for his "clemenza" (40). Another Estense, Borso, rules "in pace," and Ercole finds glory in "pace" as well as "arme" (45, 46). And the "bel regno" without term that all these Estensi will lay claim to is to be based on the "camin dritto" of a temperance based on justice; no one is to be harmed unless he has harmed some himself (44). Opposition is all, however; when Alfonso and Ippolito are characterized as Castor and Pollux, the mythical twins, each of whom was alternately in heaven and hell (50), we realize how closely Ariosto illustrated ideas of temperance and self-denial (or sacrifice) with images of time and mortality; without death, there would be no rationale for love or possibility of generation.[9] Hence, too, the "età d'oro" that Bradamante inaugurates will be predicated on mortality. Its Astraea will return but to a harsh and changeful climate, "dove può il caldo e il gielo" (51).

9. For the Dioscuri, see *Odyssey* 6.300–22.

Tristano's Castle

It is no accident that such a climate of extremes provides the setting for Bradamante's next great vision of history, which, I suggest, reflects the second way her generativity is represented. The chaste desire she learns in canto 3 is matched by the charitable justice she deals in canto 32; both of these oxymorons mirror the deeper opposition of her androgynous nature.

Bradamante arrives at Tristano's castle in a frenzy of jealousy. A Gascon knight has just told her a "buon conto" of Ruggiero's relations with Marfisa; based, he has said, on "molti segni" observed by everyone in the infidel army, the two are betrothed ("tra lor data la fede," 32.29–30). Bradamante's uncritical acceptance of this report may surprise us. She has good reason to suspect accounts based on ocular proof—Melissa had earlier cautioned her not to trust ("dar fede") what she sees (13.53). And having ignored that fairy's warning and followed a false Ruggiero, she became trapped in the "commune errore" of Atlante's third palace (77–79), a mistake all the more striking in that, never having had a close look at Ruggiero, we have to assume that Ariosto means us to conclude that she was chasing a figment of her imagination. The memory of the Gascon's story, based (as it is) on these deceptive "segni," later causes her to reflect bitterly on the unfairness of her position. She has "merto," she tells herself: Ruggiero, having vowed his devotion to her, remains in her debt. But, she admits, because he lacks "fermezza," his "valore" to her is negligible; without "valore" himself, he cannot see any in her. If he takes his faith lightly, no obligation ("peso") will have meaning to him or "weigh upon his heart" ("gravar il cor," 32.38–40). She complains that she has engaged in a commerce without reciprocity. He has taken her love without giving his in return; her vendetta, she thinks, will be confirmed by a heavenly justice (40).

As she begins her journey of revenge, she encounters Ullania, an emissary from the queen of Islanda, whose quest, a negative emblem of her own, will instruct her in the matter of administering justice. Both she and the queen seek a perfect match, but while Bradamante's is based on a mutual profession of faith exclusive of any competition for excellence, the queen's is to be the outcome of a contest—the most charming of princesses is to be joined to the most valorous of knights (32.52–53). The first of these unions is established by a sense of value that is independent of a rivalry that conduces to ranking, relative value, or pricing; the second reflects value as subject to fluctuation, as, in fact, continuously open to reevaluation. What Bradamante demonstrates at the Rocca di Tristano are the limitations of establishing value by a competitive or zero-sum game; in effect, she demonstrates that values also have meaning (and perhaps preeminent meaning) by virtue of contexts that are essentially independent of one another, however much they may also coexist in a particular situation or moment. The justice she seeks is therefore to be practiced in light of the situation it is intended to resolve. Unlike a price but like a value, Bradamante's justice in Tristano's castle is not distributive but equitable; it finds its reasons in the uniqueness of a case not in the generality of a rule. Bradamante reveals the character of her justice when she confronts and resolves the competition initiated by the custom or law of the castle.[10]

She arrives at the castle gates seeking shelter on a bitterly cold evening. Evoking comparison with the terms of Perduta's courtship, the custom of the castle requires that it shelter only the most valorous knight and the most beautiful lady. Contests end with a single winner in each category—the perfect pair. Such determination is precise, definitive, and without qualification: the weaker, the less beautiful are not to be accommodated. A crisis occurs when Bradamante, having entered and won the contest for the most valorous knight, finds herself in a second contest, now with Ullania, for the most beautiful lady. Bradamante defies the castle's law of zero-sum contest by insisting that she occupies two subject positions: her martial prowess has revealed her to be the most valorous knight and her unhelmeted face the most beautiful of princesses. But she chooses to claim her right to accommodation by identifying herself with only one of these persons: the victorious knight.

10. For this episode as a critique of custom, see Ross.

Here function, independent of whatever might be considered essential, determines identity. In cases in which multiple functions reveal complex identities, the subject has a protean latitude to shift places as circumstances require. In Tristano's castle, Bradamante exploits her complex subjectivity to interpret casuistically a single rule—superiority receives privilege—so that it has more than one application.

By insisting that her functional identity establish a perspective in which Ullania can win accommodation despite her second-rate beauty, Bradamante has discovered in the letter of the law a latitude that opens its application to the practice of equity (99–105). In the language of Aristotle, she has bent a "leaden" and general rule (malleable to a point) to fit the circumstances of a particular case.[11] The effect of her interpretation is described in climatic terms: Ullania, having withered like a flower under the oppressive sun of Bradamante's gaze, is now revivified by the rain of Bradamante's "pietade," her pity or mercy (107–8). The action recalls Merlin's description of Astraea's return to the world of heat and ice. Justice in the fallen world, in which a case may fall at any point in a spectrum delimited by extremes, must necessarily be casuistical. Bradamante insists that her mercy has moved her to equity, to make a good and correct judgment, "buono e dritto giudizio," by bending the law to circumstance. In the case she argues, her interpretation of the law is correct. By exploiting a double or perspectival identity, it has produced two winners and no losers. In earlier episodes, Bradamante has been repeatedly characterized as "generosa" or generous, a reference that implies her generativity, her role as chaste and fecund *genetrix gentis*, the mother of a race. Here these virtues acquire a moral complement, manifest in the perspectival ruling she gives rule chivalric custom without, however, dismissing its authority in future cases. In both roles, as mother and judge, she exemplifies the kinds of practice that bring about historical continuity and enable the present to build upon the past.

To see a connection between Bradamante's equitable justice and the

---

11. See Aristotle's comment on equity, *epieikeia*, as a leaden rule, *molibdinos kanon*; *Nichomachean Ethics*, 5.10.7–9.

vision of history she sees in the murals of Tristano's castle returns us to the matter of her intention in setting out from Montalbano: to revenge herself on Ruggiero's supposed infidelity. By exploiting her symbolic androgyny, Bradamante has demonstrated her willingness to play with perspective, to acknowledge that with respect to judgments a position or point of view is a variable. Such a willingness ought to be predicated on a recognition of the deceptiveness of signs generally, a recognition that would have caused her to doubt the Gascon's story of Ruggiero's betrothal to Marfisa. What Bradamante might be now moved to ask, having exploited perspective, is whether the Gascon's story is the whole story or simply a fiction based on partial evidence. What the murals tell her is that there are many perspectives to an understanding of history and that often the least satisfactory is the most rule-bound, moralistic, and judgmental.

Early stages in the series of murals depict events in the reign of King Arthur and reflect a view of history that associates events with divine will. Merlin reveals that the French king, Fieramonte, and his successors will be ruined for their ambitious attempts to conquer Italy; the sword of heaven will chastise them (33.7–15). But Charlemagne, because his invasion years later (although similar to Fieramonte's) is (inexplicably) "inoffensive," will escape divine retribution (16). This is pure exemplum history. Following its Eusebian model, it assumes first that events in history have moral meaning, and second that success (established in the historian's terms) implies divine approval. Its story is always the same: the evil are punished, the good are rewarded. Merlin's exempla both illustrate and implicitly criticize this approach to interpretation by revealing the historian's aprioristic bias: an identical action is alternatively blamed and praised. These doctrinaire interpretations contrast with an instance of Merlin's later and more sophisticated historical art, which depicts the conflict for control of Milan and other states carried on between members of the Sforza family and other parties in Italy and elsewhere (36–49). Characterized by betrayal, treason, bribery, factionalism, brutality, and revenge on all sides, these protracted struggles hardly lend themselves to a moralized interpretation nor does Ariosto attempt to give them one. Instead of pointing to the effects of heaven's sword to explain events, he invokes "Fortuna come cangia voglie" (57). This vague assertion of a nebulous and indeterminate causality suggests how difficult it is to interpret history with any degree of definition. To describe confusion, to testify to ambiguity, to record what appears to have happened may be the better part of the historian's craft.

Bradamante witnesses this transformation of historiographical norms because she must learn (and, in the course of this prodigious poem, relearn) that signs are inherently deceptive and consequently that history and story confer no more than provisional interpretations of events that are never fully comprehensible. This is, admittedly, a truth she tends to resist when her interest in securing a marriage with Ruggiero is at stake. After seeing Merlin's murals, she dreams of a reproachful Ruggiero who asks her why she has accused him of infidelity and protests that he remains true to his vows. She interprets her dream as delusionary: accusing her eyes, she asks why when they are shut she sees "il ben," and open "il mal" (63). Her willingness to leave unquestioned visual evidence recalls by inversion the truth of what is revealed in Tristano's castle: a degree of doubtfulness characterizes all experience. This truth justifies judgments that bend the letter of the law in the interest of "pietade," and, when confusion is profound and no action is required, the suspension of judgment altogether. In Tristano's castle, she demonstrated how accommodating such restraint can be; in her response to her dream, she also reveals how difficult it is to achieve when it touches matters involving deep feeling.

Cassandra's Tent

Ariosto tells us that Bradamante can read Cassandra's tent correctly, as no other human being can (46.98). Among other subjects, the prophetess has decorated the panels of her tent with the story of Ippolito's generosity, his gift-giving.[12] Her art thus calls again into question the nature of value. It is answered by the complex series of events that

---

12. For an extended interpretation of Cassandra's subject in light of the pervasive irony of the poem as a celebration of epic conquest, see Ascoli 376–93.

lead to Bradamante's eventual marriage in canto 46. Once again, Brada-mante will demonstrate the advantages that accrue to exploiting sym-bolic androgyny, oxymoronic doubleness, and perspectivism.

The visual narrative inscribed on Cassandra's tent acquires an in-terpretive context when the tent itself is considered as an object. Its transactional status eludes usual categories. Not a gift and not a loan, it does not figure as an instance of imperial magnificence, an item in a potlatch brokering obligations among powerful men. Nor is it a feature of a mercantile exchange, a loan for which interest is charged. It is a kind of gift—for which no return is expected; a kind of loan—for which there is no price. It would appear to be an end in itself, an act between disinterested parties that evades materiality and exists altogether in a symbolic mode. I shall argue that it features as a metaphor of relations of man and wife in marriage as they might be revised in a world ordered ac-cording to equitable principles, chiefly because it escapes the customary constraints upon that institution. These constraints determined much of the social practice governing aristocratic marriages.

A bride, especially a woman who had the capacity to convey property, was typically objectified as an item in a continuous exchange between men that, in potlatch fashion, took place over generations to the mutual benefit of its participants. Each gift conferred a benefit on the giver, as it obliged the recipient to reciprocate with a comparable gift. As a correlative feature of this process, the value of the nubile woman was also subject to pricing; although she functioned as a gift, her worth was also calculable in relative terms. If her father lost land or goods, she had less to offer a prospective husband. She remained the same in her per-son, but she was also always a variable, her value susceptible to rising or falling with her economic condition. To escape from such determina-tion, a woman would have to act as her own agent and thus to establish her value as invariable and absolute. She would have to become her own patriarch, to give herself away independent of any obligation other than to herself, and to make her marriage a matter of conscience and not for speculation on a fluctuating market. The action preceding and making possible Bradamante's marriage illustrates her way of coping with the challenges of the marriage market. Her nuptial status is, I think, figured in status of Cassandra's tent.

Remember that Bradamante's "gelosia" was occasioned by the thought that Ruggiero had denied her "valor"; she believed she had been replaced by Marfisa. She has deplored Ruggiero's lack of "fermezza" in relation to her "valor" as potential spouse: for him, she thinks, her value fluctuates as if she were a commodity in a market and he a potential buyer, competing among other buyers but also selecting from the best items on sale (32.38–39). To her parents, especially her mother Beatrice, she is actually up for sale. Beatrice insists that she fetch a high price, that her betrothed be rich, indeed be no less than the emperor Constantine's heir, Leone (44.37, 38). Both families will benefit from this exchange. Commodification of woman is not, of course, new to the poem. It is implicit in the terms of Perduta's courtship; as the most beautiful woman, she seeks her equal in the most chivalric man: each is a prize, each is valued in terms of a competitive market. Readers may remember a parodic instance of such commodification, strangely evocative of the terms of many dynastic marriages: Drusilla's handmaid, whom the woman-killer Marganorre transports "on a pack mule, like merchandise, tied and bound, shut in a box, and unable to speak" (37.91).

Overcoming her jealousy and disappointment, Bradamante resolves to be true to her vows to Ruggiero and, in her words, as stable as a rock by virtue of her faith, "di vera fede" (44.61). Her decision reflects the way she values her own agency: having worked to secure Ruggiero, she declares, she resists accepting the status of the bee who does not enjoy the fruits of her own labor (45). And so, in response to the idea of traffic in the marriage market, Bradamante cuts a deal with Charlemagne in order to negotiate her own interests in the business of marriage, to manage her own "valor," and to give herself where she will (or, as she says, to no man who is weaker than she is, [70]).[13] Implicit in this move is

13. Readings of Bradamante's courtship and efforts to secure Ruggiero as husband that draw on psychoanalytic and particularly Lacanian theory have tended to see the cross-dressed and symbolically androgynous Bradamante as a juvenile version of what her mature and essen-

Bradamante's sense of value as independent of the market. Were she interested in buying a husband, she could hardly do better than an emperor's heir. What she does not count on is the possibility that in the competitive combat for her hand, she will be deceived as to whom she is fighting. She counts on recognizing the identity of her opponent; she counts further on the fact that she can defeat all suitors except Ruggiero, the one to whom she is betrothed (45.71). In short, she believes she cannot lose. But Ruggiero has become the deputy of the same Leone to whom Beatrice had betrothed her, an obligation determined by a series of exchanges that are characterizable as a potlatch.

Ruggiero has earlier fought for the Bulgars and against the Greeks; his "valore" has been so conspicuous that it causes Leone to "fall in love" with it (44.91–92). Hence, when Ruggiero is captured by the Greeks, Leone arranges for his release (45.41–43). Leone's generosity obliges Ruggiero to promise to return the favor: a life for a life, he vows, acknowledging his "obligazion," his "obligo grande" (48, 52, 56). Nor can the performance of this reciprocity be mere show, "sembiante," for unless it is real, it will have no value to Leone (60). Ruggiero's execution of his obligation to Leone requires that he imitate the "fede" that has been mirrored in Bradamante's rock-like constancy. Like Bradamante, he is a "scoglio duro" in their duel (73; cf. 101); he defeats Bradamante without, however, harming her, and thus honors his debt to Leone. His action generates a further indebtedness; now Leone has an even greater "obligazione" to Ruggiero, one that may extend even to the imperial crown (84). We must assume, I think, that in exchange for Bradamante, Leone imagines he owes Ruggiero an empire. They are collectively engaged in a kind of husbandry that depends on an absolute control over

---

tially female and feminine self will become when she is a wife and mother. For a study of the narcissism in Bradamante's warrior identity, see Finucci 229–53. For Bradamante as the victim of a hysterical neurosis, see Bellamy, *Translations of Power*, 112–19. I have interpreted Bradamante's doubleness by criteria that address the poem as less the poet's reflection on psychological states of mind and more his exploration in figured language of the conditions of contemporary life.

the property they lay claim to, a property that includes objects of a political and marital nature. By resisting her function in this economy, Bradamante becomes, in Lorna Hutson's words, a "displaced marker of all that . . . would close off husbandry's potent identification with the practical mastery of temporal and spatial contingency.[14] This closure is what Ariosto illustrates in the terms of Bradamante's marriage.

With Bradamante now the intended of Leone, her efforts have been thwarted by the kind of deception so common to the poem: signs are misleading or actually ironic. Were Ruggiero to have acted in his own behalf rather than as Leone's deputy, Bradamante would have her wish. Unless she can prove that Ruggiero's obligation to her—instituted by his vow of betrothal—carries a supervening authority over all subsequent obligations, her attempt to make her agency instrumental and her value independent of the market will be frustrated. Such proof will need to be accompanied by a willingness on the part of him to whom she has been promised as a gift, Leone, to call a halt to that exchange. In short, her status as a nubile woman must be freed from materialist constraints; she must be neither a tool of dynastic greed nor a means to diplomatic power. The conditions necessary to achieve this end are forthcoming. Marfisa, who discloses that Bradamante has been given to Ruggiero once and for all by his vow, "parola," fixes her value as absolute and nonnegotiable: thus Bradamante's betrothal to Ruggiero is confirmed. And Leone—when Ruggiero offers to continue to respect his obligation to Leone by allowing himself to be killed (so freeing Bradamante for Leone)—declaring Ruggiero's "cortesia" beyond comparison, "non avrà mai pare," calls an end to their continuous and competitive gift-giving. These decisions free Bradamante's "valor" from pricing and a system implicating her in obligations and benefits. They interrupt processes that define woman as an object of variable worth to be manipulated in the interest of creating relations among men, and point to a generativity that recognizes stable values and the language of conscience. How removed this generativity is from a wealth invested in material goods or

14. See Hutson 40.

aristocratic magnificence is emblematized by the manner in which Cassandra's tent features in Bradamante's wedding. A record of gifts and benefits, it is also a prize—its price has been determined by the struggles undergone for its possession (46.80–83). But for Bradamante's wedding, an extraordinary and unique occasion, it is freely lent, borrowed from the emperor Constantine for less than twenty-four hours.[15] Neither gift nor loan, it hovers in transactional indeterminacy—supratemporal and dematerialized, it figures the absolute and essentially moral "valor" that Ariosto here attributes to the union of Bradamante and Ruggiero.

The burden of revealing the poem's complex notion of generativity is Bradamante's not Ruggiero's, because it is she in whom the most profound oppositions are registered.[16] They are generative because they function as oxymoron rather than dialectically. To convey his ideas of historical continuity, Ariosto has depicted virtues usually assigned to women—chastity, mercy, and thrift—in the idealized person of the androgynous Bradamante. But he does not represent them in terms common to the querelle or treatises on domestic government, which tended to see them as unqualified. There a chaste woman defied desire, a merciful woman ignored justice, a conserving woman remained indoors and left the business of increasing wealth to her husband. Ariosto's image of female agency is fueled by oppositions that for orthodox writers make it impossible. As exemplified by Bradamante's character and career, chastity does not reject desire but rather embraces it; mercy does not function to supplant justice but is instrumentally connected to it by equitable decisions; and finally, conservation is not understood to depend on male control of property but is rather linked to the generativity created by the shared will and agency of the married couple.

The effect of this socially revisionary vision of gender is to puncture

---

15. It is picked up at midday and returned after the wedding: "Poi finite le nozze, anco tornollo/Miraculosamente onde levollo" (46.79); that is, I assume, the morning after the wedding night.

16. For a study of Bradamante as the poem's preeminently generative character, see Marinelli 103–9. For a study of Bradamante generally, see Wiggins.

the complacency of the orthodoxy mandating male and masculine superiority by a sustained recourse to figures of thought used in expressing a *coincidentia oppositorum*. The widest application of that concept in Renaissance culture touched on matters of a mystical and cosmic nature in which images of sexuality often illustrated the generative potential of the universe.[17] For Ariosto, I think, the matter of gender—when treated as if gender admitted symbolic androgyny—allowed an approach to the reading of history that made irony a moot point. Seeing gender as independent of the physiological categories of sex provided the most obvious pretext for reading history as neither positivistic nor as an ironic denial of positivism. Reading history, or, for that matter reading the story one writes, can be the occasion for irony only if that reading is invested in an interpretation that attributes a positive and definite meaning to an event. If events are doubtful, whether vague, confused, or contradictory—as they are when centered on the androgynous being—they defy positivist interpretation and perhaps most especially interpretations that exploit allegory.[18] Doubt precludes irony; rather, it comments on irony as that which must remain moot as long as doubt prevails. Doubt invites the entertainment of figures dedicated to play: oxymoron, paradox, and perspectival description. Studies of Ariosto's style have repeatedly revealed the ways in which irony, the pervasive mood of this prodigious poem, subverts meaning; the poem's appeals to the prospective *età d'oro* to be inaugurated by the Este dynasty, and its retrospective celebrations of an epic heroism that is said to be the foundation of that family's greatness, are the focus of an obvious irony. The extent to which this irony obtains is a measure of the frustration the poem is designed to generate; to this extent the poem can be characterized as "a-generate." Its irony perplexes, baffles, and can even render interpretation ridicu-

17. The scope of this subject clearly exceeds the topic of my essay. For some introductory material, especially on the figure of the armed Venus, see Wind 81–96.

18. Bellamy argues that Ariosto's irony touches his representation of prowoman argument; "Alcina's Revenge," 64–65. Insofar as that argument is apologetic, I think her view is correct. I suggest, however, that Ariosto is not consistently interested in such apologetics and, in portraying Bradamante, represents gender as an element in a hermeneutics of history.

lous. This essay has attempted to demonstrate a limiting case: when the poet represents gender as mysteriously double, his irony loses its subject. It in these representations that generativity and the possibility of generation seem most likely.

Works Cited

Ariosto, Ludovico. *Orlando furioso.* Ed. Nicola Zingarelli. Milan: Ulrico Hoepli, 1959.

Ascoli, Albert. *Ariosto's Bitter Harmony: Crisis and Evasion in the Italian Renaissance.* Princeton: Princeton UP, 1987.

Bellamy, Elizabeth. "Alcina's Revenge: Reassessing Irony and Allegory in the Orlando Furioso" *Annali d'italianistica* 12 (1994): 61–74.

———. *Translations of Power: Narcissism and the Unconscious in Epic History.* Cambridge: Cambridge UP, 1992.

Benson, Pamela Joseph. *The Invention of the Renaissance Woman: The Challenge of Female Independence in the Literature and Thought of Italy and England.* University Park: Pennsylvania State UP, 1992.

Chojnacki, Stanley. " 'The Most Serious Duty': Motherhood, Gender, and Patrician Culture in Renaissance Venice." *Refiguring Woman: Perspectives on Gender and the Italian Renaissance.* Ed. Marilyn Migiel and Juliana Schiesari. Ithaca: Cornell UP, 1991.

Du Bois, Page. *Sowing the Body: Psychoanalysis and Ancient Representations of Women.* Chicago: Chicago UP, 1988.

Finucci, Valeria. *The Lady Vanishes: Subjectivity and Representation in Castiglione and Ariosto.* Stanford: Stanford UP, 1992.

Freccero, Carla. "Economy, Woman, and Renaissance Discourse." *Refiguring Woman: Perspectives on Gender and the Italian Renaissance.* Ed. Marilyn Migiel and Juliana Schiesari. Ithaca: Cornell UP, 1991.

Hutson, Lorna. *The Usurer's Daughter: Male Friendship and Fictions of Women in Sixteenth-Century England.* London: Routledge, 1994.

Jordan, Constance. "Boccaccio's In-famous Women: Gender and Civic Virtue in the De mulieribus claris." *Ambiguous Realities: Women in the Middle Ages and Renaissance.* Ed. Carole Levin and Jeanie Watson. Detroit: Wayne State UP, 1987.

———. *Renaissance Feminism: Literary Texts and Political Models.* Ithaca: Cornell UP, 1990.

Klapisch-Zuber, Christiane. *Women, Family, and Ritual in Renaissance Italy.* Trans. Lydia G. Cochrane. Chicago: U of Chicago P, 1985.

Kuehn, Thomas. *Law, Family and Women: Toward a Legal Anthropology of Renaissance Italy.* Chicago: U of Chicago P, 1991.

Maclean, Ian. *The Renaissance Notion of Woman: A Study in the Fortunes of Scholasticism and Medical Science in European Intellectual Life.* Cambridge: Cambridge UP, 1980.

Marinelli, Peter V. *Ariosto and Boiardo: The Origins of the Orlando Furioso.* Columbia: U of Missouri P, 1987.

Quilligan, Maureen. *The Allegory of Female Authority: Christine de Pizan's Cité des Dames.* Ithaca: Cornell UP, 1991.

Ross, Charles. "Ariosto's Fables of Power: Bradamante at the Rocca di Tristano." *Italica* 68.2 (1991): 155–75.

Shemek, Deanna. "Of Women, Knights, Arms and Love: The *Querelle des Femmes* in Ariosto's Poem." *Modern Language Notes* 104 (1989): 68–97.

Sommerville, Margaret R. *Sex and Subjection: Attitudes to Women in Early-Modern Society.* London: Arnold, 1995.

Tomalin, Margaret. *The Fortunes of the Warrior Heroine in Italian Literature.* Ravenna: Longo Editore, n.d.

Wiggins, Peter de Sa. *Figures in Ariosto's Tapestry: Character and Design in the "Orlando Furioso."* Baltimore: Johns Hopkins UP, 1986.

Wind, Edgar. *Pagan Mysteries in the Renaissance: An Exploration of the Philosophical and Mystical Sources of Iconography in Renaissance Art.* New York: Norton, 1968.

Zatti, Sergio. "Valori d'uso e valori di scambio." *Il Furioso fra epos e romanzo.* Lucca: Pacini Fazzi, 1990.

Index

Contributors

JO ANN CAVALLO is Associate Professor of Italian at Columbia University and director of its summer program in Scandiano. Her publications include *Boiardo's Orlando Innamorato: An Ethics of Desire* (1993) and articles on early Christianity, Dante, Boiardo, Ariosto, Giordano Bruno, and Elsa Morante. She is also a contributor to the *Dante Encyclopedia* and *The Encyclopedia of the Renaissance*.

VALERIA FINUCCI is Associate Professor of Italian at Duke University. She has written *The Lady Vanishes: Subjectivity and Representation in Castiglione and Ariosto* (1992), has coedited *Desire in the Renaissance: Psychoanalysis and Literature* (1994), and edited Moderata Fonte's *Tredici canti del Floridoro* (1995). She is currently completing a book on stagings of sex and gender in sixteenth-century literature and coediting a collection of essays on generation and degeneration.

KATHERINE HOFFMAN teaches English literature and European civilization at Roanoke College in Salem, Va., where she is Associate Professor of English. She has published and presented work on Ariosto, Spenser, and the Renaissance epic; her current work centers on pedagogy and early modern women writers.

DANIEL JAVITCH is Professor of Comparative Literature at New York University. His book, *Proclaiming a Classic: The Canonization of Orlando Furioso* (1991) will appear in Italian this year. He is at work on a history of genre theory in the sixteenth century.

CONSTANCE JORDAN is the author of *Renaissance Feminism: Literary Texts and Political Models* (1990) and *Shakespeare's Monarchies: Ruler and Subject in the Romances* (1997). She is currently at work on a book about representations of place and property in early modern literature.

RONALD L. MARTINEZ is Associate Professor of Italian at the University of Minnesota. Besides having written articles on Dante, Boccaccio, Machiavelli, and Ariosto, he is the co-author, with Robert Durling, of *Time and the Crystal: Studies in Dante's Rime Petrose* (1991) and author of a translation and commentary of Dante's *Inferno* (1996, *Purgatorio* and *Paradiso* are in preparation). Currently he is completing a study of Dante's career to be titled "Dante and the Vocation of Mourning," and investigating the political stakes of theatrical space in Italian Renaissance drama.

ERIC NICHOLSON, Associate Professor of Literature and Drama Studies at Purchase College, SUNY, has published several articles on early modern European theatre, its audiences, and its stagings of women and gender. A play translator and director, his productions have included Machiavelli's Mandrake and Shakespeare's Midsummer Night's Dream. He is currently preparing a book on the careers and public images of sixteenth- and early seventeenth-century Italian actresses.

WALTER STEPHENS is Paul D. Paganucci '53 Professor of Italian at Dartmouth College. He has published a number of articles on Tasso and on Renaissance literature and is the author of Giants in Those Days: Folklore, Ancient History and Nationalism (1989), a study of Rabelais, and coeditor of Discourses of Authority in Medieval and Renaissance Literature (1989). His next book, Demon Lovers: Witchcraft, Sex, and Belief, examines early modern theoretical writings on witchcraft.

SERGIO ZATTI is Professor of Italian at the University of Pisa, Italy. He has written essays on Boccaccio, Manzoni, and nineteenth-century poetry, but his major field of publication is the Renaissance chivalric romance, as exemplified in his three books: L'uniforme cristiano e il multiforme pagano: saggio sulla Gerusalemme Liberata (1983); Il Furioso fra epos e romanzo (1990); and L'ombra del Tasso: epica e romanzo nel '500 (1996). He has also published a critical commentary of Ariosto's Cinque canti (1997).

NAOMI YAVNEH is Assistant Professor of Humanities at the University of South Florida. In addition to her work on gender and theology in the Catholic Reformation, she has written on Petrarch, Leone Ebreo, Fonte, and Stampa, as well as on the reproductive body in the early modern period. Currently, she is completing a book on the body of the Virgin, and co-editing a collection of essays on female caregivers in the early modern period.

Library of Congress Cataloging-in-Publication Data
Renaissance transactions : Ariosto and Tasso / edited by
Valeria Finucci.
    p.   cm. — (Duke monographs in medieval and
Renaissance studies; 17)
Includes bibliographical references and index.
ISBN 0-8223-2275-7 (cloth : alk. paper).
ISBN 0-8223-2295-1 (pbk. : alk. paper)
1. Ariosto, Lodovico, 1474–1533. Orlando furioso.   2. Tasso,
Torquato, 1544–1595. Gerusalemme liberata.   I. Finucci, Valeria.
II. Series.   PQ4569.R46   1999
851'.309—dc21   98-23344   CIP